Modern American Drama: The Female Canon

Modern American Drama: The Female Canon

Edited by
June Schlueter

Rutherford • Madison • Teaneck
Fairleigh Dickinson University Press
London and Toronto: Associated University Presses

Associated University Presses
440 Forsgate Drive
Cranbury, NJ 08512

Associated University Presses
25 Sicilian Avenue
London WC1A 2QH, England

Associated University Presses
P.O. Box 488, Port Credit
Mississauga, Ontario
Canada L5G 4M2

The paper used in this publication meets the requirements of the American National Standard for Permanence of Paper for Printed Library Materials Z39.48-1984.

Library of Congress Cataloging-in-Publication Data

Modern American drama : the female canon / edited by June Schlueter.
p. cm.
Includes bibliographical references.
ISBN 0-8386-3387-0 (alk. paper)
1. American drama—Women authors—History and criticism. 2. Women and literature—United States—History—20th century. 3. American drama—20th century—History and criticism. I. Schlueter, June.
PS338.W6M6 1990
812.009'9287—dc20 89-45579
CIP

PRINTED IN THE UNITED STATES OF AMERICA

For my mother,

Erna Mayer

Contents

Acknowledgments

Thanks to Harry Keyishian, director of Fairleigh Dickinson University Press, for his encouragement and guidance; to Bernard Dick of Fairleigh Dickinson University for his helpful suggestions; to Richard Everett and Evangeline Bicknell of Skillman Library, Lafayette College, for their interlibrary loan assistance; and to Lafayette College for its financial support. Special and ongoing thanks to Paul Schlueter for his support, advice, and love.

I acknowledge permission to reprint the following three essays: "Megan Terry's Transformational Drama: *Keep Tightly Closed in a Cool Dry Place* and the Possibilities of Self," by June Schlueter in *Studies in American Drama, 1945–Present* 2 (1987): 59–69; " 'The Poetry of a Moment': Politics and the Open Form in the Drama of Ntozake Shange," by John Timpane in *Studies in American Drama, 1945–Present* 4 (1989): 91–101; and "Comic Textures and Female Communities 1937 and 1977: Clare Boothe and Wendy Wasserstein," by Susan L. Carlson in *Modern Drama* 27 (December 1984): 564–73.

Introduction

1

Naming this collection was not easy. To define the scope of the project, I needed a title that would identify chronology (modern), geography (American), and genre (drama) and that would record the volume's interest in female playwrights. But at the same time, I wanted a title that would, immediately and boldly, assert the value of women's writing not merely as a supplemental literature but as a primary one. In accomplishing the last of these, I kept returning to the notion of "canon," initially rejecting it as a concept of an academic culture that has habitually preferred male texts but then embracing it as the only notion that would make the goal of this collection clear. Moreover, once I decided to use "canon," I had reason to explore the implications of a concept that a collection such as this necessarily, if paradoxically, challenges.

Canon construction is a tricky business. When the literary establishment was almost exclusively male, white, capitalist, Christian, and upper middle-class, and the body of available literature less voluminous, some consensus could be expected. But this century's producers and consumers of written texts are a document in heterogeneity, made so at least in part by the ample participation in recent years of female playwrights, scholars, and teachers who feel the need of valuing the female voice, even as writers of color, for example, need to value theirs.

In the last two decades, attention given to the inherited canon has been of two kinds: deconstruction, with proposals for revalued replacements, and expansion, both to conserve the traditional fraternal order and admit new, nontraditional members. Such revisionist approaches have been successful at opening a canon that the academic community once presumed closed and in questioning its admission standards. Moreover, they have been valuable in addressing the inevitable question of whether there should be any sacred texts at all, any institutionalized body of literature that is presumed to express values that speak to all cultures at all times.

My own contribution to the discourse rests in my appropriation of the term for the title of this collection even as I offer attendant disavowals: I have no intention of proposing the body of dramatic literature discussed here, no matter how valuable, as *the* female canon. For one thing, several contributors have named female playwrights who are not treated separately in this volume—Edith Ellis, Mary Burrill, Edna Ferber, Georgia Douglas Johnson, Sada Cowan, Edna St. Vincent Millay, Mary Caroline Davies, Rita Wellman, Grace Potter, Neith Boyce, Zona Gale, Angelina Grimke, Marita Bonner, Maurine Watkins, Nikki Giovanni, Aishah Rohman, Kathleen Collins, Elaine Jackson, P. J. Gibson, Rosalyn Drexler, Mary O'Malley, Emily Mann, Tina Howe, for example—playwrights who might, I readily concede, have a claim to inclusion, as might black playwrights from the early part of the century, many other writers of the 1940s, and new voices in the theater, all of whom have been left unmentioned. For another, I have not been definitive regarding my criteria for selection, knowing that it will be years before scholarship can separate itself from the influence of institutionalized literary standards and cultural assumptions that need to be revalued to allow for a fresh, more democratically reconceived notion of canon. Finally, I realize that the word *canon* reflects not only what a culture values—the salutary part of the definition—but also what it means to fix, and I do not count myself in a position to determine which plays will speak most forcefully to readers in the year 2000, much less a century from now, nor whether "universality," however affirming its premises, can be an operative criterion in the present revisionist environment.[1] Politically, then, no other word would do for my title; philosophically, however, I must stress that "canon," for now, can be honest semantically only when it is framed by quotation marks and acknowledged as a provisional designation.

Indeed, receiving and reading the essays for this collection has reaffirmed for me the extent to which not only literary standards but literary criticism defines itself temporally. My announcement in *PMLA* requesting submissions spoke to the effort of this volume to recover and revalue texts by twentieth-century female American playwrights, noting that essays comparing lesser known female texts with better known male texts would be especially welcome. The response stands as a testament to the moment, for nearly all contributors brought feminist readings to the plays, whether expressed as a critical methodology or, more often, as an acute interest in revealing the extent to which gender perceptions have informed, shaped, and been reflected in this country's culture and drama. If this volume had been collected at another point in the intersection of drama, the feminist movement, and literary criticism, the emphasis might not have been gender. Those critics who deal with differences in the writing of double or multiple "exiles"—black women, or lesbian writers, for example, or, in one essay, Gertrude Stein, an expatriate American female writer, a Jew, and a lesbian—acknowledge the extent to which these identifying characteristics have shaped their writing. But even those essays, with one exception, affirm that, for the scholar/critic exploring female texts today, gender is *a*, if not *the*, crucial concern. As I read through the essays, I became very aware that this collection represents a particular moment in America's cultural and literary history, a time when sex difference is privileged over class and other differences and conceptions of female and male supersede—although are certainly attendant upon—conceptions of humanity. Once the definition of humanity has been adjusted and women are as central to it as men, other concerns that are marginalized by the emphasis of this volume—concerns that occupy materialist feminists, for example, and others that occupy traditional humanists—will undoubtedly attract the same scholars who have foregrounded gender here. Feminists then may better understand the caution expressed by Betsy Draine: "that a feminist literary *establishment* is by definition not feminist at all—unless . . . it has to confront the otherness of those without power, and learns (again) to be subversive."[2]

This is not to imply that historical specificity neutralizes the importance of this volume's emphasis. On the contrary, it clearly places the collection within a discourse that has established itself as a major theme of our time, a discourse that is having a decided impact on pedagogy and curriculum and on the way we and our colleagues see and behave. Recent scholarship has legitimized the reader's role in the process of literature; that the contributors to this volume draw on the cultural dynamic that informs their own perspectives endorses the richness of the moment and the value of this volume.

Further testimony to the temporal character of this collection is evident in the fact that all but two of the submissions came from women. At this juncture in the development of literary history, it is the women in the academy who are feeling, more urgently than their male colleagues, the need to acknowledge female texts. Perhaps because feminist groups, for the most part, have been operating without male members or perhaps because self-interest is a powerful incentive, these scholars have recognized and articulated the need to recover and evaluate female texts, to rescue women from what one contributor, Barbara L. Bywaters, calls the "literary anonymity of unpublished works and hasty critiques." The danger is that in operating out of self-interest, no matter how rightly conceived, female academicians may create an alternative "canon" no more balanced or representative than the one we have inherited.

Similarly, the risk involved in women reading female texts from a feminist perspective is that this provocative and productive critical approach will become the exclusive property of females. Catherine Wiley, in discussing the special circumstance involved in white women reading black women's texts, has generalized the problem. Feminist criticism, she cautions, should not be "limited to the privileged location of many of its practitioners"; we need to sensitize ourselves to understanding why our "difference makes these plays a challenge to read."

Developing strategies of reading is a major part of the agenda of this volume and its companion, *Feminist Rereadings of Modern American Drama* (Fairleigh Dickinson University Press, 1989). The earlier collection brought feminist perspectives to plays by five American male writers, all part of the traditional canon: Eugene O'Neill, Arthur Miller, Tennessee Williams, Edward Albee, and Sam Shepard. (Again, all but two of the contributors were female.) The present collection, an assemblage of criticism of twentieth-century plays by women from Rachel Crothers to Meredith Monk, invites its readers to acknowledge and value the female "canon" and, in so doing, to re-vision individual texts, critical standards, and dramatic history.

2

It is not the aim of this collection to argue for a feminist tradition in literature. Nonetheless, to provide a specifically female context for the writers in this volume, I have begun the collection with two overview essays, one on eighteenth- and one on nineteenth-century American women playwrights.

Mary Anne Schofield, whose idea it was to provide this historical context, has written on "The Happy Revolution: Colonial Women and the Eighteenth-Century Theater." Her essay discusses the colonial and revolutionary roots of the contemporary theater, identifying such playwrights as Judith Sargent Murray, Mrs. Marriott, Mercy Otis Warren, and Susanna Haswell Rowson as participants in the small but important group of women writers in this nation's early years. In particular, she explores the work of Judith Sargent Murray, author of "On the Equality of the Sexes" (written 1779, published 1790), a defense of the theater, dramatic criticism, and plays. Murray and other female writers joined in the spirit of revolution that characterized the drama of an emerging nation, extending the effort to identify an American self into an effort to identify a female self as well.

Doris Abramson's essay, " 'The New Path': Nineteenth-Century American Women Playwrights," establishes the place of women writers in the nineteenth-century theater of "spectacle, melodrama, and sentiment." Abramson identifies Marguerite Merington, Madeleine Lucette Ryley, and Martha Morton as the most frequently discussed female playwrights of the latter part of the century and Anna Cora Mowatt as the female writer whose play—*Fashion; or Life in New York* (1845)—is most frequently anthologized. She discusses Mowatt in detail and also notes the work of Louisa H. Medina, whose *Nick of the Woods* (1838) preceded *Fashion*, and Frances Wright, whose *Altorf* (1819) could, pending further discoveries, be the first commercially produced play of that century by an American woman. Abramson explores the contemporary reputations of these and other women playwrights, the relationship of their work to that of male British and American writers, and several of the plays, in both thematic and stylistic terms. She speaks as well of the impact of the commercial theater on female writers, who, like their male counterparts, often wrote for money. Despite their popularity, however, few texts by nineteenth-century female playwrights are in print, making the task of recovery and re-evaluation difficult. Abramson ends her essay by suggesting that a consideration of twentieth-century American drama need not begin with O'Neill but could justifiably begin with Rachel Crothers, thus providing the cue for her own second essay, which heads the list of contributions on twentieth-century female American playwrights.

Together, the essays on twentieth-century playwrights represent a collective inquiry into women's texts, primarily as dramatic spaces for the expression and exploration of gender concerns. Individually, they form smaller groupings as well. At least a dozen of the twenty contributors explicitly treat particular women's texts as drama of rejection and rebellion in either content or form: Susan Glaspell's plays threaten male authority; Sophie Treadwell's *Machinal* rebels against the institution of patriarchal marriage; Zoë Akins's melodramas offer subversive commentary on gender conventions; and Wendy Kesselman's maids, like Treadwell's heroine, murder their oppressor. For Glaspell and Djuna Barnes, expressionism becomes an accommodating form; Gertrude Stein, Ntozake Shange, Adrienne Kennedy, Maria Irene Fornes, Megan Terry, Wendy Wasserstein, and Meredith Monk disturb rhetorical and formal orthodoxy, redefining dramatic character. For the author of the Lillian Hellman essay, "rejection" takes the form of an "anxiety of influence," which causes male authors to diminish Hellman's achievement. The role of the critic/reviewer is discussed in the essays on Crothers, Glaspell, Akins, Stein, Hellman, Lorraine Hansberry, Fornes, and Marsha Norman; and it is implicit in the discussion of all plays proposed for the female canon, plays that have been eclipsed by male texts and male critics and that remain largely unknown.

Four contributors responded to my invitation to compare particular male and female texts. Hence another grouping may be formed of Ann E. Larabee's piece on Glaspell, Barnes, and O'Neill's *The Emperor Jones;* Charlotte Goodman's on Hellman's plays as an influence on those of Miller and Williams; Mary McBride's on patterns of loneliness and longing in Carson McCullers and Williams; and Catherine A. Schuler's on Fornes and Shepard, which questions why Shepard has been canonized and Fornes rejected.

Two essays appeal to non-American male playwrights for comparison: Joanne B. Karpinski looks at Beth Henley's *Crimes of the Heart* in the context of Chekhov's *Three Sisters,* and Bette Mandl looks at Kesselman's *My Sister in This House,* a play based on the same story as that of Jean Genet's *The Maids.* One, Susan L. Carlson's on Clare Boothe's *The Women* and Wasserstein's *Uncommon Women and Others,* compares two plays by two female playwrights separated by forty years. Katherine H. Burkman's essay on Norman's *'night, Mother* connects the play's characters to the Demeter/Kore myth, claiming more explicitly the feminine consciousness implicit in many of the texts and proposed as well for Glaspell, Barnes, Treadwell, and Wasserstein. Only two essays belong in a group unconcerned with gender issues: McBride's on McCullers and Williams, which treats the two playwrights as companions and friends; and Leonard R. N. Ashley's on Hansberry, which places that black writer in the context of other black writers and of white writers, regardless of sex, as well. Four essays on black women writers are included (Hansberry, Childress, Kennedy, Shange) and one on a lesbian writer (Stein) as well as Lynda Hart's, which explores the question of the relationship of lesbian writing to a "female" "canon."

The orientation of many of the essays is radical (or cultural) feminism, which, as Sue-Ellen Case describes it in *Feminism and Theatre,* is the dominant position in America. Radical feminism sees patriarchy as the primary cause of the oppression of women; it conceives of a separate woman's culture through which women define women. Several essays form a separate grouping, however, with their attachments to materialist feminism, most notably Dinnah Pladott's on Stein and John Timpane's on Shange. As Case describes it, materialist feminism "contradicts the essentialism and universalism of radical feminism," underscoring "the role of class and history in creating the oppression of women."[3]

Using these subgroupings as the organizing principle for this volume, however, would have created difficulties, because a number of the essays are equally at home in more than one grouping. Moreover, my own sense of this collection's function, regardless of the orientation or approach of any particular essay, is to further the conversation on the problematic cultural and theatrical relationships of sex and gender. My choice to organize the volume chronologically provides the reader with an immediate sense of the contributions of women writers in every decade of this century. The following section provides a capsule version of each of the critical essays presented here.

3

Doris Abramson's essay on Rachel Crothers explores the question of whether a female playwright could have been a commercial Broadway success, as Crothers was between 1906 and 1937, and be a feminist. Offering citations from several of Crothers's plays, including *A Man's World* (1909), *He and She* (1911/20), and *When Ladies Meet* (1932), as well as from reviews and other contemporary materials, Abramson concludes that, while Crothers wrote "commercially pleasing plays," within the form of the social comedy she raised questions about the place of women in American society. Abramson's essay provides an assessment of Crothers's place within both the early twentieth-century theater and an ongoing feminist discourse.

Barbara Ozieblo's essay, "Rebellion and Rejection: The Plays of Susan Glaspell," offers analyses of five of Glaspell's plays, all written between 1916 and 1930. Ozieblo attempts to explain why Glaspell, who, with O'Neill, was principal playwright for the Provincetown Players and whose plays "brought expressionism and social criticism to the American stage," has been excluded from the canon. Her approach is to explore those aspects of *Trifles* (1916), *Bernice* (1919), *Inheritors* (1920), *The Verge* (1921), and *Alison's House* (1930) that threaten male authority: Glaspell creates rebellious heroines who trespass on the traditionally male turf of self-definition and power, appropriating and transforming the myths of the male literary canon.

Ann E. Larabee continues and focuses the discussion of Glaspell in " 'Meeting the Outside Face to Face': Susan Glaspell, Djuna Barnes, and O'Neill's *The Emperor Jones*," considering the work of Glaspell and Barnes in relation to *The Emperor Jones*, staged by the Provincetown Players in 1920. O'Neill and Glaspell, she remarks, referring to *The Outside* (1917), *The Emperor Jones* (1920), and *The Verge* (1921), "seem to be carrying on a dialogue about the aesthetics of the liminal condition." For Glaspell and Barnes, however, the marginality of a Brutus Jones is transformed into "a position of aliveness, creativity, and linguistic freedom, constrained by society and ultimately by dramatic representation itself." In extending their feminist analysis of oppression to their own dramatic characters, Glaspell and Barnes (*Kurzy of the Sea*

[1920], *Nightwood* [1936]) pioneer "the territory stretching beyond the boundaries of staged, formal discourse."

One of the leading playwrights of the 1920s, now virtually forgotten, was Zoë Akins. Jennifer Bradley, in "Zoë Akins and the Age of Excess: Broadway Melodrama in the 1920s," offers commentary on her nine original plays and several adaptations staged in New York from 1919 to 1930—all representative of Akins's extravagant style. As Bradley states, "To an age of easy money, experiment in fashion, women's liberation, technological innovation, and general flamboyance, an exuberant romantic like Zoë Akins found melodrama the appropriate theatrical response." Bradley discusses the context for Akins's plays, the melodramatic framework, and the effects and implications of her work, which supported the careers of other theater women. Bradley notes that Akins's work consistently draws attention to "masculine-defined, middle-class moral convention about women" and often critiques "conventional notions of feminine virtue."

Barbara L. Bywaters's "Marriage, Madness, and Murder in Sophie Treadwell's *Machinal*" explores the subversive nature of Treadwell's 1928 expressionistic drama, her only commercial success. The message of that play, Bywaters claims, is clear: "the institution of marriage is a breeding ground for anger, desperation, and violence"; "female insurrection can lead to 'one moment of freedom' before the patriarchal 'machinery' crushes the revolt." Treadwell's play is a document of such protest and an exploration into the social and psychological pressures that culminate in a woman's murder of her husband. Through an "Every Woman" rather than a "New Woman" figure, Treadwell creates a formidable portrait of an "ordinary" woman capable of translating resistance into action. Bywaters works through the episodes of *Machinal*, exploring Helen Jones's rebellion as an expression of an "emerging subversive female consciousness."

Dinnah Pladott provides an analysis of Gertrude Stein's operas and plays within the context of the work of Julia Kristeva, Jacques Derrida, and Michel Foucault. In "Gertrude Stein: Exile, Feminism, Avant-Garde in the American Theater," she offers Stein's work as a new paradigm of dramatic discourse, created by an exile (expatriate, woman, Jew, lesbian) intent on proposing new forms outside the established discourse. Pladott discusses why the special character of theatrical signs provides a rich matrix for Stein's experiments in deconstructing a language insistent on patriarchal authority and social relevance. She suggests that the potential impact of Stein's avant-garde drama is not only literary but cultural as well, for new forms displace the master discourse and contribute to the breakdown of institutional codes.

Charlotte Goodman's contribution, "The Fox's Cubs: Lillian Hellman, Arthur Miller, and Tennessee Williams," identifies similarities between Hellman's *The Little Foxes* (1939) on the one hand and Miller's *All My Sons* (1947) and Williams's *The Glass Menagerie* (1945) and *A Streetcar Named Desire* (1947) on the other. She argues that Hellman remains a precursor uncredited either by critics or by the two male writers. She also speculates that "anxiety of influence" might have caused Miller and Williams to misread Hellman's work and, consequently, to fail to acknowledge her importance—a theory she feels is exacerbated because Hellman was a woman playwright. She ends by stressing the necessity of writing Hellman back into the record as a significant American playwright.

One of the two essays in this collection that makes no claim regarding special feminist perspectives is Mary McBride's "Loneliness and Longing in Selected Plays of Carson McCullers and Tennessee Williams." Working with McCullers's *A Member of the Wedding* (1946) and *The Square Root of Wonderful* (1958) and several of Williams's plays, McBride identifies similarities in the playwrights' treatment of their characters' need for acceptance. In the work of both McCullers and Williams—who were close friends and professional associates—the pattern is deprivation, loneliness, longing, and dissatisfaction, which seeks relief in the oblivion of fantasy, alcohol, or death. McBride does not offer gender distinctions but credits both her male and female characters with a sensitivity to the "anguished souls" they create.

Leonard R. N. Ashley's "Lorraine Hansberry and the Great Black Way" provides an overview of the dramatic career and reception of this black American playwright, whose *Raisin in the Sun* (1959) proved a commercial success and a "milestone in the American theater." Ashley's essay is an invitation to reevaluate the work of the youngest and first black woman to receive the New York Drama Critics' Circle Award, a playwright who, although surpassed and now out of fashion, contributed significantly to the viability and visibility of drama by and about blacks.

My own essay on "Megan Terry's Transformational Drama: *Keep Tightly Closed in a Cool Dark Place* and the Possibilities of Self" explores the efforts of Terry to redefine dramatic character, to deconstruct the notion that the dramatic self is "morally accountable, psychologically consistent, or socially defined." Terry's transformational drama "acknowledges the multiple and shifting selves that at any moment or collection of moments constitute a developing self, placing that composite in a context that is itself shifting." The discussion links transformational drama with a feminism that attempts to dismantle stereotypes and reevaluate the institutional hierarchy. As such, her drama has earned Terry the attribution (by Helene Keyssar) of the "mother of feminist theater."[4]

Susan E. Meigs's "No Place But the Funnyhouse: The Struggle for Identity in Three Adrienne Kennedy Plays" addresses the problem of the double bind of gender and race. Finding no place for expression in the Western literary tradition, Kennedy turned to African writing and particularly to mythic elements of African ritual drama. There, however, she found no female voice. Her own work, which Meigs calls "complex, surrealistic psychodramas," depicts the conflict between the two traditions as she searches for a means of resolving "the chaotic elements" that comprise black female identities. In *Funnyhouse of a Negro* (1964), *The Owl Answers* (1965), and *A Movie Star Has to Star in Black and White* (1976), she dramatizes the psychological oppression that afflicts these plays' black women protagonists. Meigs ends by suggesting that Kennedy's plays "reveal the disorientation and despair of black women who can find no other space for themselves but the funnyhouse."

In "Whose Name, Whose Protection: Reading Alice Childress's *Wedding Band*," Catherine Wiley—whose questions concerning "difference" are especially probing—offers a feminist reading of the play. Although she acknowledges the danger of preferring such a reading over one that examines the play's racial politics, she argues that *Wedding Band* (written 1966; performed in New York 1972) is more about relations among black women and between black women and white women than about interracial heterosexual relations. Wiley looks particularly at the opening incident in which Mattie, an illiterate black woman, asks her neighbor, Julia, to read the letter she has received from her merchant marine husband, who, claims Mattie, gave her "name and protection"—benefits that Julia, who has had a white lover for ten years, does not enjoy. Wiley goes on to show that neither woman attains that privilege because both are part of a 1918 South Carolina society in which blacks are oppressed and miscegenation outlawed. Instead, the women in the play learn self-acceptance and sisterhood.

Ntozake Shange's plays of the 1970s, of which *for colored girls who have considered suicide/when the rainbow is enuf* (1974) is best known, are also concerned with the process of becoming, of shaping an identity as a black and as a woman. Although written at a particular historical moment for a particular audience, Shange's plays are open texts that admit variation in performance. In " 'The Poetry of a Moment': Politics and the Open Form in the Drama of Ntozake Shange," John Timpane explores this paradox and the consequences of openness for a politically committed drama. Timpane connects Shange's linguistic subversion—"disjunction, disruption, juxtaposition, sudden illumination or recontextualization," synchronic techniques such as collage, and a resistance to closure—with political subversion; Shange, he argues, has succeeded in balancing "potential anarchy . . . with a consistent political purpose."

Susan L. Carlson frames an interesting comparison of a female playwright of the thirties and a female playwright of the seventies. In "Comic Textures and Female Communities 1937 and 1977: Clare Boothe and Wendy Wasserstein," she reads *The Women* and *Uncommon Women and Others* as plays that expose the gender conventions and assumptions common to comedy. The difference, she proposes, is one of consciousness. Unlike her predecessor, Wasserstein, writing in the 1970s, "*is aware* that comedy's built-in easy answers to women's problems are deceptive and dangerous; she *is aware* that comic conventions in and of themselves pressure characters into a limited number of roles." Boothe's play suggests why feminist comedies have been uncommon; Wasserstein's moves toward a form that frees comedy from its sexist limitations.

In "Gender Perspective and Violence in the Plays of Maria Irene Fornes and Sam Shepard," Catherine A. Schuler concerns herself with the discrepancy between the relative obscurity of Fornes and the commercial success of Shepard. Both playwrights, she notes, were experimental writers of the sixties and seventies, and both treat similar social, political, and formal concerns; yet audiences applaud the contemporary Shepard and ignore or reject Fornes. Schuler proposes an explanation in the relationship between gender and response, exploring audience reaction with respect to three features of the plays: the sex of the central characters, the depiction of male characters, and the depiction of male violence against women. She finds her examples in a range of Shepard texts, including *Fool for Love, A Lie of the Mind, Curse of the Starving Class,* and *True West,* and in several by Fornes: *Fefu and Her Friends, Mud, The Conduct of Life,* and *Sarita.* Schuler concludes that Fornes's plays have not been well received because they "deconstruct the dynamics of gender hierarchy with profoundly disturbing results."

In an effort to assess the strengths and weaknesses of Beth Henley's first work, *Crimes of the Heart* (1982), Joanne B. Karpinski places it in the context of Anton Chekhov's *Three Sisters,* a canonical play of the international theater with which it has a range of similarities. In "The Ghosts of Chekhov's *Three Sisters* Haunt Beth Henley's *Crimes of the Heart,*" Karpinski offers an extended comparative analysis of the two plays, identifying similarities in plot, setting, theme, characterization, and tragicomic tone. Finally, she offers a claim concerning the distinctive contribution of Henley to a contemporary feminist vision.

Bette Mandl also compares the work of an American woman playwright with that of a European male playwright. In "Disturbing Women: Wendy Kesselman's *My Sister in This House*," she speaks of the historical situation that formed the basis for both Kesselman's play (1980) and Jean Genet's *The Maids*, noting differences in the playwrights' treatments of the story of two servant women. Genet, intrigued by the interplay of reality and artifice, produced a dramatic study in epistomology, permitting only a surrogate and possibly fictitious murder; Kesselman, on the other hand, shapes the material to reveal "how subtle oppressions, related to gender, precipitate despair and breakdown"; her maids brutally murder their mistress and her daughter. Mandl suggests that the most disturbing element of Kesselman's play is "its insistence that we link gender and violence in unfamiliar ways."

Katherine H. Burkman argues for the presence of a feminine consciousness in Marsha Norman's *'night, Mother* (1983). In "The Demeter Myth and Doubling in Marsha Norman's *'night, Mother*," she proposes that the play may be read as a version of the Demeter/Kore myth. Such a reading, she contends, particularly with its symbolic concern with appetite, could provide insight into the relation between mother and daughter: "Jesse may be understood as both the Kore figure who feels used or raped and the Demeter figure who shares in that sense of loss and has lost the zest for life." Burkman sees the myth as a means of connecting the characters in Norman's play with an archetypal mother/daughter and of assuring the renewing effect of Jesse's suicide.

In "The Silver Lining in the Mushroom Cloud: Meredith Monk's Opera/Music Theater," Suzanne R. Westfall explores the new morphology of *The Games*, created by performance artists Monk and Ping Chong. Westfall sees the game as a female paradigm, a means of recreating children, the theater, competitive sports, and the more serious game of survival. She also sees the structure of *The Games*, a postapocalyptic drama, as representatively feminist. The work is alinear, refusing to offer closure. Its language is uncharacteristic and disruptive, removing words from their accustomed semiotic and semantic contexts. Even as its mode is feminist, it deconstructs sexual stereotyping and establishes gender neutrality.

Finally, special notice needs to be taken of Lynda Hart's essay on lesbian theater because the circumstances of its writing were special. After hearing my presentation on "The Female Canon" at the "New Languages for the Stage" conference at the University of Kansas, Professor Hart asked whether she might include in her essay, then in progress, a response to the assumptions of my introduction with which she disagreed. I welcomed the opportunity for this "intratextual" discourse and include her essay, "Canonizing Lesbians?" without attempting a summary. Its argument is challenging—not only to my introduction but to the very presence of this collection—because, in problematizing not only the term "canon," as I have done, but the term "female" as well, Hart has asked whether such a volume perpetuates the gender assumptions it seeks to question, expose, and disrupt.

Variety and vitality are the strengths of this volume. Whatever the political agenda of its individual contributors, whatever the orientation of its individual essays, whatever its questions, it invites readers to pause at this particular moment in the interplay among American theater, the female playwright, and feminism for a focused though provisional look at a body of plays by female writers that need to be revalued.

Notes

1. A concise discussion of the problems of canon reformation may be found in Betsy Draine, "Academic Feminists Must Make Sure Their Commitments Are Not Self-Serving," *The Chronicle of Higher Education*, 10 August 1988, A40.
2. Ibid.
3. Sue-Ellen Case, *Feminism and Theatre* (New York: Methuen, 1988), p. 82. See "Radical Feminism and Theatre," pp.62–81, and "Materialist Feminism and Theatre," pp. 82–94. An introduction to, and argument for, materialist feminism appears in Judith Newton and Deborah Rosenfelt, ed. *Feminist Criticism and Social Change: Sex, Class and Race in Literature and Culture* (New York: Methuen, 1985).
4. Helene Keyssar, *Feminist Theatre* (London: Macmillan, 1984).

Modern American Drama: The Female Canon

Part 1
Eighteenth- and Nineteenth-Century Backgrounds

1
The Happy Revolution: Colonial Women and the Eighteenth-Century Theater

Mary Anne Schofield

> . . . I take leave to congratulate my fair country-women, on the happy revolution which the few past years has made in their favour; that in these infant republics, where, within my remembrance, the use of the needle was the principal attainment which was thought *necessary* for a woman, the lovely proficient is now permitted to appropriate a moiety of her time to studies of a more elevated and elevating nature.[1]

In March 1790, Judith Sargent Murray, in her essay, "On the Equality of the Sexes" (written in 1779), audaciously yet questions, "Is the needle and kitchen sufficient to employ the operations of a soul thus organized?"[2] The "soul" to which she alludes is the female soul, and she goes on to castigate the littleness of man and his educational theories that continued to keep women in subordinate, subservient positions. Her notions of equality are certainly understandable; the new "united states" had just successfully waged a war to ensure those inalienable rights. Progressive thinkers like Murray insisted on extending these rights to the weaker sex as well.

Murray herself exemplified this revolutionary theory. She was able to study at home with her brother as he prepared for admission to Harvard; she wrote poems, was a frequent contributor to the *Massachusetts Magazine* and the *Universalist Quarterly,* and was the first native-born woman dramatist in America to have her plays produced professionally. During the 1780s and 1790s, she was the chief theorist of republican womanhood in the colonies. Murray, however, is just one of a small but important group of women writing for the colonial theater. Theater historians like Arthur Hornblow, Richard Moody, Montrose J. Moses, Arthur Hobson Quinn, George D. Seilhamer, and Jack A. Vaughn do not mention these women in their surveys, yet recent book-length studies by Dorothy Weil, Gresdan Ann Doty, Linda Kerber, and Mary

Beth Norton clearly indicate the growing interest in and concern with the foremothers of the twentieth-century feminine stage.[3] Briefly, then, I would like to acquaint the readers of this volume with these colonial and revolutionary roots of the contemporary theater.

The most important characteristic of this early period was its revolutionism. Regardless of their political persuasion, playwrights were absorbed by contemporary events.[4] The dramas, like the popular pamphlets, became the chief literary tool: highly propagandistic, and exclusively American, they were used in the "War of Belles Lettres." To such early male dramatists as Hugh H. Brackenridge, Jonathan Sewall, and Robert Mumford, one must add the following women previously unrecognized: Margaretta Bleecker Faugeres (1771–1801), Madam Gardie (n.d.), Mrs. Marriott (n.d.), Judith Sargent Stevens Murray (1751–1820), Mercy Otis Warren (1728–1824), and Susanna Haswell Rowson (1762–1824). The names of the popular actresses of the period also should be added: Anne Julia Kemble Hatton (1764–1838), Anne Brunton Merry (1769–1806), Mary Palmer Tyler (1775–1866), and Polly Wayne (n.d.). Certainly, the number of women involved in the early theater is not overwhelming, yet, when one considers the monetary, educational, political, and sexual obstacles that had to be overcome before they could even approach the stage, it is a wonder that any feminine theater existed at all. What I find even more noteworthy is the body of feminine dramatic criticism that was written at that time.

Judith Sargent Murray deserves the credit for the existence of such an early but essential body of criticism. In *The Gleaner. A Miscellaneous Production* (3 vols., 1798), she published not only her two plays, *Virtue Triumphant* (1795) and *The Traveller Returned* (1796), but also short stories, essays on household economy, and criticism of the contemporary stage. She severely criticizes the Commonwealth of Massachusetts for its hypocritical laws on morality that had banned dramatic performances in Boston until 1793 by emphasizing the "utility" of the theater; and she goes on to argue that time spent at the theater provides a rational use of leisure time unlike the irrationality of the tavern or gaming table. She emphasizes the hard work involved in being an actor and concludes that

> from a *chaste and descreetly regulated* theatre, many attendant advantages will indisputably result. Young persons will acquire a refinement of taste and manners; they will learn to think, speak, and act with propriety; a thirst for knowledge will be originated; and from attentions, at first, perhaps, constituting only the amusement of the hour, they will gradually proceed to more important inquiries.[5]

Murray's remarks here are revolutionary. Not only does she support the theater during its least popular period, but she clearly recognizes its educative possibilities, thus advancing her interest and support of women's education.

Her plays continue this theme of education. *The Medium, or Happy Tea Party,* retitled *Virtue Triumphant,* is about female re-education of the male, whose perception of women is dreadfully inaccurate and self-interested. The heroine, Miss Eliza Clairville, who loves Charles Maitland, unequivocably states her position. As Charles describes it,

> while she has, in the most unequivocal terms, avowed her preference, she has, *with the same breath, declared that she will never meet me at the altar, but on equal ground.*[6]

Eliza is a stock character—"the virtuous damsel of unknown parentage, who succeeds finally in proving herself the social equal of the others."[7] Yet Murray's use of her—to support female equality—removes her from stock characterization and, as Meserve notes: "the issue of the self-assertive woman is clearly stated and occurs very early in the history of America."[8]

In *The Traveller Returned,* she turns to revolutionary themes rather than feminist issues. Rambleton, the protagonist, returns to America after a nineteen-year absence; the war between Britain and America continues. He has come, he tells us, in search of the woman who betrayed him. Betrayal and war are the themes, and, although Murray masks her theories in the romance story (Camden is in love with Emily Lovegrove although affianced to Harriot Montague), Lady Liberty is the true heroine. As Camden remarks:

> America, now weeping over her desolated plains and warriors slain in battle, should be my sovereign lady. It is not thus . . . that Washington inglorious wastes his hours! Well, well—I'll haste to yon parade, and there forget my weakness.[9]

Murray is confident that she is at the brink of a new female era:

> I may be accused of enthusiasm; but such is my confidence in THE SEX, that I expect to see our young women forming a new era in female history. They will oppose themselves to every trivial and unworthy monopolizer of time.[10]

Murray writes not just to encourage the American stage but to inculcate a strong sense of the American self, especially the female self. Meserve notes that this is the real purpose of the colonial theater:

> More than other literary genres . . ., the drama sought to foster that "just pride of patriotism" of which Washington spoke. Through ridicule and satire it encouraged people in the words of de Crèvecoeur to leave behind the manners and fashions of their former countries, particularly England and

France. Taking obvious advantage of the immediate response which is peculiar to performed art, American dramatists chose material and themes to emphasize America.[11]

Her enthusiasm is contagious, and Murray attempts singlehandedly to revolutionize the importance attached to the American theater:

> The stage is undoubtedly a very powerful engine in forming the opinions and manners of a people. Is it not then of importance to supply the American stage with American scenes? I am aware that very few productions in this line have appeared, and I think the reason is obvious. Writers, especially dramatic writers, are not properly encouraged. Applause, that powerful spring of action, . . . is withheld, or sparingly administered. No incentives are furnished . . .[12]

And Murray writes to offer just such incentives. She is in the vanguard movement of the feminine, postrevolutionary theater.

This impulse toward all things American is found in Mrs. Marriott's *The Chimera; or Effusions of Fancy: A Farce in Two Acts* (1795). Although not extraordinarily long or intellectually complex, *The Chimera* is paradigmatic of the postrevolutionary feminine theater experience; it is the story of the ever-resourceful, free-willed Matilda, who disguised herself as one sort of chimera—submissive and docile—to display her "virago" tendencies, voice her independence, and yet still get her man. Marriott fuses the romance tradition with the burgeoning interest in feminine, revolutionary themes as her play moves to its happily-ever-after conclusion.

Revolutionary notes continue to be heard, as Meserve notes: "Among those dramatists who championed the cause of the Patriots, none was more concerned with the events of the Revolution than was Mercy Otis Warren."[13] Between 1773 and 1779, she wrote five plays and thus was the first American woman to write drama. Her three comedies (*The Adulateur*, 1772; *The Defeat*, 1773; and *The Group*, 1775) are characterized by a biting wit and excellent satiric propaganda. Her plays define the tensions between the patriots and the Loyalists and focus on issues of freedom versus tyranny, home versus mother country, equality versus slavery, the issues of the Revolution.

Her first play, *The Adulateur; A Tragedy; As It Is New Acted in Upper Servia* (first published anonymously in the *Massachusetts Spy*), pits Brutus (James Otis) and Cassius (Sam Adams) against Rapatio (Thomas Hutchinson); the Boston Massacre of 5 March 1770 is reenacted (act 2), and she attacks the duplicity of the Tory leaders.

Rapatio appears again in her 1773 play, *The Defeat*, and again he is defeated soundly by the Patriots. As Meserve notes: "With her heaviest satiric bursts reserved for Hutchinson, Mrs. Warren also defended those rights for which the Patriots would fight: right of assembly, freedom of the press, freedom from forced servitude, and the right to make just laws."[14] In her third play, *The Group* (1775), she continues to sound this patriotic note.

Her comedies were effective political propaganda for the Patriots' cause and allowed her to vent her own frustration with British authority in Massachusetts (and male authority in particular). Thus, although excluded from the war by her sex, she fought in it by wielding her pen. Like Murray, she also found the needle and the kitchen far too restrictive. Her independent spirit is mirrored in her plays. As she writes to her son Winslow:

> The nations have now resheathed the sword; the European world is hushed in peace; America stands alone—May she long stand, independent of every foreign power; superiour to the new spirit of intrigue, or the corrupt principles of usurpation that may spring from the successful exertions of her own sons: May their conduct never contradict the professions of the patriots who have asserted the rights of human nature.[15]

In her later years, she wrote two tragedies: *The Ladies of Castile* (1790) and *The Sack of Rome* (1791). The *Ladies of Castile* concerns the last heroic struggle for liberty in Spain before the takeover of the house of Ferdinand.

> Central in her play, as the title suggests, are women; the daughter of the tyrant is loved by a patriot; the tyrant's son loves the wife of one of the rebels; Maria, the major figure, wife and sister to patriots, defies the tyrant with a passion that suggests Mercy Warren's earlier convictions. But the revolution fails, and the play ends conventionally.[16]

Warren's focus shifts in her later tragedies, and she is more concerned with women and women's roles than with the political revolution. She argues very strongly for women's capabilities, celebrating the female sex as a moral force. She aligns herself with the women of the Enlightenment who celebrated their sex as *the* moral force in British eighteenth-century society; thus, she is closer to the dramatists of the Queen Anne period than to her own contemporaries, such as Mary Wollstonecraft.

Susanna Haswell Rowson also was concerned with the force and fate of women. Between 1794 and 1810, she wrote at least five original plays that were produced on the American stage: *Slaves in Algiers, The Volunteers, The American Tar, Americans in England,* and *Hearts of Oak*. The importance of her work is suggested by the fact that of the approximately forty plays written by Americans before 1787, no more than six were intended for presentation on the professional stage.[17] After the Revolution (1783–1800), the plays written by Americans occupied a very small part in any theater; the numbers were even fewer for women, with Murray publishing anonymously and Warren writing plays designed to be read, not acted.

Rowson clearly links the patriotic stage with the British one. Between 1780 and 1792, she and her husband appeared on the English provincial stage; by 1794, they were working for the American company in Philadelphia and by 1796 were with the Federal Street Theatre in Boston. Rowson combined dual careers of acting and playwriting. Like Murray, she was very concerned about women's education. Women characters dominate in her plays, and in 1797 she opened one of the best schools for young ladies in Boston. (She had written an essay on female education entitled *Mentoria; or, The Young Lady's Friend*, in 1791.)

She is best remembered for her first play, *Slaves in Algiers;* or, *A Struggle for Freedom: A Play Interspersed with Songs* (1794), which focuses almost entirely on the issue of liberty. In this play, she manipulates the republican outrage at the injustice of slavery (Algerian pirates had captured and enslaved American officers and seamen) and applies these conditions to that of female oppression; it becomes an important text of feminist political ideology in American drama.[18]

Of course, Rowson was unable to use contemporary feminist rhetoric in *Slaves;* instead she displays her grave interest in women's rights using plot manipulation. For example, of the four scenes in act 1, the first three are devoted entirely to women as slaves. As Dorothy Weil notes, in this play, as in the rest of Rowson's work, slavery is "a symbol of the arbitrary subordination of the female as endorsed by various social systems and organizations."[19] Therefore, the first act does not even hint at the actual conditions of the American sailors held in the Algerian dungeons but only examines the female meaning of slavery. Rowson has Fetnah, the daughter of Ben Hassan and an unwilling concubine to the Dey, define female slavery:

> In the first place I wish for liberty. Why do you talk of my being a favourite; is the poor bird that is confined in a cage (because a favourite of its enslaver) consoled for the loss of freedom. No! Tho its prison is of golden wire, its food delicious, and it is overwhelm'd with caresses, its little heart still pants for liberty; gladly would it seek the fields of air, and even perched upon a naked bough, exulting carrol forth its song, nor once regret the splendid house of bondage.[20]

The other two women characters are also prisoners: Olivia, the English woman, and Zoriana, the Dey's daughter. Olivia is held captive by the inordinate sexual desires of the Dey, and Zoriana is a prisoner of love, for she loves Olivia's fiance, Henry.

Rowson ends her play by having each female subvert an aspect of the traditional role: Fetnah rebels against her father; Zoriana rebels against the patriarchal structure of Algeria by rejecting her oppressive religion; Rebecca rebels against her fate by planning suicide. The conclusion is not brought about by traditional male control; instead it is initiated and followed through entirely by women. For the women of *The Slaves*, freedom is the right to have control over the disposal of one's person.

But this is the right that all eighteenth-century women dramatists, actresses, and characters would assert. Their desires are not very distant from their twentieth-century daughters to whom they bequeath their love of liberty. All can say, repeating the last lines of *Slaves:*

> May Freedom spread her benign influence thro' every nation, till the bright Eagle, united with the dove and olive branch, wave high, the acknowledged standard of the world.[21]

Notes

1. Constantia [Judith Sargent Murray], "Observations on Female Abilities" [Essay no. 88), in *The Gleaner. A Miscellaneous Production. In Three Volumes* (Boston: I. Thomas and E. T. Andrews, 1798), 3:188.

2. Murray, "On the Equality of the Sexes," quoted in *The Feminist Papers: From Adams to de Beauvoir*, ed. Alice S. Rossi (New York: Columbia University Press, 1973), p. 19. Mary Beth Norton, *Liberty's Daughters: The Revolutionary Experience of American Women, 1750–1800* (Boston: Little, Brown and Company, 1980), observes that, in "On the Equality of the Sexes," Murray compares "male and female mental abilities in four areas: imagination, in which women were superior; memory, in which they were equal to men; and reason and judgment, in which they were inferior—but only because of their inadequate training" (252).

3. Philip H. Highfill, et al., *Biographical Dictionary of Actors, Actresses, Musicians, Dancers, Managers, and Other Stage Personnel in London, 1660–1800* (Carbondale: Southern Illinois University Press, 1973), is an invaluable aid to our knowledge of this early period.

4. See Walter J. Meserve, *An Emerging Entertainment: The Drama of the American People to 1828* (Bloomington: Indiana University Press, 1977).

5. Murray, Letter no. 24, in *The Gleaner* 1:230.

6. Murray, *Virtue Triumphant*, in *The Gleaner* 3:50.

7. Vena Bernadette Field, *Constantia: A Study of the Life and Works of Judith Sargent Murray, 1751–1820* (Orono: University of Maine Press, 1931), p. 78.

8. Meserve, *An Emerging Entertainment*, p. 155.

9. Murray, "The Traveller Returned," in *The Gleaner* 3:135.

10. Ibid., p. 189.

11. Meserve, *An Emerging Entertainment*, p. 95. Meserve concludes that Royall Tyler (1757–1826), who created the typical Yankee character, should be credited with fostering the "American theme" for the theater.

12. Murray, "A Spirit of National Independence Recommended" (Essay no. 96), in *The Gleaner*, 3:262.

13. Meserve, *An Emerging Entertainment*, p. 65.

14. Ibid., p. 68.

15. Mercy Otis Warren, "Dedication" to *The Ladies of Castile*, in *The Plays and Poems*

of *Mercy Otis Warren*, ed. Benjamin Franklin V. (Delmar, N.Y.: Scholars' Facsimiles and Reprints, 1980), p. 101.

16. Meserve, *An Emerging Entertainment*, p. 74.

17. Robert Spiller, et al., *Literary History of the United States*, rev. ed. (New York: Macmillan, 1953), p. 185.

18. Patricia L. Parker, *Susanna Rowson* (Boston: Twayne Publishers, 1986), reads *Slaves* as a strong statement on Rowson's part about sexual dominance. She concludes: "Rowson did not here reject male sexuality but tyranny based on sex, the use of women as sexual commodities. Fetnah longs for both physical freedom from her position as slave and the freedom of a genuine sexual love" (71).

19. Dorothy Weil, *In Defense of Women: Susanna Rowson* (University Park: The Pennsylvania State University Press, 1976), p. 99.

20. Susanna Rowson, *Slaves in Algiers; or, a Struggle for Freedom: A Play Interspersed with Songs. In Three Acts* (Philadelphia: Wrigley and Berriman, 1794), pp. 5–6.

21. Ibid., p. 72.

Bibliography

Primary

Bleecker, Ann. *The Posthumous Works of Ann Eliza Bleecker, in Prose and Verse. To Which Is Added a Collection of Essays, Prose and Poetical by Margaretta V. Faugeres*. New York: T. and J. Swords, 1793.

Faugeres, Margaretta V. Bleecker. *Belisarius: A Tragedy*. New York: T. and J. Swords, 1795.

Marriott, Mrs. *The Chimera; or Effusions of Fancy: A Farce in Two Acts*. New York: T. and J. Swords, 1795.

Murray, Judith Sargent ("Constantia"). *The Gleaner. A Miscellaneous Production. In Three Volumes*. Boston: I. Thomas and E. T. Andrews, 1798.

Rowson, Susanna. *Slaves in Algiers; or, a Struggle for Freedom: A Play Interspersed with Songs. In Three Acts*. Philadelphia: Wrigley and Berriman, 1794.

Warren, Mercy Otis. *The Plays and Poems of Mercy Otis Warren*. Edited by Benjamin Franklin V. Delmar. New York: Scholars' Facsimiles and Reprints, 1980.

Secondary

Anthony, Katharine. *First Lady of the Revolution: The Life of Mercy Otis Warren*. Garden City, N. Y.: Doubleday and Company, 1958.

Bailyn, Bernard. *The Ideological Origins of the American Revolution*. Cambridge: Harvard University Press, 1967.

Benson, Mary Summer. *Women in Eighteenth Century America*. New York: Columbia University Press, 1935.

Dexter, Elisabeth. *Career Women of America*. Francestown, N. H.: Marshall Jones Co., 1950.

Doty, Gresdan Ann. *The Career of Mrs. Anne Brunton Merry in the American Theatre*. Baton Rouge: Louisiana State University Press, 1971.

Field, Vena Bernadette. *Constantia: A Study of the Life and Works of Judith Sargent Murray, 1751–1820*. Orono: University of Maine Press, 1931.

Fritz, Jean. *Cast for a Revolution: Some American Friends and Enemies, 1728–1814*. Boston: Houghton Mifflin, 1972.

Highfill, Philip H.; Burnim, Kalman A.; and Langhans, Edward A. *Biographical Dictionary of Actors, Actresses, Musicians, Dancers, Managers, and Other Stage Personnel in London, 1660–1800*. Carbondale: Southern Illinois University Press, 1973.

Hornblow, Arthur. *A History of the Theatre in America from its Beginnings to the Present Time*. Philadelphia: J. B. Lippincott and Co., 1919.

James, Janet Wilson. *Changing Ideas About Women in the United States 1776–1825*. New York: Garland Publishing, 1981.

Kerber, Linda. *Women of the Republic: Intellect and Ideology in Revolutionary America*. Chapel Hill: University of North Carolina Press, 1980.

Meserve, Walter J. *An Emerging Entertainment: The Drama of the American People to 1828*. Bloomington: Indiana University Press, 1977.

Moody, Richard. *America Takes the Stage*. Bloomington: Indiana University Press, 1955.

Moses, Montrose J. *The American Dramatist*. Boston: Little, Brown, 1915.

Norton, Mary Beth. *Liberty's Daughters: The Revolutionary Experience of American Women, 1750–1800*. Boston: Little, Brown, 1980.

Odell, George C. D. *Annals of the New York Stage*. New York: Columbia University Press, 1927.

Parker, Patricia L. *Susanna Rowson*. Boston: Twayne Publishers, 1986.

Pollock, Thomas Clark. *The Philadelphia Theatre in the Eighteenth Century*. Philadelphia: University of Pennsylvania Press, 1933.

Quinn, Arthur Hobson. *A History of the American Drama From the Beginning to the Civil War*. New York: Harper and Brothers, 1923.

Rossi, Alice S., ed. *The Feminist Papers: From Adams to de Beauvoir*. New York: Columbia University Press, 1973.

Seilhamer, George D. *History of the American Theatre: New Foundations*. New York: Haskell House Publishers, 1969.

Silverman, Kenneth. *A Cultural History of the American Revolution*. New York: Thomas Y. Crowell Company, 1976.

Smith, Thelma M. "Feminism in Philadelphia, 1790–1850." *The Pennsylvania Magazine of History and Biography* 68, no. 3 (1944): 243–68.

Spiller, Robert; Thorp, Willard; Johnson, Thomas H; and Canby, Henry Seidel. *Literary History of the United States*, rev. ed. New York: Macmillan, 1953.

Tupper, Frederick, and Brown, Helen Tyler ed. *Grandmother Tyler's Book*. New York: G. P. Putnam's Sons, 1925.

Vail, R. W. G. *Susanna Haswell Rowson, the Author of Charlotte Temple*. Worchester, Mass.: The Davis Press, 1933.

Vaughn, Jack A. *Early American Dramatists: From the Beginnings to 1900*. New York: Frederick Ungar Publishing, 1981.

Weil, Dorothy. *In Defense of Women: Susanna Rowson*. University Park: The Pennsylvania State University Press, 1976.

2
"The New Path": Nineteenth-Century American Women Playwrights

Doris Abramson

> There is an almost frenzied demand for plays, especially for the conventional "star" plays, which can be sold like potatoes. If the author is enough of a juggler to combine all the characters into one grand central light, surrounding it with shadowy, transparent forms, which act the part of echoes, or of an old Greek chorus, he will never be without work. But, for the man or woman who strikes out for himself or herself, the new path is difficult.
>
> —Martha Morton

In 1891, Laurence Hutton had this to say about native American drama:

> The American drama—such as it is—may be divided into several classes, including the Indian Drama, and the plays of Frontier Life, which are often identical; the Revolutionary and war plays; the Yankee, or character plays, like *The Gilded Age*, or *The Old Homestead*; the plays of local life and character, like *Mose, or Squatter Sovereignty*; and the society plays, of which Mrs. Mowatt's *Fashion*, and Bronson Howard's *Saratoga Trunk* are fair examples.[1]

Writing toward the end of a century noted for a theater of spectacle, melodrama, and sentiment, a theater continually adapting to an audience of newcomers and an expanding frontier, he categorized plays written for that theater, mentioning only a few by title. And a woman is one of only two playwrights acknowledged by name. Actually, women wrote plays that fit all these classes, but it is right that Anna Cora Mowatt should be named here and elsewhere—*Fashion* is the most frequently anthologized of all plays by nineteenth-century women playwrights—as the preeminent woman playwright of the century. Other plays by women of her time are worth our attention, some even our study, but only *Fashion* is securely in the canon of American dramatic literature.

Thanks to her gift for self-advertisement, we know more about Anna Cora Mowatt than about other women playwrights of the nineteenth century. Her *Autobiography of An Actress; or Eight Years on the Stage*, published in 1853, was widely read and extravagantly admired. Nathaniel Hawthorne put it on a list of a half-dozen good American books that he was recommending to Richard Monckton Milnes—along with Thoreau's *Walden* and *A Week on the Concord and Merrimac Rivers*.[2] She also wrote two autobiographical novels, *Mimic Life* (1855) and *Twin Roses* (1857). These books are detailed accounts of her personal and professional life as well as an entertaining record of the American theater at mid-century. They are self-serving by their nature—Odell complained that the author was "always making herself the heroine of a novel, which was her idea of her own life"[3]—but taken with the usual grains of salt, they are clearly informative.

Best remembered now as the author of the play *Fashion; or Life in New York* (1845), a lively social comedy, in her own period she was also noted as an accomplished actress. Born Anna Cora Ogden, descended from a distinguished American family (her grandfather on her mother's side, Francis Lewis, signed the Declaration of Independence), she married James Mowatt, a man twice her age, when she was fifteen. She had always enjoyed home theatricals, and, when her husband's health failed, she became first a public reader and then an actress. As one theater historian put it: "Anna Mowatt . . . was the first American woman of birth and breeding to identify herself with the fortunes of the stage."[4]

She became a star in an age of stars, without ever serving an apprenticeship. She saw her first play at age fourteen, when she went to the theater reluctantly (like many ladies of the period she was persuaded by her minister to view the theater as an abode of the devil) and saw the bewitching Fanny Kemble. Theater had been childhood games; later, it became an option when she was looking for ways to make a living.[5] "I pondered long and seriously upon the consequences of my entering the profession," she wrote. Her decision was not made lightly:

> I reviewed my whole past life, and saw, that, from earliest childhood, my tastes, studies, pursuits had all combined to fit me for this end. I had exhibited a passion for dramatic performances when I was little more than an infant. I had played plays before I had ever entered a theatre. I had written

plays from the time that I first witnessed a performance. My love for the drama was genuine, for it was developed at a period when the theatre was an unknown place, and actors a species of mythical creatures. I determined to fulfill the destiny which seemed visibly pointed out by the unerring finger of Providence . . . I would become an actress.[6]

She made her debut as an actress in *The Lady of Lyons* on 13 June 1845, just three months after her debut as a playwright.

According to her autobiography, her friend Epes Sargent suggested that she should move from amateur to professional status as a playwright.

"Why do you not write a play?" said E.S—— to me one morning. "You have more decided talent for the stage than for anything else. If we can get it accepted by the Park Theatre, and if it should succeed, you have a new and wide field of exertion opened to you—one in which success is very rare, but for which your turn of mind has particularly fitted you."

"What shall I attempt, comedy or tragedy?"

"Comedy, decidedly; because you can only write what you feel, and you are 'nothing if not critical'—besides, you will have a fresh channel for the sarcastic ebullitions with which you so constantly indulge us."[7]

The result, of course, was *Fashion*, a satire on American *parvenuism*, intended to be a good-humored and serviceable "*acting* comedy." She claimed she set out to write not a literary but a dramatic play. That it has stood the tests of time, in the theater especially, shows she had studied the strategies used by the best writers of comedy of the past. She wrote a thoroughly American social comedy, following the rules of British comedies of manners of the eighteenth century.

Fashion was accepted as soon as written by the Park Theatre (the manager had been a childhood neighbor), produced "without delay, and in a style of great magnificence," opening on 24 March 1845, and running for three weeks.[8] It had notable success in other American cities and played at London's Olympic Theatre in 1850, the year it was published.[9]

Edgar Allan Poe, then writing criticism for the *Broadway Journal*, did not write about *Fashion* only from the perspective of opening night. He had requested a copy of the play from Mrs. Mowatt and received one before the play's opening. His first review, then, was based on a reading of *Fashion*. Among other things, he wrote: "The general tone is adopted from *The School for Scandal*, to which, indeed, the whole composition bears just such an affinity as the shell of a locust to the locust that tenants it—as the spectrum of a Congreve rocket to the Congreve rocket itself."[10] After seeing the play in production, he became intrigued with it. Although he condemned the ways in which theatrical conventions of the day were being perpetuated—"the coming forward to the footlights when anything of interest was to be told, the reading of private letters in a loud rhetorical tone, the preposterous soliloquizing and even more preposterous asides"—he went on to say that "in many respects (and those of a *telling* character) it is superior to any American play. It has, in especial, the very high merit of simplicity of plot" (29 March 1845). By 5 April 1845, after several viewings of *Fashion*, he wrote:

> In one respect, perhaps, we have done Mrs. Mowatt unintentional injustice. We are not quite sure, upon reflection, that her entire thesis is not an original one. We can call to mind no drama, just now, in which the design can be properly stated as the satirizing of fashion *as* fashion.[11]

It was remarkable that a writer of Poe's stature paid this much attention to Mrs. Mowatt's first play. His opinions of the theater's moribund conventions as well as his judgment of *Fashion* have stood the tests of time.

Fashion's characters are not just caricatures or farcical representations uncomfortably close to those in such plays as Sheridan's *The Rivals* (1775) or Royall Tyler's *The Contrast* (1787). Mrs. Tiffany is a descendant of Mrs. Malaprop, but she is strictly American. The drawing room in which she mangles English and French is an American one. (Tyler's setting could as easily have been London as New York.)

> *Mrs. Tif.* This mode of receiving visitors only upon one specified day of the week is a most convenient custom! It saves the trouble of keeping the house continually in order and of being always dressed. I flatter myself that I was the first to introduce it amongst the New *ee-light*. You are quite sure that it is strictly a Parisian mode, Millinette?
> *Mil.* Oh, *oui*, Madame; entirely *mode de Paris*.
> *Mrs. Tif.* This girl is worth her weight in gold *(aside)*. Millinette, how do you say *arm-chair* in French?
> *Mil. Fauteil*, Madame.
> *Mrs. Tif.* Fo-tool! That has a foreign—an out-of-the-wayish sound that is perfectly charming—and so genteel! There is something about our American words decidedly vulgar. Fowtool! how refined. (3)[12]

Count Jolimaitre is recognizable as a type of scheming "foreign" fop, but he has an engaging directness in his dealings.

> *Mrs. Tif.* Count, I am so much ashamed,—pray excuse me! Although a lady of large fortune, and one, Count, who can boast of the highest connections, I blush to confess that I have never travelled,—while you, Count, I presume are at home in all the courts of Europe.
> *Count. Courts?* Eh? Oh, yes, Madam, very true. I believe I am pretty well known in some of the courts of Europe—*police courts (aside)*. In a word, Madam, I had seen enough of civilized life—wanted to refresh myself by a

sight of barbarous countries and customs—had my choice between the Sandwich Islands and New York—chose New York! (10)

Zeke (renamed A-dolph by Mrs. Tiffany for its aristocratic sound) is close to a minstrel "darky" in dialect, but he is a fully developed character who shares some of Mrs. Tiffany's pretensions.

Mrs. Tif. Silence! Your business is to obey and not to talk.
Zeke. I'm dumb, Missus!
Mrs. Tif. A-dolph, place that *fow-tool* behind me.
Zeke. *(Looking about him.)* I hab'nt got dat far in de dictionary yet. No matter, a genus gets his learning by nature. (4)

Later, failing further to understand Mrs. Tiffany's fractured French, he exits saying, "Dem's de defects ob not having a libery education" (4–5).

Gertrude (a role occasionally played by Mrs. Mowatt) is the pure, honest heroine of other plays, but with this difference: she has the sensible intelligence of an all-American girl.

Ger. I have my *mania*—as some wise person declares that all mankind have,—and mine is a love of independence! In Geneva [New York], my wants were supplied by two kind old maiden ladies, upon whom I know not that I have any claim. I had abilities, and desired to use them. I came here at my own request; for here I am no longer *dependent! Voila tout,* as Mrs. Tiffany would say. (20)

Adam Trueman is related in his outspokenness to Mr. Freeman of James K. Paulding's 1831 play, *The Lion of the West,* although he is a farmer instead of a frontiersman. He also is something beyond a stage type. Here is his final speech, just before the epilogue, in answer to the Count's objection to America's lack of *nobility:*

True. Stop there! I object to your use of that word. When justice is found only among lawyers—health among physicians—and patriotism among politicians, *then* may you say that there is no *nobility* where there are no titles! But we *have* kings, princes, and nobles in abundance—of *Nature's stamp,* if not of *Fashion's*—we have honest men, warm hearted and brave, and we have women—gentle, fair, and true, to whom no *title* could add *nobility.* (61)

Anna Cora Mowatt created a play, then, that works on the level of farce comedy but that also attacks folly at every turn.[13]

Fashion is not the first nineteenth-century play by a woman. Louisa H. Medina's melodrama *Nick of the Woods,* based on Robert Montgomery Bird's novel of that title, was first produced in 1838 at the Bowery Theatre in New York.[14] If we were to adopt Frances Wright as she so wholeheartedly adopted America, we could even count her play *Altorf*

(1819) as the first play of the century authored by an American woman.[15] It seems easier to speak of foremost than to speak of first. *Fashion* is foremost, and in view of still undiscovered scripts, it is wiser not to try to establish who or what came first.

A later play about the *gaucheries* of social-climbing New Yorkers at mid-century is *Self* (1856) by Mrs. Sidney Bateman. Mrs. Bateman was born Sidney Cowell, daughter of comedian Joe Cowell, in New York City in 1823. She went on stage at age fourteen and married theater manager H. L. Bateman at sixteen. Together they managed theaters for the rest of their lives—in St. Louis, New York, and finally London. (Four of their eight children had careers in the theater, most notably Kate and Ellen, who were billed as The Bateman Children.) Mrs. Bateman's careeer as an actress-manager is well documented, and we know the titles of some of her plays.[16] It seems safe to assume that *Self* was the best of them.

Only Montrose J. Moses has published *Self* in an anthology, putting it for comparative reasons with *Fashion*.

> There is no doubt that Mrs. Bateman must have had "Fashion" in mind as to plot and characterization. Of the two, I should say that Mrs. Mowatt is more spontaneous in her style, and that "Fashion," for its fame was less dependent on E. L. Davenport's success in the role of *Adam Trueman*, than "Self" on the wonderfully creative acting of John E. Owens, in the title role of *John Unit*.[17]

This is a good blend of literary and production criticism.

In one of the most detailed reviews of *Self*, when it moved from St. Louis to New York, the drama critic for *Porter's Spirit of the Times* wrote that he was convinced that "it was a most extraordinary comedy to be written by a lady" and that it was "replete with gentle womanly feeling and sentiments, and at the same time abounding in expressions, situations and points which one would suppose none but a very 'strong-minded' person of the opposite sex could conceive."[18] Calling it a "serio-comic drama of modern life" (it is more blatantly moralistic than *Fashion*), he told the play's involved story from beginning to end. When he finally gave a résumé of the characters, comparing them to characters in other plays, he paired John Unit with Sir Oliver Surface, Mrs. Radius with Lady Sneerwell, and he called Mrs. Codliver "the cockney Mrs. Malaprop." It seems not to have occurred to him to reach back only eleven years to characters in Mowatt's *Fashion*.

Mrs. Bateman, born into the theater, a practical manager whose husband thought her "the best writer and judge of plays in existence,"[19] no doubt knew *Fashion* as well as she knew Sheridan's and Congreve's plays. She borrowed from several sources in writing *Self*, and it does move between sentiment and sense (feminine and masculine poles to the critic). Here is Mary, the play's sweet heroine, in a scene with her devoted "colored nurse" Chloe. (Chloe is a larger role than Zeke but a more demeaning one finally; he at least can seem to be "puttin' on de massa," but she apparently covets her place in this society.) Mary is teaching Chloe to read and laughing at her attempts to say the alphabet.

> *Chloe.* A—B—C—D—*(Repeat)* See, hea', 'tain't worth while spending your precious words on this hea' ole woman; kase I neber could learn, no how. Dey done tried to teach me when I was a little bit of a gal, but I never could get further than D, and dat am de berry place whar I sticks yit. I was a right cute little nigga, too, I was dat; but de readin'—dat got me, shure.
>
> *Mary.* Never mind, mammy, you know I always read to you; so, it don't make much matter; and, by-and-bye, when you grow very old, I'll be as good as a pair of spectacles for you: you shall see out of my eyes, and hear with my ears; . . . we will have a nice, quiet cosy little home, and you, dear mammy, shall order everything your own way. (723)

John Unit, who represents "us Republicans," is answering Mrs. Radius, who has warned him that the world doesn't think much of his thrifty ways:

> Don't care, and that is more to the purpose, ma'am! I know all about the world's opinion—opinions are bought with dollars, ma'am—have *got* the dollars, ma'am—could buy opinions with them, if it paid—but I don't believe it would pay. (739)

These rhythms suggest why John Unit was the star's role: the freshness in his diction lifts him above the typical.

Self joined the sentimental, rhetorical melodramas that crowded nineteenth-century stages, but unlike *Fashion* it did not become part of a literary canon. Forgotten even in the author's own time—*Self* is not listed among Mrs. Bateman's plays by English theater historians and was not among works named in her obituary in 1881—it is rarely cited today.

Laurence Hutton claimed:

> Scores of native writers, during the past decade or two, have presented American plays which have been clean and clever, even if they have not yet become a classic. But it is a striking fact that the first three "society plays" which were in any way successful upon the American stage were from the pens of women—Mrs. Mowatt's *Fashion*, Mrs. Bateman's *Self* and Miss Heron's *The Belle of the Season*[20]—and that since their production the name of a woman has very rarely appeared upon the bills as the author of a play.[21]

By the time he wrote these words, in 1891, the names of women playwrights had been on countless playbills for sentimental comedies, farces, dramas, melodramas, and romantic verse dramas—many written for stars of the day. (As early as 1857, E. A. Sothern had starred in Julia

Ward Howe's *Leonora or The World's Own*, a romantic verse drama.[22]) Marguerite Merington wrote *Captain Lettarblair* (1892) for E. H. Sothern[23]; Madeleine Lucette Ryley wrote *Christopher Junior* (1894) for John Drew[24]; Martha Morton wrote *A Bachelor's Romance* (1896) for Sol Smith Russell and *A Fool of Fortune* (1897) for William H. Crane. These three were among the best known women writing for the professional theater. Others were Mrs. Romualdo Pacheco, Alice E. Ives, Mrs. C. A. Doremus, Ada Lee Bascom, Mary Stone, Anita Vivante Chartres, and Lottie Blair Parker. These names were mentioned most frequently in articles of the late nineteenth and early twentieth centuries.

Here is a sampling of authors and titles (dates when given) from Esther Singleton's 1898 article, "American Women Playwrights"[25] (from which Theodore Dreiser liberally plagiarized the following year):

Mrs. Charles Avery Doremus . .	*The Sleeping Beauty* (1878)
	The Circus Rider
	Pranks
Mrs. Romualdo Pacheco	*Loyal Till Death*
	Nothing But Money
	Incog (1892)
Miss Martha Morton.	*Helene* (1889)
	The Refugee's Daughter (1890)
	The Merchant (1891)
	His Father's Wife (1895)
	A Fool of Fortune
	A Bachelor's Romance (1896)
Miss Marguerite Merington . . .	*Captain Lettarblair* (1892)
	A Lover's Knot
	Good-Bye
Mrs. Madeleine Lucette Ryley	*Christopher, Jr.* (1894)
	Lady Jemima
	A Coat of Many Colors (1897)
Miss Ada Lee Bascom	*The Bowery Girl* (1896)
	The Queen of Spades
Miss Alice Emma Ives	*Lorine* (1874)
	The Village Postmaster (1896)
	The Brooklyn Handicap (1894)
Mary Stone.	*House of the Wolf*
	The Social Highwayman (1895)
Mrs. Frances Hodgson Burnett	*The First Gentleman of Europe* (1897) [in collaboration with George Fleming/Miss

	Constance Fletcher]
	Little Lord Fauntleroy (1888)
Lottie Blair Parker............	*White Roses* (1892)
	Way Down East (1896)[26]

Singleton gave her readers personal insights into the playwrights' lives. Mrs. Pacheco's husband "has been Governor of California and United States Minister to Central America." Miss Marguerite Merington showed *Captain Lettarblair* to Joseph Jefferson, who praised it highly. Mrs. Ryley, born in London, sang in comic opera; married to J. H. Ryley, the comedian, she was the "original 'Patience' in America." Miss Ives of Detroit used to write for the newspapers, and she lived on the racetrack for several months and read the "sporting papers" in order to write *The Brooklyn Handicap.*

Perhaps more important are the comments she solicited from playwrights about their work habits. Martha Morton's were described in this way:

> Miss Morton writes rather slowly and cautiously, taking great pleasure in forging the tiny links in the chain of events out of which the plot is developed, and in fitting together the great and small points with mathematical precision. To balance everything accurately she finds it a help to demonstrate her scenes on a chessboard, but she intends to have a theatre in the house she is now building, where she can try the effects of her combinations, exits, and entrances . . . Her manuscripts are carefully written and contain many directions for the players.

Mrs. Ryley is quoted directly:

> "When I put on my thinking cap, and set to work on the evolution of a plot, I first draw out an elaborate sketch of each individual character so that each one's peculiarities and qualities are stamped indelibly on my mind, and I am as familiar with them as I might be with living persons. I then write out my plays in the form of a narrative, and jot down scraps of dialogue as it occurs to me. All my efforts are concentrated upon this narrative, which is cut afterwards. The writing of this dialogue is the easiest part of the work."

We learn that *Little Lord Fauntleroy* was played simultaneously by several touring companies here and in Europe and "produced for its author more than $200,000 in royalties." Ada Lee Bascom's *The Bowery Girl* earned her $40,000 in its first season in New York. The emphasis, finally, is on the women's financial success in the commercial theater. Dreiser's subtitle says it all: "A Path to Fame and Prosperity Not Always Strewn with Roses—The Stories of Leaders Who Have Won Celebrity and Fortune as Authors of Plays of the Period—Lofty Standards of

Dramatic Art."[27] Those lofty standards were measured monetarily, a thoroughly American determination of success.

What about the plays? Unfortunately, very few are available today. (They appear in collections or tattered copies of Samuel French or Walter Baker scripts found in auctions or flea markets.) Martha Morton's *A Bachelor's Romance*[28] is one that we can read, although it is not anthologized. It is a delightful if sentimental comedy, with a cast of characters who talk about books and paintings and make literate jokes. They are bored city folk who become countrified in an attempt to renew their strength through nature. The plot resembles a Pinero plot. David Holmes, hero and literary critic, is forty and has a ward of seventeen. She woos him away from his books and restores his youth. The dialogue is reminiscent at times of Shaw's *Pygmalion*—but *Pygmalion* was not written until 1912. One also thinks of Wilde's *The Importance of Being Ernest*, which was written the year before *A Bachelor's Romance*. But rather than reach to British male authors, we might look ahead to Clare Kummer, whose breezy, witty style in the teens and twenties is similar to Morton's. Something of Kummer, even of Rachel Crothers, is seen in this exchange after Gerald has offhandedly asked Harriet to marry him:

> *Gerald*. Well—Harriet—what do you say?
> *Harriet*. I say no—I will not—marry you.
> *Gerald*. Harriet!
> *Harriet*. You do not care for me enough to marry me. You have simply accustomed yourself to think—that some day—you should ask me to be your wife—there is nothing in it for either of us—nothing.
> *Gerald*. You don't mean it.
> *Harriet*. I do mean it—it's unalterable. (37–38)

When *A Bachelor's Romance* moved from New York to London in 1898, this bit appeared in a column by "The Lounger" in an American publication, *The Critic:*

> Another American playwright has made a success in London—Miss Martha Morton with her "Bachelor's Romance" in which Mr. John Hare is adding to his laurels. *The Daily Mail* says that the play is "full of Dickens tenderness and full of Dickens laughter, and it is never for an instant dull." Not only do the critics agree that the play is a good one, but the public has taken it up enthusiastically.

Then, after announcing that "Paris has established a Théâtre Féministe for the purpose of giving women playwrights a chance," he wrote:

> In this country we have not found it necessary to establish a women's theatre, for the reason that women are given the same opportunities as men in all our theatres. It does not take a woman manager to know that Mrs. Riley [*sic*] and

> Miss Martha Morton write clever plays, and it is the play, not the playwright's sex, that our managers are interested in.[29]

Tell that to Martha Morton, who sent her first manuscripts out in the 1880s under the pseudonym of Henry Hazelton and who recalled a man giving her the "comforting assurance," early in her career, "that a woman would have to do twice the work of a man to get one-half the credit. Since then I have been treated just as well, and just as badly as a man."[30]

It is impossible to judge plays we have not read or seen on a stage. Critics of her day seem to have found Martha Morton's plays (she wrote thirty between 1888 and 1908) the most successful of those being written by women. But if it is true, as Singleton and Dreiser claimed, that some of her plays present "social problems," those scripts have not become accessible to scholars. Our evidence is that not until Rachel Crothers is there an American woman playwright who begins to address feminist issues. Of her published plays, only *Criss Cross*[31] was written before 1900. The heroine of this one-act play, Ann Chadwick, makes a living as a writer, and she gives up the man she loves to her cousin Cecil, who needs a man to lean on more than she does. There are elements of melodrama in Ann's sacrifice, but real questions are posed about female independence. This little play points clearly in theme to the twentieth century. Perhaps some of Martha Morton's do, too.

Some critics do not begin to consider American drama until Eugene O'Neill. Perhaps feminist critics should wait for Rachel Crothers, yet it seems important to acknowledge that there were women writing plays in the nineteenth century. They were not Ibsens or Strindbergs, but neither were their playwright brothers. They worked hard at their craft, writing in the variety of styles demanded by the voracious theaters of the day. It is somehow gratifying that they were often well rewarded financially. Only Mowatt early and Crothers late seem canonically secure, but others also deserve our attention, because they learned the needs of the theater of their day and wrote well for it.

Notes

1. Laurence Hutton, *Curiosities of the American Stage* (New York: Harper and Brothers, 1891), p. 8.

2. Caroline Tichnor, *Hawthorne and His Publisher* (1913; reprint ed., Port Washington, N.Y.: Kennikat Press, 1969), p. 135.

3. George C. D. Odell, *Annals of the New York Stage*, 15 vol. (New York: Columbia University Press, 1927–49): 5 (1931), p. 99.

4. Mary Caroline Crawford, *The Romance of the American Theatre* (New York: Halcyon House, 1940), p. 455. Mowatt's career as an actress, novelist, memoirist, and play-

wright is particularly well documented by Marius Blesi, whose 1938 dissertation has been respectfully plundered by scholars for years.

5. Between 1842 and 1845, usually under the name of "Helen Berkley," Mowatt wrote pieces for *Godey's Lady's Book*, *Graham's*, *The Ladies Companion*, et al. She wrote them to order, for a profit. In the same way, she wrote etiquette books, cook books, and novels. But all this scribbling did not bring in enough money, nor did it put her considerable energies to good enough use. See Anna Cora Mowatt, *Autobiography of an Actress; or Eight Years on the Stage* (Boston: Ticknor, Reed, and Fields, 1854), pp. 184–86.

6. Mowatt, *Autobiography of an Actress*, p. 216.

7. Ibid., p. 202.

8. Ibid., pp. 203–4.

9. Both of her professionally produced plays were published in one volume in an American edition in 1854. Her second play, *Armand; or, the Peer and the Peasant*, was first produced at the Park Theatre in 1847, subsequently in Boston and London. A historical blank verse play, *Armand* is scarcely known and never revived in our time.

10. In *Broadway Journal*, 20 March 1845, quoted in *Israfel: The Life and Times of Edgar Allan Poe*, by Hervey Allen (New York: Farrar and Rinehart, 1934), p. 517.

11. James A. Harrison, ed., *The Complete Works of Edgar Allan Poe*, 17 vol. (1902; reprint ed., New York: AMS Press, 1965), pp. 121, 124.

12. Anna Cora Mowatt, *Fashion*, in *Plays* (Boston: Ticknor and Fields, 1854), pp. 1–62. Subsequent references are cited parenthetically by page number.

13. See Daniel F. Havens, *The Columbian Muse of Comedy: The Development of a Native Tradition in Early American Social Comedy: 1787–1845* (Carbondale: Southern Illinois University Press, 1973), 129–48.

14. L. [Louisa] H. Medina, *Nick of the Woods* (New York: Samuel French, 1838). See illustration in Stanley Appelbaum, ed., *Scenes From the 19th Century Stage in Advertising Woodcuts* (New York: Dover Publications, 1977), p. 4. Shown is "Act II, scene 5: Nick, the Avenger, scares off hostile Indians by shooting the falls in a blazing canoe."

15. Frances Wright—feminist, radical, reformer—emigrated from Scotland to America at twenty-one, in 1818, and brought with her several play scripts in progress. *Altorf* (a version of the William Tell story) was produced in New York and Philadelphia; although a theatrical failure, it made money as a book. She sent a copy to Thomas Jefferson, then living in retirement, who sent her words of praise and grateful thanks. See Richard Stiller, *Commune on the Frontier: The Story of Frances Wright* (New York: Thomas Y. Crowell, 1972), pp. 43–51.

16. Montrose J. Moses, ed., *Representative Plays by American Dramatists, From 1765 to the Present Day*, vol. 2 (New York: E. P. Dutton & Company, 1925), pp. 7–8, bibliography; 697–703, notes; 704–64, text of *Self*.

17. Ibid., p. 697.

18. Review of *Self*, in *Porter's Spirit of the Times*, 1 November 1856, n.p., New York Public Library Theatre Collection clipping.

19. Clement Scott's impression, quoted in Moses, *Representative Plays by American Dramatists*, p. 703.

20. Matilda Heron was an accomplished actress, best known for her role as Camille in her own translation of the play of that title. I have been unable to find a copy of the society play cited by Hutton.

21. Hutton, *Curiosities of the American Stage*, pp. 75–76.

22. Arthur Hobson Quinn, *A History of the American Drama From the Beginning to the Civil War* (New York: Harper & Brothers, 1923), p. 365.

23. As *Lettarblair; Or, Loves Me, Loves Me Not*,it played for a special author's matinee on 22 October 1891.

24. Madeleine Lucette Ryley, *Jedbury Junior* (New York: Samuel French, 1900), p. 3. In London in 1896, it starred Frederick Kerr and was retitled *Jedbury Junior* because Christopher Columbus was the subject of several burlesques that season.

25. Esther Singleton, "American Women Playwrights," *Evry Month*, July 1898, n.p., New York Public Library Theatre Collection clipping.

26. *Way Down East*, originally titled *Annie Laurie*, was successful on Broadway and then all across the country on professional and amateur stages; it was the basis for D. W. Griffith's classic 1920 film, *Way Down East*, starring Lillian Gish. On stage and screen, it was a great money-maker. (In addition to commercial plays, women wrote didactic dramas; e.g., James Russell Lowell's sister, Mary Lowell Putnam, wrote an anti-slavery play in blank verse, *Tragedy of Errors* [1862]. They also wrote parlor dramas for their own amusement; e.g., Louisa May Alcott and her sister wrote plays published in 1893 as *Comic Tragedies*, and in 1875 Harriet Hosmer wrote *1975, A Prophetic Drama* for private theatricals in Rome.

27. Theodore Dreiser, "American Women as Successful Playwrights," *Success* 2 (17 June 1899): 485–86.

28. Martha Morton, *A Bachelor's Romance* (New York: Samuel French, 1912).

29. [The Lounger], *The Critic* 29 (5 February 1898): 94.

30. Martha Morton, quoted in Lucy France Pierce, "Women Who Write Plays," *World Today* 15 (July 1908): 725.

31. Rachel Crothers, *Criss Cross*, in *A Century of Plays by American Women*, ed. Rachel France (New York: Richards Rosen Press, 1979), pp. 25–29.

Bibliography

[Alcott, Louisa May.] "Jo" and "Meg." *Comic Tragedies*. Boston: Roberts Brothers, 1893.

Allen, Hervey. *Israfel: The Life and Times of Edgar Allan Poe*. New York: Farrar & Rinehart, 1934.

Appelbaum, Stanley, ed. *Scenes From the 19th Century Stage in Advertising Woodcuts*. New York: Dover Publications, 1977.

Blesi, Marius. "The Life and Letters of Anna Cora Mowatt." Ph.D. dissertation, University of Virginia, 1938.

Crawford, Mary Caroline. *The Romance of the American Theatre* [1925]. New York: Halcyon House, 1940.

Dreiser, Theodore. "American Women as Successful Playwrights." *Success* 2 (17 June 1899): 485–86.

Frame, Virginia. "Women Who Have Written Successful Plays." *The Theatre* 6 (October 1906): 264–66, ix.

France, Rachel, ed. *A Century of Plays by American Women*. New York: Richards Rosen Press, 1979.

Frost, S. Annie. *The Parlor Stage: A Collection of Charades and Proverbs*. New York: Dick & Fitzgerald Publisher, 1866.

Harrison, James A., ed. *The Complete Works of Edgar Allan Poe*, vol. 12. New York: AMS Press, 1965.

Havens, Daniel F. *The Columbian Muse of Comedy: The Development of a Native Tradition in Early American Social Comedy: 1787–1845*. Carbondale: Southern Illinois University Press, 1973.

[Hosmer, Harriet.] *1975, A Prophetic Drama*. Rome: printed privately, 1875.

Hutton, Laurence. *Curiosities of the American Stage*. New York: Harper & Brothers, 1891.

[The Lounger]. *The Critic* 29 (5 February 1898): 94.

Medina, L. [Louisa] H. *Nick of the Woods*. New York: Samuel French, 1838.

Merlington, Marguerite. *Captain Lettarblair*. Indianapolis, Ind.: The Bobbs-Merrill Company, 1906.

Morton, Martha. *A Bachelor's Romance*. New York: Samuel French, 1912.

Moses, Montrose J., ed. *Representative Plays by American Dramatists, From 1765 to the Present Day*, vol. 1. New York: E. P. Dutton, 1925.

Mowatt, Anna Cora [Ritchie, Anna Cora (Ogden)]. *Autobiography of an Actress; or Eight Years on the Stage*. Boston: Ticknor, Reed, and Fields, 1854.

———. *Plays*. Boston: Ticknor and Fields, 1854.

Odell, George C. D., *Annals of the New York Stage*, vol. 5. New York: Columbia University Press, 1913.

Pierce, Lucy France. "Women Who Write Plays." *World Today* 15 (July 1908): 725–31.

Porter's Spirit of the Times (1 November 1856), n.p. New York Public Library Theatre Collection clipping.

Putnam, Mary Lowell. *Tragedy of Errors*. Boston: Ticknor and Fields, 1862.

Quinn, Arthur Hobson. *A History of the American Drama From the Beginning to the Civil War*. New York: Harper & Brothers, 1923.

Ryley, Madeleine Lucette. *Jedbury Junior*. New York: Samuel French, 1900.

Singleton, Esther. "American Women Playwrights ." *Evry Month* (July 1898). n.p. New York Public Library Theatre Collection clipping.

Stiller, Richard. *Commune on the Frontier: The Story of Frances Wright*. New York: Thomas Y. Crowell, 1972.

Ticknor, Caroline. *Hawthorne and His Publisher* [1913]. Port Washington, N. Y.: Kennikat Press, 1969.

Part 2
Twentieth-Century Playwrights

3
Rachel Crothers: Broadway Feminist

Doris Abramson

> If you want to see the sign of the times watch women. Their evolution is the most important thing in modern life.
>
> —Rachel Crothers

When Rachel Crothers's play *He and She* was revived at the Brooklyn Academy of Music in 1980, the *New York Times* published an article by Jean Ashton intended to introduce Crothers to a new audience. Although her plays were on Broadway stages between 1906 and 1937—twenty five plays in all, many of them critical as well as popular successes—even her name had been forgotten by all but students of American theater history and criticism. The caption for Ashton's article was startling: "The Neil Simon of Her Day—And an Ardent Feminist."[1] Could that be? Could a woman playwright have a long career on Broadway and write from a feminist perspective? The answer is yes if we are not too stringent, too doctrinaire in defining feminism. Crothers fits the definition given in Alice Duer Miller's 1915 rhyme:

> "Mother, what is a Feminist?"
> "A Feminist, my daughter,
> Is any woman now who cares
> To think about her own affairs
> As men don't think she oughter."[2]

Her plays for the most part meet Megan Terry's criteria for feminist drama: "Anything that gives women confidence, shows themselves to themselves, helps them to begin to analyze whether it's a positive or negative image. . . ."[3] Crothers tucked woman-centered questions into her social comedies, yet, like Neil Simon, she made a good living turning out a string of well-crafted Broadway productions. Ashton states:

> Few men, let alone women, have had a comparably full and rewarding professional career. Although she was neither an innovator nor a genius, Miss Crothers brought to the theater a high degree of dramatic efficiency and technical skill. She wrote gracefully about articulate people attempting to adjust to new social values and shifting sexual mores. Most often, she wrote about women and their relationships with men, with their children, and with one another.[4]

Crothers was born in Bloomington, Illinois, in 1879.[5] Writers of articles about her and reviewers of her early plays mention that both her parents were doctors, that she had written a play at age 12 or 13, that she participated in a dramatic club in high school, that she studied elocution in Boston after graduating from the State Normal School in Bloomington and that—after giving recitals and teaching elocution in her home town—she went to New York to embark on an acting career. Sometimes they mention that she appeared with E. H. Sothern's company, the Lyceum Stock Company, but one gets the impression that writing scenes for her students (after one term she became an instructor at Stanhope-Wheaton) meant more to her than acting on the professional stage. No doubt, time spent with a professional stock company served her well, however, when she started writing plays and later when she directed them.[6] A reviewer of her first Broadway play, *The Three of Us* (1906), has this observation:

> Miss Crothers' working days have been passed entirely in the artificial atmosphere of the playhouse, yet no successful drama of recent years is as free from theatrical fustian and claptrap as hers.[7]

In this first play, she used what suited her from the melodrama that she had observed and in which she had participated, but she already seemed intent upon making a statement. Another reviewer went so far as to say that "*The Three of Us*. . . . possesses in a marked degree those elements which some day may give us an American drama." The discussion that follows is a reminder that 1907 is not so far removed from Anna Cora Mowatt's time:

> In our drama, as in our dinners and our dress . . . we still look abroad for the leading fashions, but (says John Corbin of *The Sun*) "Miss Rachel Crothers's maiden effort will serve to remind us that there is another half to our makeup, and one worthy of more attention than it often gets . . . a bourgeois realism which, while not new to the drama, comes very near being a native and spontaneous growth with us."[8]

As she would be for the next three decades, Crothers was praised widely by the critics, although few of them on this occasion mentioned the new note she brought to the stage when her young heroine did not hide after being discovered in a gentleman's rooms. Having nothing to conceal, she stood her ground, thus breaking with a long-established stage convention. It seems a small victory, but in 1918 a writer for *The Nation* was still commenting on it: "Her first successful play, *The Three of Us*, gave the deathblow to the cherished theatrical convention that a woman's honor must be fatally injured because she happens to be alone in a room with a man after sundown."[9] It was the first but not the last time that Crothers dealt with a double standard of morality, one for men and another for women. She went on to write plays that called attention to career versus marriage, religious skepticism, divorce, trial marriage, the generation gap, and, many times over, a woman's right to live out her own destiny in honesty and freedom.

Emma Goldman, who quoted with approval Strindberg's statement that the modern artist is "a lay preacher popularizing the pressing questions of his time," said of the American theater in 1914: "Unfortunately, we in America have so far looked upon the theater as a place of amusement only, exclusive of ideas and inspiration."[10] It is unlikely that Crothers set out consciously to answer this challenge, but she did choose to create commercially pleasing plays into which she folded ideas; and at times those ideas may have inspired audiences witnessing these problem plays in the guise of social comedies to think about the pressing questions of her time.

Critics took Crothers seriously from the beginning. In 1910, reviewing *A Man's World*, Walter Prichard Eaton wrote of the play's "searching truth of feminine psychology, its air of quiet but studied realism, its obvious significance as a comment on the feminist movement of the day—a thoughtful, sympathetic intelligent comment."[11] Reviewing *Ourselves* in 1914, Arthur Ruhl concluded, "The play throughout was the statement of a conviction, but the passionate statement of it, fused into dramatic action; the work of a woman of sophisticated intelligence and fine feeling who brought to the revolt shared by most American women of her class the power of expression generally supposed to belong to men."[12] Standards of excellence were inevitably masculine. In the Eaton review just cited, he noted in passing that *A Man's World*, although "an interesting and at times a moving play, frankly and honestly written from a woman's point of view . . . just misses the masculinity of structure and the inevitableness of episode necessary to make it dramatic literature."[13]

Florence Kiper, writing in 1914 about several plays that she considered to be written from the feminist viewpoint—of the ten playwrights whose work she discussed, only two were women, Marion Fairfax (who has left no easily discovered tracks) and Rachel Crothers—said this about *A Man's World:*

> *A Man's World* is honest, well-built drama, interesting to feminists not only because of its exposition of a modern sex-problem, but also because it is written by a woman—one who does not attempt to imitate the masculine viewpoint, but who sees the feminine experience through feminine temperament.[14]

Yet Kiper gave three times as much space to Augustus Thomas as she did to Crothers, without even mentioning her influence on his play *As A Man Thinks* (1911), which she analyzes here. In that play, Mrs. Seelig, in an argument with her husband, says: "And that woman dramatist with her play was right. It is 'a man's world.' "[15] It would have been interesting for her readers to have had this comparison drawn, but one cannot fault Kiper, because to this day women's works—whether fiction, poetry, or drama—are rarely seen to influence men's. Yet men over the years must have been reading women's writing (not just Virginia Woolf and George Eliot) and been affected by it.

Over the years Crothers was praised for craftsmanship, variety of subject matter, and topicality—for plays Barrett Clark called "well-bred, witty, and wise."[16] In 1929, Richard Cordell wrote: "Her plays are all aimed directly at stage presentation; her eye is on the contemporary audience; she knows precisely how to utilize legitimate stage business, how to balance nicely her use of sentiment, humor, and irony: she is a master of dramatic economy."[17] Brooks Atkinson, Arthur Hobson Quinn, Burns Mantle, Joseph Wood Krutch, R. Dana Skinner, and Thomas Dickinson were among the many who sang her praises. She had her detractors, of course, but they were few, among them George Jean Nathan, whose specialty was the put down. He referred to Crothers's plays as "box office trivialities" and called her "a successful second-rater at best."[18]

The University of Pennsylvania invited her in 1928—along with Jesse Lynch Williams, Langdon Mitchell, Lord Dunsany, and Gilbert Emery—to give a lecture entitled "The Construction of a Play."[19] On this occasion, she was a singular woman in a world of men, acknowledging her debt to Ibsen, praising Sheldon, O'Neill, Howard, and Barry. No mention of feminism was made, and no reference was given to her plays and their subject matter. The significant thing is that she was invited and taken seriously even in academe.

It is not easy to imagine what it was like for Crothers when she began her career as a Broadway playwright. There were many women writing plays for Broadway at the turn of the century, so many that one Washington critic was quoted as saying: "Women don't write plays; they put them in a squirt gun and push the plunger."[20] They were turning out plays written to formula for the stars of the day. To get an idea of how they were viewed by the newspapers, one need only notice that interviews with and articles about "lady playwrights" were often placed on the society page. Here is the opening of an account of "Women Dramatists' Night" at the Hungry Club in 1910:

> "Women Dramatists' Night" at the one hundred and eighty-second dinner of the Hungry Club Saturday evening at the Hotel Flanders, was an unqualified success.
>
> More than one hundred and fifty were present to greet the guests of honor, who were Mrs. Anne Crawford Flexner, Mrs. Edith Ellis Furness, Miss Alice E. Ives, Miss Cora Maynard, Mrs. Chauncey Olcott, Miss Katherine Stagg and Mrs. Rida Johnson Young. Mattie Sheridan, the club's president and toastmaster, explained that the guests of honor were placed on the prettily printed program in alphabetical order that no favorites might be played. Each dramatist present made a happy little speech. . . .[21]

We are told that Mrs. Chauncey Olcott was introduced as "the baby dramatist" because she had just writen her first play. Among those invited but "prevented by absence from town" from accepting was Rachel Crothers.

All very charming and more than a little patronizing, this account tells us much about women playwrights in the commercial theater of the time. Rachel Crothers—Zoë Akins, Susan Glaspell, and a few others—had to get off the society pages to be taken seriously as playwrights. There was always the danger that, being female, they would be characterized as "girls" (Nathan's name for them) or praised for their homemaking in an article about their playmaking. As late as 1941, Charlotte Hughes wrote that "Rachel Crothers, Zoë Akins and Rose Franken are inordinately proud of being good housekeepers." She said of Rachel Crothers, whom she called "the dean of the women playwrights," that "she reminds you of the finest type of very human, understanding teacher." She assured her readers that these playwrights were not militant, they were "simply beyond all that." To show how the women "bristle noticeably at feminist talk," she quoted the one most often called a feminist, Crothers, as saying, "What a picayune, self-conscious side all this woman business has to it."[22] She seems to have been reacting against being interviewed yet again as a *woman playwright*, not just as a *playwright*.

By 1941, Crothers had given many interviews, beginning in 1910 when she was interviewed by Ada Patterson of *Theater Magazine*. That piece began:

> "I have convictions, but I am not a reformer." Rachel Crothers, the author of "A Man's World" and "The Three of Us," smiled a serious little half smile. . . . "I have convictions," she went on. "I believe every playwright has, or no play could be written. But try to reform the world, to reform men"—her

slim hand waved away the possibility. It was an eloquent gesture, showing the helplessness and hopelessness of such an effort.

Asked if she believed, with the heroine of *A Man's World*, that a man should have the same standard of morals as a woman, she answered:

> "I believe it with all my soul, but I am not trying to force that opinion upon the world. The playwright's province is not reform. If a conviction of the playwright can be clothed in a dramatic story and make an entertaining play, very good. But it never was my intention to preach."[23]

When Charlotte Hughes asked her thirty years later if women writers are particularly good at creating women characters, she answered:

> "I've been told that my plays are a long procession reflecting the changing attitude of the world toward women. If they are, that was completely unconscious on my part. . . . I suppose I call upon the way-deep-down insides of women more than I do men."[24]

The women in her plays are intelligent, attractive, and witty. They are, for the most part, "well-bred, well-read, and well-to-do."[25] Many have careers: there are writers (Ann Chadwick in *Criss Cross*, Frank Ware in *A Man's World*); a sculptor (Ann Herford in *He and She*); a singer (Lione in *A Man's World*); an actress (Mrs. Dan Raymond in *Peggy*); a dancer (in *39 East*), to mention a few. When they are married, they may be questioning that state; and although much has been made of her heroines moving back into matrimonial security at the final curtain (Lucile in *As Husbands Go* is the best example), it is never without argument or attempts at rational discussion of marriage. Her women try on ideas, but few of them are unequivocally brave. One reason why Eleanor Flexner expressed her disappointment in Crothers's later plays, preferring the very early *A Man's World*,[26] is that the heroine of that play, Frank Ware, takes a stand that comes out of rational arguments witnessed by the theater audience. (The question then arises: Did Crothers give her a man's name to remind us that women writers frequently took men's names to get an initial hearing from publishers?) The playwright's empathy with Frank prompted audience empathy through careful construction of a discussion similar to those of G. B. Shaw. Frank Ware, like Major Barbara, has to stand up to wrong ideas even when they are embodied in a man who, in other respects, is attractive.

That time after time in her plays Crothers wrote about women who were trying to decide between a career and marriage is not surprising in view of the period in which she was writing for the commercial theater. Well into the thirties, magazines and popular songs were filled with references to "the womanly woman" who married, had babies, and was dutiful to husband and children. In other words, the ideas of the nineteenth century that were being challenged in many areas of art and life had to be supported by the conservatives who always contend that a woman's place is in the home. "The woman as Mother was made in heaven," says Martha Banta, "a heaven relocated 'down here' in the American home." She goes on to observe:

> But turn-of-the-century American women were, after all, human, and humans are volatile and possess energies that roll away from under the idealizing thumb like pellets of mercury. The conservative imagination was in trouble once women began to unfix themselves from the conceptual containers set by posters, murals, and the home-hearth.[27]

Crothers's plays reflect the conflict arising at that moment in our history when women were beginning to assert their individuality in careers, and when some were trying either to have an equal partnership with men or to find a way to sustain an old-fashioned marriage while being a New Woman.

One of the strengths of *A Man's World* is that not all the women are at the same level of emancipation, although each has to make decisions about how to live as a woman early in the twentieth century. Each is given new freedoms, but these are endangered by customs that die hard. For example, Clara is an old maid. There have been many old maids in American drama before and since her, but she is not a stage stereotype; we attend her pitiful outcry because she is really trying to understand the state she finds herself in.

> *Clara*. . . . I've tried just as hard as I can for ten years—and scrimped and scraped and taken snubs and pretended I was ambitious and didn't care for anything but my work, and look at me—don't even know how I am going to pay my next month's rent. I'm so sick and tired of it all I don't know what to do. I'd marry any man that asked me.
> *Frank*. Now, you're not going to lose your nerve like this.
> *Clara*. I would. I'd marry anything that could pay the bills.
> *Frank*. Poor little girl. It is a hard fight, isn't it?
> *Clara*. It doesn't pay. I've been too terribly respectable and conventional all my life to succeed. If I were like you—you're so strong and independent—you believe in women taking care of themselves.
> *Frank*. I believe in women doing the thing they're most fitted for. You should have married, Clara, when you were a young girl—and been taken care of all your life. Why didn't you? Don't you believe in that?
> *Clara*. No man has ever asked me to marry him. I've never had a beau—a real beau—in my life. I—I've always been superfluous and plain. Absolutely superfluous. I'm not necessary to one single human being. I'm just one of those everlasting women that the world is full of. There's nobody to take care of me and I'm simply not capable of taking care of myself. . . . If I were a man—the most insignificant little runt of a man—I could persuade some woman to marry me—and could have a home and children and hustle for

> my living—and life would mean something. Oh, I can't bear it, Frank. I can't bear it! I often wish I were pretty and bad and could have my fling and die.[28]

Her case is made, and even Frank's offer to have her work in the "new club we're opening," to become someone of use to others—"Oh, do you think I could help anybody?", she asks Frank—cannot take away the poignancy of her cry, "I've always been superfluous and plain."

Lione, an opera singer in the same play, is another matter. Here she is on a double standard of morality:

> I've never thought much about the whole business myself. Men are pigs of course. They take all they can get and don't give any more than they have to. It's a man's world—that's the size of it. What's the use of knocking your head against things you can't change? I never believed before that you really meant all this helping women business. What's the use? You can't change anything to save your neck. Men are men.[29]

A Man's World is the bravest, perhaps even the best of Crothers's plays. Eleanor Flexner certainly thought so when she praised it above Crothers's later plays; "Miss Crothers has come increasingly to sacrifice dramatic force and honesty of thought for sprightliness and well-turned phrases."[30]

But even in the sprightly comedies, Crothers wrote about women and their problems in a striking fashion. Here are two women talking in a one-act comedy of the twenties:

> *Nancy.* No man on earth could possibly be as important to me as I am to myself.
>
> *Connie. (lighting another cigarette from the one she has just finished).* Yes, dear—you're a superwoman—we all know that—president of more organizations, with your fingers in more uplifts and a larger income flowing into your check-book than most *men* have who have worked like dogs all their lives. Still, my darling—you *are* an old maid—and that's an awfully stupid thing to be.
>
> *Nancy.* I'm not an old maid. I'm a woman who hasn't married and I'm not sure that it isn't the most distinguished thing a woman *can* be.
>
> *Connie.* It takes an awfully big woman to be unmarried and not be an old maid. . . . I don't think you're quite up to that.
>
> *Nancy.* Who *is* in that class if I'm not? I haven't slipped back one inch since the war. Most women who sort of rose to something then have slumped into themselves again, but I've gone *on*. My life gets much fuller and wider all the time. There's no room for men. Why—*why* should I give up my own personal life—or let it be changed in the slightest degree for a man?[31]

When Connie tells her that no woman is complete without a man in her life, Nancy says that is "rank old-fashioned outlived nonsense."[32] The lightness of touch does not betray the ideas tossed out here.

Crothers then drops this observation about divorce into a scene in *Let Us Be Gay* (1929):

> *Mrs. Boucicault.* I always knew my husband wasn't faithful to me, but I lived in hell with him for fifty years because divorce wasn't respectable. My only daughter had three divorces—which I was tickled to death to see her get—and here's my grandchild in the middle of this moral revolution and I'm helpless—can't do a thing for her.[33]

The irony of the old woman insisting on her granddaughter marrying—"She's got to walk up that aisle a perfectly decent girl"[34]—is a clever device for getting an audience to consider attitudes toward divorce and marriage in the twenties.

When Ladies Meet, Crothers's best written comedy of the thirties, is basically a study of infidelity in which the wife, Claire, and the "other woman," Mary, both give up sharing Roger because they have come to know each other. Claire tells her husband: "I've always been glad to get you back before—and thankful it was over—always thinking of *you*—never of *her*—but now—I've *seen her*—and something has happened *to me*. I've seen *all* of her—her whole heart and soul and self. And I know—*so well* how you made her love you like that."[35] A light comedy swirls around an intriguing message about the double standard.

In addition to *A Man's World*, the Crothers play that seems most likely to belong in the twentieth-century canon of significant works by women playwrights is *He and She*. It was first written in 1911, tried out on the road, revised several times, and brought to New York in 1920. In this play, Crothers speculated on the price in human relationships that women artists pay to practice their art. Both Tom and Ann Herford are sculptors; yet the play is not about their professional rivalry but about Ann's need to be a mother when their child requires her to be. She sets aside her career to be with a teenage daughter whom she comes to believe she has neglected. Alexander Woollcott was outspoken in his review, calling the play a true tragedy:

> . . . for something fine and strong dies in the last act. It is the hope, the ambition and all the future work of a genius—deliberately slain in order that the "she" of *He and She* may be able to play more attentively and more whole-heartedly what she is driven to regard as her more important role—that of wife and mother. For this play by Miss Crothers rehearses the tragedy of the new woman, with her longing for a creative career and the obligations of her home warring within her.[36]

When Ann turns her work over to her husband (he will complete her prize-winning frieze for her), her last substantial speech before the final curtain is in response to her husband's saying that "there'll be times when you'd eat your heart out to be at work on it—when the artist in you will *yell* to be let out."

> I know. I know. And I'll hate you because you're doing it—and I'll hate myself because I gave it up—and I'll almost—hate—her. . . . You needn't tell me. Why, I've seen my men and women up there—their strong limbs stretched—their hair blown back. I've seen the crowd looking up—I've heard people say—"A woman did that" and my heart has almost burst with pride—not so much that *I* had done it—but for *all* women. And then the door opened—and Millicent came in. There isn't any choice, Tom—she's part of my body—part of my soul.[37]

Woollcott cautioned his readers not to assume too hastily that Crothers was advocating domestic existence over a career as an artist, "for the woman in her play is already a wife and mother, already under moral contract to play that role as well as it can be played." He then adds that Crothers no doubt believes that the road taken depends on the woman and that "there are enough women in the world to keep both roads fairly congested."[38]

Was Rachel Crothers, then, an ardent feminist? Speeches in *A Man's World* and *He and She* make her seem so, and yet one hesitates at the word *ardent*. A woman who had her eye on Broadway success—and who achieved it over a long period of time—had to disguise her ardor for a feminist message. She put critics off guard at times by giving them the polished comedies that Broadway audiences wanted, and inserting into them some questions about women's position in American society. She took time-worn themes and breathed new life into them by approaching questions a bit differently, always from a woman's point of view. Her popularity in her own time should not keep us from acknowledging her contribution to American theater.

Notes

1. Jean Ashton, "The Neil Simon of Her Day—And An Ardent Feminist," *New York Times*, 25 May 1980, sec. 2, pp. 3, 16.
2. Alice Duer Miller, "Feminism," in *Are Women People?: A Book of Rhymes for Suffrage Times* (New York: George H. Doran Company, 1915), p. 64.
3. "Megan Terry." Interview with Dinah L. Leavitt, in *Women in American Theatre: Careers, Images, Movements: An Illustrated Anthology and Sourcebook*, ed. Helen Krich Chinoy and Linda Walsh Jenkins (New York: Crown Publishers, 1981), p. 288.
4. Ashton, "The Neil Simon of Her Day," p. 3.
5. Throughout her lifetime and for many years after her death in 1958, her birth date was given as 1878, but both the 1900 U. S. Census and her death certificate confirm 1870. See Barbara Sicherman and Carol Hurd Green, eds., *Notable American Women: The Modern Period: A Biographical Dictionary* (Cambridge: Harvard University Press, 1980), p. 176.
6. Lois C. Gottlieb, *Rachel Crothers* (Boston: Twayne Publishers, 1979), pp. 17–18. This study stands as the best Crothers criticism we have to date.

7. *Appleton's*, April 1907, n.p., New York Public Library Theatre Collection clipping.
8. *Current Literature*, January 1907, n.p., New York Public Library Theatre Collection clipping.
9. M. C. D. [Mary Caroline Davis], "Women and the American Theatre," *The Nation* 106 (1 June 1918): 665.
10. Emma Goldman, *The Social Significance of the Modern Drama* (Boston: Richard G. Badger, 1914), pp. 3, 5.
11. Walter Prichard Eaton, "Miss Crothers Champions Her Sex," in *At The New Theatre and Others: The American Stage: Its Problems and Performance, 1908–1910* (Boston: Small, Maynard, 1910), p. 155.
12. Arthur Ruhl, *Second Nights: People and Ideas of the Theatre To-day* (New York: Charles Scribner's Sons, 1914), pp. 139–40.
13. Eaton, "Miss Crothers Champions Her Sex," p. 156.
14. Florence Kiper, "Some American Plays: From the Feminist Viewpoint," *The Forum* 51 (1914): 928.
15. Augustus Thomas, *As A Man Thinks*, in *Modern American Plays*, ed. George P. Baker (New York: Harcourt, Brace, 1921), p. 65.
16. Quoted in Sicherman and Green, eds., *Notable American Women*, p. 175.
17. Richard A. Cordell, ed., *Representative Modern Plays: British and American from Robertson to O'Neill* (New York: Thomas Nelson and Sons, 1929), p. 499.
18. George Jean Nathan, "Why Women Can't Write Plays" (New York: King Features Syndicate, 1937), n.p., New York Public Library Theatre Collection clipping.
19. Rachel Crothers, "The Construction of a Play," in *The Art of Playwriting* (Philadelphia: University of Pennsylvania Press, 1928), pp. 115–34.
20. Quoted in Virginia Frame, "Women Who Have Written Successful Plays," *The Theatre* 6 (October 1906): 264.
21. "Women Dramatists Tell How Easy It Is to Write a Play That Is a Success," *New York Telegraph*, 7 February 1910, n.p., New York Public Library Theatre Collection clipping.
22. Charlotte Hughes, "Women Playwrights," *New York Times Magazine*, 4 May 1941, pp. 10, 11.
23. Ada Patterson, "Woman Must Live Out Her Destiny," *The Theatre* 40 (May 1910): 134.
24. Hughes, "Women Playwrights," p. 27.
25. Joseph Mersand, *The Play's The Thing* (1941; reprinted, Port Washington, N. Y.: Kennikat Press, 1968), p. 66.
26. Eleanor Flexner, *American Playwrights, 1918–1938: The Retreat from Reality* (New York: Simon and Schuster 1938), pp. 239–48.
27. Martha Banta, *Imagining American Women: Idea and Ideals in American Cultural History* (New York: Columbia University Press, 1987), pp. 678–79.
28. Rachel Crothers, *A Man's World*, in *Plays By American Women: 1900-1930*, ed. Judith E. Barlow (New York: Applause Theatre Book Publishers, 1985), pp. 52–53.
29. Ibid., p. 57.
30. Flexner, *American Playwrights, 1918–1938*, p. 239.
31. Rachel Crothers, *The Importance of Being a Woman*, in *Six One-Act Plays* (Boston: Walter H. Baker, 1925), pp. 70–71.
32. Ibid., p. 71.
33. Rachel Crothers, *Let Us Be Gay* (New York: Samuel French, 1929), p. 32.
34. Ibid.
35. Rachel Crothers, *When Ladies Meet* (New York: Samuel French, 1932), p. 133.
36. Alexander Woollcott, "The Play," *New York Times*, 13 February 1920, p. 16. Earlier titled *The Herfords*, when it reached Broadway as *He and She*, Crothers played the role of Ann Herford for a brief time.
37. Rachel Crothers, *He and She* (Boston: Walter H. Baker, 1933), p. 126.
38. Woollcott, "The Play," p. 16.

4
Rebellion and Rejection: The Plays of Susan Glaspell

Barbara Ozieblo

Susan Glaspell (1876–1948) is a prime example of the "peculiar eclipsing" so frequently suffered by women writers.[1] She devoted eight years to the Provincetown Players, and her plays alone would have justified the claim that the sand dunes of Provincetown were the birthplace of modern American drama.[2] But Glaspell's voice was silenced, and although feminist literary criticism has rediscovered some of her work, she is still largely unknown.[3] Experimental in form and content, her plays brought expressionism and social criticism to the American stage, and her contribution on this count is so significant that it cannot be treated adequately in a short essay. Here I have set a less ambitious goal: by focusing on those facets of her work that threaten male authority, I hope to account for Glaspell's exclusion from the dramatic canon.

The American dream is undeniably a man's dream: "the green breast of the new world" flowered for Dutch sailors while Margaret Fuller's earlier cry in vindication of women's rights, "Let them be sea-captains," became the butt of sexist jokes.[4] As Nina Baym points out in her work on American fiction, "the essence of American culture means that the matter of American experience is inherently male" and that it is conditioned by a deeply romantic promise, the myth that "a person will be able to achieve complete self-definition."[5] In American literature, this quest for identity has traditionally been the quest of men, with society, symbolically embodied in woman, identified as the obstacle. Glaspell's protagonists are women; they are superior to the male characters and have a disturbing habit of arrogating to themselves divine powers over life and death. Clearly, Glaspell's female characters threaten patriarchal authority. We should not be surprised, then, that many of Glaspell's reviewers dismissed her plays as nonsense and that the management of the Players deleted them from their repertoire after she had left.

Glaspell started her writing career in the Midwest as a newspaperwoman, short-story writer, and novelist; it was not until her marriage to George (Jig) Cram Cook catapulted her into the heart of Greenwich Village bohemia that she tried her hand at playwriting. In the summer of 1915, Cook's enthusiasm for the theater, which he saw as the life-giving force of ancient Greece, culminated in the first productions of the Provincetown Players—in a rickety old fishhouse on the end of an abandoned wharf. The following summer, Glaspell wrote *Trifles*, which was an immediate success and is still her best-known play. That autumn, Cook galvanized the Players into opening their first season in a converted warehouse on MacDougal Street, New York, where their principal playwrights were Eugene O'Neill and Susan Glaspell. O'Neill had joined the Players that summer with a "trunkful" of plays awaiting performance; Glaspell, not similarly equipped, conceived her plays specifically for the Provincetowners, experimenting with their 'untramelled little stage" and working out "her ideas in freedom."[6]

A stint on the *Des Moines Daily News* had early aroused Glaspell's interest in local and domestic politics; she was assigned to the statehouse and legislature, and this experience gave her material for many short stories and plays. It also convinced her that the local socialist party was too conservative, and she readily abandoned it when Jig Cook founded the more liberal Monist Society. New York City widened Glaspell's horizons further; but whereas Cook plunged joyfully into the "New Bohemia"—an exotic amalgam of the old Parisian bohemia, the Industrial Workers of the World, and the New Feminist Movement—Glaspell's poor health, which included a weak heart and gynecological problems, forced her to remain on the sidelines. In an interview in 1921, she justified her position by saying, "I am interested in all progressive movements, whether feminist, social or economic, but I can take no very active part other than through my writing."[7] And it was indeed through her work that she voiced her dissatisfaction with right-wing politics, forcefully expressing the "concern with wrongs to human beings in their times" that marks her as a feminist writer.[8]

At a time when the established American theater refused to deal with social problems (excepting those of marriage), Glaspell dared to tackle controversial issues, among them political dissent and the ambitions of a female Zarathustra.

The 1917 and 1918 Espionage and Sedition Acts, for example, outraged her democratic spirit, and she responded with *Inheritors*, which the Provincetown Players produced in 1920. The setting is a midwestern college campus that had been founded by the idealist Silas Morton, one of the earliest settlers, and Felix Fejevary, an exiled Hungarian revolutionary whose son is now on the board of trustees. The play opens in 1879 with a discussion of the pioneer days and of the importance of learning, and act 1 ends with Morton's decision to bequeath his best land to the building of a college. Act 2 shows how the expansion of the college brings about financial problems that must be solved. Felix Fejevary Junior does his best to convince Senator Lewis that the state should appropriate the college and so assure its future. Lewis agrees but imposes one condition: Professor Holden, a radical idealist and supporter of conscientious objectors, must go. By act 4, Fejevary has persuaded Holden of the advantages of silence, but he then is defeated by his niece—the granddaughter of both Silas Morton and Felix Fejevary Sr.—who insists on supporting Hindu students in their fight for independence. As the play ends, Madeline Morton leaves for the court hearing; there is no doubt that she will be imprisoned for her ideals.

This play is a feeling riposte to a historical moment, and although it is the least overtly feminist of Glaspell's plays, the surface plot thinly disguises her disappointment with patriarchal society, with man's weakness and his readiness to forego his ideals under pressure. Discretely, Glaspell mocks several male myths: the frontier myth; the myths of progress, learning and civilization; and in particular, the myth of male superiority. Her "leading" men, although endowed with redeeming virtues, are far from being supermen and frequently frustrate the expectations of the female protagonists. In *Inheritors*, Glaspell intelligently refuses to condemn or praise the individual outright, and her sympathies waver between Holden and Madeline, finally settling on the side of the female character. Holden's pusillanimous decision is excusable in the light of Mrs. Holden's costly illness, and Madeline's action, although it will bring sorrow to the family, is seen in the idealistic terms of the individual's self-sacrifice in the cause of freedom.

As a result of her first-hand experience, Glaspell was never tempted to sentimentalize pioneer life. She was a Midwesterner by birth and spent many years on Cape Cod, only a few miles from the Mayflower Pilgrims' reported first landing place and still a rough place to live in the 1910s. Thus, she could authoritatively expose the frontier myth of machismo, with the white man defending his women from savage Indians and wresting the land from barbarity, and she did so in a number of her novels and plays, but nowhere so incisively as in *Inheritors*. Silas Morton's grandmother used to give cookies to the Indians, who, in her words, were "mostly friendly when let be"; they did not attack or rape till the white man had "roiled them up" by taking their land (104).[9] Grandmother Morton had observed in the white man a similar attachment to the land, and her sympathetic understanding of his weaknesses is mingled with disgust at his love of violence. She herself had always been prepared to feed and help strangers, and she finds it difficult to accept that "nothing draws men together like killing other men" (106). She knew the hardships of pioneer life for a woman, and the news of the death of a Civil War veteran's wife provokes from her the heavily laden comment, "Well, I guess she's not sorry" (107). Self-reliant and hard-working, Grandmother Morton is reminiscent of Willa Cather's Alexandra in her love of the land: "A country don't make itself. When the sun was up we were up, and when the sun went down we didn't" (106).

The learning myth also is stripped of its romantic fallacies. Morton's generous spirit, love of the land, hard work, and initial friendship with the native Indians inspired him to build a college on a hill, visible for miles "for the boys of the cornfields—and the girls. . . . 'Twill make a difference—even to them that never go" (113–14). In Silas Morton's "dreams for the race," the college offered a "vision of what life could be," and it atoned for the wrong the white man had done to the native: "That's what that hill is for! Don't you see it! End of our trail, we climb a hill and plant a college" (113). Echo of the Puritan City on a hill and founded with the explicit purpose of redeeming the white man's bloody role in the Blackhawk War, the college ultimately generates the overwhelming desire for expansion and state appropriation—a "sivilization" that not all are free to reject. Holden's Whitmanesque vision of each man "being his purest and intensest self" is sourly compromised by financial interests—a consequence of patriarchal society Glaspell deplored (134).

Founder Morton's expansionist dream fails on another count. He had worked the fields to bring wealth to his family and community, but now his son Ira, who has experimented with corn and created an improved variety, curses the wind for carrying seeds to his neighbor's farm. The community tries to excuse Ira's obsession as a mental disorder and believes he is the price the white man pays for progress and growth, the "scar" left by the "lives back of him," that were too hard (141).

Ira's daughter Madeline compensates for his mean spirit when she takes up the cause of a group of Hindu students who have been inconsiderately preaching "the gospel of free India—non-British India" (122) on the day when Senator Lewis visits the college. Madeline is depicted first as a carefree, fun-loving, tennis-playing college senior who has no time or respect for her ancestors or elders. By play's end, however, she has shed her egotism and consciously adopted ideals that will require her to sacrifice her freedom. Madeline's first act of rebellion is to hit a policeman with a tennis racket: this childish reaction to the police harassment of the Hindu students sends her to prison. Released almost immediately after her uncle intervenes, she is shocked to discover that Fejevary has done nothing for the Hindus and horrified at their imminent deportation. The ensuing argument with Fejevary transforms the naive and impetuous college girl into an articulate adult aware of her feelings for her grandfather, the college, freedom, and what she always, although only half-consciously, believed to be the ideal of American democracy:

> *Madeline. (In a smoldering way.)* I thought America was a democracy.
> *Fejevary.* We have just fought a great war for democracy.
> *Madeline.* Well, is that any reason for not having it? (140)

Moments later, when the gang of students led by Fejevary's son provokes the Hindus and the police intervene again, Madeline has so far learned to control her impulses that she can respond without reverting to childish tantrums to express herself. Her impassioned speech proves her worthy of both of her grandfathers: "My grandfather gave this hill to Morton College—a place where anybody—from any land—can come and say what he believes to be true!" (142).

Although she does not come anywhere near the "superwoman" stature achieved by the protagonists of the later plays, Madeline does prefigure them, particularly the heroine of *The Verge* (1921). Claire is an older Madeline, weighted down by social and moral pressures; whereas Madeline is ingenuously prepared to sacrifice her physical freedom for the ideal of democracy, Claire despairs of ever attaining real freedom for woman, artist, or humanity. She realizes that the older order—symbolized in the play by a plant that grows in the shape of a cross—has failed her, but she is still afraid of challenging it; she finds it difficult to believe in the existence of a new and better dispensation or to express her vision of it coherently.

The Verge is Glaspell's most provocative play. The Provincetown Players "kept alive a stage dedicated to the experimental production of plays by American playwrights," and by 1921 Glaspell was sufficiently self-confident to use the many innovations both in content and stagecraft that the Players had adopted from Europe.[10] They took Strindberg, Ibsen, and Shaw for their models, although the Players' insistence on their own nationalistic aesthetics made them very reluctant to stage the Europeans; they assimilated the work of Stanislavski and Reinhardt, and they were ready to incorporate at least some of the tenets of expressionism then coming to the fore in Germany. Cook insisted on building a dome for O'Neill's *The Emperor Jones* to create an illusion of expanded space, for example, and he was impatient to try out the ideas of Adolphe Appia and Gordon Craig. *The Verge* is an example of the assimilation of European trends in using characteristically expressionistic settings to reveal the mind of the protagonist. Concerning content, the play criticizes the stifling doll's house a marriage can become; but by not insisting on the gender of the protagonist, it portrays successfully the lot of humankind, trapped by established norms and unable to overcome itself.

The play opens in a luscious and overheated greenhouse in which Claire experiments with plants. She believes she can exploit a technique of transplanting to create new organisms that are liberated from the previous forms and functions of plant life. Tom, Dick, and Harry (confidant, lover, and husband) violate this sanctum when they seek a warm spot for breakfast. Hoping to end the farcical bickering that follows, Claire attempts to express her Nietzschean desire to overcome established patterns and to break into whatever lies beyond; of the three men in her life, only Tom gropes toward an understanding of her disjointed sentences. In act 2, Claire's sister Adelaide invades her study, a strangely twisted and uncannily lit tower that is an outward sign of Claire's disturbed mind. Adelaide's mission is to convince her sister to play the part of the dutiful mother and wife, but Claire is too close to transcendence to take heed. On the brink of uncovering her latest experiment, the plant she calls "Breath of Life," she is staggered by fear of the retaliation of the God whose life-giving powers she has appropriated. Claire seeks a haven in consummating her relationship with the sympathetic Tom, but, in deference to her superior spirit, he denies her that ordinary human refuge. The second act ends with Claire's hysterical plea for "Anything—everything—that will let me be nothing!" (92). In act 3, back in the greenhouse, we witness the unveiling of the new plant and Claire's success in creating a hitherto unknown life form. Yet the achievement is clearly ambivalent; any organism is condemned to repetition and stagnation unless it continually overcomes itself. Claire is fully aware of that baleful dilemma; when Tom finally offers his love, she is appalled at the prospect of being engulfed by mediocre patterns and relentlessly chokes him to death. The murder parallels the suffocating norms of society, that inevitably silence the creative urge in those who refuse to conform, but the family sees Claire's convulsive action as final proof of her insanity. The play ends on a savagely ironic note as Claire chants the hymn "Nearer, my God, to Thee," which Adelaide, intuiting blasphemy, had refused to sing previously in her presence. Claire, a female Faust, now is her own God and cannot be reached by societal structures and compunctions; she has broken out and is free existentially, alone in the transcendental beyond. Like the protagonist of *Inheritors,* Claire rejects the laws of the patriarchal world, but unlike her she refuses to deal with them on their own terms.

Glaspell is careful in *Inheritors* not to be too harsh on the male characters, but in *The Verge* she is not so generous; she allows each in turn to prove his inferiority to Claire. As their names suggest, Tom, Dick, and Harry are stereotypes; they are incapable of helping Claire define herself fully in a patriarchal society or of protecting her from the consequences of transcending it. Harry, the husband, does his utmost to understand her, but his down-to-earth character is an impossible barrier to comprehension or communication. Dick paternally dismisses Claire's strange behavior as "the excess of a particularly rich temperament" (65); Tom commits the unforgivable error of offering her a bourgeois relationship. In the earlier play, which is less fiercely feminist, Fejevary and Holden are neither dim-witted nor guilty of paternalism; they are motivated by less idealistic concerns than Madeline, and Fejevary duly convinces Holden that his wife's health is more important than his ideology: "You'd like, of course, to be just what you want to be—but isn't there something selfish in that satisfaction?" he asks (136).

Claire is selfish—a male prerogative in the 1920s—and it is precisely her determination to create a satisfactory life for herself that aroused the fervent admiration of the Greenwich Village feminists and brought "religious excitement" to their voices and eyes when talking of *The Verge.*[11] This was Glaspell's most impiously feminist play, although she had touched on the same issues in *Inheritors;* in the earlier play, she had established Madeline's need for the freedom to define herself as an individual, contrasting physical with mental imprisonment and allowing her to choose the former. As a result of her death-dealing, Claire also will be confined to four walls, but she too will have the satisfaction of a mind free of the restrictions society imposes. Both women rebel against conventional roles in their determination to make themselves new (96); and although the author approves their defiance, she presents it as meriting social punishment.

The protagonist of an earlier play, *Bernice* (1919), escapes society by literally moving into another life: she dies, and in death wields absolute power over her husband. Neither the husband Craig nor the trusted friend Margaret who "sees everything" arrives in time to hear Bernice's last words (10).[12] The cause of death is never revealed; a long illness and a sudden, unexpected death are all we know. Bernice's marriage had not been successful; she was too independent to need Craig, an inferior writer whom she could never admire, and he accordingly sought admiration from other women and was openly unfaithful to her. As in Claire's case, patriarchal society imposes a twofold denial of self-definition on Bernice: as a woman in her own right, she is trapped by marriage; as a woman bound to her husband's love and professional failure, she is trapped by his inadequacy. Craig is a more dangerous opponent to Bernice than any of Claire's to her; he wishes for the power to destroy and reshape the terms of existence, but that is a faculty only Glaspell's female protagonists are given to exercise. Craig had presumably battled with Bernice for this power and had always lost; "her life wasn't made by my life," he tells Margaret (17). In death, Bernice wins the battle once and for all. Before dying, she extracts from Abbie, her servant, the promise to tell Craig that she had taken her own life. Through this ruse, she hopes to confer on him the delusion of power over herself that he had always coveted, and Craig convinces himself that he was "*everything* to Bernice" (19). On the other hand, Margaret cannot believe that her friend could have committed suicide and finally works out Bernice's Freudian logistics. Even from the grave, the female protagonist assumes power over the living; as in the later plays, the principal male character is shown to be undoubtedly weaker than his female counterpart.

Glaspell's men cannot understand their women; with the exception of Silas Morton, they are vastly inferior intellectual and moral beings.[13] The logical corollary of this inequality would be that the women join forces against them, creating a higher caste. But Glaspell has no preconceived notions of women's superiority. In *The Verge,* Claire cannot bond with her daughter, that creditable young American who goes with all the girls, or with her sister, the prototypical self-sacrificing Mother. Bernice and Margaret, whose bonding ensures the latter's final comprehension of her friend's action, must contend with Craig's sister, who is prepared to defend him come what may, while in *Inheritors* Mrs. Fejevary, in spite of her maternal feelings toward Madeline, can only echo her husband's arguments. Nonetheless, the possibility of real understanding between women attracted Glaspell, and her first play was a study of female bonding.

Trifles (1916) opens with the sheriff and his men looking hopelessly for clues to the murder of Minnie Temple's husband, who has been strangled with a rope. Although they cannot bring themselves to believe that a woman—Minnie herself—could have done the deed, their wives, who visit the house to collect some clothes for Minnie to wear in prison, spot and interpret certain clues: a dirty kitchen, bread not made, crooked sewing, a broken canary cage, a dead canary. The women had been prepared to condemn Minnie, but as they talk of her they learn to give credit to old Grandmother Morton's knowledge of pioneer life and realize how they could have helped: "Oh, I *wish* I'd come over here once in a while! That was a crime! That was a crime! . . . We live close together and we live far apart. We all go through the same things—it's all just a different kind of the same thing" (44). They begin to perceive that

Minnie Temple has "effectively triumphed over a cruel male jailer" and to understand that the annihilation of male authority, which oppresses them too, depends on their bond.[14]

Although Glaspell never again used female bonding as the main theme of a play, it surfaces in *Bernice* and is significant in the later *Alison's House* (1930). This thinly disguised life of Emily Dickinson begins after the protagonist's death, when we learn that Alison, the poet, had long ago sacrificed her forbidden love to avoid bringing scandal on the family. Elsa, her niece, has run off with a married man, and although that is precisely what Alison had not done, Elsa feels a special understanding between them. When a cache of unpublished poems by Alison is discovered, Elsa claims them for herself because she alone can "know their value." Alison, the seer, the one who always "knew" and understood and had the courage to sacrifice love and find "victory in defeat," has left a legacy for all women in the form of her poetry.[15]

Glaspell's attitude to society and to women's duty toward it is ambivalent. Rejection of responsibility to a society that "exerts an unmitigatedly destructive pressure on individuality" is the inescapable consequence of the American myth.[16] In men's writings, society is assumed to be the adversary, the obstacle to self-definition, and is depicted as female. In Glaspell's plays, society is not simply the enemy that must be defeated but an integral part of her protagonists' lives, to be examined and, if possible, understood. Glaspell's women seek self-definition as women at home and beyond; that is, they enter the male sphere, thus being both inside and outside society. Glaspell is caught between the patriarchal myth she had been taught to respect and her realization that it is false. Although women must choose between their individuality and their role in society, Glaspell never presents this choice clearly—in terms of right and wrong. Madeline must satisfy either herself or her family; Claire's impulse to create new forms of life is commendable, and yet it brings anguish to her and to those who love her; Bernice's lie, viewed from the outside, is wicked, but it gives Craig confidence in himself. Alison rejected love, gave her life to her family and poetry, and achieved self-definition, which love alone, as Elsa learns, cannot offer. Glaspell cannot condemn her women for opposing society, but she is painfully conscious of the consequences of their rebellions.

Glaspell's protagonists do rebel: they insist on appropriating to themselves the traditionally male quest for self-definition. They are aware that they transgress the laws of society and that retribution will follow. This is abundantly clear in *Trifles* and in *Inheritors*, in which the law steps in bodily. Retribution in *The Verge* is more subtle and ironic; Claire is conscious that she has gone too far and that the law of man no longer applies to her. Yet she has put herself under the supposedly higher law of a man-made God and realizes that her only salvation lies in insanity.

In her plays, Susan Glaspell challenges the prevailing patriarchal myth and pays the consequences. While she enjoyed the "protection" of her husband and the circle of friends that had originally formed the Provincetown Players, her plays were produced, published, and praised. In 1922, however, just before the first night of *Chains of Dew*, she left for Greece with Cook; when she returned after his death two years later, the Provincetown Players had already forgotten their founder and his wife. Lacking support, Glaspell retired to her clapboard cottage in Provincetown and returned to writing fiction, the only medium in which she could examine her discontent with society in relative independence.

Notes

1. Tillie Olsen, *Silences* (New York: Dell Publishing, 1978), p. 40.

2. The Provincetown Players produced their first plays in Provincetown, Cape Cod, in the summer of 1915. George (Jig) Cram Cook had cajoled Mary Heaton Vorse into letting him take over an unused fish shed on her wharf for the repetition of performances of *Suppressed Desires* (Cook and Glaspell) and *Constancy* (Neith Boyce), previously done in Boyce's drawing room before an audience of friends. The next summer, Cook organized a whole season of plays, and in the autumn, with the support of John Reed and Eugene O'Neill, he founded the Playwrights' Theatre in Greenwich Village. (For a firsthand history of the Players, see Helen Deutsch and Stella Hanau, *The Provincetown: A Story of the Theatre* [New York: Farrar and Rinehart, 1931]. A more recent and objective account is Robert Karoly Sarlós, *Jig Cook and the Provincetown Players: Theatre in Ferment* [Amherst: University of Massachusetts Press, 1982].) In her autobiographical *Time and the Town: A Provincetown Chronicle* (New York: The Dial Press, 1942), Mary Heaton Vorse quotes the critic William Archer: "In the region of Washington Square or Greenwich Village, or . . . among the sand dunes of Cape Cod—we must look for the real birthplace of the American Drama" (p. 126).

3. Sandra M. Gilbert and Susan Gubar include *Trifles* in *The Norton Anthology of Literature by Women: The Tradition in English* (New York: W. W. Norton, 1985), pp. 1388–99. Of Glaspell's work, this play, and the short story it gave rise to, "A Jury of Her Peers," are the most frequently chosen for comment by feminist critics. Both the play and the story are generally seen as early attempts to signal gender marking in language. See, for example, Annette Kolodny, "A Map for Rereading: Gender and the Interpretation of Literary Texts," in *The New Feminist Criticism: Essays on Women, Literature, and Theory*, ed. Elaine Showalter (New York: Pantheon Books, 1985), pp. 46–62. Gilbert and Gubar adopt a somewhat different attitude in *No Man's Land: The Place of the Woman Writer in the Twentieth Century, Vol. 1: The War of the Words* (New Haven: Yale University Press, 1988), p. 91. For a fuller treatment of Glaspell's life and work, see Arthur Waterman, *Susan Glaspell* (New York: Twayne, 1966), and Marcia Noe, *Susan Glaspell: Voice from the Heartland* (Jacksonville: Western Illinois University, 1983).

4. F. Scott Fitzgerald, *The Great Gatsby* (Harmondsworth, England: Penguin, 1967), p. 187; Margaret Fuller, *Woman in the Nineteenth Century* [1845] (New York: W. W. Norton, 1971), p. 174.

5. Nina Baym, "Melodramas of Beset Manhood: How Theories of American Fiction Exclude Women Authors," in *The New Feminist Criticism: Essays on Women, Literature, and Theory*, ed. Elaine Showalter (New York: Pantheon Books, 1985), pp. 70, 71.

6. Provincetown Players Announcement 1917–1918, in the Provincetown Scrapbook held by the Beinecke Library, Yale University. Gerhard Bach offers a methodical study of Glaspell's work with the Provincetown Players, showing how her development reflects theirs, in "Susan Glaspell—Provincetown Playwright," *Great Lakes Review* 4, no. 2 (1978): 31–43.

7. Alice Rohe, "The Story of Susan Glaspell," *New York Morning Telegraph*, 18 December 1921.

8. Olsen, *Silences*, p. 42.

9. Quotations from *Inheritors*, *The Verge*, and *Trifles* are from *Plays by Susan Glaspell*, ed. C. W. E. Bigsby (Cambridge: Cambridge University Press, 1987). Subsequent references are to this edition and are cited parenthetically by page number.

10. Provincetown Interim Announcement, 1922–1923, in the Provincetown Scrapbook held by the Beinecke Library, Yale University.

11. Hutchins Hapgood, *A Victorian in the Modern World* (New York: Harcourt, Brace and Company, 1939), p. 377.

12. Susan Glaspell, *Bernice: A Play in Three Acts* (London: Ernest Benn, 1924). Subsequent references are cited parenthetically by page number.

13. Isaac Goldberg, *The Drama of Transition: Native and Exotic Playcraft* (Cincinnati, Ohio: Stewart Kidd, 1922), compares the plays of Eugene O'Neill and Susan Glaspell: "O'Neill's women do not understand their menfolk . . . Glaspell's men do not understand their women" (477).

14. Gilbert and Gubar, *No Man's Land*, p. 91.

15. Susan Glaspell, *Alison's House: A Play in Three Acts* (New York: Samuel French, 1930), pp. 145, 147.

16. Baym, "Melodramas of Beset Manhood," p. 71.

5
"Meeting the Outside Face to Face": Susan Glaspell, Djuna Barnes, and O'Neill's *The Emperor Jones*

Ann E. Larabee

Brutus Jones, who first appeared in the famous and fatal production of *The Emperor Jones* at the Provincetown Playhouse in 1920, is a liminal figure caught at the threshold of culture and its languages. Inscribed by a privileged white society (including the author himself), Jones wanders through the terrifying, prelinguistic terrain of the Other, constructing his own silence and death. Provincetown playwrights Susan Glaspell and Djuna Barnes also were fascinated with the exiled and—in Barnes's term—the "repulsive." In works after *The Emperor Jones*, Glaspell and Barnes revised marginality into a position of aliveness, creativity, and linguistic freedom, constrained not only by society but by dramatic representation itself. Both playwrights extended their feminist analysis of oppression to include the stage, which they viewed as a prison of structural language and cultural inscription. Thus, they rewrote the liminal figure of Jones as one who does not engage in self-destruction but rather pioneers the territory stretching beyond the boundaries of staged, formal discourse.

The ability to control language and, therefore, to create a social identity, is an essential consideration of *The Emperor Jones*. From his first conversation with Smithers, Jones asserts his linguistic power, for he has built his empire by manipulating the "bush niggers" by "talkin' big." Learning his techniques from "de white quality talk," Jones views words as an economic investment, deriding Smithers for failing to learn the "lingo" of the natives: "You ain't never learned ary word er it, Smithers, in de ten years you been heah, dough yo' knows it's money in yo' pocket tradin' wid 'em if you does." Jones's pride is in "talkin' big" rather than "talkin' wild" (14–15)[1]; he can back up his claims of power and invulnerability with a real silver bullet, making his language currency in a silver-based economic system.

A skilled storyteller, Jones accumulates power and wealth through fictions of his mysterious and violent identity, terrifying even the cynical Smithers. Jones's inflated language is accompanied by his cunning control over the language of others. In shows of force, he insists that Smithers "talk polite" and "talk plain" and warns him against repeating what he has heard. Only Jones is allowed to relate his past, a tale that parades on the border between reality and fiction: "It's a story I tells you so's you knows I'se de kind of man dat if you evah repeats one word of it, I ends yo' stealin' on dis yearth mighty damn quick!" (18). Using rhetorical strategies, he sets himself up as sole interpreter of his own history and inflationary creator of his own social identity.

Jones's ability to manipulate the languages of power is ultimately revealed as self-destructive pride, as he stands on the dangerous border between the lingo of the natives and white English. Even his name suggests the seam between the adopter of white culture (Jones) and white culture's Other: the ambitious betrayer and fantastic savage brute (Brutus). Jones himself sees a distinction between his affected, fictional language, geared for social transaction, and "dat ole woman's talk" about "ghosts an' ha'nts" produced by "devil spells and charms" (24, 23). Throughout the play, Jones's attempt to shape himself through languages of a dominant culture is viewed as "puttin' on 'is bloody airs" (26), and his hubris must be purged by his reduction to an abject, prelinguistic, original state as he kneels and cringes like his Doppelgänger: the old woman embracing Smithers's knees in the first scene.

Jones's liminality, his "in-between" position in a borderland between the native and the colonized, is, in part, a unique position for linguistic creation, borrowing codes from both worlds. (The silver bullet, for instance, is both a metaphor for domination and a heathen "charm.") But O'Neill, unlike Glaspell and Barnes, does not see this liminality as a radical freedom. Rather, language is a loaded gun for culture's marginals: Jones tells Smithers to "shoot his piece" (relay news), and the silver bullet is reserved for Jones's self-destruction. Jones's invention of Self—to which he has no apparent right—is suicide, and he is dragged back to his original state of Otherness, perceived by the author as mechanical, biological, preordained, and outside of language.

Thus, the demise of Brutus Jones is largely his loss of language and strategies of interpretation. He is first unable correctly to read the signs of his servants' defection from his place, believing they are "drinkin' rum and talkin' big down in de town" or "sleepin' under de trees" (10, 18). But even after this slip, Jones remains convinced of his interpretive abilities. Jones tells Smithers, "I'se gone out in dat big forest, pretendin' to hunt, so many times dat I knows it high an' low like a book. I could go through on dem trails wid my eyes shut" (21). But the forest—a metaphorical book—with its "brooding, implacable silence" and mute visions, conquers Jones's ability to map its signs: "White stone, white stone, where is you?" (27, 29). He is reduced from powerful constructor and facile animator of the multi-layered silver bullet—"Don't she shine pretty?"—to a simpleton who carries on conversations with his feet: "Feet, you is holdin' up yo' end fine" (15, 28). Gradually, Jones loses his ability to project and his power of speech along with his clothes: wailing on the slave ship, speaking in an "*incoherent mumble*" as he watches the witch doctor who croons "*without articulate word divisions*," "*whimpering with fear*" at the Crocodile God, and finally collapsing in the silence of death (51, 52, 54).

Jones's strip-down is not a complete return to the state of the "woods nigger," for that would be an education in another language: the language that informs the drum (a "roll call") and the scripted pantomime of the witch doctor. O'Neill only suggests the language of the "African type"—the "heathen charms and spells"—through drum beats that seem to come from some mysterious place outside of the stage. Lem is opaque, communicating primarily through gesture and only reluctantly conversing with Smithers. Then, with an appearance that belies his powerful conjuring, he "simply" states the facts. Thus Jones seems at the mercy of an anonymous, inarticulate force without—a "*baffled but revengeful power*" (54).

George Cram Cook, patriarch of Provincetown, was so committed to this notion of transcendental force that he nearly bankrupted the Provincetown Playhouse to build a dome—an illusion of "pure space"—for the forest scenes of *The Emperor Jones*. At an opening night party for the play, he boasted that "groups like ours are about to inherit the whole duty of dramatic man." Susan Glaspell reported: "Some of us laughed, saying that was a large order."[2]

It is impossible to say exactly how Glaspell, a formidable and ambitious writer herself, might have felt about the hoopla surrounding *The Emperor Jones*—a play that clearly borrowed from her own metaphysical meditations on the transcendental "Outside." The set for *The Emperor Jones*, upon which so much depends, seems often to be taken outright from Glaspell's play *The Outside*, produced at the Provincetown in 1917. In scene 2 of O'Neill's play, for instance, "*The foreground is sandy, level ground dotted by a few stones and clumps of stunted bushes cowering close against the earth to escape the buffeting of the trade wind.*" In the background, the forest stands, "*dividing the world*" with a "*brooding, implacable silence*" (27). This hostile world mirrors the set for *The Outside*, which contains a slightly different configuration of the same elements:

> . . . *the line where woods and dunes meet stands out clearly and there are indicated the rude things, vines, bushes, which form the outer uneven rim of*

the woods—the only things that grow in the sand. At another point a sandhill is menacing the woods. (48)[3]

In both plays, the "outside" is "the edge of life," a marginal physical and psychological space suited to the liminal characters who are forced to inhabit it. However, as Linda Ben-Zvi has pointed out, Glaspell believed in the pioneer thrust that was part of her heritage, while O'Neill longed for roots.[4] In *The Outside*, Allie Mayo, who has been thrown out of the domestic sphere by the death of her husband and lives in an abandoned "life-saving station" (ironically the later abode of O'Neill himself), sees herself as a "stunted straggly line that meets the Outside face to face" (54). Like Brutus Jones, she has lost her articulateness "outside" but struggles for a new language to name the experience of her "strange shape" and marginality. Not simply a restoration of fluency, Allie Mayo's lines are borders between silence and the social contract of language. She herself is a "lonely line" struggling for poetic life outside of women's usual domestic condition: "Outside sea—outer shore, dark with the wood that once was ships—dunes, strange land not life—woods, town and harbor. The line!" (54). For Allie, the struggle for a language in exile is laden with creative potential.

The figure of Allie Mayo is doubled not only in Brutus Jones, whom O'Neill punishes for his linguistic hubris, but in Glaspell's Claire Archer, heroine of *The Verge* (1921). O'Neill and Glaspell seem to be carrying on a dialogue about the aesthetics of the liminal condition, because *The Verge* is strikingly similar to *The Emperor Jones*. *The Verge*, however, has a sardonic tone that seems to parody O'Neill's heavy-handed ritualism. Claire Archer, like Brutus Jones, is something of a monomaniac—the only monomaniac in any of Glaspell's plays—who constructs a world for herself out of ambition. She is a self-sufficient biologist who is attempting to breed a new and exotic plant, the Edge Vine, that grows along the glass wall of her greenhouse and has produced a bud called Breath of Life. Claire's scientific investigation of "strange new comings together" is interrupted continually by her well-meaning lovers and relatives, who remind her of her past—her "hymn-singing ancestors"—and eventually drive her insane (64, 77). Breath of Life finally blooms, but Claire is disappointed that her creative process, the "flow" as she calls it, has hardened into form. She finally crushes the Edge Vine, strangles her lover, shoots a revolver through the ventilator in her greenhouse, and sings "Nearer My God to Thee" as the curtain falls.

The Edge Vine is clearly an emblem for Claire herself: "*The leaves of this vine are not the form that leaves have been. They are at once repellent and significant*" (58). The plant pointedly grows on the greenhouse wall between inside and outside—between safe enclosure and a hostile, snowy, windy world. Also at the threshold between domestic confinement and creative projection, Claire is the New Woman, engaged in the business of self-creation, struggling against social expectations. She has three lovers, rejects motherhood, and ambitiously pursues her own career. Like Brutus Jones, she denies cultural definitions of "naturally" submissive behavior. Claire's tragedy, however, is not an exile to the "outside" but a confinement within social structures, created by "those gentlemen of culture who—" "Moulded the American mind!" (6). Her psychic journey is acted out in a seemingly inescapable prison of language, created by patriarchy. Claire's ultimate linguistic collapse, however, signals the new, tentative freedom of a feminist discourse that opens up a territory of limitless combinations, fulfilling Claire's own prophecy: "We need not be held in forms moulded for us. There is outness—and otherness" (64).

Claire's theory of language is exacting, and she sees an investment in direct correspondences and metaphors as a capitulation to the "old men" and the "hymn-singing ancestors." Her worst insults, directed at her "creditable" daughter and civic-minded sister, suggest that they are figuratively simple: "She is a tower that is a tower" and "She's just like one of her father's portraits" (79). Claire sees potentialities in language besides the repressive, socially conditioned "this is it" and "we are that." Her language, she says, comes from "outside," otherness, agony, risk, and sexual passion, and erupts at the edge or the verge. Her idea is to make "patterns that haven't been" (86), articulating self-difference rather than the "unity" of things perceived by her sister, Adelaide. But the fortifications, she suggests, are unassailable: "If one ever does get out, I suppose it is—quite unexpectedly, and perhaps—a bit terribly" (63).

The stage itself represents a fortification of inscription rather than a "pure space" beyond the forest. Claire's greenhouse, on whose wall the Edge Vine is caught between inside and outside, is etched with "*—as Plato would have it—the patterns inherent in abstract nature*" (58). In the first act of *The Verge*, Glaspell sets up an odd pantomime in which Claire's three clownlike lovers (Tom, Dick, and Harry) try to communicate with each other through this glass wall. Tom approaches the greenhouse from the outside and shoots a revolver to get Dick and Harry's attention. Harry, however, can't open the door, and Tom puts the gun desperately to his head as if to shoot himself. Harry tries to get Tom to read his lips using gestures and then explains their dilemma using pantomime. This form of communication is arduous and almost ineffectual, mocking the efficacy of performance through the illusory fourth wall. Unlike the witch doctor in *The Emperor Jones*, who pantomimes the actions of Brutus Jones and ideally—with O'Neill—raises his audience to a nonverbal, interactive intensity, the mimes of *The Verge* are unable to communicate through a wall of inscription, which is like Plato's cave.

The only way to get through such a wall, Claire suggests, is to pierce it. Her thwarted, Gothic tower in the second act shows the results of this violent "stabbing to awareness":

> *The whole structure is as if given a twist by some terrific force—like something wrong. It is lighted by an old-fashioned watchman's lantern hanging from the ceiling; the innumerable pricks and slits in the metal throw a marvellous pattern on the curved wall—like some masonry that hasn't been.* (78)

The "terrific force" is clearly Claire's own subversive personality—her feminism, which batters against the civilized structures that confine her and allow only pricks of light. Claire's violent and anguished discourse is intended to stab others to awareness that they are caught in "a form too long repeated."

Perhaps reflecting Brutus Jones's last-minute reliance on prayer, Clare's final words are a hymn—"Nearer My God to Thee." But she is not referring to an angry Eye, but to a specific historical event—the sinking of the Titanic. Claire strangles her lover, Tom, after he offers his chivalrous protection—"Darling! I can keep you. I will keep you—safe" (99). Claire explains that with this violent eruption she has "saved" herself. After the sinking of the Titanic, a controversy arose over whether women—demanding sexual equality—should have gone down with the ship or accepted the self-sacrifice of chivalrous men. This was a no-win situation—either one accepted one's lot as the weaker sex or one drowned. By the end of *The Verge*, Claire has clearly chosen drowning as preferable to accepting male protectionism and so haltingly recites "Nearer My God to Thee," the legendary song that serenaded the sinking Titanic.

But the hymn is tentative and searching, as though Claire is investing each word with new complexities: "Out. *(as if feeling her way)* Nearer, *(Her voice now feeling the way to it.)* Nearer—*(Voice almost upon it.)*—my *God*, *(Falling upon it with surprise.)* to Thee, *(Breathing it.)*" (100). No longer a rote performance from the hymn-singing ancestors, the song becomes an expression of Claire's emotionally-charged freedom. She does not, like Brutus Jones, go through the motions of religious ritual to curry favor, pragmatically using religious language as a material investment in salvation. Rather, Claire's recitation breaks the continuity and traditional rhythms of a rigidly social language.

Both Glaspell and Barnes saw those who fall outside of normative culture as thieves of language, who are in a unique position to experiment with new forms "outside." Barnes, perhaps, had more hope for this project than Glaspell, although she distrusted severely any cultural representations of the Other. Fifteen years after she left the Provincetown in 1921, Barnes wrote, through the discourse of Dr. O'Connor in *Nightwood*, a portrait of "Nikka, the nigger who used to fight the bear in the *Cirque de Paris*":

> There he was, crouching all over the arena without a stitch on, except an ill-concealed loin-cloth all abulge as if with a deep-sea catch, tattooed from head to heel with all the *ameublement* of depravity! (244)[5]

Nikka's similarities to Brutus Jones, who gives his subjects "de big circus show for deir money" and fights a monstrous crocodile in nothing more than a "breech cloth," are striking (12, 48).

Barnes satirizes the cloaked racism and voyeurism of the audience for these "performances," uncovering the implicit sexual fear and desire of the spectators. Nikka has "Desdemona" tattooed on his penis, but "he couldn't have done a thing . . . if you had stood him in a gig-mill for a week. . . ." (245). Jones, too, despite his strip-tease, is given no sexual life (an aspect of the play that Dudley Murphy, in 1933, tried to remedy in his odd film, *The Emperor Jones*, with Paul Robeson). Nikka and Jones are nonthreatening as passive sexual objects, a position that Barnes is obviously parodying.

Nikka is also tattooed on each knee with the anagrammatic "I" and "can," which put together spell "Cain." O'Neill's remark that Charles Gilpin was "all 'Ham' and a yard wide" after Gilpin altered O'Neill's script (he changed "nigger" to "black boy") suggests the same marking of the exiled and the untouchable.[6] Despite the rosebuds, point lace, angels, and hearts that decorate Nikka, his "*dos*" is covered with a "terse account in early monkish script . . . of the really deplorable condition of Paris before hygiene was introduced, and nature had its way up to the knees" (245). Nikka, like Jones, thus bears the inscription of his captivity in "nature" and biology—marks that make him suitable for the circus and the stage.

The cynical Barnes, even in her Provincetown days, did not have much faith in the stage as an arena for changing the social contract of language: the inscriptions that hold both Nikka and Jones in captivity. In her early plays, she portrayed disenfranchised types who remain unchanged throughout the plays, as if to call attention to their inviolability. Her characters seem to gain life only after vacating the stage, as in *Kurzy of the Sea*, produced in 1920.[7] Kurzy seems to be a mermaid—one who exists between water and land. She is caught in a net and brought home by Rory, a man searching for "a Queen or a Saint or a Venus, or whatever it is comes in with the tide." The "real sea-going Venus" at first will not utter a word, "save for a few whispers like the sound in shells," but eventually explains that she has come "to the surface" because she was tired of the incantations of Rory's mother. After giving her a red shawl, Rory takes her back to the sea and throws her in to see if she is a real mermaid. Rory returns and reports to his mother that, as Kurzy swims away, she reveals that she is really a barmaid at the White Duck. Taunting him, Kurzy says: "It's long distance swimming you'll be learning this summer, but it will do you little good, for by the time you can hold your own, I shall be half way to Cork with a lover on my arm." Kurzy is a trickster, who, offstage and unbound from Rory's labels and the net of cultural "fairy tales," becomes both articulate and strong enough to swim long distances.

Kurzy's natural medium is the "outside," and she is a heroine of the marginal—unsilenced and untamed. O'Neill's "emperor" takes his tragic plunge into silence in the terrifying terrain "outside," Glaspell's Claire remains paralyzed on the "inside," and Barnes imagines a character who achieves a radical freedom offstage. Her subject is the impossibility of representing the Other on stage, because the stage is built on paralyzing social inscriptions.

Ironically, the ceremonial silencing of Brutus Jones signalled the ultimate silencing of Provincetown's "amateurs." Glaspell never recovered fully, writing only tentatively and occasionally for the stage and never with the force of her early work. Djuna Barnes produced brilliant works offstage (with the exception of *The Antiphon*, a cryptic and highly literary play). They were joined by others of the Provincetown: Edna St. Vincent Millay, Mary Caroline Davies, Rita Wellman, Grace Potter, Neith Boyce—the first significant women playwrights in the American theater. Like Brutus Jones, they had the hubris to steal the language of a culture that excluded them, and, like him, they were eventually exiled from the stage.

Notes

1. Eugene O'Neill, *The Emperor Jones, in Three Plays: The Emperor Jones, Anna Christie, The Hairy Ape* (New York: Modern Library), pp. 1–58. Subsequent references are cited parenthetically by page number.

2. Susan Glaspell, *The Road to the Temple* (New York: Frederick A. Stokes, 1927), p. 290.

3. C. W. E. Bigsby, ed. *The Outside* and *The Verge*, in *Plays by Susan Glaspell* (Cambridge: Cambridge University Press, 1987). Subsequent references are cited parenthetically by page number.

4. Linda Ben-Zvi, "Susan Glaspell and Eugene O'Neill: The Imagery of Gender," *Eugene O'Neill Newsletter* 10 (Spring 1986): 22–27.

5. Quotations from *Nightwood* are from *Selected Works of Djuna Barnes* (New York: Farrar, Straus and Cudahy, 1962). Subsequent references are cited parenthetically by page number.

6. Arthur Gelb and Barbara Gelb, *O'Neill* (New York: Harper & Brothers, 1962), p. 449.

7. Djuna Barnes, *Kurzy of the Sea*, typescript, Djuna Barnes Collection, University of Maryland.

6
Zoë Akins and the Age of Excess: Broadway Melodrama in the 1920s

Jennifer Bradley

> "I want an ambiguous thing—romance. . . . For you and I—we have, each of us, something of the incommunicable technique of magnificence."
>
> Zoë Akins

Although Zoë Akins's dramatic work has not recently excited much critical attention, from 1919 to 1930, fourteen of her original plays and adaptations appeared in Manhattan, and critics called her a leading playwright of the decade. From the perspective of generic and social literary criticism, Akins's brand of melodrama—what Peter Brooks has called "the mode of excess"[1]—played well against the backdrop of an age of excess. Her characteristic melodrama supported the careers of other women of the theater and prepared her for later stage work and a career in film. In the 1920s, especially in the nine original plays, excess was Akins's personal preference, social environment, and theatrical technique. For her, less was never more.

The Woman and the Era

Zoë Akins was born in the 1880s, when, as Frank Rahill explains, post-Civil War and far west themes, grafted onto European patterns, defined the genuine American version of the melodramatic mode. She left New York at the end of the 1920s, when the last "simon-pure melodrama" appeared on Broadway.[2] She knew the form early; what tale is more romantic than the source for her first play, *Iseult the Fair*? Akins and melodrama were contemporaneous.

Boston critic H. T. Parker believed instead that Akins was born too late. To him her drama sounded like something out of Ouida, a curiosity in the age of stripped-down realism. In an earlier day, Akins "could have indulged to the full her passion for flamboyant rhetoric, ornate symbolism, recondite allusion, her ceaseless delight in the furbelows and the fustian of words."[3]

Despite her luxuriance in language, Akins did not admire excess in all forms. Nor did she use it consistently to subscribe to the dominant conventional values, as melodrama often does. She recognized in Prohibition, for example, a national misdirected "intemperate extravagance."[4] When it came to excess, she preferred the private, nonlegislated kind; of her friends the Scott Fitzgeralds, she wrote, "Their extravagances of feeling, and behaviour were sometimes a nuisence—but the sort of nuisence made by petals falling from flowers . . . [*sic*]."[5] A reclusive cousin believed that Akins's flamboyant friends influenced her career too much; "whether you know it or not," the cousin wrote, "you dramatize your associates and on that account it is specially important that you should know and associate with noble people."[6]

Part acculturated unawares, part intentionally cultivated, Akins's personal style during these years was just as extravagant as her writing and her associates. She was sartorially splendid, for example, affected a generic Eastern European accent, and spent wildly on European antiques for her apartment. (Her writing room, however, was bare as a nun's cell.) She also was sentimental, but selectively so; she wept regularly and ostentatiously at the opera and was positively soggy about dogs, but she happily forgot her Missouri home.

Once established in New York, Akins won the admiration of many critics, the ticket-buying audience, her fellow dramatists, and others in the theatrical community. Comparing her with Eugene O'Neill, Edna St. Vincent Millay, Booth Tarkington, and Philip Moeller, a 1920 *Vanity Fair* article declared that Akins added "a vivid and distinctive wit and genuine poetic feeling to whatever she touches."[7] A Boston reviewer placed her in the company of Molnar and Schnitzler.[8] Throughout the decade, H. L. Mencken continually promoted Akins's career in print, as did Alexander Woollcott, who admired almost everything she wrote. In 1927, *Theatre Arts* compared Akins with Eugene O'Neill, Rachel Crothers, Philip Barry, Susan Glaspell, and others; Akins was "still the chief romancer on Broadway."[9]

Akins's colleagues honored her as well. Among her more celebrated supporters were Crothers, who produced *Thou Desperate Pilot* (1927), and Ethel Barrymore, who starred in three Akins plays of the decade and directed one of them, an adaptation, *The Love Duel* (1929). Producer Winthrop Ames told Akins's agent, "I'd rather do a Zoë Akins play than almost any other . . ." (as he turned one down).[10] Renowned as a fast writer, Akins was also valued as a useful play doctor. She rewrote Elmer Rice's *For the Defense* (1919), for example, and several times virtually collaborated with Edward Sheldon, probably the period's most romantic dramatist.[11]

Akins's involvement in a production was unconventionally energetic. A practicing poet, she fought especially hard for the integrity of her text. For her, romantic melodramas were not interchangeable; she admitted the similarity of their plots but emphasized the individuality of their language and characterization. Hence she acquired a temperamental reputation. This notoriety was compounded because she wanted to be involved in all phases of production, rather than focusing on her writing. She once wrote George Tyler, "I suppose you never had an author worry about EVERYTHING from the star's wig to the butler's underwear before—but that's the way I am. I go through one million agonies in order to get everything ideal."[12] To many of her colleagues, Akins seemed professionally excessive.

To an age of easy money, women's liberation, technological innovation, and general flamboyance, an exuberant romantic like Zoë Akins found melodrama the appropriate theatrical response.

The Melodramatic Framework

In melodrama's history is a bimodal tradition, from both popular culture and the bourgeoisie. An important scholar of melodrama and women's film, Christine Gledhill cogently summarizes cultural and theatrical episodes in this development.[13] In Europe before Akins's time, to compete with licensed, "legitimate" theaters, popular theatrical producers had to become increasingly extravagant; they needed heftier doses of spectacle to attract a house and then to maintain audience interest. Although the New York theater-goer of the 1920s had lost much capacity to be dazzled, the late-nineteenth-century realist tendency contributed to precision and magnificence in set designs. Modern technical innovation afforded increasingly gorgeous execution of those designs.

Akins's work participates in this "popular" tradition; all her original plays between 1919 and 1930 use glamorous settings, flamboyant histrionics, remarkable coincidence, or all three. No wonder the younger Boucicault admired Akins so. Her settings were luxurious (casinos, greathouses, castles, penthouses); her characters' activities sensational, their occupations spectacular (opera star, matador, gambler, mistress). For, as Woollcott said, "the poetess of Humansville, Missouri," wanted "her woe well dressed."[14] Parker noted that young playwrights usually avoided being "highbrow"; Akins "shares not these faiths and fears."[15] Of the nine original plays between 1919 and 1930, only one focuses on ordinary Americans who work for a living.

If popular taste influenced melodrama's mechanics, middle-class culture determined its effect. Unlike tragedy, melodrama externalizes conflict;[16] it breeds more readily in a nonhierarchical culture. Moreover, as Brooks's important study indicates, melodrama results from a "desacralization" of ethics.[17] With no overriding metaphysical system, values reside in personality. After the revolution in France, for example, melodrama tended to pacify its audience, and in melodrama's American incarnation, the moral worth of characters was judged by their feelings.[18] Hence modern melodrama developed its proverbial excesses: its dramatization of conventional morality, and its sentimentality. Melodrama not only externalizes protest; it also trivializes it. By expressing desire, it gains some control over it and effectively tranquilizes it.

But melodrama itself also has a subversive strain.[19] In the 1920s, melodrama was a superannuated art in a Freudian age, and it incorporated new materials and symbolic behaviors. In Akins's work, the heroines and heroes are rarely faultless; more important, the villains are selfish or disturbed but usually not evil. Arthur Hobson Quinn called the result Akins's "romance of sophistication."[20] Akins described her qualified complicity with the status quo. "[I am] not radical enough to trade the past for the present," she wrote. "But I am radical enough to want to burn down houses too much alike . . . I want everybody to live his own life."[21]

The disposition of women characters provides one way to gauge how much Akins's plays comply with social convention. Many of Akins's heroines are women of virtue more or less lapsed. In one way or another, the resolution of such moral exoticism invariably acknowledges masculine-defined, middle-class moral convention about women. In the weepy texts, Akins subscribes to convention. Even noble women in nasty situations—victims of circumstance—suffer expected punishment. But Akins's frothier plays critique conventional notions of feminine virtue. Either way, Akins ensured herself an attentive female audience.

The Plays

Although the titular focus of Zoë Akins's 1919 financial failure seems to be a man, in fact, *Papa* is the story of his two daughters. Indeed, Papa himself is a portrait of Akins's delightfully daffy mother.[22] The plot is a search for someone to marry one of the daughters and thereby act as father to her illegitimate child. Here Akins is neither realistic nor romantic; instead, she took the stuff of melodrama and parodied it. As a result, a fairly sophisticated drama seemed to mix styles and confuse emotions; it pleased neither the public nor the critics. First produced in Los Angeles in 1914, the play is one of Akins's best reads, but it failed on Broadway.

Déclassée, starring Ethel Barrymore, was Akins's first genuine success. The play ran 251 performances. Among the fifteen biggest hits of the 1919–1920 season, *Déclassée* earned critical acclaim as well as financial success; both Heywood Broun and Burns Mantle placed it on their annual "best play" lists.[23] The play has glamour, sentimentality, middle-class values, a couple of startling reversals, and incidentally an affecting use of music to underscore emotion.

The heroine is a titled woman from a sensational family; more than a few times she reminds the audience that she is the last of the "mad Varicks." Trapped in a loveless marriage, she denounces the man she loves when he cheats her boorish husband at cards. In revenge, the lover betrays her so that the husband divorces her. She lives only by selling off her jewels one by one. The act 2 curtain gesture is typically gallant: she leaves her last pearl on a restaurant check. A wealthy American suitor, who declares that she has the "technique of magnificence," might well have been speaking of Akins's own work.

The ending of *Déclassée,* which relies in part on coincidence, is a paradigm of what James L. Smith has called "melodrama of defeat." After the World War, few people could believe in poetic justice, but the drama of excess still stimulated the emotions.[24] Distraught by what she misconstrues as a cruelly abrupt withdrawal of the wealthy American's marriage proposal, Lady Helen rushes into the street, is hit by a motorcar, and gorgeously dies at length in the drawing room to an air of Mozart.

As David Grimstead points out, splendor can "give a veneer of excitement and dignity to situations, sentiments, and people that were in their nature ordinary rather than extraordinary."[25] Although Lady Helen is titled and glamorous and her surroundings exotic (two gorgeous townhouses, the middle act with circus performers), she demonstrates bourgeois virtues: she is quietly responsible for all her own debts, does not want to marry for convenience, and confronts a cheat no matter how emotionally and socially punishing the choice. By dressing up middle-class responsibilities, *Déclassée* makes them more affecting. Its three years on Broadway and on tour argues the savvy of playing to audience sentiments and values.

Akins's next play was the first of her five adaptations of the decade.

When producer George Tyler planned a season around Emily Stevens and their first play failed, Akins sped through the 1886 play, *Forget-Me-Not*, turning it into the 1920 *Footloose*. The heroine, who lacks Lady Helen's long-suffering nobility, had virtually begun the American tradition of déclassée females; she was the "mother" of the dramatic "bad lady."[26] Along with skill at fast writing, sympathy with this tradition made Akins an excellent choice for Tyler.

Her next original play was a melodrama that Ludwig Lewisohn in *Nation* called less "meanly pretentious" than *Déclassée*.[27] *Daddy's Gone A-Hunting* works from more complicated, but still melodramatic conflicts. Ostensibly the main dramatic struggle belongs to Julien Fields, who must balance an artist's career with middle-class family responsibility—a familiar tension to Akins. In actuality, the emotional focus is on the wife Edith, played by Marjorie Rambeau. When middle-class American Julien returns from a year of study in Paris, he seems more interested in his bohemian friends and his art than in his wife Edith and little girl. Edith tolerates him through act 2, but in act 3 she moves in with another, wealthy man. Like Lady Helen, fallen-woman Edith pays. The Fields's daughter, not Edith herself, dies in perhaps the most bathetic episode of the Akins canon.

Akins never forgot that the first act was played "to a word" as she had drafted it at one sitting.[28] She was proud to have sold the play to Arthur Hopkins virtually on one of its structural tricks—each act ends with someone saying "God knows."

The structural manipulation of *The Varying Shore* is more extreme. The action runs backward, Akins's attempt to recreate the workings of human memory. A frame tale is set in the present (1921), when the heroine Julie has just died at ninety; the three acts work from 1870, to 1859, to 1847, when at seventeen she refuses to marry her fiancé, whose child she carries, because he does not love her. Like Ethel Barrymore's appearance in Sierra's *Kingdom of God*, the range of ages presented a striking challenge for Elsie Ferguson.

Alexander Woollcott's review of Akins, as usual, is curmudgeonly and affectionate. For him, the play by this "gifted glutton for romance" was "written with a kind of gusto and elation that the theatre began to lose when the naturalists swarmed into it."[29] But other critics were less kind. As a result, for several performances acts 1 (1870) and 3 (1847) were switched, restoring ordinary chronology. Akins admitted that Julie's story is "sentimental," the situations "banal, enough—but they are used as conventions. . . . And I am a little proud of the way I have managed them."[30]

The Texas Nightingale (1922), also known as *Greatness—a Comedy*, was personally important to Akins because her dearest friend Jobyna

Howland was its star. The plot is melodramatic: a famous diva has a reunion with the second of her four husbands, the father of the grown son he had never known about. Akins was proud of her work and wrote to the editor of *Cosmopolitan* that it was "quite unlike anything I've ever done, a comedy that is called 'Greatness', (that is really a tragedy underneath). . . ."[31] Given the heroine's flamboyance and the sentimentality of the family plot, melodrama becomes a rambunctious mode—it could combine many moods.

Akins's first purely comic piece after *Papa* was *A Royal Fandango*. Ethel Barrymore starred as princess of a fictional land, who has a flirtatious affair with a dizzy matador. The princess is just as dizzy—Barrymore took her role as a challenge, but Akins's friend Billie Burke would have been more to type. This play is Akins's least melodramatic in form: it seems bent on promulgating conventional ethics but does not do so melodramatically.

This play is bent on not taking itself seriously, as melodrama does almost by definition.[32] The royal setting, of course, is elaborate, as is the final disposition of Princess Amelia, whose husband rescues her in an aeroplane. The princess drops an artificial flower to the matador, and someone explains this ersatz-Brechtian author's message: "It isn't real."[33] Although Akins felt that critics had not understood *A Royal Fandango*, she called it her best play.

By the mid-1920s, New York critics knew Akins's work well enough to find unity in its diversity. A few pinpointed the extravagance and the mixture of motives that contribute to melodrama's exuberant attitude. John Corbin of the *Times* described *A Royal Fandango* this way: "Miss Akins . . . attempts no middle flight." But she needed to control herself; "there must also be pin feathers."[34] Woollcott also saw a mixture of motives in Akins's work. "Miss Akins strokes such scenes with a relish that is half an amused sophistication and half a naive, wide-eyed enjoyment of . . . great and elegant goings on. It is a curious compound which gives us a little of lost romance, salted with a saving irony."[35] Heywood Broun said, "The author's sense of humor is dampened by her own tears."[36]

Three years and two adaptations later, Akins wrote another original drama. For a while in the late 1920s, she again seemed more interested in the melodramatic motifs of adultery and death, as her next two plays show. *Thou Desperate Pilot* (1927) is probably one of Akins's soggiest and weakest dramas; not surprisingly, it was the least successful of her 1920s Broadway plays and lasted only eight performances. Even Woollcott, now at the *New York Tribune*, could not applaud. Like *Daddy's*, this play has parallel curtain business for each of the three acts: Lord Eric and his wife Lady Lisa each threaten suicide, but at the end of act 3,

Lord Eric's unstable, inexperienced American girlfriend, Zelda, dashes herself on the rocks at Monte Carlo. Here is an example of a play that has a full complement of melodramatic ingredients: aristocracy, recklessness, feminine victimization, and musical punctuation of especially emotional scenes.

Exactly one year after the opening of *Thou Desperate Pilot*, Akins's next play began its short Broadway run. Superficially a murder mystery, *The Furies* is one of her most expressionistic pieces. George Cukor, a close friend, directed *The Furies* (1928) and would later direct such Akins films as *Girls About Town* (1930), *Camille* (1936), and parts of *Desire Me* (1947); he recalled *The Furies* as "a melodrama written in partly blank verse. . . . We played a sort of 'modern jazz' with this romantic play. And she struck out a new form. . . ."[37] *The Furies* begins, for example, with an innovative soliloquy that Thornton Wilder said inspired *Our Town* ten years later;[38] the play calls for symbolic musical interludes, intense colored spots, masks, and interior monologue.

More than *A Royal Fandango*, this is a "kitchen-sink play"; along with ultra-modern techniques, Akins seems to have had fun including every melodramatic cliché she could think of. Speeches, for example, are baroque. In her script, the villain says, "You and I are the kind of people God made death for," which Cukor trimmed to "God—the air's good!"[39] *The Furies* provided Laurette Taylor and Estelle Winwood superb acting challenges. The last act's coincidence—a gust of wind blows papers, revealing the murder weapon—demanded precise technical skill.

After two more adaptations, Akins again turned to comedy and one of her most interesting plays, *The Greeks Had a Word For It* (1930). The word is hetaera—these women are never passive victims of male dominance. *The Greeks* does not focus on a single woman but, like Akins's earlier comedy *Papa*, creates a sisterhood of gold-diggers. As comedy does, *The Greeks* relies on incongruity, recursion, profanation of the sacred; in its way, it also affirms comedic values of cultural loyalty. The language is occasionally lyrical but more often coarse and realistic. Unlike the 1954 film *How to Marry a Millionaire*, which it inspired, the young woman about to be married steps out of her wedding dress, skips out on the groom, and joins her friends and three aviators on a cruise to France. When little Julie in *The Varying Shore* does not marry, the effect is sentimental; when this gold-digger does not, it's a critique of sentimentality.

Brooks Atkinson of the *New York Times* gave a mixed review, but he did understand the mixture of motives in the play itself. "It is a comic conception," he wrote; "Miss Akins as enlivened it with wryly humorous dialogue and considered it dreamily in terms of romantic adventure."[40] It is not surprising that Akins later experimented with several sequels to *The Greeks*. Because it is a female picaresque, the plot is easily extended.

By the time this play opened, Zoë Akins had lived in California for a year and a half. Her bread and butter for much of her Hollywood career was screen adaptations of the fallen-woman plot. In its gold-digger manifestation, like *The Greeks,* were the comedy *Girls About Town* and the melodrama *Anybody's Woman* (1930); in its illegitimate baby incarnation were *Sarah and Son* (1930), *The Right to Love* (1930), *Working Girls* (1931), *Christopher Strong* (1932), and *Lady of Secrets* (1936). At MGM she adapted costume drama infidelity in *The Toy Wife* (1938) for Luise Rainer and *Zaza* (1939) for Claudette Colbert. She was born to write *Camille*.

Effects and Implications

Zoë Akins's "technique of magnificence" influenced the careers of actresses, the development of theater criticism, and the development of the form itself. Because Akins's roles demanded much of an actress, they promised an actress much in experience and honor. Akins's versatility helped make or rescue several women's careers. The revival-adaptation *Footloose,* which saved Tyler's Emily Stevens seasons, also provided the first notable Broadway role for Tallulah Bankhead. Hermione Baddeley, who starred with her sister Angela in the three-year London run of *The Greeks*, credited the play with "the part that would take me back to the top of my profession."[41] (Later, in Hollywood, Akins continued to initiate women's careers; according to its director, Dorothy Arzner, *Sarah and Son* made Ruth Chatterton a screen star,[42] and an adaptation of Akins's play *Morning Glory* earned Katharine Hepburn her first Oscar.) Akins was proud of her creations for women; in an unpublished article called "I Write Good Parts," she lists more roles that began, advanced, or saved careers.[43] So celebrated were Akins's scene-chewing roles for women that Woollcott parodied her work as "Zowie; or, The Curse of an Akins Heart."[44]

Because she knew both her craft and her audience, Akins became a useful and successful scenarist as spoken dialogue transformed the film industry and appropriated the female-centered, female-oriented American melodrama. For this reason, too, her adaptation of Edith Wharton's novella, *The Old Maid,* a period drama about a mother and her illegitimate child, won the 1935 Pulitzer Prize as the American play produced in New York that best demonstrated the theater's power to raise tastes and values. But so incensed were the established critics with the Pulitzer committee's choice (one clear contender was Lillian Hellman's *Children's Hour)* that in protest they founded the New York Drama Critics' Circle Award.

Zoë Akins's melodrama is conservative and expansive. Although it tolerates a synthesis of styles and techniques (including romance, realism, tragicomedy, expressionism, music, verse, spectacle), it relies heavily on the viewer's awareness of traditional values. Finally, as a mode of excess, dramatizing a range of emotions, melodrama represents what Eric Bentley said it did: "the theatrical impulse itself."[45] Perhaps with its New World expansiveness and its admiration of Old World materials, melodrama in Akins's hands is also quintessentially American.

Notes

1. Peter Brooks, *The Melodramatic Imagination: Balzac, Henry James, Melodrama, and the Mode of Excess* (New Haven: Yale University Press, 1976).
2. Frank Rahill, *The World of Melodrama* (University Park: The Pennsylvania State University Press, 1967), p. 297.
3. H. T. Parker, "Strange Case of Zoë Akins in a New Play," review of *The Furies*, by Zoë Akins (hereafter ZA) *Boston Evening Transcript*, 2 April 1928. Clipped review in ZA Collection, Box 28, Henry E. Huntington Library (hereafter HEH), San Marino, California.
4. ZA to Dave Epstein, n.d., ZA Collection, Box 1, HEH.
5. ZA, "Scott and Zelda," radio talk, typescript ZA Collection, Box 13, HEH.
6. Genevieve McEnerney to ZA, c. 20 March 1924, ZA Collection, Box 11, HEH.
7. *Vanity Fair*, August 1920, p. 48.
8. Review of *Anything Might Happen*, by Edgar Selwyn, *Brooklyn Eagle*, 25 February 1923. Clipped review in ZA Collection, Box 28, HEH.
9. "Some Playwright Biographies: A Cross-section of the American Theatre," *Theatre Arts Monthly* 11 (July 1927): 531–32.
10. Quoted in Alice Kauser to ZA, 11 July 1923, ZA Collection, Box 10, HEH.
11. Elmer L. Rice to ZA, 19 November 1919, ZA Collection, Box 12a, HEH. The same collection includes many letters from Sheldon, Box 12a.
12. ZA to George Tyler, n.d. [April 1920], George Crouse Tyler Collection, Theatre Collection, Princeton University Library.
13. Christine Gledhill, "The Melodramatic Field: An Investigation," in *Home Is Where the Heart Is: Studies in Melodrama and the Woman's Film*, ed. Christine Gledhill (London: British Film Institute, 1987), pp. 5–39.
14. Alexander Woollcott, "Zoë Akins Must Have Her Woe Well Dressed," review of *Thou Desperate Pilot*, by ZA, reprinted in *St. Louis Post-Dispatch*, 13 March 1927. Clipping in ZA Collection, Box 28, HEH.
15. H. T. Parker, "Artifice and Acting," review of *Déclassée* (road), by ZA, *Boston Evening Transcript*, 11 October 1921, p. 8.
16. Robert Bechtold Heilman, *Tragedy and Melodrama: Versions of Experience* (Seattle: University of Washington Press, 1968), pp. 79–80.
17. Brooks, *The Melodramatic Imagination*, pp. 15–16.
18. Gledhill, "The Melodramatic Field," pp. 17, 31.

19. Ibid., pp. 20, 37.
20. Arthur Hobson Quinn, *A History of the American Drama From the Civil War to the Present Day*, 2 vols. (New York: Harper and Brothers, 1927), 2:142.
21. ZA, Notebook [1925], manuscript, ZA Collection, Box 13, HEH.
22. ZA, "Others Than Myself," typescript, ZA Collection, Box 15, HEH, p. 122.
23. "Broadway's 15 Biggest Hits Gross $7,000,000 During Greatest Show Year," *Daily Variety*, 14 May 1920; Heywood Broun, "As We Were Saying," *New York Tribune*, 25 April 1920; Burns Mantle, "Which Were the 10 Best Plays," *New York Evening Mail*, 8 May 1920. Clippings from ZA Collection, Box 28, HEH.
24. James L. Smith, *Melodrama* (London: Methuen, 1973), p. 46.
25. David Grimstead, "Melodrama as Echo of the Historically Voiceless," in *Anonymous Americans: Explorations in Nineteenth-Century Social History*, ed. Tamara K. Hareven (Englewood Cliffs, N. J.: Prentice-Hall, 1971), p. 88.
26. " 'Stephanie' Comes Back as in *Forget-Me-Not*," *Pittsburgh Leader*, 30 May 1920. Clipped article from the ZA Collection, Box 28, HEH.
27. Ludwig Lewisohn, "Drama: Homespun and Brocade," *Nation* 113 (21 September 1921): 325.
28. ZA, *Daddy Goes A-Hunting*, manuscript, ZA Collection, Box 15, HEH, i.
29. Alexander Woollcott, "The Play," *New York Times*, 6 December 1921, p. 24.
30. ZA, "My Own Opinion of 'The Varying Shore,' " typescript, ZA Collection, Box 21, HEH: 3, 4
31. ZA to Verne H. Porter, 8 July 1921, ZA Collection, Box 7, HEH.
32. Northrop Frye, *Anatomy of Criticism* (Princeton: Princeton University Press, 1957), p. 47.
33. ZA, *A Royal Fandango: A Comedy in Three Acts*, typescript, ZA Collection, Box 4, Special Collections, UCLA, Los Angeles, 3: 36.
34. John Corbin, "Comedy and Farce," *New York Times*, 18 November 1923, sec. 8, p. 1.
35. Alexander Woollcott, "Rue on the Riviera," review of *The Moonflower*, by ZA, *New York Herald*, 27 February 1924. Clipped review from ZA Collection, Box 28, HEH.
36. Heywood Broun, "At the Astor, Elsie Ferguson in *The Moon-Flower*," review of *The Moonflower*, by ZA, *New York World*, 26 February 1924. Clipped review from ZA Collection, Box 28, HEH.
37. George Cukor, interviewed by Ron Mielech, personal cassette recording, 27 July 1972.
38. Thornton Wilder to ZA, 18 November 1940, ZA Collection, Box 12b, HEH; see also Wilder to ZA, 13 November 1940, ZA Collection, Box 12b, HEH.
39. ZA, *The Furies*, typescript, Special Collections, UCLA Library, Los Angeles, 3: 40.
40. Brooks Atkinson, "Vine Leaves in a Heap," review of *The Greeks Had a Word For It*, by ZA, *New York Times*, 26 September 1930, p. 16.
41. Hermione Baddeley, *The Unsinkable Hermione Baddeley* (London: Collins, 1984), p. 98.
42. Gerald Peary and Karyn Kay, "Interview with Dorothy Arzner," *Cinema* 34 (Fall 1974): 4, reprinted in *The Work of Dorothy Arzner: Towards a Feminist Cinema*, ed. Claire Johnston (London: British Film Institute, 1975), p. 23.
43. ZA, "I Write Good Parts," typescript, ZA Collection, Box 13, HEH.
44. Alexander Woollcott, "Zowie; or, The Curse of an Akins Heart," in *Shouts and Murmurs: Echoes of a Thousand and One First Nights* (New York: Century, 1922), pp. 254–64.
45. Brooks, *The Melodramatic Imagination*, p. xi.

7

Marriage, Madness, and Murder in Sophie Treadwell's *Machinal*

Barbara L. Bywaters

> don't touch me—please—no—can't—must—. . .
> I want to rest—no rest—earn . . . all girls—most
> girls—married
>
> Let me alone—I've submitted to enough . . . Vixen
> crawled off
> under bed—eight—there were eight—a woman crawled off
> under the bed . . . one two three four . . . I'll not
> submit any more—
>
> I put him out of the way—yes . . . To be free. . . .
>
> When I did what I did I was free!. . . . my child . . .
> Let her live! Live! Tell her—[1]

Sophie Treadwell's *Machinal* transmits a terse, telegraphic message: the institution of marriage is a breeding ground for anger, desperation, and violence. This 1928 expressionist drama imparts the story of an ordinary young woman's marriage to her employer and the societal and psychological pressures that lead her ultimately to murder him. Trivialized by theater critic Robert Brustein in 1960 as "one of those banal tabloid stories . . . about how a sensitive dish of cream is curdled in the age of the machine," Treadwell's slighted work often has been characterized as a derivative drama of social criticism targeted at the effects of mechanization on the individual.[2] Treadwell's social protest, however, reaches beyond the machine age of the twentieth century. Augmenting a female tradition of literature that dissects the restrictive institution of marriage and its effects on women, *Machinal* stands as an early twentieth-century piece of subversive drama, conveying the message that female insurrection can lead to "one moment of freedom" before the patriarchal "machinery" crushes the revolt.

Born in Stockton, California, in 1885, Treadwell belongs to a group of early modern American women writers who flourished in what Elaine Showalter has labeled "feminism's awkward age."[3] A respected journalist, actress, playwright, as well as producer and director of her own work when necessary, Treadwell could pose as a prototype for the independent and adventuresome "New Woman" of the early twentieth century. Graduating from the University of California at Berkeley in 1906, Treadwell, like many women writers in the first half of the century, began her writing career in journalism, working as a staff writer for the San Francisco *Bulletin*, where she covered as well as participated in the marches for women's suffrage. After her marriage to journalist William O'Connell McGeehan, she moved to the New York *Herald Tribune*, which sent her to Europe as a war correspondent during World War I.[4] Alternating between journalism and playwriting, Treadwell had her first professional production in 1922 with the drama *Gringo*, influenced by her exclusive interview with the Mexican revolutionary Pancho Villa a year earlier. Although Treadwell wrote thirty full-length plays before her death in 1970, only seven were performed on Broadway, and of this handful, only *Machinal* and *Hope for a Harvest* (1941) were ever published. Performed in European theaters and produced for television in 1960, *Machinal* remains Treadwell's only commercial success, and yet it also has been largely overlooked in traditional drama surveys by critics.[5]

Although an analysis of Treadwell's dramatic canon reveals a broad spectrum of dramatic forms ranging from light comedy to melodrama to social criticism, it is her longstanding "partisanship of feminism" that marks the majority of her works.[6] Plays such as *Oh Nightingale* (1925), a conventional comedy about an aspiring actress in New York City; *Lone Valley* (1933), a melodrama of a reformed prostitute; and *Hope for a Harvest*, a realistic drama of a woman's attempt to restore her family's farm, all feature female protagonists who struggle for autonomy (albeit not always successfully) in a male-dominated society. Perhaps the strongest declaration of Treadwell's commitment to feminist concerns is her play *Rights*, an unpublished biographical drama of Mary Wollstonecraft, the eighteenth-century author of the seminal feminist work *A Vindication of the Rights of Woman*. Copyrighted in 1921 but never produced, *Rights* frames Wollstonecraft's bid for personal freedom against the broader struggle of the French Revolution.[7] Criticized as didactic and unfocused, *Rights* nevertheless capsulizes some feminist issues that receive powerful, searing dramatization in *Machinal* seven years later, particularly the role of women in the institution of marriage.[8] The bold, vibrant character of Wollstonecraft in *Rights*, who lashes out, "I am opposed to marriage. . . . I will not submit to an institution I wish to see abolished," stands behind the docile wife portrayed in *Machinal*.[9]

Like *Rights*, *Machinal* (French for "mechanical") voices Treadwell's feminism with a particular vehemency and radicalism that is softened in many of her other plays. Combining expressionistic techniques, such as repetitive dialogue, audio effects, numerous short scenes, and the distortion of inner and outer reality, Treadwell creates, with the evocative disorientation of an Edvard Munch, the picture of an ordinary young woman driven by desperation to murder. Using her newspaper writing experiences, Treadwell based her play in part on the celebrated 1927 murder trial of Ruth Snyder and Judd Gray, two lovers convicted of killing Mrs. Snyder's husband. With this sensational crime as her foundation, Treadwell builds the story of a young woman forced by economic and societal pressures to marry her employer. Trapped in a loveless mariage, the young woman drifts into an extramarital affair with a handsome adventurer. After her lover's return to Mexico, the woman's sense of confinement and anguish overwhelm her and lead her to murder her husband by striking him over the head with a bottle of stones, a method related to her by the lover. The young woman is convicted of murder when her lover informs the police of their affair in an effort to keep himself from punishment. The play ends with the execution of the young woman.

Coming eight years after the extension of the franchise to women in 1920, *Machinal* occupies an unusual place in early twentieth-century drama by women. Although a number of theatrical works by women from 1910 to 1920 focused on women characters and feminist themes, by the late 1920s the figure of the independent, daring "New Woman" who challenged the traditional roles for women had been subdued.[10] The "New Woman" who declared in Jesse Lynch Williams's 1918 hit play, *Why Marry?* had by as early as 1925 metamorphosed into the neurotic housewife of George Kelly's critically acclaimed *Craig's Wife*, who sought not just independence but "control *over* the man [she] married."[11] In this respect, the portrayal of women in the dramatic productions of the 1920s and 1930s mirrored the changes in women's roles in the social and economic structures of the time. After the crucial success of achieving the vote in 1920, the feminist movement began to wane, partly because of the conservative backlash prompted by the economic and social turmoil of the late 1920s and early 1930s.[12] A decline in women's enrollment in colleges and in their participation in the work force and professional fields all contributed to an increasing return to traditional domestic roles for women after 1920.[13] Within this more conservative context in both society and the theater, Treadwell's drama of the restrictive nature of traditional marriage for women indeed stands alone as an "isolated expression[] of 'feminist' theatre."[14]

Focusing on the social and psychological restrictions imposed on women in a male-dominated society, *Machinal* features not a "New Woman" of extraordinary talents and determination, but an "Every Woman," one who is neither politically motivated nor ambitious or creative. Opening with the simple statement, "The plot is the story of a woman who murders her husband—an ordinary young woman, any woman" (173), Treadwell begins to construct her "strategy of resistance" against the patriarchal system.[15] Emphasizing the average rather than the special woman, Treadwell implies that it is not the extraordinary "New Woman" of the suffrage movement that the patriarchal system has to fear but rather the outwardly docile, ordinary woman who can be transformed by the social pressures of the patriarchy to act. This accent on the ordinary constitutes the radical in Treadwell's work.

Divided into nine episodes, *Machinal* opens with a business scene, replete with office workers and cacophonous office machinery, but the topic of the office conversation centers less on business accounts than marriage. Almost like an Austen novel, the characters speculate on whether the female protagonist, Helen (referred to throughout the play as the "Young Woman" to emphasize her anonymity), will marry the boss, George Jones: "Will she have him? . . . will he have her?" (182) Early in the play, this juxtaposition of business with marriage establishes Treadwell's concentration on the economic basis of marriage. On one hand, Helen would be free of economic pressures if she marries her employer; on the other hand, she would be subordinate in every sense, legally, physically, emotionally, and economically, to a man she does not love or respect. Neither alternative—a life of work or marriage—meets her personal needs.

Helen recognizes that the dilemma posed by the two alternatives is compounded by the social pressure to conform to marriage: "all girls—most girls—married" (186). This emphasis on traditional domestic roles for women accompanied the political and social conservatism of the late 1920s and 1930s. After the early successes of the women's movement in the first decade of the century, many women again began to view marriage as their only option. As Jane F. Bonin stresses in her analysis of prize-winning American plays, many major plays of the 1920s and 1930s, especially those by male playwrights, reinforced the belief that marriage was a necessary goal in a young woman's life:

> Again and again, these plays insist that marriage, to any man and under any conditions, is better than none. Especially during the twenties and early

> thirties, a period when many women were questioning whether a life exclusively preoccupied with home and family was necessary or desirable, the important plays seemed to assume that salvation for women could be found only in marriage, even an unhappy one.[16]

In the expressionistic, telegraphic style that characterizes *Machinal,* Helen's disjointed monologue at the end of the first episode summarizes this social and psychological conflict confronting the average, young working woman in the early twentieth century:

> Mrs. George H. Jones—money—no work—no worry—free!—rest—sleep till nine—sleep till ten—sleep till noon—now you take a good rest this morning—don't get up till you want to—thank you—oh thank you—oh don't—please don't touch me—I want to rest—no rest—earn—got to earn—married—earn—no—yes—earn—all girls—most girls—ma—pa—ma—all women—most women—I can't—must—maybe—must—somebody—something—ma—pa—ma—can I, ma? Tell me, ma—something—somebody. (186)

Helen's vague but desperate need for "something—somebody" to tell her how to resolve the conflicts she faces in a male-dominated society resurface throughout the play.

Helen's cry for "somebody" to rescue her from a life of work or marriage merges in episode 2 with her dreams of romance, of "somebody young—and—and attractive—with wavy hair" (192). While at dinner with her mother in their shabby apartment, Helen tries to express her inner turmoil about love and marriage. But Helen's mother, hardened and worn by the rigors of work and an unhappy marriage herself, scoffs at her daughter's romantic idealism, "Love!—what does that amount to! Will it clothe you? Will it feed you? Will it pay the bills?" (191) She exposes with brutal pragmatism the economic basis of the traditional marriage, which often negates romantic love. In this way, Helen's mother is a poorer, less frivolous Mrs. Bennet, but underneath her motivations are the same as Austen's characters'. They both know that for the impecunious young woman, marriage, even a flawed one, is preferable to being alone in a male-dominated society. The absence of Helen's father (he is never mentioned in the play) and her mother's financial dependence on her daughter illustrate in this episode how the traditional marriage can fail to provide the woman with economic or emotional support. Because her mother's financial welfare plays a part in Helen's decision to marry Mr. Jones, it symbolizes how the burden of the marriage devolves on to the next generation of young women trapped in the system.[17]

The metaphor of marriage for women as confinement or imprisonment is introduced in the first two opening scenes and reinforced throughout the play. Using psychosomatic disorders such as claustrophobia and anorexia, which feminist critics Sandra M. Gilbert and Susan Gubar have interpreted as expressions of escape in women's writing, Treadwell conveys her female protagonist's inability to cope with the social pressures placed on women.[18] In the first episode, Helen experiences a "stifling" feeling in the subway that makes her repeatedly late for work, an unconscious avoidance of Mr. Jones's attentions. This sense of claustrophobia or suffocation returns in the discussion of marriage with her mother in episode 2. Here, not only does Helen have difficulty breathing; she is unable to swallow her meal. These psychological reactions reappear at key moments in the play whenever Helen feels especially threatened by the inexorable pressures of the marriage.

If Helen's need to escape the confines of marriage is represented by the "stifling" and "gagging" she experiences, her rebellion against male-dominated society can be read in her "madness," which results in the murder of her husband near the end of the play. Gilbert and Gubar's first volume in their critique of modernist works, *The War of the Words*, describes the madwoman figure of nineteenth-century women's texts who escapes from the attic to take center stage in a number of works by twentieth-century women writers. Linked with militant feminism and violence against the patriarchy, Gilbert and Gubar's madwoman embodies female anger and anxiety over male dominance and, most importantly, the power to resist the formidable pressure to conform to male-prescribed roles.[19] Helen, identified at the outset of the play as an ordinary woman, seems to incorporate little of the madwoman-rebel figure. But her resistance to marriage and, later in the play, to maternity, causes her to be labeled as "crazy" and "neurotic" by those about her. Helen's act of murder, however, injects a mad-like dimension to her behavior that most strongly links her to the rebel figure.

Repeatedly chastised by her mother in the second episode as "crazy" for her refusal to marry Mr. Jones, Helen ultimately displays a level of repressed anger and despair that clashes with her earlier passivity. Marriage is again the catalyst. Throughout episode 2, Helen searches for an escape from marriage to love. Resigning herself to marriage at one point in the scene, Helen dully concedes, "And I suppose I got to marry somebody—all girls do" (192). But as the inevitability of her marriage to Jones looms larger, her feelings of claustrophobia intensify: "it's like I'm all tight inside" (193). Her mother's unsympathetic response, "You're crazy," in the face of her desperation causes Helen to explode in violent anger: "Ma—if you tell me that again I'll kill you! I'll kill you!" (193). This uncharacteristic response is difficult to reconcile with the passivity and tractability that Helen displays throughout the earlier part of the scene. The almost monster-like quality to Helen's explosion indicates another side, a "mad double" that many women writers have used to allow their "proper" heroines to express the violent acts of rebellion they dare not express otherwise.[20] Although Helen Jones is not given a "mad double" in the play, there is some indication in both this scene and in the murder scene of a "darker side" that lurks within her, foreshadowing the murder of her husband that follows.

Episode 2 closes with Helen's numb capitulation to marriage, leading to the honeymoon scene of episode 3. Staging a harsh, unromantic honeymoon night in a tawdry hotel room with jazz music from the dance casino next door intruding in the background, Treadwell again connects economics to marriage in this scene in a way that sharply exposes the traditional patriarchal marriage. Jones's obsession with money, "Twelve bucks a day! They know how to soak you in these pleasure resorts," is coupled with his crass, sexual humor, "Say, what you got under there?" (196, 197). Helen, unprepared for the sexual realities of the night and repelled by a man she does not love, is seized with claustrophobic reactions and ends the scene weeping in terror. Despite the criticism of Freudian scholar W. David Sievers, who has characterized Helen as a "sexually baffled" woman with an unnatural fear of sex communicated by her mother's own sexual frigidity, Helen can more accurately be interpreted as a young woman who feels pressured by the "rules" of the traditional marriage to be intimate with a man against her will.[21]

Here Treadwell charges that the basis of the patriarchal marriage, an exchange of intimacy for economic security, is tantamount to prostitution. The tone of Jones's comment on the cost of the hotel room, "Twelve bucks! Well—we'll get our money's worth out of it all right," seems more appropriate for the brothel than the honeymoon suite. At the conclusion of the episode, Helen pleads for her mother, for "somebody," to save her, but the throbbing rhythm of the jazz music overpowers her cries as the scene blacks out. Criticized in 1931 as "revolting" in British reviews of the play, the honeymoon episode depicts the sexual relationship between husband and wife with a degree of verisimilitude that was considered too "true to life" for public presentation.[22] Treadwell's portrayal of marital intimacy *is* "revolting" in this episode in a way that the critics failed to realize. Helen's plea for "somebody" to help her suggests the possibility of a rescue, a revolution against a tradition that requires a woman to submit to a kind of "legalized rape" that is truly "revolting."

Following a natural progression, episode 4 opens in a maternity ward of a major hospital. Here Treadwell presents one of the most critical portraits of motherhood in modern literature. The claustrophobic set design—one room closed in by a corridor, the window view blocked by the construction of a tall, phallus-like building—and the jarring audio effects of the riveting machine that permeate and overpower the dialogue characterize the sacred institution of motherhood, creating a truly radical vision of what western society considers woman's primary function, maternity. The scene opens with the nurse making her rounds. She tries to engage Helen in routine conversation, "No pain? . . . Such, a sweet baby you have, too. . . . Aren't you glad it's a girl? Your milk hasn't come yet—has it?" (202), all questions to which Helen signals "no" in a counter rhythm of negation against the nurse's trite observations on motherhood and the sound of the riveting machine in the background. Helen's responses to motherhood, as an Every Woman figure, are particularly telling. Her refusal to communicate, only gesturing "no," and her inability to eat as she gags on her food both imply a rejection of motherhood. Helen's power to choose what she does with her life, however, is limited. Pressured and pressed into the "machinery" of the patriarchal marriage in the opening scenes and forced by her coarse husband in the honeymoon episode, Helen becomes solidly "riveted" into the system by giving birth. Her severe reaction, the repeated negation of "self," tragically emphasizes her total subsumption by the institution. Treadwell illustrates the totality of Helen's subjection by stressing the lack of control she has over even her own body in this scene.

Helen confronts three male guardians of patriarchy in the maternity ward who claim authority over her. First her husband visits, exhorting her to just "brace up," and "face things." He minimizes the pain of her pregnancy and assumes a measure of authority over the birth process itself, "Everybody's got to brace up and face things! That's what makes the world go round. I know all you've been through but—Oh, yes I do! I know all about it!" (202). Despite his overbearing assertions, Jones understands as little about Helen's experience of childbirth as he did of her distress on their honeymoon night. Helen reacts to this statement with a "violent gesture" of negation and then withdrawal. It is when Jones states with male arrogance, "Having a baby's natural! Perfectly natural thing—" (203) that Helen gags and emphatically gestures for her husband to leave. This is the potent truth that Helen tries to reject throughout the maternity episode: as a woman she has little control over her fate; she is bound to reproduction.

Helen's lack of power is underscored by the male doctor's entrance immediately after the exit of her husband. The doctor usurps jurisdiction over her body in a very literal way. He immediately commands, "Put the child to breast" (203), although she has no milk and refuses to breast-feed. Then, when informed of Helen's nausea, the doctor ignores the protests of both Helen and the nurse and prescribes food for her anyway in a kind of forced feeding. Helen's reaction is one of desperation and despair, and her response to the doctor is simply, "Let me alone." This cry for autonomy then forms the theme of her closing interior monologue. In a stream-of-consciousness flow, Helen remembers the pregnancy of a pet dog of her childhood. The string of associations that follow link the woman to dog as breeding animals in an inescapable bond of biological determinism. In melding the past with present, Helen even expresses a death wish for her own child[23]:

> I won't submit to any more—crawl off—crawl off in the dark—Vixen crawled under the bed—way back in the corner under the bed—they were all drowned—puppies don't go to heaven—heaven—golden stairs—long stairs . . . all the children coming down—coming down to be born—dead going up—children coming down—going up—(204–5)

As the dog and the woman fuse in a form of reproductive destiny, the paternal authority reaches its zenith when the earthly patriarch, Helen's husband, merges with the ultimate patriarchal authority, God the Father,

> What kind of hair has God? no matter—it doesn't matter—everybody loves God—they've got to—got to—got to love God—God is love—even if he's bad they got to love him—even if he's got fat hands—fat hands—(205)

Helen objects that "God never had [a baby]"; Mary was the one who gave birth. "God's on a high throne," and Mary's place is "in a manger—the lowly manger" (205). Clearly the position and the power, God on top and Mary underneath, is with the male. Helen's recognition and indictment of a male society based on biology is underscored with her final lines of the scene, "I'll not submit any more—I'll not submit—I'll not submit—" (206). But as the sound of the riveting machine overpowers her final cry, it is already too late for this ordinary young woman to escape.

Instead of the ardent figure of the newly bound prisoner, episode 5 depicts a Helen Jones whose despondency and restlessness ("I want to keep moving") (211) lead her to an encounter in a bar with a stranger and a subsequent affair. Treadwell's skillful use of setting and the interplay of background dialogues in this scene, significantly entitled "Prohibited," reveals the illusion of escape from marital restrictions that the extramarital affair appears to offer. In addition, Treadwell stresses the subversive side of the intimate encounter that places it outside the boundaries of the legal and sanctioned union of marriage and labels it as an "outlaw" relationship. Helen's initial meeting with her lover occurs in a darkened bar with the mechanical tunes from an electric piano and exchanges between a series of other couples in the bar counterpointed against the main dialogue. One such conversation between a man and woman centers on the possible abortion of her child, which she reluctantly agrees to after being reminded harshly by her lover that she will lose her job if she keeps the child. Again, Treadwell emphasizes that economics and biology play a central role in male-female relationships even outside of marriage.

Against this bleak backdrop, Treadwell stages Helen's love affair. Played by Clark Gable in the original production, the man Helen falls in love with fulfills all the requirements of the romantic lead: he is an experienced lover ("They all fall for you") with "coarse wavy hair" and an adventurer from Mexico who tells stories of his daring escapades, "I got the two birds that guarded me drunk one night, and then I filled the empty bottle with small stones—and let 'em have it!" (214). Trapped in a marriage that provides no emotional or physical fulfillment, Helen yields easily to a man with a handsome face and quick tongue who represents to her a form of outlaw freedom. During their intimate encounter in a dismal basement room in episode 6, Helen experiences a fleeting moment of release and fantasizes a romantic escape with her lover in a series of childhood associations that combine romance with the fairy tales and nursery rhymes told to children: "And the dish ran away with the spoon—I never thought that had any sense before—now I get it" (221). But like marriage and motherhood, romance in a patriarchal society offers neither happiness nor freedom, but an illusion or a momentary feeling of being "on top of the world," "purified." Helen is merely one of many women for her lover—"Jeez, honey, all women look like angels to me" and these few illicit hours have brought her no closer to the freedom she craves—"I'll never get—below the Rio Grande—I'll never get out of here" (222–23). This grim realization that as a woman she must play out the submissive role determined for her leads Helen from one subversive act, an illicit affair, to the ultimate subversive act of killing her husband—a bid for self-liberation that results simultaneously in self-destruction.

The place of action for Helen's violence is again domestic. Episode 7 portrays a typical evening conversation between Jones and Helen that focuses on his business deals and the news from the daily newspaper. The mechanical and repetitive quality of the exchanges on business illustrates the absence of any real communication between them and the emptiness of their union. Treadwell's integration of newspaper material into the dialogue, however, exposes the true schism between not just this particular married couple but between the male perception of what is significant, "newsworthy," and the conflicting female view of reality. In the opening exchange, both Jones and Helen "read" their own versions of what constitutes the "news," the record of the times:

Husband: Record production.
Young Woman: Girl turns on gas.

Husband: Sale hits a million—
Young Woman: Woman leaves all for love—
Husband: Market trend steady—
Young Woman: Young wife disappears—
Husband: Owns a life interest—(227)

Helen "reads" a woman's story of anguish and escape while her husband sees only economic prosperity. As the scene progresses, Helen interprets a more radical version of the female story, "Prisoner escapes—lifer breaks jail—shoots way to freedom," and finally, "Woman finds husband dead" (229–30). The possibility of freedom through revolution in these lines indicates the presence of an emerging subversive female consciousness that undermines the male version of what is "real" and which, if acted upon, would threaten the male-dominated social structure. As the weight of her role as wife and mother intensifies, Helen feels "stifled" and "drowned," painfully conscious of her confinement. The background music and internal voices escalate at the conclusion of the scene, and as the possibility of freedom possesses Helen, the "mad double," the agent of rebellion, takes control of her actions. In the middle of night, when the moon is full, she fills a bottle with stones and strikes at her husband in his sleep.

Judged and punished by "The Law" in episodes 8 and 9 for the murder of her husband, Helen completes her metamorphosis from a passive young woman who succumbs to economic and social pressures at the beginning of the play to the militant rebel of the final scenes. Helen's initial description of the killers indicates how far she has moved beyond passivity to actor. Helen tells the prosecutor that she was awakened by hearing "somebody—something—in the room" (237). These two words, "somebody—something," which have formulated her "motif of yearning" in the marriage and honeymoon scenes, are reiterated here with telling significance.[24] Her repetition of the words "somebody," "something" to describe who killed her husband link her violent act with rescue or liberation. In these earlier episodes, the rescuer is vague, an indeterminate pronoun—Helen is the one who is acted upon. But when she identifies her husband's killer as "something," "somebody," "a big dark looking man," on one level she is describing herself because she is the killer. The "somebody," "something," that rescues her from the prison of marriage is this time within herself, something big and dark from within.

Machinal ends with the same kind of understated rebellion that marks Treadwell's first lines. Although Helen confesses her crime, there is no act of contrition and submission as in episode 2 when she begs for her mother's forgiveness and obediently agrees to marry Mr. Jones. Instead, in the final scene before her death, Helen declares to the priest that her only free moment on earth was when she killed her husband:

"When I did what I did I was free!" (252). This lack of penitence, almost to the point of exaltation, must be punished by death. Moments before the execution, her mother enters for a final goodbye, and Helen's exclamation, "But she's never known me—never known me—ever—," changes to reconciliation, and her last entreaty is for her own daughter,

> Wait! Mother, my child; my little strange child! I never knew her! She'll never know me! Let her live, Mother. Let her live! Live! Tell her—(253)

Generation to generation of women seem alienated, "never known" to one another, each new mother raising her daughter to conform to her expected role in a male-dominated social structure. Helen's plea to communicate to her daughter the realities that Helen has discovered, to "Tell her—," holds the hope of change, of solidarity among generations of women, but this message is cut off abruptly, left uncompleted as Helen is forced to the electric chair. Given the subversive possibilities, that Helen Jones is "any woman, any ordinary woman" who murders her husband, it is imperative that the machine works at the end of *Machinal:* "It'll work!—It always works!" (254). Otherwise, Helen Jones might be able to pass the message on to her daughter that "somebody," "something," this emerging female consciousness, can help her live.

Sophie Treadwell belongs to the coterie of early modern women playwrights who portrayed with relentless honesty women's struggle for autonomy against a patriarchal system. Concentrating on women's issues and employing the male-dominated mode of drama, feminist playwrights such as Treadwell have threatened to subvert the traditional theater by seeking their own powerful public voice.[25] Their efforts until now have condemned them to a literary anonymity of unpublished works and hasty critiques such as that suffered by Treadwell. The contributions of Sophie Treadwell and women dramatists like her merit reassessment. The story in *Machinal* of one ordinary woman's attempt to strike back at a repressive institution needs to be communicated. Perhaps instead of being misread or misinterpreted by male critics, *Machinal* has been comprehended all too well. Silenced for decades by the literary "machine," Sophie Treadwell still has a message to telegraph to her "daughters."

Notes

1. Sophie Treadwell, *Machinal*, in *Plays by American Women: 1900–1930*, ed. Judith E. Barlow (New York: Applause, 1985). Subsequent references are cited parenthetically by page number.

2. Robert Brustein, "A Director's Theatre: *Machinal* by Sophie Treadwell," in *Seasons of Discontent: Dramatic Opinions 1959–1965* (New York: Simon and Schuster, 1965), p.

38. If Treadwell's play is mentioned at all in drama studies of the period, it is usually linked to Elmer Rice's critically acclaimed *The Adding Machine* (1923), which also uses expressionistic techniques to stage the effects of mechanization on an office worker. Winifred L. Dusenbury, *The Theme of Loneliness in Modern American Drama* (Gainesville: University of Florida Press, 1967); Thomas Allen Greenfield, *Work and the Work Ethic in American Drama, 1920–1970* (Columbia: University of Missouri Press, 1982); John Gassner, ed., *Twenty-Five Best Plays of the Modern American Theatre* (New York: Crown, 1949); and Ethan Mordden, *The American Theatre* (New York: Oxford University Press, 1981), all discuss *Machinal* as an anti-mechanization play that substitutes a female employee for the male protagonist of Rice's play.

3. There is some discrepancy concerning Treadwell's date of birth. According to Nancy Edith Wynn, *Sophie Treadwell: The Career of a Twentieth-Century American Feminist Playwright* (Diss., City University of New York, 1982), various sources give a 3 October 1890 date, and the Census Report of 1900 and Treadwell's application to Berkeley list her birth as October 1885. Treadwell herself was responsible for the confusion (1). The designation "feminism's awkward age" appears in Elaine Showalter, ed., Introduction to *These Modern Women: Autobiographical Essays from the Twenties* (Old Westbury, N. Y.: Feminist Press, 1978), p. 9.

4. Ishbel Ross, *Ladies of the Press: The Story of Women in Journalism by an Insider* (New York: Harper and Brothers, 1936), provides information on several early women journalists, including Treadwell.

5. Judith Olauson, *The American Woman Playwright: A View of Criticism and Characterization* (Troy, N. Y.: Whitston Publishing, 1981), examines the lack of attention historically accorded women playwrights. Treadwell receives one line or no mention in the following drama surveys: Arthur Hobson Quinn, *A History of the American Drama From the Civil War to the Present Day* (New York: Harper and Brothers, 1923); Joseph Mersand, *The American Drama, 1930–1940: Essays on Playwrights and Plays* (New York: Modern Chapbooks, 1941); Eleanor Flexner, *American Playwrights: 1918–1938: The Theatre Retreats from Reality* [1938] (Freeport, N. Y.: Books for Libraries Press, 1969); and C. W. E. Bigsby, *A Critical Introduction to Twentieth-Century American Drama: Vol. 1. 1900–1940* (Cambridge: Cambridge University Press, 1982).

6. Louise Heck-Rabi, *Sophie Treadwell: Subjects and Structures in 20th Century American Drama* (Diss., Wayne State University, 1976), p. 18.

7. Wynn, *Sophie Treadwell*, p. 66.

8. Ibid., p. 72.

9. Sophie Treadwell, *Rights*, quoted in Wynn, *Sophie Treadwell*, p. 71.

10. Cynthia Sutherland, "American Women Playwrights as Mediators of the 'Woman Problem,'" *Modern Drama* 21, no. 3 (September 1978): 325–26; Deborah S. Kolb, "The Rise and Fall of the New Woman in American Drama," *Educational Theatre Journal* 27 (1975): 149–60; Judith L. Stephens, "*Why Marry?*: The 'New Woman' of 1918," *Theatre Journal* 34 (1982): 183–84.

11. Jesse Lynch Williams's *Why Marry?* (1918) portrays a "New Woman" character who rigorously challenges the traditional role of women in marriage. George Kelly's *Craig's Wife* (1925) is a critical picture of a wife obsessed with housekeeping, who dares to control her husband. Both plays won Pulitzer Prizes.

12. Rayna Rapp and Ellen Ross, "The Twenties' Backlash: Compulsory Heterosexuality, the Consumer Family, and the Waning of Feminism," in *Class, Race, and Sex: The Dynamics of Control*, ed. Amy Swerdlow and Hanna Lessinger (Boston: G. K. Hall, 1983), pp. 93–107.

13. Kolb, "The Rise and Fall of the New Woman," pp. 158–59. See also William L. O'Neill, *Everyone Was Brave: The Rise and Fall of Feminism in America* (Chicago: Quadrangle Books, 1969).

14. Sutherland, "American Women Playwrights," p. 330.

15. Sharon Friedman, "Feminism as Theme in Twentieth-Century American Women's Drama," *American Studies* 25 (1984): 71. Friedman identifies murder and madness as strategies of resistance in such feminist plays as Susan Glaspell's *Trifles* (1916), a compel-

ling one-act drama of a farm wife's murder of her oppressive husband. A number of interesting parallels can be traced between Glaspell's play and *Machinal*.

16. Jane F. Bonin, *Major Themes in Prize-Winning American Drama* (Metuchen, N. J.: Scarecrow Press, 1975), pp. 6–7.

17. The marriage of Treadwell's parents provides some insight into the negative portrayal of traditional marriage in her works. When Treadwell was eight years old, her parents separated. Although divorce was avoided, Treadwell's father, a prosperous judge, failed to provide for them as promised, forcing Mrs. Treadwell, and later a teen-age Treadwell, to seek employment to support themselves. During her last year of high school, Treadwell began to experience physical and nervous breakdowns that plagued her the rest of her life. For further discussion see Wynn, pp. 1–10.

18. Sandra M. Gilbert and Susan Gubar, *The Madwoman in the Attic: The Woman Writer and the Nineteenth-Century Literary Imagination* (New Haven: Yale University Press, 1979), p. 86.

19. Sandra M. Gilbert and Susan Gubar, *No Man's Land: The Place of the Woman Writer in the Twentieth Century, Vol. 1: The War of the Words* (New Haven: Yale University Press, 1988), pp. 67, 14.

20. Gilbert and Gubar, *The Madwoman in the Attic*, p. 85.

21. W. David Sievers, *Freud on Broadway: A History of Psychoanalysis and the American Drama* (New York: Hermitage, 1955), pp. 90–91.

22. Reviews of *Machinal* (retitled *The Life Machine*) in the *London Daily Mail* (1931), *Evening Standard* (1931), *The Morning Post* (1931), and *Daily Sketch* (1931), quoted in Wynn, *Sophie Treadwell*, pp. 144–45.

23. Sievers, *Freud on Broadway*, p. 91.

24. Wynn, *Sophie Treadwell*, p. 126; see also Heck-Rabi, *Sophie Treadwell*, p. 72.

25. Michelene Wandor, "The Impact of Feminism on the Theatre," *Feminist Review* no. 18 (1984): 85–86.

8
Gertrude Stein: Exile, Feminism, Avant-Garde in the American Theater

Dinnah Pladott

How does one live and create while in exile? The life and work of Gertrude Stein, exiled several times as an expatriate American woman, a Jew, and a lesbian, make the question especially pressing. Her decision to experiment with unprecedented forms of writing gives resonance to the notion of exile formulated by Julia Kristeva, also a double exile. In "A New Type of Intellectual: The Dissident," Kristeva comments that physical banishment implies a dissenting metaphysics: "Exile is already a form of *dissidence,* since it involves uprooting oneself from a family, a country or a language."[1] According to Kristeva, this initial form of exile is compounded in women, who are excluded from participation "in the consensual law of politics and society." A woman, argues Kristeva, is by definition "trapped within the frontiers of her body and even of her species, and consequently always feels *exiled* both by general clichés that make up a common consensus and by the very powers of generalization intrinsic to language."[2] The same terms apply by inference to the Jew and the lesbian, living permanently outside the consensus. The effect of this multiple exile on Stein's contribution to American drama is considerable.

Regrettably, Kristeva never mentions Stein among the writers she valorizes—Joyce, Kafka, Beckett—who "pluralize meaning and cross all national and linguistic barriers."[3] Yet her discussion of avant-garde writing and its ability to use exile as a vantage point from which it displaces established literary forms by "the eruption of the languages of modernity" situates Stein perfectly.[4] Moreover, Kristeva insists that the displacement accomplished by such dissidence is not confined to the purely literary or aesthetic realm but always has political implications. Under the pressure of avant-garde writing, "the master discourses begin to drift and the simple rational coherence of cultural and institutional codes breaks down."[5]

Kristeva provides a belated description of the defiant creative project

Stein has already carried out,[6] demonstrating that exile from the mainstream opens for women and avant-garde artists a similar enterprise—undertaking to interrogate and destabilize the most sanctified and most entrenched assumptions about what constitutes reality, knowledge, beauty, and truth. As Stein explains in "Composition As Explanation," the experimental writer composes differently than her contemporaries, and in so doing shatters the habitual modes of seeing and showing, as well as the received emphases and perspectives. In a typical humorous deflation, Stein comments on the refusal of the majority to accept the minority's (re)vision until the artistic innovation has become abstracted from its spatiotemporal context, thus rendering the upstart artist an "outlaw" or exile from the communal framework:

> "Those who are creating the modern composition authentically are naturally only of importance when they are dead because by that time the modern composition having become past is classified and the description of it is classical. That is the reason why the creator of the new composition in the arts is an outlaw until he is a classic . . ."[7]

Faced with the choice of being "an outlaw" or "a classic," Stein unhesitatingly chose the former. I suggest that her creative project of realizing "the new composition" is most central and radical in her operas and plays, which have received much less critical attention than her fiction.[8] It is most radical because Stein takes on the tendency of the theatrical medium to mask more effectively than any other art the fact that it is a structured and codified process of signification. The convergence of the spectator with the physical presence of iconic signs (in Peirce's terms), namely, the actors and the performance's sights and sounds, fosters the illusion that the staged play is an unmediated reality rather than a rule-governed semiotic exchange. Stein repeatedly foregrounds and unmasks this illusion. By refusing to abide by the traditional rules of dramatic writing, she also calls into question many assumptions about the means whereby meaning is produced and about the relationship of signification to the object signified. Furthermore, as we shall see, she confirms Kristeva's prediction that the dissidence from one system of "consensual laws" bears inevitably on a number of theoretical projects. In Stein's case, dissident innovation is pertinent to feminism on the one hand and to theories of art and criticism on the other, because she raises questions about the presumed authority of any text (most notably, "the master discourse") to represent reality.[9]

Stein's dramatic scripts anticipate the deconstructive terminology and methods of Jacques Derrida and Michel Foucault, because she set out intentionally to disrupt all structures or systems that presuppose the existence of a stable, inherent, and infallible meaning (patriarchal structures particularly), including her own writing. The operas and plays exemplify writing that is conscious of its own provisional authority; that is, aware of its own contingency, of its being *sous rature* (under erasure), in Derrida's words.[10] Stein and her practice in her operas and plays, therefore, come into the discussion as both illustrating (although antedating) Kristeva's points and moving the discussion toward a consideration of the relation of the woman-writer-exile to feminism, the avant-garde, deconstruction, and signification. I propose that the capacity to interrogate the signifying practices of theater and other types of discourse establishes an analogy between feminism and the avant-garde in art as well as in science. Moreover, this capacity collapses categories central to the historiography of American drama and theater, such as "the play of social relevance."

The New (Syntax-Free) Composition

At first glance, Stein's operas and plays appear opaque, fragmented, chaotic, and undecipherable. No cohesive signified object or action takes shape. The difficulty arises from the absence of hierarchical ordering. This disorienting discourse formation is intentional. In explaining the direction and extent of Picasso's dissidence, Stein notes that "the composition of living had extended and each thing was as important as any other thing."[11] The comment elucidates her own art as well as his. Stein describes the "new composition" as one that eschews both subordination and classification into associated paradigmatic groups.[12] In painterly terms, this amounts to the relinquishing of perspective, equalizing center, and periphery. But if we invoke a linguistic metaphor, this strategy disestablishes syntax. In the absence of codified association and subordination, the syntactical ordering of the elements in the sentence is derailed (deruled), and signification in the habitual sense becomes impeded. Consider a standard passage:

Scene 2

Elizabeth Henry having been left to the encouragement of George Henry who said they are following they may be left to have it been heard or borne.

Elizabeth Long hears Elizabeth Henry repeating that she will be told that they were hearing it themselves.

George Henry and Elizabeth Long made it a part of their arrangement that they would wait till Monday.

The sea shore and they wished to remember that it had had a name as well as afterwards.

Who came to be left to have it helped as they were preparing to accustom them to their arrangement.[13]

The opacity of this passage, its failure "to make sense" in any traditional manner, is a feature of all Stein's operas and plays. The scene illustrates Stein's refusal to abide by traditional meaning-producing organizations and syntax. First, the passage is one of many that confound and deflate any generic division between drama and narration. Therefore, we are uncertain about the codes that might be applicable in deciphering it. Second, no gradations of diction and activities provide the reader-viewer with any grounds for differentiating among the *dramatis personae*. Here and elsewhere, attempts to reconstruct a stable identity, a dramatized character, from the words spoken by a certain named individual (e.g., Elizabeth Long) is doomed to failure. We can conjure neither a psychological being nor a fabulous, archetypal, or even cartoon figure. Similarly, it is impossible, here and elsewhere, to connect words to actual deeds and thus to reconstruct a represented action—what the speakers enact on stage—as a correlation of their words.[14] Finally, there is no structuring of moments into a sequence of deeds that cohere or are at least related to one another. Such a structuring, with a beginning, middle, and end, or with an alternation of complication and dénouement, constructs a plot. Instead, we witness a mosaic of fragments that invites comparison to cubism.[15] If any spatial metaphor may be applied to Stein's unstructured structure, it is the circle.[16] Finally, at any point in the play, the reader-viewer must imagine or determine which parts of the text are stage directions, establishing an exchange between author and reader, and which parts belong to a represented dialogue among the fictive *dramatis personae*. The first type of text is outside the represented action, and the second is an integral part of it. A contrasting example from the same play may illustrate the difficulty of trying to distinguish between the internal and external discourses:

Scene 4

George Henry and William Long

It is better.
To be most
Most and best
Finally
As it does happen
To matter enough to be that.
They will hope to eat slowly.
Always on account.
If they go
They will seem
To be mine.

In a way
All of it
Very well.[17]

The breakdown of "meaningful sense" and the blurring of hierarchical and generic distinctions observed earlier are thematized in this scene. Stein deflates the obsession with being "better," "most," and "best," because these categories cannot be defined meaningfully against the empty demonstrative "that."[18] The persistent valorization of the "hierarchy-free" or "syntax-free" composition turns out, moreover, to undermine the authority of depiction. In the examples cited, Stein pokes fun at the serious presumption of authorial (and authoritative) reference to describe or transcribe reality into the theatrical medium, replete with meaning and truth. The gambit of *Say It With Flowers* is repeatedly reenacted in other operas and plays as the relationship between the signifying chain and its object becomes the subject of comedy. The comedy is enacted on all levels of the text: micro and macro, local and global. It appears in the witty (dis)organization and fragmentation of the smallest unit of the verbal continuum (e.g., phoneme and lexeme), as well as in the amusingly arbitrary division into acts and scenes; and it deforms and transforms the largest units of theatrical reference, such as dialogue, monologue, and diegesis.[19] All signifiers are simultaneously fragmented and doubled in a confusing multiplication of mirrored shreds, a carnival of signs. A representative passage, from *They Must. Be Wedded. To Their Wife,* assails our ear with the musical assonance of phonetic echoes and doublings and assaults our cognition with the accretion and subtraction of pronouns, the modulations of "may" and "can," and the concomitant dissolution and multiplication of represented selves:

Scene 7

Josephine. Can be. Respectfully. Left free.
Julia. She may be. Respectfully. Free.
Guy. She. May Be. Respectfully. Left free.
Paul. She may be. Respectfully left free.
Josephine. May be. Respectfully left free.
Josephine. May be. With three Josephine Julia and Guy.
Josephine. May be. With them. With the. Three Josephine Therese John and Guy.
Josephine. She may be. One of. Three. Josephine Julia John and Guy.
Julia and Guy. They may be. Very sleepy. And again. They may not be.[20]

In structure and content, the passage is emblematic of Stein's artistic and theoretical concern with modes of depiction and with their relation(s) to signification. The equation of primary and subsidiary, or inside and outside, noted above, is enacted here as the refusal to discriminate between the important and the trivial or between the one and the many. "Being left free" and "being very sleepy" are equally weighty where "each thing is as important as any other thing." Furthermore, the passage dramatizes Stein's concern with the relationship of description (or depiction) to its object. The various speakers offer here their conflicting portrayals and counts of what Wallace Stevens terms "things as they are," which in this scene appear variously as "she," "they," or versions thereof. The absence of a definite or stable opposition between an "original" (reality) and a double (copy, depiction) and the refusal to valorize the former in accordance with Platonic conceptions are characteristic of Stein's dramas and mark her bold departure from traditional modes of seeing, showing, and composition.[21]

Mimesis and Its Discontents

It is in relation to the notion of *mimesis* or the transcription of reality that Stein's work is most radical and most provocative. The dramas embody an intuition that has remained controversial even in its later theorization by Foucault and Derrida, that the depiction or description of the "thing itself" does not re-present an entity that exists a priori but precedes the model and gives it shape and life. In the 1934-35 *Lectures in America,* she articulated this intuition as the reason for her changing modes of writing. Stein recalls her disenchantment with the earlier achievement of *The Making of Americans,* in which knowledge of the object ("all I knew about everything") preceded and prescribed its description. In the next stage, she changed her priorities. Contingency and mutability replaced certainty and stability. Consequently, "what if not was not not to be known about any one about anything," that is, the absence of preconceived ideas about the object became the dominant concern. This "clean slate" approach opened the space for the process-oriented "what is happening to come" to take shape in the interstices of the description:

> "And so The Little Gay Book little by little changed from a description of any one of any one and everything there there was to be known about any one, to what if not was not not to be known about any one about anything. And so it was necessary to let come what would happen to come because after all knowledge is what you know but what is happening is inevitably what is happening to come."[22]

This assertion that description or composition precedes the object and gives it shape as well as reality has ramifications on the level of aesthetics as well as on that of ideology and politics. In "The Double

Session," Derrida discusses the concept of *mimesis* as a complex system of trifurcations and proliferating doubles in which original and copy enter into a multiplicity of relationships, most notably the copy as double, replacement, and supplement.[23] In relating the "discourse about what is" to the artistic "text," Derrida makes his most telling contribution to our own discussion.[24] This connection is crucial to critics of the literary art as well as to theorists of criticism. It enables us to reverse the shift Foucault has noted: "From the Romantic revolt . . . literature becomes progressively more differentiated from the discourse of ideas."[25] I shall use the term "representation" rather than *mimesis* to emphasize this intimate relationship or analogy between the critical text, a "discourse of ideas" that undertakes to describe or represent "what is" in the discourse it question(s), and the artistic (or literary) text, which sets out to represent "what is" in "reality" (in nature? in the world? in life?). If we believe, Derrida points out, that "a discourse about what is" is possible, then we accept the presence, the authority, of "the deciding and decidable *logos* of or about the *on* (being-present)."[26] We then accede willy-nilly to the claim that the "real" is distinguishable from the appearance, the image, the phenomenon, etc., that is, from anything that, presenting it *as* being-present, doubles it, re-presents it, and can therefore replace and de-present it."[27] The conclusion from these assumptions, Derrida points out—if we accept them—is the adherence to a rigid system of polarities: true/false, real/imitated, original/double, order/disorder, anterior/posterior, imitator/imitated. "And obviously," concludes Derrida sarcastically, "according to 'logic' itself, . . . what is imitated is more real, more essential, more true, etc., than what imitates. It is anterior and superior to it."[28]

Our preliminary analysis has shown that Stein does not subscribe to such a view of description and composition. Her practice questions all imperial and imperialist attempts to represent "things as they are" in the fictive work of art or in the discourse of ideas. Thus, she foregrounds an issue raised by feminist critics, who disputed the presumed objectivity of male literary critics, as well as the authority or validity of the disparaging classification such critics accorded to women artists. As we shall see in the last section of this paper, the feminist objections have a general relevance: the "master discourse" will always tend to distort, devalue, and, whenever possible, exclude (exile) all discourses that do not follow its own discursive practices.[29]

The Play of the InterPlay

We do a gross injustice to Stein, however, if we describe her as a philosopher in disguise. One of her most radical moves is her insidious refusal to associate herself with authority or irrefutable wisdom by aligning herself with "the serious" in the familiar oppositions "serious/ frivolous" (insignificant, trivial). Her disorienting procedures, it turns out, do not merely undermine aesthetic criteria such as Beauty, Truth, "verisimilitude" and "realism," or underscore the contextual and relative nature of all perceptions. They also valorize "play," one of the terms exiled from the discourse of metaphysics.

In Stein's practice, "play" covers a variety of prankish, clowning, and witty operations. It includes all the definitions advanced by Webster's dictionary: "jest," "the act of playing on words and speech sounds," "recreational activity," "the stage representation of an action or story"; in addition, it is also "games," "merry-making" and the like. Stein's playfully irreverent model refuses to engage in a confrontational debate with "the master discourse." Instead, she undertakes to pervert as well as subvert the Platonic hierarchical system by invoking irony and humor.[30] If, as Nancy Miller suggests, "feminists have no sense of humor" when confronted with male-centered denigration of women in literature and art,[31] Stein provides an alternative and highly humorous model. In complete harmony with her "syntax-free" composition, she farcically and subversively collapses a series of consecrated categorizations and antinomies, a series on which the hegemonic discourse founds its authority. "Play," therefore, becomes a pivotal word, as a hinge or a Derridean "hymen," at once separating and uniting two entities. It is a means, or rather a whole arsenal of means, for humorously collapsing any claim for a serious and absolutely truthful and objective representation.

Stein often plays mischievous structural games with her readers-spectators. For example, she inserts an "Interlude: Susan B. A Short Story" into her opera *The Mother of Us All* (1946), whose heroine is Susan B. Anthony. Stein replaces the antithetical exclusion "either play or story" by the inclusion "both play and story" or "neither play nor story." In a jest worthy of Derrida, she hinges the polarity play/story on a membranous "hymen" that differs/defers them rather than separates them. Thus in creating what Foucault terms not an exclusion or subtraction but an "interplay" between opposites,[32] Stein invites us to see whether each term in the binary opposition play/story is not, in the final analysis, an accomplice, or even a twin, rather than an enemy.

Is Stein suggesting that the polarization drama/narrative no longer holds for her? Probably. Is she toying with Henry James's famous distinction between "showing" and "telling"? Possibly. Is her theatrical practice underscoring the equivocal relation between the so-called primary and secondary texts? Does Stein play the text that encircles against the one that is injected into its middle, refusing to accord either of them a more "objective," "authoritative," or "transcendental" status (using irony, humor, parody, and comic confusion to stress this effect)? Definitely. In the absence of absolutes, exclusionist opposites become doubles. Consider the hilarious manner in which the sanctified antinomy right/wrong is collapsed:

> Susan B. was right, she said she was right and she was right. Susan B. was right. She was right because she was right. It is easy to be right, everybody else is wrong so it is easy to be right, and Susan B. was right, of course she was right . . . in a way yes in a way yes really in a way, in a way really it is useful to be right. It does what it does, it does do what it does, if you are right, it does do what it does.[33]

Play is also "the (anagrammatic, hymenographic) play"[34] that throws into relief language exuberantly and joyfully wrenched out of its "normal" usage, its minimal units perceived independently of the habitual contexts and organized in novel sequences to reveal their phonic, graphic, or semantic affinities. Nothing remains sacrosanct in this disintegrative process, in which words as well as sentences are composed, decomposed, and recomposed in an incessant dis-play of wit and musicality, a shimmering cascade of puns and sound effects:

> All of it to be not to be not to be left to be to him and standing.
> Saint Theresa seated.
> Left to be not to be not to be left to be left to be and left to be not to be.[35]

> *Ernest and Josephine*. All who may know. A march. Will know.
> That willows blow. When they mean.
> *Josephine and Ernest*. They will compare. Their.
> They will. Compare. Their.
> *Josephine and Paul*. They will. Compare. It. With their.
> Advantage. They will even. Compare.
> *Paul and Josephine*. They. Will compare.
> Compare add. And they. Compare. Com-
> panion. They will compare. Adding.
> With. Seen. Them.[36]

> *Susan B*. What is marriage, is marriage protection or religion, is marriage renunciation or abundance, is marriage a stepping stone or an end. What is marriage.[37]

These excerpts are fun to read and hear. Burlesquing one of the most grave and sacrosanct soliloquies in drama is a characteristic impish jest. Stein capitalizes, moreover, on the sound kinship of unrelated terms as "will know" and "willows." She also plays on the contraries of "to be" and "not to be," "standing" and "seated," "protection or religion," or "renunciation or abundance," etc. Stein makes it clear that extreme opposites converge rather than exclude and override one another. This central point also is dramatized in *A Circular Play* (1920). Here Stein defines the notion of the play as a dramatic structure with no beginning or end and in the process decenters the seminal opposition certain (right)/mistaken (wrong), echoing and redoubling the cited passage from *The Mother of Us All:*

> A circular play.
> Cut wood cut wood.
> I hear a sore.
> Stop being thundering.
> I meant wondering.
> He meant blundering.
> I have been mistaken.
> No one is so certain.
> She is certain.
> Certainly right.
> Can I be so sorry.[38]

"Play" collapses categoric dichotomies, a process that permeates the operas and plays,[39] and so also provides a link between actual action and verisimilitude, between literature and truth.[40] Having disrupted the traditional dramatic strategies for engaging reality and imposing order on its flux (e.g., plot, action, Character(ization), unity, completion, complication, unraveling), Stein sets in motion a dynamics that refuses both stability and solemnity. Even the freshly minted verbal compositions and the dislodged categories of drama do not aspire to replace the old with an irrevocable finality or to provide a new transcendental center.[41] Instead, the entertaining games point out the uninterrupted, ever-receding and self-decentering mirroring effects.[42] The refusal to "characterize" a stable identity and the decentering mirroring process both are operative in the following scene, in which Stein parodies the antinomy big-little in *The Mother of Us All,* making a little man see himself reflected/doubled in a mirror as a big man:

> *Andrew J.* I wish to say that little men are bigger than big men, that they know how to drink and to get drunk. They say I was a little man next to that big man, nobody can say what they do say nobody can. . . .
> *Chorus of Men.* You can.
> *Andrew J.* I often think, I am a bigger man than a bigger man. I often think I am. *(Andrew J. moves around and as he moves around he sees himself in a mirror.)* Nobody can say little as I am I am not bigger than anybody bigger bigger bigger *(and then in a low whisper)* bigger than him bigger than him.[43]

Semiosis in the Theater

The preceding examples manifest that Stein capitalizes on the distinctive semiotic property of the theater, in which every element of the staged performance—even the most concrete—is semiotized, that is, charged with signification or meaning(s). This signification is encoded using a double rather than a single reference. The figure we see cavorting on the stage is merely an actress representing a *dramatis persona* called "Desdemona," who is, in turn, a fiction. This make-believe entity could be played (or acted) by a man, a child, or even a marionette, or by lighting and sound effects. The costume she wears may stand for a dress, a coat, or a uniform and could be represented effectively by a piece of sacking. The chair she sits down on might denote anything from an actual chair to a scaffold or a mountain. The double semiosis is most evident in "non-illusionist" productions, in which the relation of signs to referents is arbitrary. But it is equally present in the most iconic approximations of verisimilitude. Even if we have an aromatic soup simmering in a well-appointed kitchen on stage, they still function merely as signs for the imaginary kitchen in which Linda Loman is cooking dinner. Two Prague structuralists sum up the double semiosis that distinguishes the theater: "All that is on the stage is a sign."[44] Everything on the stage functions as "a sign of a sign and not a sign of a material thing."[45] This means that every sign occupies a place that is twice removed from reality. Therefore, we are presented with a simulated, or imitated, reference. The stage naturally contains, to borrow Foucault's term, a "series of liberated simulacrum."[46]

Stein turns the representation of theatrical reality upon itself so that the tantalizing double reference of the theater becomes redoubled and questioned even further. This deflates the dichotomy simulation/reality. In *The Mother of Us All*, for example, Stein gleefully mixes historical characters such as Daniel Webster or Susan B. with contemporaries and friends such as Virgil Thompson and with totally fictive figures such as Jo the Loiterer. Stein, whose reliance on several forms of ambiguity is legendary, invokes here an ambiguous relationship that blurs even more radically the distinction/boundary between the real and the imitated, between the true and the seemingly true (or is it the false?).

This phenomenon underscores the fact that throughout Stein's operas and plays, the ambivalent relationship between representation and its referents is ubiquitous. Stein achieves a deconstruction of a whole system of oppositions, beginning with the antinomy "reality-illusion." In her operas and plays, there is no a priori "reality" except the simulated reality or the simulacrum of reality that Stein conjures up on her madcap stage, where the "real" and the fabricated have equal status.

There is no stable point of reference, no Platonic sun of truth against which the shadows of the cave can be measured and judged deficient, and this has revolutionary consequences. The "seeming" or the reflected "double" is not given priority. Instead, the category "antithesis" is deflated. This erasure of absolute dichotomy becomes thematized as characters declare the coexistence of opposite "facts" or of irreconcilable states of being. The contradictions, for example, between being twice divorced but never married or between having joined and not having joined cease to be significant in Stein's universe as the thing and its antonym (e.g., kneeling and refusing to kneel) become synonymous:

> *John Adams.* I never marry I have been twice divorced but I have never married . . .
>
> *Daniel Webster.* When I have joined and not having joined have separated and not having been separated have led, and not having led have thundered, when I having thundered have provoked and having provoked have dominated, may I dear Angel More not kneel at your feet because I cannot kneel my knees are not kneeling knees . . .[47]

The result in Stein's operas and plays is the phenomenon of the pirouetting signifiers.[48] Everything can and does become the representation of something else, giving a vivid and lighthearted demonstration of the instability of theatrical reference and of the instability of all categoric divisions. "I who was once old am now young, I who was once weak am now strong, I who have left every one behind am now overtaken," "explains" Daniel Webster.[49]

Thus discourse creates and shapes reality rather than being shaped by it. Impishly capitalizing on the device of mirroring, Stein foregrounds the constitutive power of discourse in an astounding inversion of habitual (and stable) reference. She achieves this feat by giving the character Susan B. (*The Mother of Us All*) some nasty and sexist lines. It takes a minute to grasp the satiric thrust of the situation in which a woman turns the instrument of sexist stereotyping against men by mimicking the categorically dismissing terms usually used by males in their representation or description of females:[50]

> Men said Susan B. are so conservative, so selfish, so boresome and said Susan B. they are so ugly, and said Susan B. they are gullible, anybody can convince them . . .Men can not count, they do not know that two and two make four if women do not tell them so. There is a devil creeps into men when their hands are strengthened. Men want to be half slave half free.[51]

It might appear that Susan B. is represented as what Kristeva terms (pejoratively) "man's homologous equal."[52] Closer scrutiny reveals, however, that we are faced with a miming of reference.[53] The more outrageous the "facts" enumerated in this speech, the clearer the gap between the representation and the hypothetical referents. Stein invokes this mimed reference not merely to mock habitual male sexist descriptions of women. Her critique is equally relevant to any attempt to set oneself (and one's discourse) up as the arbiter of value, significance, and, above all, of Truth, while relegating others (and their discourses) to the realm of the "untrue," the "inconsequential," or any similar derogatory category. Here and elsewhere, Stein is repudiating all notions of a central and objective, definite and defining, authorial authority (her own or her characters' included) by simulating and mocking the notion of representation or reference.[54] The playful chain of self-transforming signs "*gets caught in*, but thereby disorganizes, the whole ontological machine," as Derrida explains. "It dislocates all oppositions. . . . setting them out of phase, more or less regularly, through unequal displacements.[55] "I must choose I do choose," complains Susan B. of the folly of the inflexible organization into antinomies, "men and women women and men I do choose. I must choose colored or white white or colored I must choose, I must choose, weak or strong, strong or weak I must choose."[56] Needless to say, the feminist refusal to abide by these antinomies is the foundation of Susan B.'s revolutionary activity. Her reply to the question of what distinguishes the rich from the poor is: "there is no wealth nor poverty, there is no wealth, what is wealth, there is no poverty, what is poverty."[57]

Because the feminist demand for equality has progressively been augmented by explorations of feminine difference,[58] it is irreverently but playfully pertinent that Stein's strategies suggest that even such investigation must avoid falling into the trap of inflexible classification of male and female. In *The Mother of Us All*, an opera concerned with a suffragist leader of hallowed fame, Stein once more assigns a sexist speech to a female character, reiterating that a fallacy inheres in any definition of gender that is posited on a simplistic antithesis between men and women, labeling some traits "masculine" and others "feminine."[59] "How," asks Susan B. with apparent naivete, "can anything be really mixed when men are conservative, dull, monotonous, deceived, stupid, unchanging and bullies, how said Susan B. how when men are men can they be mixed. Yes said Anne, yes men are men, how can they when men are men how can they be mixed yes how can they."[60] The answer is that things cannot be "really mixed" in a situation in which negative labeling still occurs. As we have seen, Stein's operas and plays consistently emphasize that the condition of the "really mixed" provides the only true freedom: the freedom to be and to create oneself and one's discourse. It cannot be attained without prior renunciation of all antinomial categorizations. Valorizing the female while remaining within the rigid sexist dichotomy means enslavement rather than liberation and falls short of the fruitful negation or questioning of traditional assumptions envisioned by Stein or Kristeva. The exile's dissidence must be expressed instead as an ongoing operation of decentering, taking fresh and flexible positions and readjusting its aims as additional portions of the "new" are reclassified as "classic" and coopted by the "master discourse." This holds true both in the artistic discourse and in the discourse of ideas. Emphasizing dynamic process rather than static polarity, Stein's practice corroborates Kristeva's reminder that sexual difference may be most productively experienced "not as a fixed opposition ('man'/'woman'), but as a process of differentiation."[61]

Discourse and/or Reality

It becomes clear that Stein's operas and plays sabotage the mainstay of authority in theory as well as aesthetics, namely, the assumption that being and truth exist independently of discourse. If the object comes into existence only in the process of perception and description, then any discourse about "what is" or "things as they are" constitutes the very objects it purports to delineate and classify. Stein, in other words, gives early dramatic rendering to Foucault's analyses of the ways in which discursive practices defined scientific terms and delineated "legitimate" and "illegitimate" fields of inquiry, and his illumination of the power of the scientific account to shape and misshape the object it describes in the name of objectivity and authority.[62] What falls outside the delimited/prescribed scope is *propter hoc* presumed to be nonexistent/and/or of no ontological value. Prescription thus precedes description: the self-regulating representation is anterior to the objects it presumes to describe.[63]

Stein's operas and plays reveal representation to be provisional, bereft of any stable axiological center. Like Foucault's analyses, they reveal that the objections raised by feminist critics against the myopic and distorting practice of male-centered critical theory apply to a universal characteristic of discourse. This truth, however, is perceptible only by the exiles, including the innovative thinkers and artists. Consequently, I concur with Catherine Stimpson, who does not subscribe wholeheartedly to feminist critical attempts to classify Stein's experimental writing from a point of view that "profoundly genderizes the world," emphasizing dualism even in the process of rejecting male assumptions.[64] The mainspring of experimental writing in general, and Stein's in particular, is the repudiation of more than just "patriarchal, conventional speech."[65] It questions all so-called "stable and traditional" dichotomies on which the mainstream constructs its norms and values, including gender dichotomy. Therefore, it embodies the recognition that it is time to provide another model for the depiction of reality.

But if discourse shapes reality in its own subjective manner, is it not possible to change reality by reshaping our discourse?[66] Although there is no unequivocal answer, because economic and political realities exert a pressure of their own, feminist scholars have suggested that "we make our own knowledge and are constantly remaking it in the terms which history provides—and . . . in making knowledge we act upon the power relations in our lives."[67] In convincing us that there is no stable axiological, epistemological, or ontological center, no "true discourse," and no single truth (the [in]famous "transcendental signified") Stein also suggests that we appropriate the freedom to scribe our own discourse, inscribe our own objects, and transcribe our own knowledge. Furthermore, Stein's example urges us to recognize the great affinity or similarity between feminism on the one hand and the avant-garde and insurgent in art as well as in science on the other. Exiled from mainstream institutions that lay down the law, they are similarly in a position to review and revise such laws. Feminists, as well as the innovative artist or scientist, claim the freedom to construct different models of description and composition.[68] Feminist scholars and artists are free, in Carolyn Heilbrun's felicitous term, to "reinvent womanhood," describing/inscribing "what is" in a radically independent and novel manner.[69]

The grandeur of this common project motivates Kristeva's choice of sonorous rhetoric:

> the exile cuts all links, including those that bind him [or her] to the belief that the thing called life has A Meaning guaranteed by the dead father. For if meaning exists in a state of exile, it nevertheless finds no incarnation, and is ceaselessly produced and destroyed in geographical or discursive transformations.[70]

Stein, on the other hand, presents us with a comic model of self-deconstruction in her playfully suspended and continually transforming simulated simulacra, insubstantial phantasms joyfully created within her fiction, by her fiction, yet more real than any "reality." This model, as Foucault puts it, perverts and subverts the Platonic system using its invocation of irony and humor: "it is the decentering of oneself with respect to Platonism so as to give rise to the play (as with every perversion) of surfaces at its borders. Irony rises and subverts, humor falls and perverts."[71] Like Stein, fortified with humor and irony, all exiles—feminists, avant-garde artists, innovative critics and theorists—need never be thrown into paralysis by this "decentering of oneself."

Notes

1. Julia Kristeva, "A New Type of Intellectual: The Dissident" [1977], in *The Kristeva Reader*, ed. Toril Moi (New York: Columbia University Press, 1986), p. 298.

2. Ibid., p. 296.

3. Ibid., p. 299.

4. Ibid., pp. 293–94, 298. Kristeva's omission underscores the fact that Stein has been effectively excluded—that is, exiled—from mainstream criticism of modernism and innovative writing in the twentieth century, which merely adds an additional facet to her basic exile(s).

5. Ibid., p. 294.

6. In "Oscillation between Power and Denial" [1974], Kristeva asserts: "If women have a role to play in this on-going process, it is only in assuming a *negative* function: reject everything finite, definite, structured, loaded with meaning, in the existing state of society. Such an attitude places women on the side of the explosion of social codes: with revolutionary moments." Quoted in *New French Feminisms: An Anthology*, ed. Elaine Marks and Isabelle de Courtivron (Amherst: University of Massachusetts Press, 1980), p. 166.

7. Gertrude Stein, "Composition as Explanation," in *Selected Writings of Gertrude Stein*, ed. Carl Van Vechten (New York: Modern Library, 1962), p. 514. The idea that "the new" interacted with the established system of norms and expectations, producing a continuous modification of the existent aggregate of suppositions and presumptions against which the work of art is perceived and judge, fascinated Russian formalists Juri Tynjanov and Roman Jakobson. Their work led to Czech structuralist Jan Mukarovsky, *Aesthetic Function, Norm, and Value as Social Facts*, trans. Mark E. Suino (Ann Arbor: University of Michigan, 1970), and to the contemporary H. R. Jauss, *Toward an Aesthetic of Reception*, trans. J. Schulte Sasse (Minneapolis: University of Minnesota Press, 1982).

8. The operas *Four Saints in Three Acts* (1927) and *The Mother of Us All* (1946) have been set to music by Virgil Thompson and have been performed in New York, causing both consternation and excitement. It is interesting that later generations of avant-garde theater practitioners (first The Living Theatre, which performed one of her plays, and later Richard Foreman and Robert Wilson) expressed conscious indebtedness to her inspiration.

9. Stein's dramas are permeated by the awareness of the relativity and the inherent bias of all perceptions, including aesthetic judgments and theoretical dogmas. The "new," she explains, for example in "Composition as Explanation," is perceived by the "indolent" majority as "irritating annoying stimulating," and is judged as beautiful only after its classification as "classic" and sanctification as an institutional artifact (515).

10. Stein's decentering of traditional concepts of representation and signification may be described as a deconstructive project that antedates the formulation of deconstruction. Especially instructive and illuminating about Stein's experimentalism is Jacques Derrida, "The Double Session," in *Dissemination*, trans. Barbara Johnson (Chicago: University of Chicago Press, 1981), which treats certain texts of Mallarmé on theater, especially *Mimique*. I find Derrida and Foucault most congenial in application to Stein because they follow the example she has set, namely, eschewing linear progressions and deductions in favor of circularity and repetition. Like them, I trace "concentric circles, moving sometimes towards the outer and sometimes towards the inner ones" (Michel Foucault, *The Archaeology of Knowledge* and *The Discourse on Language*, trans. A. M. Sheridan Smith [New York: Pantheon Books, 1972], p. 114).

11. Gertrude Stein, "Picasso" [1938], in *Gertrude Stein on Picasso*, ed. Edward Burns (New York: Liveright, 1970), p. 19. Stein explains her affinity with Picasso as follows: "I was alone at this time in understanding him, perhaps because I was expressing the same thing in literature" (p. 23).

12. Ibid., pp. 51, 52.

13. Stein, *Say It With Flowers*, in *Selected Operas and Plays of Gertrude Stein*, ed. John Malcolm Brinnin (Pittsburgh, Pa.: University of Pittsburgh Press, 1970), p. 138.

14. Stein's texts refuse to yield signifieds, or "meaning." When we consider that "the stream of consciousness" or the interior monologue has been naturalized as signifying

meaning on the level of "the chaotic functioning of the psyche," we may appreciate Stein's uncompromising break with referential signification.

15. See Randa Dubnik, *The Structure of Obscurity: Gertrude Stein, Language and Cubism* (Urbana: University of Illinois Press, 1984). For a perceptive analysis of Stein's revolutionary method in portraying individuals (in the Portraits, rather than in the dramas), see Wendy Steiner, *Exact Resemblance to Exact Resemblance* (New Haven: Yale University Press, 1983).

16. Stein's pervasive use of repetition underscores the erasure of linearity in favor of circularity. Consider one of her numerous recommencements in *The Making of Americans:*

> As I was saying every one always is repeating the whole of them. As I was saying sometimes it takes many years of hearing the repeating in one before the whole is clear to the understanding of one who has it as a being to love repeating, to know that always every one is repeating the whole of them (Gertrude Stein, *The Making of Americans*, in *Selected Writings of Gertrude Stein*, ed. Carl Van Vechten [New York: Modern Library, 1962], p. 267).

In "Picasso," Stein suggests a critique of positivism as a reason for the refusal of linear progression. She equates the new composition with the repudiation of the traditional view "that things seen are real, that the truths of science make for progress" (19–20).

17. Stein, *Say It With Flowers*, p. 134.

18. See Julia Kristeva's discussion of demonstratives in "The True-Real" [1979], in *The Kristeva Reader*, ed. Toril Moi (New York: Columbia University Press, 1986), p. 232.

19. The value of both Marianne DeKoven's and Randa Dubnik's work lies precisely in their focus on Stein's artistic decentering of the signifier rather than on that of the signified (although they both concentrate on the fiction rather than on the drama).

20. Gertrude Stein, *They Must. Be Wedded. To Their Wife*, in *Selected Operas and Plays of Gertrude Stein*, ed. John Malcolm Brinnin (Pittsburgh, Pa.: University of Pittsburgh Press, 1970), p. 108.

21. The decentering of Platonic and Aristotelian notions of *mimesis* may be traced back to Richard Wagner, who first pointed to the tenuous link between theatrical signs and their referents and consequently celebrated subjective "expression" rather than objective "imitation" in the theater. (See Dinnah Pladott, "The Semiotics of Postmodern Theatre: Gertrude Stein," in *A Collection of Essays on Semiotics of the Theatre*, ed. Andre Helbo [Paris: Didier, 1989.]) Recent developments in the theoretical debate underscore the subjective nature of all representational modes. See Mieke Bal, "Mimesis and Genre Theory in Aristotle's *Poetics*," *Poetics Today* 3, no. 1 (1982): 171–80, and Mieke Bal, "The Rhetoric of Subjectivity," *Poetics Today* 5, no. 2 (1984): 337–76.

22. Gertrude Stein, *The Making of Americans*, in *Selected Writings of Gertrude Stein*, ed. Carl Van Vechten (New York: Modern Library, 1962), pp. 256–57. Stein's descriptions as well as her plays, therefore, illustrate the insight that being (or presence) does not antedate the representation but comes into existence in the process of composition. Cf. Stein's portrait by Picasso, which resembled her as she was going to be years from the time of the painting. Cf. also Derrida, *Disseminations*, p. 190.

23. Derrida, *Disseminations*, p. 186n.

24. Ibid., p. 191.

25. Michel Foucault, *The Order of Things: An Archeology of Human Sciences* (New York: Pantheon Books, 1970), p. 300.

26. Derrida, *Disseminations*, p. 191.

27. Ibid.

28. Ibid.

29. See Michel Foucault, *The Birth of the Clinic: An Archaeology of Medical Perceptions*, trans. A. M. Sheridan Smith (New York: Pantheon Books, 1972); *Language, Counter-Memory, Practice: Selected Essays and Interviews*, ed. Donald F. Bouchard (Ithaca: Cornell University Press, 1977); *The History of Sexuality: Vol. 1: An Introduction*, trans. Robert Hurley (New York: Pantheon Books, 1978); and *The Order of Things.*

30. Cf. Foucault, *Language, Counter-Memory, Practice*, p. 168.

31. Nancy Miller, "Rereading as a Woman: The Body in Practice," *Poetics Today* 6, no. 1-2 (1985): 291.

32. Foucault, *The Archaeology of Knowledge*, p. 185.
33. Gertrude Stein, *The Mother of Us All*, in *Selected Operas and Plays of Gertrude Stein*, ed. John Malcolm Brinnin (Pittsburgh, Pa.: University of Pittsburgh Press, 1970), p. 169.
34. Derrida, *Disseminations*, p. 259n.
35. Gertrude Stein, *Four Saints in Three Acts*, in *Selected Operas and Plays of Gertrude Stein*, ed. John Malcolm Brinnin (Pittsburgh, Pa.: University of Pittsburgh Press, 1970), p. 48.
36. Stein, *They Must. Be Wedded. To Their Wife*, pp. 102, 106.
37. Stein, *The Mother of Us All*, p. 185.
38. Gertrude Stein, *A Circular Play*, in *Selected Operas and Plays of Gertrude Stein*, ed. John Malcolm Brinnin (Pittsburgh: University of Pittsburgh Press, 1970), p. 144.
39. The same is true of the fiction. See, for example, Stein's repeated invocation of the modifiers "dependent independent" and "independent dependent" in *The Making of Americans*, pp. 285, 286, 288, 290.
40. See Derrida, *Disseminations*, p. 183.
41. "There is no heart," as Foucault, referring to Gilles Deleuze, says, "but only . . . a distribution of notable points" *(Language, Counter-Memory, Practice*, p. 165).
42. In the quoted passage from *Four Saints*, for example, "to be" is immediately mirrored and questioned by "not to be" due to the tell-tale omission of the pivotal "or" from the original literary phrase. In this parodic wordplay at *Hamlet's* expense (which both mirrors and inverts), both facets of the tragic and/or existential dilemma are displaced from center to margin.
43. Stein, *The Mother of Us All*, p. 175.
44. Jiří Veltruský, "Man and Object in the Theater" [1940], in *A Prague School Reader on Esthetics, Literary Structure and Style*, ed. and trans. Paul Garvin (Washington, D.C.: Georgetown University Press, 1964), p. 84.
45. Petr Bogatyrev, "Semiotics in the Folk Theatre" [1938], in *Semiotics of Art: Prague School Contributions*, ed. Ladislav Matejka and Irwin R. Titunik (Cambridge: M. I. T. Press, 1976), p. 33.
46. Foucault, *Language, Counter-Memory, Practice*, p. 171.
47. Stein, *The Mother of Us All*, p. 184.
48. Derrida, *Disseminations*, p. 240.
49. Stein, *The Mother of Us All*, 182.
50. Feminist/comic writers like Marietta Holley (who published between 1873 and 1917) have shown in the past the power of irony and humor to deconstruct the series of antinomies on which the dominant patriarchal ideology is founded. See Marietta Holley, *Samantha Rassles the Woman's Question*, ed. Jane Currie (Urbana: University of Illinois Press, 1983).
51. Stein, *The Mother of Us All*, pp. 168, 183.
52. Kristeva, "A New Type of Intellectual," p. 296.
53. Derrida, *Disseminations*, p. 219.
54. In *Dr. Faustus Lights the Lights*, an artificial viper takes a central part in the action by stinging and killing. Similarly, a prominent place is given to the wordplay on the question of how many individuals are represented by a woman named Marguerite Ida Helena Annabel (pp. 101, 104, passim). In *A Manoir: An Historical Play in which They are Approached More Often*, the "manoir" (manor?) is depicted and defined, for example, as "a temporary home" (279), "a house for a gentleman" (281), but also as "A Manoir / Anything that is and it is a dish / Is amusing" (312) (in *Last Operas and Plays by Gertrude Stein*, ed. Carl Van Vechten [New York: Rinehart, 1949]). In *A Play Called Not and Now*, Stein revisions both difference and distinction by commenting "The difference between not and now. That is what makes any one look like some one." When the characters are introduced, "Hullo they say and the do each go away. Not that that makes any difference, *as the real one is not there but just the one that is just like him*" (in *Last Operas and Plays by Gertrude Stein*, ed. Carl van Vechten [New York: Rinehart, 1949]), p. 422; emphasis mine). The list of examples is endless.
55. Derrida, *Disseminations*, p. 236.

56. Stein, *The Mother of Us All*, p. 174.
57. Ibid., p. 179.
58. See, for example, Elaine Showalter, "Toward a Feminist Poetics," in *The New Feminist Criticism: Essays on Women, Literature and Theory*, ed. Elaine Showalter (New York: Pantheon Books, 1985), pp. 125–43. The provocative explorations of *écriture féminine* by Hélène Cixous and Luce Irigaray are cases in point.
59. Two examples from *The Making of Americans* illustrate Stein's vision of flexible gender differentiations: "every one is a kind of men and women, . . . More and more I love it of them, the being in them, the mixing in them, the repeating in them, the deciding the kind of them every one is who has human being . . . There are many ways of making kinds of men and women. Now there will be descriptions of every kind of way every one can be a kind of men and women. . . ." (262). "There are many ways of making kinds of men and women. In each way of making kinds of them there is a different system of finding them resembling" (263).
60. Stein, *The Mother of Us All*, p. 170.
61. Kristeva, "Oscillation between Power and Denial," p. 165.
62. Foucault points out that the texts that presume to describe/transcribe "what is" in an unbiased manner are regulated by discursive principles that delimit the "field of objects" for study, define "a legitimate perspective" from which the objects may be studied, and fix "norms for the elaboration of concepts and theories" (*Language, Counter-Memory, Practice*, p. 199). His analyses reveal that the notions "sex," "madness," "illness," "representation," "literature," or even "truth"—to which we would add "woman" and "aesthetic values"—turn out to be the product of discourse rather than its object or model ("The Discourse on Language," in *The Archaeology of Knowledge*, appendix).
63. A pertinent example is found in Foucault's most recent *The History of Sexuality*, a discussion of "transformation of sex into discourse" (61). Foucault outlines this transformation as one that took place within a specific cultural and ideological context, a specific "economy of bodies and pleasures." He points out, for example, that Freud's so-called "liberating" and "antirepressive" pronouncements on sex have on the contrary put sex "at one of the critical points marked out for it since the eighteenth century by the strategies of knowledge and power . . . giving a new impetus to the secular injunction to study sex and transform it into discourse" (159).
64. Catherine R. Stimpson, "The Somagrams of Gertrude Stein," *Poetics Today* 6, no. 1–2 (1985): 77.
65. Marianne DeKoven, *A Different Language: Gertrude Stein's Experimental Writing* (Madison: University of Wisconsin Press, 1983).
66. This position has been advocated by Foucault. In *The Order of Things*, he sees our modern preoccupation with recurrence, repetition, and recommencement as a form of disenchantment with the linear structure of representation. The newly shaped nonlinear texts (such as Stein's) represent a new reality, from which the illusion that an origin can be found, that time can be apprehended in all its transcendental entirety, has been expunged (334–35).
67. Judith Newton and Deborah Rosenfelt, "Introduction: Toward a Materialist Feminist Criticism," in *Feminist Criticism and Social Change: Sex, Class and Race in Literature and Culture*, ed. Judith Newton and Deborah Rosenfelt (New York: Methuen, 1985), p. xv.
68. For a provocative analysis of the complexity of the avant-garde stance, see Timothy Murray, "The Theatricality of the Van-Guard," *Performing Arts Journal* 24 (1985): 93–95.
69. It is invigorating to discover that in the field of history and historiography, scholars now are acknowledging the subjective and relative nature of historiographic representation. Cf. Gebhard Rusch, "The Theory of History, Literary History, and Historiography," *Poetics* 14 (1985): 257–77; Harro Müller and Nikolaus Wegman, "Tools for a Genealogical Literary Historiography," *Poetics* 14 (1985): 229–41.
70. Kristeva, "A New Type of Intellectual," p. 298.
71. Foucault, *Language, Counter-Memory, Practice*, p. 168.

9
The Fox's Cubs: Lillian Hellman, Arthur Miller, and Tennessee Williams

Charlotte Goodman

> A drama worthy of its time must first, knowingly or by instinctive means, recognize its major and most valuable traditions and where it has departed from them.[1]

The 1947 theater season on Broadway was, by all accounts, an extraordinarily exciting one. Tennessee Williams followed his triumph of 1945, *The Glass Menagerie,* with a play that was more dazzling, the Pulitzer Prize winning *A Streetcar Named Desire;* and Arthur Miller, whose first Broadway attempt, *The Man Who Had All the Luck,* had failed dismally after four performances in 1944, now contributed *All My Sons.* The play won the New York Drama Critics' Circle Award that year and helped to launch the career of a writer destined to become one of America's most celebrated dramatists. However, neither the critics who applauded these two exciting new American playwrights nor the playwrights themselves acknowledged the debt both Miller and Williams owed to an important female precursor: Lillian Hellman, author of two successful plays produced on Broadway in the thirties, *The Children's Hour* (1934) and *The Little Foxes* (1939).

Although both Miller and Williams are securely ranked among American twentieth-century playwrights, the same cannot be said of Hellman. Always the subject of controversy during her lifetime, Hellman remains a controversial figure today. Five years after her death, critics continue to debate the merit of her work and especially of her plays, although most would not deny her celebrity status. Writing about the drama of the thirties in 1967, Warren French said of Hellman's *The Children's Hour* and *The Little Foxes* that they would "never become period pieces as long as malice and greed make the world wobble round."[2] Contrary to French's assertion that "Miss Hellman's best work can look out for itself,"[3] however, her plays often are ignored in discussions of the American theater, and, when they are mentioned, they are usually dismissed as melodramas or "well-made" plays. Although feminist critics such as Judith E. Barlow, Sandra M. Gilbert, and Susan Gubar consider Hellman "one of America's leading dramatists,"[4] theirs is a minority opinion. As Jackson Bryer recently noted in his introduction to *Conversations with Lillian Hellman*, "Her place in modern American literary history has yet to be satisfactorily explored and defined."[5]

My purpose in this essay is not to extol Hellman's virtues as a playwright, although it certainly would be possible to do so. Rather, I want to describe some intriguing parallels between Hellman's *The Little Foxes* and the plays by Miller and Williams that appeared less than a decade later: *All My Sons*, *The Glass Menagerie*, and *A Streetcar Named Desire*. Critics have frequently associated Miller with Ibsen and Williams with Chekhov, but I believe that Hellman is an important and much more immediate precursor who should be cited as well. As meticulously crafted as Ibsen's domestic dramas, Hellman's *The Little Foxes*, like Ibsen's *Hedda Gabler* and *A Doll's House*, also addresses important social questions. And in its portrait of the effete turn-of-the-century Southern aristocracy about to be overrun by the emerging merchants of the middle class, Hellman's *Little Foxes* also resembles Chekhov's brilliant depiction of the effete but cultured Russian upper class at the turn of the century in *The Cherry Orchard* and *Three Sisters*. Although Miller can be said to write in the Ibsen tradition and Williams can be described as a disciple of Chekhov, both also might have been indebted to Hellman, whose Ibsenian-Chekhovian *The Little Foxes* had a significant impact during the decade when both Miller and Williams were coming of age.

In 1960, mentioning the plays of Clifford Odets and Hellman that appeared during the thirties, Miller spoke favorably of Hellman, commending her for "a remorseless rising line of action in beautifully articulated plays."[6] Although he qualified his praise of both Odets and Hellman by observing that, after the "cataclysm" of the depression was followed by war, "their world seemed out of date," he also acknowledged, ". . . I was deeply moved by these plays and remember them with love."[7] Some years later, however, in his autobiography, *Timebends* (1987), he appears less charitably disposed toward Hellman. After commenting on how impressed he had been by the plays of Odets and Eugene O'Neill in his youth, Miller writes, "Lillian Hellman's work didn't seem to me and other younger writers I knew to belong with these impassioned, challenging plays. . . . No doubt unjustly, she seemed to some of us preeminently Broadway rather than an outsider, with plots that never faltered and a certain deliberateness that we were probably too young and careless as writers to appreciate."[8] Even more hostile were the remarks Miller made about Hellman during an interview with Hellman's biographer, William Wright. Declining to discuss Hellman at length, he nevertheless remarked, "Lillian always resented my emergence on the playwriting scene and she resented even more my not making a quick exit from it." Then Miller added snidely, "Lillian came on with every man she met. I wasn't interested and she never forgave me for it."[9] Wright conjectures that Miller's hostility toward Hellman might have been triggered by a savage parody of *After The Fall* that Hellman wrote after the play appeared in 1964. But whatever the cause for Miller's rancor, it is evident that Miller came to dislike Hellman actively. Furthermore, the more successful he himself became, the less generously he spoke of her achievements.

There is, unfortunately, no personal testimony from Miller about Hellman's influence on his own plays. Nevertheless, I believe the striking parallels between his work and Hellman's suggest that she was an important if unacknowledged precursor. Although one might also fruitfully compare Hellman's *The Children's Hour* and Miller's *The Crucible*, I shall focus here on Hellman's *The Little Foxes* and Miller's *All My Sons*, two plays reminiscent of the social dramas of Ibsen. Both plays dramatize the sinful acts of parents and the coming of age of idealistic offspring who ultimately feel they must separate themselves from the tarnished world of their elders.

The protagonist of Hellman's *The Little Foxes*, Regina Giddens, and the protagonist of Miller's *All My Sons*, Joe Keller, are both preoccupied with money. In their efforts to acquire it, however, both commit misdeeds that their children cannot forgive. Regina sins against society as well as the family. Not only does she join her two rapacious brothers, Ben and Oscar, in promoting a business deal that will pit poor white cotton mill workers against poorer black ones, but, in the process of trying to acquire the necessary capital for this venture from her desperately ill husband, she succeeds in angering him to such an extent that he has another heart seizure. Then, when Regina refuses to get his medicine, he collapses and later dies. Thus, Regina is indirectly responsible for her husband's death. Miller's Joe Keller also sins both against society and the institution of the family. During World War II, he allows cracked airplane cylinders to be shipped from his munitions plant and then compounds this crime by placing the blame on his partner, who goes to jail in his stead. Not only does Joe put an unbearable burden on his wife, a silent collaborator in the cover-up, but he also indirectly causes the death of twenty-one pilots who are killed when their defective planes crash. In addition, his criminal act results in the death of his own son, Larry, who decides to kill himself after reading that his father's firm was implicated in the deaths of the pilots.

Although Hellman and Miller expose the wrongdoings of their respective protagonists, they also want their audience to comprehend what motivated the unscrupulous behavior of these erring characters, for whom they appear to have had a great deal of sympathy. Dominating the respective plays in which they are found, neither Regina Giddens nor Joe Keller emerges as a one-dimensional villain of melodrama, despite their morally reprehensible behavior.

After *the Little Foxes* was produced, Hellman insisted that she had not conceived of Regina as a villain. Much to Hellman's distress, however, both Tallulah Bankhead, who played Regina in the original production, and Bette Davis, who assumed that role in the William Wyler film version, emphasized the perfidy and sangfroid of Regina at the expense of her humanity. Recalling her reaction to the play in *Pentimento,* Hellman said, "I sat drinking for months . . . trying to figure out what I had wanted to say and why some of it got lost."[10] Perhaps her dissatisfaction with Bankhead and Davis's interpretations of Regina helps to explain why Hellman subsequently chose to direct her second play about Regina, *Another Part of the Forest,* herself. Insisting that although she might have disapproved of Regina, she did not dislike her,[11] Hellman observed on another occasion, "I think Regina's kind of funny. If anything, I was amused with her."[12]

What "amused" Hellman was Regina's cleverness and tenacity, her ability to hold her own with her scheming brothers, who are determined to keep her helpless and dependent. Like Medea or Hedda Gabler, Regina, whose name means "queen," is frustrated by her lack of power and autonomy. Despite being her father's favorite, she is cheated of her inheritance when he leaves his money to her brothers. "Ah, Ben, if Papa had only left me his money," she says to her brother after she has helped to hasten her husband's death (223).[13] It is probably no accident that during the first few minutes of the movie version of *The Little Foxes,* for which Hellman herself wrote the screenplay, the camera pans on the words "Hubbard Sons" printed on bails of cotton and then focuses on the sign "Hubbard Sons" at the entrance to the family business. A daughter rather than a son, Regina has no access to the power that money, which is passed on from father to son, provides. The patriarchal society in which she is raised in effect disinherits her, and consequently she must depend on the largess of her brothers or her husband. "Money's been the subject of a great deal of literature because it . . . isn't only money of course it's power, it's sex; it's a great many other things," Hellman said in 1968.[14] Without any money of her own,

Regina cannot hope to escape from the stifling small town in Alabama where she was born and go to live in Chicago; although she longs to begin her life again in the more sophisticated city of Chicago, it seems as distant to her as the "Moscow" for which Chekhov's provincial three sisters constantly yearn.

Hellman reveals in *Another Part of the Forest* that Regina was forced by her father and her brothers to marry Horace Giddens. The more entrapped Regina feels, the more mean-spirited she becomes. When explaining her behavior to her daughter Alexandra, Regina says, "Too many people used to make me do too many things" (225). She believes that her dead husband's money will give her the means to change not only her own life but that of her daughter. "You're young, you shall have all the things I wanted. I'll make the world for you the way I wanted it to be for me," she tells Alexandra (223). Thus, although Hellman ultimately does not sanction the lengths to which Regina is willing to go to acquire money and power, she nevertheless enables us to comprehend what motivates this frustrated woman whose aspirations have been thwarted at every turn.

Miller, in *All My Sons*, also creates an erring protagonist with whose struggles we are nevertheless meant to empathize. Described as a "man among men" (59),[15] Joe Keller, like Regina Giddens, is preoccupied with money. Both the dependent Regina and the self-made businessman, Joe Keller, equate money with power, and both want to pass on to their children the power they themselves have struggled to attain. Echoing the comment Regina makes to her daughter, Joe Keller says plaintively to his son after he has uncovered the truth about Joe's criminal act, "Chris, I did it for you, it was a chance and I took it for you" (115). In act 1, when Chris hints that he might want to leave the business, an alarmed Keller stammers, "Well . . . you don't want to think like that. . . . Because what the hell did I work for? That's only for you, Chris, the whole shootin' match is for you!" (69). Most people would probably find Joe Keller a far more sympathetic figure than Regina Giddens, for he commits a crime outside the boundaries of family life, while Regina's crime directly involves her own family. As Hellman reveals, however, the patriarchal structure of the family denies Regina any access to power. In contrast to Regina, Joe Keller is able to create a power base for himself outside the family. When he is forced to behave unethically rather than risk a business failure, however, he too is willing to dirty his hands.

Not only are Regina and Joe parallel figures, but so are Alexandra and Chris. Both plays conclude with a dramatic confrontation between a parent and a child. The moral center of their respective plays, Alexandra and Chris each utter a sententious speech that questions the actions of an erring parent. Announcing her intention to leave, Alexandra tells her mother,

> Addie said there were people who ate the earth and other people who stood around and watched them do it. . . . Mama, I'm not going to stand around and watch you do it. (225)

Hellman, who confessed that she "felt sentimental" about Alexandra, observed, "I felt very strongly that the girl had to leave. . . ."[16] Identifying with the plight of Alexandra, she paid tribute to her spirit by having Regina utter the very words to Alexandra that Hellman's Uncle Jake once had said to the young Hellman: "Well, you have spirit after all. I used to think you were all sugar water."[17] Hellman, however, insisted in *Pentimento* that she also in part had meant to half-mock her own "youthful high-class innocence in Alexandra,"[18] who would, she said, "never have the force or vigor of her mother's family."[19] Nonetheless, it is to Alexandra that Hellman gives the final lines. When Regina asks Alexandra whether she would like to sleep in her room, Alexandra asks, "Are you afraid, Mama?" (225), intimating that she has concluded her mother is not as impervious to fear as she would have others believe.

Like Alexandra, Chris Keller also is the moral spokesperson. After discovering what his father has done, he announces his intention of leaving his parents' house. Although Joe Keller pleads with him to remain, insisting that what had always been most important to him was to be able to leave a flourishing business to his son, Chris explodes "with burning fury" (115):

> For me! Where do you live, where have you come from? . . . What the hell do you think I was thinking of, the Goddam business? Is that as far as your mind can see, the business? What the hell do you mean, you did it for me? Don't you have a country? Don't you live in the world? (116)

As the violent ending of *All My Sons* suggests, Miller is more critical of the moralizing Chris than Hellman was of the somewhat naive Alexandra. During the final moments of the play, the guilt-ridden Keller shoots himself, and now Chris must confront his own guilt. "Mother, I didn't mean to—" a devastated Chris moans (127).

In response to the intricately plotted *The Little Foxes* and *All My Sons*, Hellman and Miller were both called to task for their reliance on coincidence and their heavy-handed Ibsenesque exposition. Defending her writing of "well-made" plays, Hellman asserted in 1968:

> I don't think the well-made play is fashionable this minute but I'm not sure that it won't be in fashion again, and it doesn't really seem to matter whether

> it is or it isn't. It's simply a fashion. I can't believe Ibsen is going to be thrown aside in the end by cultivated men or serious men. He certainly was the master of the well-made play. Anything any good is well-made. It's just a different kind of making.[20]

Although the action of *The Little Foxes* spans only two days, Hellman, like Ibsen, made the past of Regina and her other characters a palpable reality. She became so intrigued by Regina's past that seven years later she dramatized Regina's early years in a second play, *Another Part of the Forest*. Miller also defended his use of dramatic techniques he claimed to have learned from Ibsen. Insisting that he had "no vested interest in any one form," he observed that what he valued most in Ibsen was the way his plays "reveal the evolutionary quality of life. . . . a viable unveiling of the contrast between past and present, and an awareness of the process by which the present has become what it is."[21] The ineluctable impact of the past on the present is an important consideration for both Hellman and Miller, as it was for Ibsen. However, although it is possible that Ibsen was a common source, it is also possible that Hellman was the more immediate source for *All My Sons*. After he succeeded in winning an audience by writing the kind of realistic play with which the Broadway audience was already familiar via Hellman's plays and those of some of her contemporaries, Miller then had the courage to blend past and present in a more innovative fashion in *Death of a Salesman*.

More obvious than the similarities between *The Little Foxes* and *All My Sons* are the parallels between *The Little Foxes* and the two plays that represent Williams's finest achievement as a playwright: *The Glass Menagerie* and *A Streetcar Named Desire*. As William Wright has implied, Williams, like Hellman a Southern writer, might well have based two of his most memorable Southern female characters, Amanda Wingfield and Blanche Dubois, on Hellman's fragile, alcoholic Birdie.[22] Yet Wright is the only critic who has suggested that a vital link exists between the plays of Hellman and Williams. Ibsen, Strindberg, Chekhov, Rilke, Crane, Lawrence, and Lorca—these are the writers that Donald Spoto lists in the index under "Literary Influences On" in his biography of Williams.[23] Nor does Harold Bloom mention Hellman in his introduction to the recent collection he edited on Williams's work.[24]

When Hellman presented Williams with the gold medal of the National Institute of Arts and Letters in 1970, he might have taken this occasion to mention the continuities between her work and his own. Instead, in his brief acceptance speech, he told a pointless, humorous anecdote about a lesbian bride and a homosexual bridegroom.[25] Although Williams spoke enthusiastically during his lifetime about the plays of contemporaries such as Miller, William Inge, Edward Albee, and John Osborne, his only recorded comment on the plays of Hellman was in an interview with Dotson Rader in 1981: "I know you think Lillian Hellman's a somewhat limited playwright. But *Hellman* doesn't think so, does she? No!" Then he added, "She's a funny woman, and a skillful playwright. Several of her plays are enormously skillful."[26]

Although Williams failed to comment on any similarities between his work and hers, one cannot help noticing some striking parallels. A case could be made for the resemblance between Hellman's Marcus Hubbard in *Another Part of the Forest* and Williams's Big Daddy in *Cat on a Hot Tin Roof;* however, in this discussion, I shall focus on Hellman's Birdie Hubbard. A relic of the antebellum South, the flaccid Birdie is a foil for the steely Regina. Like Regina, she married a man with whom she had nothing in common, Regina's unimaginative, foolish younger brother, Oscar. Retreating into the past and fortified by alcohol, Birdie serves as a reminder to Alexandra of what she too might become if she remains in her parents' home. Hellman maintained that she had intended Birdie to be merely "silly"; after the play was produced, however, she discovered that she had created a character who was touching as well.[27] It is precisely this combination of silliness and pathos that one finds in both Williams's Amanda Wingfield and Blanche Dubois.

More resilient and resourceful than Hellman's Birdie, Williams's protagonist in *The Glass Menagerie* nevertheless sounds like Birdie, particularly in the scene in which she recalls the lost days of her youth. Compare, for example, Birdie's speech about her past and Amanda's. Birdie reminisces to her niece, Alexandra:

> I remember. It was my first big party, at Lionnet I mean, and I was so excited, and there I was with hiccoughs and Mama laughing. . . . You know, that was the first day I ever saw Oscar Hubbard. (204)

Traces of this speech, its very rhythms, appear in Amanda's description of her glamorous youth to her daughter Laura:

> This is the dress in which I led the cotillion. . . . I wore it on Sundays for my gentlemen callers! I had it on the day I met your father. . . . I had malaria fever all that Spring. . . . "Stay in bed," said Mother, "you have a fever!"—but I just wouldn't. (71)[28]

Also reminiscent of *The Little Foxes* is Amanda's warning to Laura that unless she makes an effort to control her life, she will end up helpless and dependent. "Don't love me," Hellman's Birdie cautions Alexandra. "Because in twenty years you'll just be like me. . . . And you'll trail after them, just like me, hoping they won't be so mean that day or say something to make you feel so bad. . . ." (206) Similarly, Amanda cautions Laura, "I know so well what becomes of unmarried women who aren't prepared to occupy a position. I've seen such pitiful cases in the South—barely tolerated spinsters living upon the grudging patronage of sister's husband or brother's wife! . . . . little *birdlike* women without any nest [emphasis added]—eating the crust of humility all their life!" (34) After having been forced by poverty to abandon a way of life that they now recall with longing, both Birdie and Amanda are compelled to eat "the crust of humility."

Also resembling Hellman's Birdie is the genteel alcoholic woman in *A Streetcar Named Desire*, whom Stanley Kowalski sarcastically addresses as "canary bird" (105).[29] A secret drinker like Birdie and a woman who values culture as Birdie does, Blanche Dubois is as lost in the world of the coarse Stanley Kowalski as Birdie is in the world of the avaricious nouveau-riche Hubbards. Blanche's recollection of the loss of the family plantation, Belle Reve, is reminiscent of Birdie's lamentations about the decline of her own family's plantation, Lionnet.

Hellman's use of the South as setting, the character types she introduces, her creation of various speech patterns to differentiate her characters, and her pungent blend of humor, pathos, and irony are also found in Williams's plays. When one considers that Hellman was the first American playwright to make productive use of the mores of the changing South in the theater, it is ironic that some reviewers accused Hellman of imitating Williams. As Katherine Lederer has noted, this was true especially of Hellman's 1960 play, *Toys in the Attic*.[30] In Hellman's defense, William Wright points out that "Hellman, a Southerner with as good a claim to familiarity with decadence as anyone, may well have felt Williams had invaded a turf as much hers as his."[31] Because Hellman and Williams were both writing during the same decades, it is difficult to determine in most instances who was influenced by whom. Nevertheless, *The Little Foxes* became a Broadway hit in 1939, whereas *The Glass Menagerie* did not appear until 1945. Surely Hellman deserves credit for creating a compelling play about a Southern family that antedated Williams's plays about Southern characters.

If my supposition that Hellman influenced Miller and Williams has validity, the failure of both Miller and Williams to acknowledge Hellman as a precursor needs to be considered. An explanation for their silence might be that both experienced what Bloom has termed "the anxiety of influence":

> But nothing is got for nothing, and self-appropriation involves the immense anxieties of indebtedness, for what strong maker desires the realization that he has failed to create himself.[32]

Bloom goes on to explain that strong writers often misread the works of their precursors "to clear imaginative space for themselves."[33] It is plausible that this "anxiety of influence" caused both Miller and Williams not only to "misread" Hellman's work but also never to mention that it had a bearing on their own.

The discomfort that Hellman aroused in Miller may be detected in some of his observations. In his autobiography, Miller speaks of the effect of winning the Hopwood Award from the University of Michigan in 1936:

> With the 1936 Hopwood award, my psychic sun on the rise, I had no difficulty pitting myself in imagination against the reigning writers of the Broadway theatre—Clifford Odets, first of all, and Maxwell Anderson, S. N. Behrman, Sidney Howard, Sidney Kingsley, and Philip Barry, and a dozen others whose names have disappeared with their season. However, there were no Americans who seemed to be working a vein related to what I had come to sense was mine, except for Odets and for a few weeks Anderson . . .[34]

It is fascinating that Hellman's name has been omitted from this list, despite the great success of her 1934 play, *The Children's Hour.* When Miller does mention her elsewhere in his autobiography, however, he is quite candid about how awed he was by the "mystique" of this "southern American noblewoman who at the same time espoused pro-Soviet positions." Describing Hellman's "salon,"which was frequented by influential people, Miller confesses:

> I was never quite at my ease there, I suppose partly because it was still difficult for me to relax with people of distinction, for there was inevitably a kind of ranking in the air that tended to disturb concentration upon whatever subject was at the moment; one felt the depressing obligation to shine with a clever remark or some rare story. . . .[35]

For Miller, the anxiety that Hellman aroused in him might have been exacerbated because she was not only a successful playwright but a woman playwright. As Sandra M. Gilbert and Susan Gubar have claimed in *No Man's Land*, the first volume of their projected three-volume study of twentieth-century women writers, many modern male writers were alarmed by what they perceived as "women's unprecedented invasion of the public sphere. . . ."[36] In the theater, Miller would have to contend not only with male precursors but with such formidable women playwrights as the Pulitzer Prize winning Zona Gale, Susan Glaspell, and Zoë Akins, as well as the highly successful Hellman, who, like himself, was an American Jew with a social conscience.

By the time Miller began *All My Sons*, he had written eight or nine plays, but only *The Man Who Had All The Luck* had been produced professionally, and that play failed after four performances. Determined to abandon his career if *All My Sons* did not succeed, Miller experienced anxiety in writing it. One source of that anxiety might have been Hellman's *The Little Foxes*. If Miller feared that critics would make invidious comparisons between his play and Hellman's, he probably realized that he would have to reconceive his own play—which is precisely what he did. In the introduction to his *Collected Plays*, Miller reveals that the idea for *All My Sons* originated with a story a relative had told him about how a family in her neighborhood was destroyed when a daughter turned her father into the authorities after discovering he had been selling defective machinery to the Army. By the time the speaker was finished, Miller said, "I had transformed the daughter into a son and the climax of the second act was full and clear in my mind."[37] Once this crucial change was made, Miller's play did not concern the confrontation between a mother and daughter or the powerlessness of both mothers and daughters in a patriarchal society, as Hellman's *The Little Foxes* had done; instead, Miller's play dramatized the Oedipal conflict between a father and son, a theme he also was to explore in *Death of a Salesman*. Miller's feelings of rivalry with Hellman might have been aroused again after the play was completed, after the influential Herman Shumlin, producer of Hellman's *The Children's Hour* as well as *The Little Foxes*, turned down Miller's *All My Sons*.[38]

Williams's anxiety about his precursor, Hellman, might have been even more acute than Miller's, because when she succeeded in dramatizing the changes that were taking place in the South, Hellman staked out a territory that Williams wished to appropriate for his own plays. Williams, who never referred to connections between his work and *The Little Foxes*, forged a distinctive style of his own. Moreover, he seldom created aggressive female characters like Regina, focusing instead on victims like Amanda, Laura, and Blanche, and giving more weight than Hellman did to strong male figures who shatter the fragile illusions of these vulnerable women.

In Kathleen Betsko and Rachel Koenig's recent *Interviews with Contemporary Women Playwrights*, several of the women playwrights interviewed invoked the name of Hellman. Marsha Norman, for example, said that as far as women playwrights were concerned, Hellman was her "only indication that this kind of life was possible." Referring to her May 1984 interview of Hellman for *American Theatre Magazine*, Norman observed, "I went to say thank you."[39] But whereas Norman and other women playwrights have valued Hellman as a role model, male critics and playwrights have frequently belittled her contributions to the American theater. As Judith Olauson points out in her study of American women dramatists, ". . . women have made extensive contributions to the body of American dramatic literature but apparently have been presumed to be second-rate and undeserving of thorough critical attention."[40]

Now that literary history is being rewritten to include discussions of the works of groups heretofore excluded from the literary canon, it is imperative that an important figure like Lillian Hellman be written back into the record. Instead of describing twentieth-century American drama exclusively in terms of the contributions of male playwrights such as O'Neill, Odets, Miller, Williams, Albee, David Mamet, and Sam Shepard, the important contributions of Hellman and other women playwrights also must be acknowledged. The inclusion of Hellman in American literary history should serve to remind us not only of her substantial achievements as a playwright but of the relevance of her work to that of younger American dramatists such as Miller and Williams.

Notes

1. Arthur Miller, Introduction to *Collected Plays* (New York: Viking Press, 1957), p. 54.
2. Warren French, *The Thirties: Fiction, Poetry, Drama* (Deland, Fla.: Everett/Edwards, 1969), pp. 177–78.
3. Ibid., p. 178.
4. Judith E. Barlow, ed., *Plays By American Women: The Early Years* (New York: Avon, 1981), p. xxxi; Sandra M. Gilbert and Susan Gubar, eds., *The Norton Anthology of Literature by Women: The Tradition in English* (New York: W. W. Norton, 1985), p. 1704.
5. Jackson R. Bryer, Introduction to *Conversations with Lillian Hellman*, ed. Jackson R. Bryer (Jackson: University Press of Mississippi, 1986), p. xv.
6. Henry Brandon, "The State of the Theater" [1960], in *Conversations with Arthur Miller*, ed. Matthew C. Roudané (Jackson: University Press of Mississippi, 1987), p. 62.
7. Ibid., p. 63.
8. Arthur Miller, *Timebends: A Life* (New York: Grove Press, 1987), pp. 230–31.
9. William Wright, *Lillian Hellman: The Image, The Woman* (New York: Simon and Schuster, 1986), p. 295.
10. Lillian Hellman, *Pentimento*, in *Three: An Unfinished Woman, Pentimento, Scoundrel Time* (Boston: Little, Brown, 1979), p. 482.
11. Peter Adam, "Unfinished Woman" [1978], in *Conversations with Lillian Hellman*, ed. Jackson R. Bryer (Jackson: University Press of Mississippi, 1986), p. 223.
12. Richard G. Stern, "An Interview with Lillian Hellman" [1958], in *Conversations with Lillian Hellman*, ed. Jackson R. Bryer (Jackson: University Press of Mississippi, 1986), p. 35.
13. *Six Plays By Lillian Hellman* (New York: Vintage, 1979). References from *Another Part of the Forest* and *The Little Foxes* are cited parenthetically by page number.
14. Fred Gardner, "An Interview with Lillian Hellman" [1968] in *Conversations with Lillian Hellman*, ed. Jackson R. Bryer (Jackson: University Press of Mississippi, 1986), p. 116.

15. Arthur Miller, *Collected Plays* (New York: Viking Press, 1957). Subsequent references are cited parenthetically by page number.
16. Stern, "An Interview with Lillian Hellman," p. 35.
17. Carl Rollyson, *Lillian Hellman: Her Legend and Her Legacy* (New York: St. Martin's Press, 1988), pp. 128–29.
18. Hellman, *Pentimento*, p. 482.
19. John Phillips and Anne Hollander, "The Art of the Theater I: Lillian Hellman—An Interview" [1964], in *Conversations with Lillian Hellman*, ed. Jackson R. Bryer (Jackson: University Press of Mississippi, 1986), p. 56.
20. Lewis Funke, "Interview with Lillian Hellman" [1968], in *Conversations with Lillian Hellman*, ed. Jackson R. Bryer (Jackson: University Press of Mississippi, 1986), p. 94.
21. Miller, Introduction to *Collected Plays*, p. 21.
22. Wright, *Lillian Hellman*, p. 301.
23. Donald Spoto, *The Kindness of Strangers: The Life of Tennessee Williams* (Boston: Little, Brown, 1985), p. 408.
24. Harold Bloom, ed., *Tennessee Williams* (Modern Critical Views) (New York: Chelsea House, 1987).
25. Spoto, *The Kindness of Strangers*, p. 278.
26. Dotson Rader, "The Art of Theatre V: Tennessee Williams" [1981], in *Conversations with Tennessee Williams*, ed. Albert J. Devlin (Jackson: University Press of Mississippi, 1986), pp. 350–51.
27. Stern, "An Interview with Lillian Hellman," p. 35.
28. Tennessee Williams, *The Glass Menagerie* (New York: New Directions, 1945). Subsequent references are given parenthetically by page number.
29. Tennessee Williams, *A Streetcar Named Desire* (New York: New American Library, 1947). Subsequent references are given parenthetically by page number.
30. Katherine Lederer, *Lillian Hellman* (Boston: Twayne, 1979), p. 93.
31. Wright, *Lillian Hellman*, p. 281.
32. Harold Bloom, *The Anxiety of Influence: A Theory of Poetry* (New York: Oxford University Press, 1973), p. 5.
33. Ibid.
34. Miller, *Timebends*, pp. 227–28.
35. Ibid., p. 256.
36. Sandra M. Gilbert and Susan Gubar, *No Man's Land: The Place of the Woman Writer in the Twentieth Century, Vol. 1, The War of The Words* (New Haven: Yale University Press, 1988), p. 4.
37. Miller, Introduction to *Collected Plays*, p. 17.
38. Miller, *Timebends*, p. 134.
39. Kathleen Betsko and Rachel Koenig, *Interviews with Contemporary Women Playwrights* (New York: Beech Tree Books, 1987), p. 341.
40. Judith Olauson, *The American Woman Playwright: A View of Criticism and Characterization* (Troy, N.Y.: Whitston Publishing, 1981), p. 6.

10
Loneliness and Longing in Selected Plays of Carson McCullers and Tennessee Williams

Mary McBride

In the play version of *The Member of the Wedding,* written by Carson McCullers in 1946 while she worked across the table from Tennessee Williams in his Nantucket home, twelve-year-old Frankie Addams—restless, longing, lonely—speaks with innocent depth in a moment of introspection: "The trouble with me," she proclaims, "is that for a long time I have been just an 'I' person. . . . All people belong to a 'we' except me" (51).[1] The irresistible need expressed by Frankie, the need to belong, to be accepted and loved, lies at the base of McCullers's dramatic works. It is also central to the drama of Williams, McCullers's close friend and professional associate. From this naturalistic urge and denial of its satisfaction arise the complexities of character and action in works of these two dramatists. Characters denied satisfaction of this compelling need react with individual complexity. Nevertheless, a common pattern of action may be observed among the plots of these two authors' plays: deprivation of acceptance and love brings about loneliness, longing, and dissatisfaction so intense that the character is driven to seek relief; and if relief is not found in satisfaction of the need, the character turns to other means of escape—flights into time or space or into fantasy and alcoholic oblivion, even into suicide.

This is the pattern of action in McCullers's play *The Member of the Wedding* (a dramatic version of her novel with the same title). Frankie Addams lives in a motherless home, with little attention from her hardworking father, a widower of many years. She is cared for by the cook Berenice, a motherly black, who, despite her devoted protection, is unable to fill the need of this restless, developing child to belong to a "we," to be loved, accepted, considered important by her father, brother, and peer acquaintances. The opening scene of the play introduces this need. Frankie's brother, now serving in the Army, has brought his prospective bride Janice home for a betrothal visit, and Frankie, starved for love and attention, gushes and attempts to attract attention. She perches on the ground at the feet of the betrothed Jarvis and Janice and stares adoringly at them; then she pretends to be drunk. She reminds her brother that he has never answered her letters or acknowledged the many boxes of homemade candy that she sent him. And Jarvis dismisses the accusation with "Oh, Frankie. You know how it is" (5).

Frankie's restlessness is even greater after this scene. Her child mind is not able to understand the love of Janice and Jarvis, but she is stirred by the mystery of their attachment, their belonging to each other: "My heart feels them going away—going farther and farther away—while I am stuck here by myself. . . . I remembered them more as a feeling than as a picture" (15). She worries about the impression that she has made, and her unsatisfied need, already deep, becomes deeper. Her natural, unseasoned reaction is expressed in dissatisfaction and in her wishes to escape. She fluctuates between reality and fantasy as she trails off into reverie during a card game with her young cousin John Henry and Berenice. "You don't have your mind on the game," Berenice tells her, and Frankie retorts, "I have some of my mind on the game" (15). Soon she wishes for literal escape, stating that she wishes she could leave the town and never see it again.

This escape not immediately practical, she continues to wish for what is not and to express her unmet need through condemnation of reality. "I wish I was somebody else except me" (18) she says, and this wish is augmented when she is not chosen as the new member of an exclusive girls' club. Later she is dissatisfied with her name (she wants to change it to Jasmine) and still later with her age (she wants to be grown) and, before the wedding, with her short haircut and her height (she wants to be shorter). These desires ungratified, she wishes for escape into death. "I just wish I would die" she cries in despair (31).

Her misery increases. She becomes more lonely when she recalls good times with a friend who has moved away or when she remembers the death of her favorite cat. Further, she continues to be haunted by her reaction to the love that she observed between Janice and Jarvis and is increasingly disturbed by her feeling of loneliness. Frankie decides that she will run away with them after the wedding and will become a part of their sense of belonging: "The bride and my brother," she says, "are the 'we' of me" (52). Thus, her longing unresolved, she plans escape.

Frankie also wonders whether her father loves her, since, immersed in his business, he is seldom at home, never listens to what she has to say, never pays any serious mind to her, and never seems to see or care. In a conversation with Berenice, she becomes so frustrated by her own inability to define and verbalize her ideas and feelings that she knocks her head against the door jamb and looks up at the ceiling. Berenice pities her but is unable to assuage her loneliness and longing.

On the day of the wedding, Frankie's attempt to escape with the bride and groom is aborted. Prized out of the wedding car by her father, she sobs. Her hope of escape into a world of belonging dies temporarily, and she exclaims that her exclusion from the couple's "we" is not fair. "I wish the whole world would die" (101), she cries, and later she runs out of the house with her father's pistol in her suitcase and stays overnight in the alley behind her father's store. People search frantically for her until she returns exhausted. She had attempted suicide, she reports, but her nerve had failed.

Unable to escape, Frankie seems at last to begin to accept reality. She identifies with Honey Camden, Berenice's wayward foster brother, who is running from the law and who later hangs himself in jail—free at last. And she is softened by the death of young John Henry, her cousin and playmate. When the story ends, Frankie talks excitedly with friends and anticipates moving with her father into the home of John Henry's parents. Ironically, it is the devoted Berenice, no longer employed as cook, who at the end of the play sits in the kitchen alone and motionless, singing a song about being happy and free.

The pattern of action in this play may also be traced through various works in the dramatic canon of Williams.[2] Although McCullers's sensitivity to the adolescent complexity revealed in the character of Frankie is not required in the often more predictable reactions of Williams's adults, both dramatists portray the irresistible force of the basic human need for acceptance and the desperation of characters denied fulfillment of this need.

Williams's character Blanche, for example, in *A Streetcar Named Desire*, is blocked by her sordid past from social acceptance; and to ease the loneliness and longing caused by this denial of acceptance, she attempts unsuccessfully to hide her past. This means of escape having failed, she seeks refuge in madness.

Like Blanche, Amanda of Williams's *The Glass Menagerie* is denied the social acceptance that is her deep need. Reared in the upper social level of a class-conscious Delta town, she had been a popular and charming belle. Now, deserted (and thus denied acceptance) by her husband, she is forced into obscure existence with her son and daughter in a St. Louis tenement house. While Amanda attempts to escape into the past, her crippled daughter Laura seeks refuge in a fragile glass collection of animal figurines, and her son Tom first finds diversion from a grimly laborious job by engaging in literary activity and ultimately escapes by deserting both his job and his family.

Cat on a Hot Tin Roof presents a similar pattern. Here Williams submits the character Brick to unresolved pressures so great that Brick brings about his own lack of acceptance by cutting himself off from other people, one of whom is his wife Margaret, who is also vying for acceptance in order to inherit the family estate. Brick seeks escape in alcohol and ultimately finds peace in truthfulness, but Margaret tells a blatant lie to gain acceptance and thus becomes ensnared in the maze of her deceit.

Mrs. Goforth in *The Milk Train Doesn't Stop Here Anymore* also withdraws from society and thereby induces her own lack of human bonding, which, in turn, brings about the loneliness and longing characteristic of isolation in other Williams plays. To achieve physical isolation, she moves to a previously uninhabited mountain, where, like Amanda, she withdraws into her past to escape the present—society, illness, and impending death. In the loneliness and longing of self-imposed isolation, she succumbs to the ultimate reality of death—her final escape.

Such characters illustrate a thread of tension between isolation and desire for acceptance that runs through the plays of Williams and McCullers. In both authors' plays, the healing, transcending force is, or would be, love—assured acceptance. Most of their tragic characters fail to grasp this healing force and, as a result, withdraw into destructive, sometimes violent, escape.

This failure is at the core of the chief tragedy in Carson McCullers's second and last play, *The Square Root of Wonderful* (first published 1958), in which the pattern of loneliness and longing continues. In this play, as the family name Lovejoy implies, the naturalistic magnetism of sexual attraction, treated with less emphasis in *The Member of the Wedding* and presented variously in the works of Williams, plays a major role in character relationships. But love deepened into acceptance is the unfulfilled need that leads to Phillip's tragic fate in McCullers's *Square Root*.

Love's mystery is introduced in the first scene of the play when Mollie Lovejoy, now divorced from Phillip, accepts affection from John Tucker, an architect whom she had picked up on a lonesome road ten days earlier. Her twelve-year-old son Paris (also the son of Phillip) observes this affection and offers his youthful assessment that love is "goofy," and, because it can't be eaten, it is a big fake. At this early age, Paris is more concerned with the need for food and parental love than with romantic love.

Mollie explains to John that she picked him up because she felt lonely, uncared for, unprotected. She implies a mysterious compulsion to relieve her loneliness when she says that picking him up somehow seemed inevitable the moment she saw him walking down the road. John's response is that he, too, was attracted to her by something magical. But Mollie's need, she tells John, is a love beyond the physical. She needs more now: somebody who will accept her wholly, not only her body, but also her mind and soul. Phillip, she thinks, had loved her only for her body.

Virtually every other character in the play also exhibits need for varied kinds of love and acceptance. Like Laura in Williams's *The Glass Menagerie,* Loreena Lovejoy, Phillip's maiden sister, lives with a domineering mother and has few suitors. Loreena assuages her longing for love by imagining affairs with foreigners. Mother Lovejoy, more seasoned and less passionate, has been deprived of a husband's love since the time when Phillip's father abandoned her and their two children many years before, and, in addition to being harshly critical and demanding, she is inordinately attached to these two children, although they have become adults. Even the child Hattie Brown, who figures only briefly in the play, reveals her need for acceptance in her bold young effort to persuade Paris to kiss her goodbye.

But the play's most problematic need is in the soul of Phillip, a tragic character obsessed by his need for professional acceptance and torn by his inability to achieve it. He considers a deep, accepting love from and for Mollie to be necessary for his success, yet his solipsistic desire to succeed prevents him from experiencing this kind of love. Like Tom in *The Glass Menagerie,* Phillip is a frustrated writer. Years earlier, Phillip had published *The Chinaberry Tree,* a book so successful that he was afraid to write again for years. When he did produce another play, it was so unsuccessful that the audience started leaving during the first act, and, after the final curtain, he went to the hotel and slashed his wrists. After this, his mother sent him to a sanitorium.

Love between Phillip and Mollie was, for Mollie, largely physical. She recalls that after their first divorce, she had remarried him because she was "under a spell—a strange spell" (23).[3] She confesses that she has broken the ten commandments with Phillip, but, she adds, "it wasn't me doing it" (37). She compares their love with two magnets running together and says that she responds to him as if she is drunk or "drugged or somehow powerless" (99).

But when he returns from the sanitorium, Phillip can no longer love. His failure to achieve professional success extends to failure in love, and his dilemma is full: he is unable to write without love, yet he can no longer love. He returns to the farm with Mollie, hoping to fill his need of love so that he can write, but he tells her that he can no longer smell or feel or love, that he feels surrounded by loneliness and can no longer touch when he reaches out. He has needed Mollie's protection, he says, and he longs to return to the safety of escape into a cocoon with her. For Phillip, their love had been more than physical; it was a place and time of escape, a refuge from fear of nonacceptance, a place of acceptance, where he might write again.

He had sought relief in drinking, leaving home, divorce, other women; and these having failed to supply his need, he sought to recapture the past when, with Mollie, he had written *The Chinaberry Tree*. Unlike Frankie Addams in *Member of the Wedding*,who has no past love to recall, but like Amanda and other Williams characters, Phillip can retreat into the comfort of memory. He wonders where his talent has gone and from where it came. Not from the brain, he decides, but from "some strange little motor in the soul. And now the motor has stopped" (111). In desperate need to resurrect this talent in his soul, he recalls to Mollie some of their past erotic scenes, but his illusive hope is dashed when Mollie tells him that she will marry John Tucker. This said, his soul cries out in nihilistic agony that without her there is nothing. "But nothing is not blank," he adds. "It is configured hell" (121). He still pleads with her to save him; she has saved him many times before. When Mollie concludes that he must be drunk, he replies that he is not drunk, but lost. Nothing remains for him but terror, and he wonders about its source. Is it fear of losing Mollie, he wonders; is it fear of time or space, or the trickery between the two? "To the lost," he says, "all that is in between is agony immobilized." Although he smashes the clock, it chimes on and on, as "time, that endless idiot goes screaming around the world" (123).

Because he cannot escape with Mollie, Phillip turns to his son for acceptance. Awakening Paris on the morning of Mollie's departure, Phillip says to the child, "I need you," and pours out his despair, veiled in parabolic figure and talk of a mysterious journey into an unknown land—his last voyage. Sensing that his father should not be making this journey alone, Paris offers to go with him, and Phillip, desperate in loneliness, agrees. But Paris remembers his plan to fish at the pond with Hattie Brown that day and chooses not to accompany his father. Now Phillip's final hope of acceptance is dashed. For a moment he escapes into the past as he recalls "when a song on the street and a voice from childhood all fitted" (138), when he could love and did not struggle against being loved, when he was not alone. But as it always must, past gives way to present, and Phillip drives himself into the water and drowns. The longing, lonely soul of Phillip, driven by needs that he could neither curb nor satisfy, finds ultimate escape in the permanent darkness of death.

This resolution of Phillip's dilemma, although tragic in its desperation, may nevertheless be construed as comic, if the reader accepts the logic of *raisonneur* John Tucker in the last act of the play. Suffering from guilt, Mollie is deeply disturbed by the idea that by choosing John she has caused Phillip's death. Fifteen years she had helped Phillip, and in the end she had driven him to death. But John reasons with her, telling her that she had been responsible for keeping life in a man who no longer wanted to live. His point is supported by illustration; he tells of an incident in the Navy when he tried, but failed, to save a boy who fell overboard. The boy had struggled and pulled him down repeatedly until John had to let him go, and so did Mollie have to release Phillip. Thus death, in the case of Phillip (as in Williams's story of Mrs. Goforth), may be construed as comic realization of his goal: to escape from the unbearable reality of a life tortured by denial of acceptance and love. More clearly comic is the resolution of Mollie's dilemma. She, along with Paris, receives from John the acceptance and beneficent love that Phillip could not give.

The close tension between tragedy and comedy in McCullers's plays is also evident in the works of Williams, but Williams wrote of gentle pathos rather than high tragedy. In most of his plays, characters move through quiet desperation, torn by their effort to live in a state of illusion amid the demands of a world in which cold reality rides roughshod over illusive dream. This is also the central problem of McCullers's characters, although to escape, many of Williams's characters retreat into prisons of their own making (Blanche, Amanda, Mrs. Goforth, for example),[4] while characters in McCullers's drama are more often propelled into complex directions by deterministic forces beyond their control. Naturalistic urges play a part in both authors' plays, especially the urges to experience sex, love, and self-preservation, but each author portrays individualized, rather than stock, reactions of characters to these urges. Specific character types, however, may be found in both canons: the dominant mother (e.g., Mother Lovejoy, Amanda), the frustrated writer (e.g., Phillip, Tom), divorced characters, and children in the care of one parent (e.g., Frankie, Paris, Laura).

Yet the most striking similarity in the drama of these two contemporaries and friends may be found in their common themes of loneliness and longing, their sensitivity to the anguished soul that cries out for acceptance which it does not receive, for love which, although made essential by nature, is denied by circumstance. The human hearts of their plays are indeed lonely hunters—restless, kindred souls in need.

Notes

1. Carson McCullers, *The Member of the Wedding: A Play* (New York: New Directions, 1951). Subsequent references are cited parenthetically by page number.
2. Further studies relating the works of McCullers to those of various other writers are

listed in Adrian Shapiro, Jackson R. Bryer, and Kathleen Field, *Carson McCullers: A Descriptive Listing and Annotated Bibliography of Criticism* (New York: Garland Publishing, 1980).

3. Carson McCullers, *The Square Root of Wonderful* (Boston: Houghton Mifflin, 1958). Subsequent references are cited parenthetically by page number.

4. For other examples, see Mary McBride, "Prisoners of Illusion: Surrealistic Escape in *The Milk Train Doesn't Stop Here Anymore*," in *Tennessee Williams: A Tribute*, ed. Jac Tharpe (Jackson: University Press of Mississippi, 1977), pp. 341–48.

11
Lorraine Hansberry and the Great Black Way

Leonard R. N. Ashley

It is odd that when Philip Rose wanted to produce Lorraine Hansberry's *A Raisin in the Sun* and made the rounds with the script, he was told the play was not what Broadway wanted. Yet *Raisin* is a quintessentially commercial Broadway drama. It is old-fashioned: Brooks Atkinson called it a "Negro *The Cherry Orchard*,"[1] and Tom Driver said that "the effect that it produces is comparable to that which would be had in a concert hall if a composer of today were to write a concerto in the manner of Tchaikovsky."[2] It is safe: it is Clifford Odets or Arthur Miller in blackface in a conventionally naturalistic and well-made drama about people who could be of any racial minority, what Atkinson identified as "human beings who want, on the one hand, to preserve their family pride and, on the other hand, to break out of the poverty that seems to be their fate."[3] It is relevant without being radical and sweet without being saccharine, uplifting and not too disturbing. C. W. E. Bigsby put his finger precisely on the play's commercial appeal when he wrote:

> For all its sympathy, humour and humanity, . . . [*Raisin*] remains disappointing. . . . Its weakness is essentially that of much of Broadway naturalism. It is an unhappy crossbreed of social protest and re-assuring resolution. Trying to escape the bitterness of Wright, Hansberry betrays herself into radical simplification and ill-defined affirmation.[4]

Originally prompted by Sean O'Casey's *Juno and the Paycock*,[5] which dramatizes the hardships and hopes of the ghetto, and by Langston Hughes's "Mother to Son," in which a black matriarch asserts that "Life for me ain't been no crystal stair,"[6] Hansberry finally put the emphasis on "a dream deferred" in Hughes's poem "Harlem," in which he asks whether such a dream will "dry up / like a raisin in the sun"—or "explode."[7] Hansberry was dedicated to political activism: she met her

Jewish husband on a picket line and worked for Paul Robeson's radical journal *Freedom*, writing such pieces as "Harlem Children Face Mass Ignorance in Old, Over-crowded, Understaffed Schools" and "Noted Lawyer Goes to Jail: Says Negroes' Fight for Rights Menaced."[8] However, she was not about to talk of the dream exploding into violence. As *Raisin* ends, the black Younger family, who have been planning to move from their dilapidated Chicago apartment to suburbia, decide not to accept money to stay out of the white neighborhood; if the battle awaits them, it takes place conveniently after the curtain falls.

Raisin opened at the Ethel Barrymore Theatre on 11 March 1959 and ran for 530 performances on Broadway. It became a favorite on liberal college campuses, was made into a movie starring Sidney Poitier, and won the 1961 Cannes Film Festival award.[9] Most significantly of all, *Raisin* was hailed as the Best Play of the Year, although it competed with a middle-brow success (Archibald MacLeish's *J.B.*), a minor Eugene O'Neill play (*A Touch of the Poet*), and a major Tennessee Williams play (*Sweet Bird of Youth*). Hansberry became the youngest and the first black woman recipient of the New York Drama Critics' Circle award. *Raisin* became a milestone in the American theater. It was made into a musical by third-rate talents (her former husband Robert Nemiroff, composer Judd Woldin, lyricist Robert Brittain, and Charlotte Zatzberg) in 1973 and ran for three years on Broadway, and in 1988 it was revived for a new season of "American Playhouse" on television.[10] It got into drama anthologies and up-to-the-minute college courses, becoming a mainstay of such new disciplines as Black Studies and Women's Studies.

Raisin immediately caused *Variety* and many others to rank Hansberry as the most promising playwright as the fifties ended. True, the structure of *Raisin* was conventional and the plotting clumsy. Why would Walter Younger give a partner in the liquor store deal all his share of the inheritance, $3,500, when only approximately a tenth of that was needed to bribe the venal (white) licensing authorities? And isn't the insurance money itself too obvious a "generating circumstance" to stir up the drama? Isn't the powerful and lovable Lena Younger just a copy of Hattie McDaniel or Ethel Waters? Doesn't the dialogue too often sound a little more New York Jewish than South Side Chicago black? (Did Nemiroff, with his own dreams derived from the English Department at New York University, do more than rescue his wife's pages from the wastepaper basket, encourage her to rewrite, abandon the other plays and the opera and the other projects she was toying with, and make a Broadway script for success?) Nonetheless, the play does deal with blacks—one critic complains they are "light-skinned" ones—and was a distinct advance on the few black playwrights who had been seen on Broadway in the thirty years after Wallace Thurman's forgotten *Harlem* (1929).

After 1929, New Yorkers had seen Garland Anderson's *Appearances* (1939), Hall Johnson's *Run, Little Chillun* (1933), Frank Wilson's *Meek Mouse* (1934), Langston Hughes's *Mulatto* (1935) and *Simply Heavenly* derived from his short stories (1957), Richard Wright's *Native Son* (1941) (better known as a novel), Theodore Ward's *Our Lan'* (1947), Louis Peterson's *Take a Giant Step* (1953), and Charles Sebree's *Mrs. Patterson* (1954).

Of these, *Take a Giant Step*, first presented at The Lyceum Theater on 24 September 1953, was probably the most important in terms of the reiterated theme of what Lindsay Patterson, in his anthology of *Black Theater* (1971), defined as "the specific moment when a black discovers he is a 'nigger' and his mentality shifts gears and begins that long, uphill climb to bring psychological order out of chaos."[11] Hansberry had her own flawed but notable way of addressing that concern and reaching out to middle-class theatergoers, both black and white. Other black women (such as Arna Bontemps) had come before her, and other black women (such as Adrienne Kennedy) would come after, along with black men with messages reaching the mainstream (such as Ossie Davis) and others of great significance to emergent black theater (such as Ed Bullins and Douglas Turner Ward) and black radical thought (such as James Baldwin and Amiri Baraka). But Hansberry came at a crucial time and had an undeniable impact, making a historic contribution to what W. E. B. DuBois decades before had called for: black writers dedicated to presenting the black man to the world as both artist and a subject of art.[12]

Off-Broadway black writers had been successful: Langston Hughes at The Suitcase Theater with *Don't You Want to Be Free?* and Alice Childress at Club Baron with *Just a Little Simple* and at Greenwich Mews with *Trouble in Mind* were but two. It was *Raisin*, however, with a Jewish push from Nemiroff and his friends Burt D'Lugoff and Philip Rose, who recognized Hansberry as a champion of all the downtrodden regardless of race, that made Broadway and history.[13]

Next came *The Sign in Sidney Brustein's Window* (1965), a direct attack on the bohemians of Greenwich Village. Sidney Brustein is a cynical and rather crass intellectual who can see through everyone's pretentions but his own. His unattractive wife Iris, who has more desire than talent to be an actress, has two sisters: Gloria (an expensive prostitute) and Mavis (a middle-class housewife). Alton Scales (a black activist in love with Gloria) and David Ragin (a gay playwright) create a very Village atmosphere. Perhaps it's a *Village Voice* atmosphere that prevails, because Scales wants Brustein to support the political reform candidate Wally O'Hara. The sign in the window gives the main message—"Vote Reform." Brustein discovers that the candidate he helped elect has sold out to the political bosses. Iris becomes an actress in commercials, Gloria decides to retire from "the profession" to marry Alton but commits suicide when he discovers her past, and Sidney and Iris reunite in the end. The good news (perhaps the bad news, because they are somewhat despicable types) is that they will somehow survive.

If this was to be a "play of ideas," the problem was that there were too many ideas and no firm idea of how to make a coherent drama out of them. *Raisin* had been described unkindly as soap opera with contrived climaxes and problems not of blacks but of people who just happened to be black. *Brustein* leaves black questions aside and jumps on the horse of social satire and rides off in several directions. Although Hansberry was never reliable with dialogue and her screenplay (nominated for an Oscar) for *Raisin* shows how bad she could get when she really worked at it with collaborators, *Brustein* has some effective lines, mostly what comedians call *zingers*, concise and cutting. What it lacks is a character as complex as Walter Lee Younger of *Raisin*, who is at least as fully conceived as Miller's Willy Loman.

Sidney Brustein proves the inadequacy of two polar opposite liberal views, fleeing from the crowd, dwelling with quietness (à la Thoreau), and losing himself in wild-eyed political activism. But we are never asked to feel with or for Sidney, as we do with and for Walter Lee even when he is most confused. Of course, dimwit Iris's idea of "live and let live, that's all" is a selfish and stupid lack of what later is deified as Involvement, but Sidney is simplistic in thought and contemptuous of others, just as Alton is brutal and Mavis is prejudiced. Sidney, unlike Lena in *Raisin*, may transcend stereotype, but the more we learn of him the more we legitimately despise him. Sidney is more engaged than engaging. He and Iris deserve each other, and they take up a lot of time that might have been devoted to minor characters such as David or Max (a sandaled bohemian).

Time also should have been spent conveying the message of this would-be intellectual play, which Harold Taubman reviewed in the *New York Times* as "uneven" and having charm and some good performances and "intelligence and ardor" but this basic fault:

> Miss Hansberry has tried to cover too much ground and to touch on too many issues. There is the theme of the three sisters, daughters of an unusual, poetic Greek, who are haunted in different ways by the memory of their father. There is the theme of the intellectual who knows nearly everything and scoffs at most of it and who learns that he must make a commitment. There is a theme of the opportunist who uses the Reform movement in local politics to get ahead. . . .

> The principal themes do not coalesce comfortably, and the tangential ones, while occasionally amusing, stay the forward progress of the play.[14]

The reviews that *Brustein* received would have closed the play had it not been for a massive sympathy campaign by her friends. Since 1963, Hansberry had known she had cancer. She was dying when she attended opening night at the Longacre Theatre on 15 October 1964. Nemiroff and she had recently divorced, but this was kept secret, and he continued to act as her manager. He organized people who admired and loved Hansberry, and they all generously contributed the promotion, word of mouth, and hard cash that kept *Brustein* running for 101 performances on Broadway until Hansberry died on 12 January 1965. Although John Braine had greeted *Brustein* as "a great play," it wasn't one. But keeping it alive as long as its author was alive was a great gesture, and it became a cause that opened hearts and wallets.

It also became Nemiroff's charge to enhance the memory of his former wife after her death. He arranged for the publication of *Brustein* (1969), and he participated in a marathon memorial to her broadcast on radio station WBAI that he later made into the stage presentation *To Be Young, Gifted and Black: Lorraine Hansberry in Her Own Words* (1969). This was a collage of bits of her plays, articles, public speeches, diaries, personal letters, and tape recordings billed as theatre. Gerald Weales in *Commonweal* was furious: "Whatever Nemiroff intended, the play made a mockery of Miss Hansberry's talents, destroyed everything that is good and subtle in her work." He added that "if Nemiroff's mosaic were taken at face value, it would be necessary to assume that Miss Hansberry was a gushy little girl, oohing and ahing in much the same voice of Wisconsin snow and ghetto courage, a dramatist who turned out clumsy genre pieces or broad comedy put-downs."[15]

To Be Young, Gifted and Black, however, became *the* show to be associated with to show one's idealism and liberalism, and it also became *the* off-Broadway hit of 1969 and later toured more than 200 college campuses. Hansberry's nonviolent black voice was eventually drowned out by louder and more angry cries for Black Power; it was, however, of political and artistic interest for a time and for a certain constituency.

Practically no one read her text in the book *The Movement: Documentary of a Struggle for Equality* (1964), which also appeared in Britain under the title *A Matter of Colour: Documentary of the Struggles for Racial Equality in the USA* (1965). That was just as well, because she was a creative artist of the theater, not a clear theorist of the political arena. She had as little real talent for politics as she had for drawing or painting, although she had dabbled in radicalism and in pictorial art.

For some years before her death, Hansberry had been toying with an answer to Genet's *Les Negres* (1960), which she disliked very much. It was called *Les Blancs*, and, with characteristic hyperbole, Nemiroff described it as "the first major work by a black American playwright to focus on Africa and the struggle for black liberation."[16] In 1970, Nemiroff "edited" the script and had it produced to very mixed reviews.

Hansberry had regarded it as her most important work, and Richard Watts in the *New York Post* immediately proclaimed it "the one first-rate new American play of the season."[17] Clive Barnes in the *Times* said it was flawed but "on a vital subject.[18] John Simon in *New York* damned it as "not only the worst new play on Broadway, of an amateurishness and crudity unrelieved by its sophomoric jabs at wit, it is also, more detestably, a play finished—or finished off—by white liberals that does its utmost to justify the slaughter of whites by blacks."[19]

I agree that it encourages the kind of black revolution that bloodied Africa soon after and, to some at the time, seemed to be "the fire next time" due to break out in America. It is gauche as much as leftist; it substitutes anger and artiness for articulateness and art. But if the label *racist* is to be put on it—as many people thought right—then it is as critical of black opportunists as it is of the white Establishment. It was more "controversial" than the ninety-minute television drama *The Drinking Gourd* (1960), which dealt with slavery and the Civil War and which, after telling Hansberry to make it "as frank as it needs to be," Dore Schary then dropped.[20] (In 1965 Claudia McNeil, who had starred with Poitier in the film of *Raisin*, and Frederic Marc and Florence Eldridge tried to get it on the air, but by then it was no longer "contemporary," the Civil War centenary being over and the immense popularity of a program such as *Roots* not yet imagined.) However, whites were treated objectively in *The Drinking Gourd*, and in *Les Blancs* they were not.

Hansberry always had a number of ambitious projects in mind. Something on the feminist Mary Wollstonecraft was one of them, but it never came to fruition. Another was a short play for television, *What Use Are Flowers?*, an optimistic view about the aftermath of nuclear war. (A seventy-eight-year-old English professor survives the holocaust and emerges into a destroyed world to try to give civilization back to a motley crew of nine children. He dies after he teaches them about the wheel and they destroy it in a quarrel. But as the play ends, they are cooperating to rebuild it.) NBC rejected that, so Hansberry revised it as a stage play.[21] She had so much optimism that she hoped it would be a positive response to the negativity (as she saw it) of Beckett's *Waiting for Godot*, and she had so little critical taste that she believed it was better.

A Raisin in the Sun was published in 1959, and, although the movie did not get the acclaim that greeted the play, her screenplay of it was published in 1961. *The Sign in Sidney Brustein's Window* was published in 1965 and in Penguin's *Three Negro Plays* (1969). *To Be Young, Gifted and Black: Lorraine Hansberry in Her Own Words* was published in 1969 by Nemiroff, who also edited *Les Blancs: The Collected Last Plays of Lorraine Hansberry* (including *Les Blancs, The Drinking Gourd*, and *What Use Are Flowers?*) in 1972. Also in 1972, Nemiroff produced *Lorraine Hansberry Speaks Out: Art and Black Revolution* for Caedmon's Spoken Arts series, and Robert M. Fresco adapted *To Be Young, Gifted and Black* for National Educational Television. Since that time, there have been a special issue of *Freedomways* (with a bibliography, 1979), a biography (Catherine Scheader's *They Found a Way: Lorraine Hansberry*, for Children's Press, 1978), appearances in anthologies, and numerous mentions in literary studies. Most recently, her importance in the modern theater and in the raising of black consciousness has been less valued than it once was.

Her importance is minor but must not be ignored. Hansberry's last play, *Les Blancs*, may have lasted only forty-seven performances (opening at the Longacre Theatre on 15 November 1970), but *A Raisin in the Sun* had a long and well-deserved run in its time and assures her a place of respect in the history of the modern American theater.

Her papers (Nemiroff is her literary executor) contain a novel, a screenplay based on the Haitian novelist Jacques Roumain's *Masters of the Dew*, and political articles and dramatic fragments, including *The Arrival of Mr. Todog*, a skit satirizing *Waiting for Godot*. She was always the outspoken enemy of anything she regarded as absurdist, pessimistic, or determinist, and of the problems of blacks and whites profoundly convinced that "We Shall Overcome."

"Miss Hansberry," wrote Professor Bigsby in *Confrontation and Commitment*, "weds an understanding of historical causality to a genuine belief in the possibility of change—a faith which necessarily rejects art formed out of despair and finding its genesis in individual suffering." She was able "to transcend parochialism and social bitterness"[22] and to create at her best what Clive Barnes and other critics praised as effective theatrical scenes[23] if not balanced and always carefully crafted dramas. She was not at her best with propaganda about plantation slavery or African revolution, any more than she was in her venture into philosophical drama in *What Use Are Flowers?* But with a nonagitprop and compassionate view of her fellow Americans from Chicago, she was powerful and memorable.[24] *Raisin in the Sun* is not a great play, but for various reasons it has an enduring place in American theater history, like *The Contrast* or *The Fantasticks* or other milestones. It will remain and draw interest to itself as a period piece and record-breaker, but it also will help our theater to remember what it was like to be a young, moderately gifted, more than usually successful black woman playwright at a time when that meant pioneering on two fronts at least. Hansberry did notably more in her work than Mrs. Scales, the black domestic mentioned in a strong speech in *The Sign in Sidney Brustein's Window*, who brought home leftovers from the white family's table to feed her black children.

Notes

1. Brooks Atkinson, "The Theater: *A Raisin in the Sun*," *New York Times*, 12 March 1959, reprinted in *New York Theatre Critics' Reviews* 1959, p. 345.
2. Tom F. Driver, "Theater: *A Raisin in the Sun*," *The New Republic* 140 (13 April 1959): 21.
3. Atkinson, "The Theater: *A Raisin in the Sun*," p. 345.
4. C. W. E. Bigsby, *Confrontation and Commitment: A Study of Contemporary American Drama 1959–1966* (Columbia: University of Missouri Press, 1969), p. 156.
5. See Peter L. Hays, "*Raisin in the Sun* and *Juno and the Paycock*," *Phylon* 33 (Summer 1972): 175–76.
6. Langston Hughes, "Mother to Son," in *The Weary Blues* (New York: Alfred A. Knopf, 1926), p. 107.
7. Langston Hughes, "Harlem," from *Montage of a Dream Deferred*, in *Selected Poems of Langston Hughes* (New York: Alfred A. Knopf, 1959), p. 268.
8. Some other politically oriented essays by Hansberry include "Willy Loman, Walter Younger, and He Who Must Live," *Village Voice*, 12 August 1959, pp. 7–8; "This Complex of Womanhood," *Ebony* 15 (August 1960): 40; "Genet, Mailer, and the New Paternalism," *Village Voice*, 1 June 1961, pp. 10–15; "Images and Essences: 1961 Dialogue with an Uncolored Egghead Containing Wholesome Intentions and Some Sass," *The Urbanite* 1 (May 1961): 10–11, 36; "A Challenge to Artists," *Freedomways* 3, no. 1 (Winter 1963): 33–35; "Black Revolution and the White Backlash" (transcript of Town Hall Forum), *National Guardian*, 4 July 1964, pp. 5–9; "The Nation Needs Your Gifts," *Negro Digest* 13, 10 (August 1964): 26–29; "The Legacy of W. E. B. DuBois," *Freedomways* 5, no. 1 (Winter 1965): 19–20; "The Negro Writer and His Roots: Toward a New Romanticism," *Black Scholar* 12 (March/April 1981): 2–12; and "All the Dark and Beautiful Warriors," *Village Voice*, 16 August 1983, pp. 1, 11–16, 18–19.
9. Reviews of the 1961 Columbia Pictures film of *Raisin in the Sun* include *America* 105 (8 April 1961): 133–34; *BFI/Monthly Film Bulletin* 28 (July 1961): 95; *Commonweal* 74 (7 April 1961): 46; *Ebony* 16 (April 1961): 53–56; *Film Daily*, 29 March 1961, p. 6; *Filmfacts* 4 (5 May 1961): 77–79; *Films in Review* 7 (May 1961): 298; Alvin H. Marill, *The Films of Sidney Poitier* (Secaucus: Citadel, 1978), pp. 97–100; Daniel J. Lear, *From Sambo to Superspade: The Black Experience in Motion Pictures* (Boston: Houghton Mifflin, 1975), pp. 226–27; *Life*, 21 April 1961, p. 52D; *Magill's Survey of Cinema, Series I*, 3, pp. 1422–24; *The New Republic*, 20 March 1961, p. 19; *New York Times*, 30 March 1961, p. 24; *New York Times*, sec. 2, 17 July 1960, p. 5; *New York Times*, sec. 2, 2 April 1961, p. 1; *The New Yorker*, 8 April 1961, p. 164; *Newsweek*, 10 April 1961, p. 103; *Saturday Review*, 25 March 1961, p. 34; *Time*, 31 March 1961, p. 64.
10. The American Playhouse production, Robert Nemiroff/Jaki Brown/Toni Livingston/

Josephine Abady Productions, was directed by Bill Duke; its cast included Danny Glover (Walter Lee Younger), Starletta DuPois (Ruth Younger), Kimble Joyner (Travis Younger), Kim Yancey (Beneatha Younger), Esther Rolle (Lena Younger), and Lou Ferguson (Joseph Asagai). For Black History Month in (February) 1988, Channel 13 New York (PBS) presented R. Tangney's (producer and director) "Lorraine Hansberry: The Black Experience in the Creation of Drama" (1975), narrated by Claudia McNeill.

11. Lindsay Patterson, ed. *Black Theater: A 20th Century Collection of the Work of Its Best Playwrights* (New York: New American Library, 1971), p. ix.

12. Essays on Hansberry's contributions to black theater include Theophilus Lewis, "Social Protest in *A Raisin in the Sun*," *Catholic World* 190 (October 1959): 31–35; Harold R. Isaacs, "Five Writers and Their African Ancestors, Part II," *Phylon* 21, no. 4 (December 1960): 317–36; Ossie Davis, "The Significance of Lorraine Hansberry," *Freedomways* 5, no. 3 (Summer 1965): 396–402; Jordan Y. Miller, "Lorraine Hansberry," in *The Black American Writer, Vol. 2: Poetry and Drama*, ed. C. W. E. Bigsby (Baltimore, Md.: Penguin Books, 1969), pp. 157–70; Robert Willis, "Anger and Contemporary Black Theatre," *Negro American Literature Forum* 8 (Summer 1974), 213–15; Jeanne-Marie A. Miller, "Images of Black Women in Plays by Black Playwrights," *CLA Journal* 20 (June 1977): 498–500; Glenda Gill, "Techniques of Teaching Lorraine Hansberry: Liberation from Boredom," *Negro American Literature Forum* 9 (Summer 1987): 226–28. See also Gwendolyn S. Cherry, et al., *Portraits in Color: The Lives of Colorful Negro Women* (Paterson, N.J.: Pageant Books, 1962), pp. 149–52; Harold R. Isaacs, *The New World of Negro Americans* (New York: The John Day Company, 1963), pp. 277–87; Harold Cruse, *The Crisis of the Negro Intellectual* (New York: William Morrow, 1967), pp. 267–84; Loften Mitchell, *Black Drama: The Story of the American Negro in the Theatre* (New York: Hawthorn Books, 1967), pp. 180–82; Harold Clurman, "Theater: *Les Blancs*," *The Nation* 211, no. 18 (30 November 1970); Arthur P. Davis, *From the Dark Tower: Afro-American Writers 1900 to 1960* (Washington, D.C.: Howard University Press, 1974), pp. 203–7; Tom Scanlan, *Family, Drama, and American Dreams* (Westport, Conn.: Greenwood Press, 1978), pp. 195–201. Hansberry herself speaks to the issue in *Lorraine Hansberry: The Black Experience in the Creation of Drama* (Princeton: Films for the Humanities, 1976) and *Lorraine Hansberry Speaks Out: Art and the Black Revolution* (Caedmon, 1972), both recordings.

13. See Gerald Weales, "Thoughts on *A Raisin in the Sun*," *Commentary* 27, no. 6 (June 1959): 527–30, and Lloyd W. Brown, "Lorraine Hansberry as an Ironist: A Reappraisal of *A Raisin in the Sun*," *Journal of Black Studies* 4 (March 1974): 237–47.

14. Harold Taubman, "Theater: *Sidney Brustein's Window*," *New York Times*, 16 October 1964, p. 32. See also Walter Kerr, "*Sign in Sidney Brustein's Window*," *New York Herald Tribune*, 16 October 1964, reprinted in *New York Theatre Critics' Reviews* 1964, pp. 192–93; Robert Nemiroff, "The One Hundred and One 'Final' Performances of *Sidney Brustein*: Portrait of a Play and Its Author," in *A Raisin in the Sun / The Sign in Sidney Brustein's Window*, by Lorraine Hansberry (New York: Signet/New American Library, 1966), pp. 138–85; Orley I. Holton, "Sidney Brustein and the Plight of the American Intellectual," *Players* 46 (June/July 1971): 222–25; Clive Barnes, *The Sign in Sidney Brustein's Window*," *New York Times*, 27 January 1974, p. 44.

15. Gerald Weales, "Losing the Playwright," *Commonweal* 90 (5 September 1969): 542–43.

16. Robert Nemiroff, quoted in Michael Adams, *Dictionary of Literary Biography* 7, p. 252; see also Julius Lester, Introduction to *Les Blancs: The Collected Last Plays of Lorraine Hansberry*, ed. Robert Nemiroff (New York: Vintage Books, 1973), pp. 25–32.

17. Richard Watts, *New York Post*, 16 November 1970, reprinted in *New York Theatre Critics' Reviews* 1970, p. 154.

18. Clive Barnes, *New York Times*, 16 November 1970, reprinted in *New York Theatre Critics' Reviews* 1970, pp. 154–55.

19. John Simon, quoted in *Dictionary of Literary Biography* 7, p. 252.

20. The information on Dore Schary and *The Drinking Gourd* is from *Dictionary of Literary Biography* 7, p. 252. Schary called it "a powerful, marvelous script . . . that says something about the peculiar institution of slavery." CBS claimed it was "not contempo-

rary enough" and no television executives could see that the topic was box office (as it proved to be in *Roots*). Hansberry's script was racist (although she presents whites favorably), but it was trash, not treasure. See also Bertie J. Powell, "The Black Experience in Margaret Walker's *Jubilee* and Lorraine Hansberry's *The Drinking Gourd*," *CLA Journal* 21, no. 2 (December 1977): 304–11.

21. *The Drinking Gourd* and *What Use Are Flowers?* published separately by Random House in 1972, are included in *Les Blancs: The Collected Last Plays of Lorraine Hansberry*, ed. Robert Nemiroff, pp. 217–310, 323–70.

22. Bigsby, *Confrontation and Commitment*, pp. 168–69, 172.

23. Barnes, *The Sign in Sidney Brustein's Window*.

24. Two interviews of interest are "Playwright," *The New Yorker*, 9 May 1959, pp. 33–34, containing information on Hansberry's early life; and Studs Terkel, "An Interview with Lorraine Hansberry," *WFMT Chicago Fine Arts Guide* 10, no. 4 (April 1961): 8–14. Primary and secondary materials are listed in Ernest Kaiser and Robert Nemiroff, "A Lorraine Hansberry Bibliography," *Freedomways* 19, no. 4 (1979): 285–304 [special Hansberry issue]. The latest study of Hansberry is by Elizabeth Brown-Guillory, *Their Place on the Stage: Black Women Playwrights in America* (Westport: Greenwood Press, 1988). It is written from a feminist perspective, while this present article, without ignoring her feminine or black interests, attempts to place Hansberry in the mainstream of the American popular theater and to stake her historical claim, along with successful plays as different as *Lightnin'* and *Abie's Irish Rose*, for an enduring if minor place in the pantheon of Broadway.

12

Megan Terry's Transformational Drama: *Keep Tightly Closed in a Cool Dry Place* and the Possibilities of Self

June Schlueter

> In order "to make it," we need to make images of ourselves. We compose ourselves from our cultural models around us. We are programmed into a status hunger. Once we have masked ourselves with the social image suitable to a type, we enter the masquerade of the setup. Even the masquerade of our ethnic and sex roles permeates our life so thoroughly that many of us are afraid to give them up. In giving them up we fear we would be giving up our identity, and even life itself.[1]

Joseph Chaikin's comment represents part of his response to what he and others involved in the Open Theatre of the 1960s called the "setup." In advertising for an "ingenue," a "leading lady," a "character actress," a "male juvenile character," and so on, trade papers reflected a disturbing coincidence between theatre and society: both based their vocabulary of character on the stereotype. Both assumed there were "fixed ways of telling one person from another" and found security in institutionalizing that assumption. As a consequence, Chaikin points out, "Each element of the societal [or theatrical] disguise, the acceptable image, can be assessed on an almost absolute and exploitative scale of values: 'It is better to be Caucasian': 'it is better to be heterosexual and male'; 'it is better to be rich'; 'it is better to be Protestant.' "[2]

Megan Terry's early transformation plays—*Eat at Joe's, Calm Down Mother, Keep Tightly Closed in a Cool Dry Place, Comings and Goings,* and *Viet Rock*—represent a further response of the Open to the "setup." Abjuring the rigidity of appointed and anointed roles, the Open made transformational drama a staple of its early repertory, creating theatrical exercises and plays in which actors shifted freely and suddenly from one character, situation, time, or objective to another. As Terry's col-

Reprinted by permission from *Studies in American Drama, 1945–Present* 2 (1987): 59–69.

league Peter Feldman put it, "Whatever realities are established at the beginning are destroyed after a few minutes and replaced by others. Then these are in turn destroyed and replaced."[3] From the perspective of two decades of subsequent theater, it should now be clear that Terry's work with transformation challenged more than the individual actor seeking versatility and range. In freeing the actor from the prescriptiveness of the assigned role, transformational drama challenged the prevailing character of realistic theater, which reinforced social and theatrical expectations. Terry's work in neutralizing fixed assumptions, dismantling the stereotype, and reevaluating the institutional hierarchy proved seminal in forming the emerging principles and modes of New York's alternative theatre.

Chief among these emerging principles was off-Broadway's conception of character. Until Beckett's *Waiting for Godot* startled Broadway in 1956; until Joseph Cino opened the Caffe Cino in 1958; until the Becks went public with the Living Theatre in 1959, with Jack Gelber's *The Connection;* until Edward Albee turned to playwriting, staging *The Zoo Story* in New York in 1960; until Ellen Stewart opened La Mama in 1962; and until the Open Theatre became a presence in 1963, the prevailing mode of American drama was realism. The principle of construction was the cause-and-effect relationship, the plot proceeding neatly through units of action that raised a dramatic question, satisfied that question, and raised another, even as a dominant dramatic question sustained itself throughout the sequence. Character became clear through motive, often discovered in a past event that justified a character's present perversions. The social-psychological-moral paradigm pursued by Ibsen in *A Doll House* and *Ghosts* remained the model for postwar American drama, which placed its faith in causality and its attendant claims.

Modern American drama took little notice of Pirandello's radical assault on the theater in 1923, when *Six Characters in Search of an Author* rocked its Paris audience and changed Europe's theatrical vocabulary. In his 1953 study of "*Modernism*" *in Modern Drama,* Joseph Wood Krutch needed only to append a brief chapter on American drama, asking how modern it was, even while he was expressing moral outrage over Pirandello. The Italian playwright, he argued, of all the moderns, made "the most inclusive denial of all, namely, the denial that the persistent and more or less persistent character or personality which we attribute to each individual human being, and especially to ourselves, really exists at all."[4] For Krutch, the "dissolution of the ego" that Pirandello's plays present obviated all moral systems, "since obviously no one can be good or bad, guilty or innocent, unless he exists as some sort of continuous unity."[5]

Krutch's reaction might be justified if one assumes the moral function of theater, in which case consistency, plausibility, and growth are all essential elements of the continuous self. But a play, as Terry and others have shown, might also be designed to play with the epistemological question of how the self takes form, without identifying a self that is morally accountable, psychologically consistent, or socially defined.

Transformational drama acknowledges the multiple and shifting selves that at any moment or collection of moments constitute a developing self, placing that composite in a context that is itself shifting. The consequence is a drama of perception analogous to a Picasso painting of a woman's profile seen in the same frame as the woman's frontal view. Neither has priority, neither negates the other, both suggest the complexity of the dynamic process that we can only tentatively call the self. Moreover, transformational drama acknowledges the extent to which the modern self is shaped by popular culture—advertising, movies, fictional heroes, romanticized history, TV commercials-the stereotypes provided by the media that steal into ordinary lives and shape expectations. In its involvement with media propaganda as the living artifacts of our culture, transformational drama becomes a kind of found art, a collage of the objects that insipiently form, reform, and transform models of self. And, finally, although transformational drama of necessity negates Krutch's concept of an identifiable and continuous self, it curiously affirms the relationships between self and others that Krutch's more traditional analysis of character would also affirm. As Feldman points out in his "notes for the Open Theatre Production," rehearsals for *Keep Tightly Closed* began with improvisations dealing with "dependency, enclosure, and isolation."[6] And as Bonnie Marranca notes in her study of *American Playwrights, Keep Tightly Closed* explores "confinement, dependency, domination-submission, ritual, friendship, deprivation, and loneliness."[7] Terry's approach to these relationships is, of course, different from Arthur Miller's, but like realistic drama, it affirms the invariables of human experience. Unlike the dominant paradigm, however, transformational drama accommodates and affirms the variables as well.

Any of Terry's transformation plays might serve to illustrate the Open's contribution to redefining dramatic character, although her technique is not always the same. In *Comings and Goings*, randomly selected actors replace other actors, often in midsentence, and are themselves replaced, continually subverting the identification of actor and character or audience and character. In *Calm Down Mother*, three actresses assume changing roles, becoming first one character and then another. In *Viet Rock*, the technique, as Richard Schechner describes it, is variously used:

> In the opening scene the actors become, in rapid sequence, a human, primordial flower, mothers and infants, army doctors and inductees, inductees and mothers. In the Senate Hearing scene actors replace other actors within the framework of a single scene.[8]

In *Keep Tightly Closed in a Cool Dry Place,* not only do the three inmates change into other characters as the play progresses, but the situation being dramatized changes as well. Schechner sees Terry's techniques in *Keep Tightly Closed* as accomplishing three functions: "They explode a routine situation into a set of exciting theatrical images; they reinforce, expand, and explore the varieties of relationships among the three men; they make concrete the fantasies of the prisoners."[9] It is this play, mounted in 1965 in a double bill with *Calm Down Mother,* that I find most diverse, most fascinating, and most representative of the potential and the impact that Terry's work with transformational drama has had on the American theater. I would like to look at the transformations in that play more closely and then offer some comments on Terry's contribution to off-Broadway's redefinition of the definition of self.

Keep Tightly Closed in a Cool Dry Place, like all transformation plays, does not ask its actors to find some coincidence between themselves and the characters they are portraying, nor does it ask its actors to create subtexts. In place of this psychological work, it offers a sequence of opportunities for verbal and nonverbal behavior, each involving an abrupt shift in roles. Transformational drama is clearly both a challenge and an opportunity for the actor wanting to see himself or herself not as a trade magazine type but as an actor capable of moving with facility among diverse roles. Yet transformational drama is not simply "for the actors," as Gerald Weales suggests in his unappreciative assessment of Terry's work.[10] Transformational drama, like all drama, is for the audience, whose response to the abrupt changes the form demands helps create this alternative model of presenting dramatic character, one that says more about the epistemology of character, onstage and off, than realistic drama can.

The three men who share a prison cell in *Keep Tightly Closed,* all sentenced for their part in the collective murder of Jaspers's wife, provide a centering situation—not necessary for transformational drama but immensely effective here. Jaspers, an attorney in his thirties, hired Michaels to hire Gregory to murder his wife so he could collect half a million dollars in insurance pay-offs. Although Gregory accomplished the deed, he was apprehended, offering a confession that also implicated the other two. Now cellmates, Michaels has taken refuge in illness, Gregory in dreams and orgasms; but Jaspers is restless and angry. Although confined as the other two are, the lawyer still attempts to exercise his authority and to use whatever strategy might help him get free. He bullies Michaels into agreeing to torture Gregory. When Michaels frustrates Gregory by repeating everything he says, Jaspers offers calculated comfort, advising the humiliated man not to sign the confession when he is upset. Still later, he contrives to get Gregory to join him in persuading Michaels to confess.

As the drama of Jaspers's power struggle progresses, the three remind themselves of the circumstances that led to their incarceration. At one point, Jaspers assumes the role of prosecuting attorney/judge/arresting officer, interrogating Gregory and attempting to reshape the arrest and trial into the scenario he would have liked to have seen. The three speak of the murder, reproaching and comforting one another, and Gregory tells stories: one of a dream he had of raping a woman, the other a fantasy of a woman who swallowed a snake's egg and was eaten away inside by the snake. Although arranged with no special respect for chronology of causality, each of the episodes in the centering situation contributes to the audience's conception of the three cellmates: Jaspers is arrogant, authoritative, angry. Michaels, a server rather than a leader, is burdened by conscience and compassion. Gregory is a weak but dangerous sexually preoccupied underling.

But if presentation of the socially/psychologically/morally recognizable character were all transformational drama achieved, it would be indistinguishable in effect from realistic drama. What is special about transformational drama is that it provides multiple perspectives through providing alternate situations and roles. In *Keep Tightly Closed*, the centering situation which itself admits recollection, wishful thinking, and fantasy, is punctuated repeatedly by actions among other characters outside the cell, played by the same three actors. Hence at one point, Jaspers becomes General Custer, Michael a bluecoat, and Gregory their Indian victim. At another, the three become characters in a Jamestown drama, with a dying fifteen-year-old begging for water from Captain Smith. In one especially chilling vignette, Gregory recreates the moments in Jaspers's kitchen immediately preceding the crime, while Jaspers becomes his soon-to-be-murdered wife and Michaels his eight-year-old son. Three times, the trio become mechanical devices, and in one sequence they are transformed into a vaudeville trio, drag queens, and movie gangsters.

In none of the transformations is an audience to see the three as Rosalind playing Ganymede playing Rosalind (Shakespeare, *As You Like It*) or Solange playing Claire while Claire plays Madam (Genet, *The Maids*), even when Gregory as the murderer replays the kitchen drama. For each transformation, the three actors, not the characters, assume different roles or join in the mechanical representation of a container, a lead pencil (?), and a labeling machine—all identifiable through the prescriptions and restrictions spoken by the actors. Even if the transformation is completely convincing, however, and the audience understands that Jaspers is not General Custer or the dying boy but that the actor has merely shifted roles, its perception of character changes, in a number of ways. For one thing, as Chaikin points out, the wearing of a disguise affects the actor:

> In former times acting simply meant putting on a disguise. When you took off the disguise, there was the old face under it. Now it's clear that the wearing of the disguise changes the person. As he takes the disguise off, his face is changed from having worn it.[11]

The face that is changed from having worn the disguise is the face the audience sees. But that face is a Picasso. Although an audience understands that it is not Jaspers who is playing General Custer but an actor shifting roles, the after-image of the character that actor has just played necessarily informs the next. Hence an audience's perception of Custer is affected by the after-image of Jaspers, and the after-image of Custer, in turn, changes the audience's perception of Jaspers. As the actor who plays Jaspers assumes other roles as well, the layering multiplies: images and after-images combine in a densely layered portrait that challenges the clear, sharp outlines of the realistically drawn face.

Moreover, as it is creating the Picasso face, transformational drama is also engaging, even exploiting, the special double vision that an audience brings to every theatrical experience. Even as the transformation requires the actor to abandon one role for another, it plays on the knowledge that an audience never achieves the same abandonment. Although willing by convention to believe the masquerade and to enter the fiction of the play, an audience watching Olivier playing Lear never forgets that it is watching both Olivier and Lear. Nor do recidivist playgoers discard their recollection of Olivier playing Hamlet when they watch Olivier playing Lear or, for that matter, their image of Olivier playing Hamlet when they watch Jacobi in that role. Transformational drama demands that the audience not only be aware of the multiplicity of selves generated by a multiplicity of roles but that it becomes an active participant in the process of definition and redefinition that never ends.

Were we talking of *Comings and Goings*, which shifts arbitrarily from one situation to the next and randomly appoints actors to assume specific roles, we might stop our discussion here, without attention to context. But *Keep Tightly Closed* presents a nuclear trio of characters whose prison experience is central to the play. Given this centering situation, it is safe to assume that Terry's choices of transformations in

Keep Tightly Closed are not random but contribute in their specific content both to an audience's perception of Jaspers, Michaels, and Gregory and to its understanding of how character takes form. In shifting to the situation with Custer, a bluecoat, and a redskin, for example, Terry provides a vignette that might well have served as a subtext or a preparatory improvisation for the trio had the group been operating under the Method. Jaspers—arrogant, authoritative—changes into the General, "buckles on sword, tips hat forward, climbs on horse, gallops in circle, comes back to Michaels" and commands: "Tie that redskin up." Michaels, who followed Jaspers's orders in securing a hired murderer, now changes into the obedient bluecoat, responding with a "Yes, sir!" Gregory, who is about to be interrogated by Jaspers and coerced into signing a confession, becomes the Indian, laughing derisively and refusing to sign the treaty even when tortured (163–64).[12] Or Jaspers, exhausted from Gregory's refusal to sign, becomes a fifteen-year-old dying in Jamestown: "Please, water . . . a taste . . . only one . . . then I'll ask for nothing more . . . a drop. . . ." The others take verbal jabs at the absent Captain Smith, creating a portrait of a hellish old "pisspot"—not unlike Michaels's and Gregory's perception of Jaspers—and cursing the day they "signed on this voyage." As the lad's life fades, Gregory becomes Captain Smith, assuming the position of authority figure and father (173–74). In both cases, history provides an analogy that works through association of the relationships and emotions of the past with those of the present. In this duo of vignettes, the actor (and, by association, Jaspers) becomes both father and son, tormentor and tormented, the dominant figure and the submissive one.

If history provides a subtext for the centering situation, so also do the collection of offbeat characters recognizable to any contemporary audience: the vaudeville trio, drag queens, and gangsters. Earlier I spoke of how at times the prisoners discuss and act out events of the recent past, sometimes reshaping them in response to their needs, and how Gregory, when encouraged by Michaels, speaks of his dream and, on his own initiative, tells the story of the woman whom an interior snake emaciated and killed. In describing two of the play's alternate situations—the General Custer and Captain vignettes—I spoke of shifting situations and roles, in which the audience is asked to think of the historical characters and relationships in the context of the centering situation and the characters and relationships of the centering situation in the context of the historical vignettes. Halfway through the drama, Terry has the actors wrap themselves in a prison blanket, lock arms, and break into a song and dance, then shift into a vignette as drag queens, then into one as gangsters; thus, she is introducing another order of transformation, one that crosses the line between the centering situation and the alternate situation through more than analogy. In these vignettes, the actors retain their identities as Jaspers, Michaels, and Gregory even as they engage in the transformation, so that style and tone reflect the drag queen or gangster even as content betrays their prison identities. The shift between role playing and transformation is subtle and ill defined, a tactic that requires the audience to think of the three cellmates at the same time it is thinking of the offbeat figures.

Here again, we have relationships similar to those profiled in the historical vignettes: Jaspers becomes the dominant queen; joined by Michaels, he torments Gregory, who tries to swallow an embarrassing love note. But "Swinging Woolf's" love note was "sent to this cell" (179), apparently by a prisoner, or perhaps by a guard, attracted to one of the three cellmates. In the gangster vignette, Michaels's movie gangster discusses his seduction of Gregory's movie gangster as he primed him for the murder assignment. To Michaels's gangster's "I buy lots of slobs drinks when I want a few laughs," Gregory's gangster, or Gregory, replies, "Some laugh. You're in for life for a few laughs. You aren't laughing now" (180).

These offbeat vignettes comment as well on the peculiar way in which a uniquely modern character, both national and individual, takes form. These products of Hollywood—singers and dancers, drag queens, and movie gangsters—are merely another part of the propaganda machine that advertises for an ingenue or a leading lady. These seemingly harmless representations of humanity are surface rather than substance, which, through mass dissemination, acquire legitimacy of form. Terry's introduction of these recognizable pieces of Hollywood celluloid wrenches us away from the individual confinement of the prisoners and reminds us of the social and personal confinements that media stereotyping prescribes.

The culminating vignette of the play, in which Jaspers becomes a preacher, his cellmates altar boys, and then the three become father and sons, brings together the centering situation, the transformation vignettes, and the vignettes in which role playing and transformation are difficult to divide. Having just tried to persuade Gregory to help him get Michaels to confess, the actor playing Jaspers, or Jaspers, changes abruptly into a preacher, speaking before a congregation about a man "in our midst" (194) accused of murdering his wife. After delivering an exhausting sermon that warns the congregation of impending losses and urges community as a countering strength, the preacher collapses into the arms of Michaels and Gregory, who become Jaspers's eight-year-old son, Richard, and his ten-year-old, Mark. Both offer comfort to their father, assuring him that "Mommie's in heaven" (196); then all three engage in a chanting prayer to "Our father, Our Father" (197–98).

In his notes to the Open Theatre production, Feldman remarks that he took it that "Jaspers' mind cracks completely at the end, and the 'Dearly Beloved' speech shows him in the midst of a wild, pseudo-religious, ecstatic delusion."[13] Yet Walters's notes reveal that he told his actor not to play Jaspers playing a priest but simply to play a priest.[14] That the two directors approached the moment with opposing assumptions suggests the complexity of this culminating vignette, in which a preacher who looks just like Jaspers says what Jaspers would have said had Jaspers been in the pulpit—or in which Jaspers himself (or a Jaspers who has lost touch with himself) orates. The figure in the pulpit is at once a preacher before his congregation, one of any number of TV evangelists (Feldman used a Cardinal Cushing oration as his model),[15] Jaspers in prison adopting the role of a preacher, and a mentally incompetent Jaspers who has collapsed under the moral weight of confinement, isolation, and loss. The vignette curiously accommodates the social-psychological-moral inscriptions of realistic drama, urging affirmation of the invariables of human relationships and experience that the previous vignettes individually and collectively record. But it departs from the realistic model in not yielding to the static face. This shifting portrait of Jaspers provides a stage image not of the morally accountable, psychologically consistent, socially defined self that Krutch values but of the dynamic process of character formation and the multiple layers that constitute an anatomy of self.

Terry's understanding of transformational drama as more than an acting exercise, as an opportunity to explore with intelligence and with force the modes of self-definition in a contemporary arena, helped move American theater beyond the cliché. A decade after Terry's work with transformational drama at the Open, Sam Shepard, acknowledged high priest of off-Broadway, framed a note to actors in *Angel City:*

> Instead of the idea of a "whole character" with logical motives behind his behavior which the actor submerges himself into, he should consider instead a fractured whole with bits and pieces of characters flying off the central scheme. Collage instruction, jazz improvisation. Music or painting in space.[16]

Shepard might have been describing Terry's transformational drama, created a decade earlier at the Open.

If Terry's work with redefining character has found legitimacy in the American theater, so also has it been instrumental in establishing feminist theater. In *Feminist Theatre,* Helène Keyssar calls Terry the mother of the phenomenon.[17] Yet in the sixties, when Terry was active in New York, feminist theater did not even have a name. Today's Terry calls herself a feminist—and a humorist, and a humanist, and, most importantly, a theater person[18]—yet her motherhood rightly began at the Open, not because she was writing plays for and about women (which she was) nor because she was shaping a feminist party line (which she wasn't), but because she was writing transformational drama. That form's theatrical efforts at dismantling the stereotype, freeing the actor from the prescriptiveness of an assigned role, and re-evaluating the institutional hierarchy speak with force to the comparable goals of feminism. Whether or not Terry was writing plays at the Open that we would now call feminist, her work in neutralizing fixed assumptions was seminal in preparing off Broadway for the gender deconstructions of the burgeoning phenomenon we now call feminist theater. In an interview with Diane Leavitt in 1977, Terry spoke of her desire to "explore the possibilities of what a woman could be." "We don't know what a woman could be like" she said, "because we've had so many outlines and definitions forced upon us."[19]

Terry dedicated *Keep Tightly Closed* to Chaikin, whose words began this paper. Perhaps it would be appropriate to end as well with a quotation from Chaikin's *The Presence of the Actor:*

> The joy in theatre comes through discovery and the capacity to discover. What limits the discoveries a person can make is the idea or image he [or she] may come to have of himself [or herself].[20]

Terry's theater is a theater of discovery, in which all things, and joy, are possible.

Notes

1. Joseph Chaikin, *The Presence of the Actor: Notes on the Open Theater, Disguises, Acting, and Repression* (New York: Atheneum, 1972), p. 13.
2. Ibid., pp. 12–14.
3. Peter Feldman, "Notes for the Open Theatre Production," in *Viet Rock: Four Plays by Megan Terry* (New York: Simon and Schuster, 1967), p. 201.
4. Joseph Wood Krutch, *"Modernism" in Modern Drama: A Definition and an Estimate* (Ithaca: Cornell University Press, 1953), p. 77.
5. Ibid., p. 78.
6. Feldman, "Notes for the Open Theatre Production," p. 199.
7. Bonnie Marranca and Gautam Dasgupta, *American Playwrights: A Critical Survey*, vol. 1 (New York: Drama Books Specialists, 1981), p. 185.
8. Richard Schechner, "The Playwright as Wrighter," in *Viet Rock: Four Plays by Megan Terry* (New York: Simon and Schuster, 1967), p. 16.
9. Ibid., p. 13.
10. Gerald Weales, *The Jumping-Off Place: American Drama in the 1960's* (London: Macmillan, 1969), p. 240.
11. Chaikin, *The Presence of the Actor*, p. 6.
12. Megan Terry, *Keep Tightly Closed in a Cool Dry Place*, in *Viet Rock: Four Plays by Megan Terry* (New York: Simon and Schuster, 1967), pp. 153–209. Subsequent references are cited parenthetically by page number.

13. Feldman, "Notes for the Open Theatre Production," p. 204.

14. Sidney S. Walter, "Notes for the Firehouse Theatre Production," in *Viet Rock: Four Plays by Megan Terry* (New York: Simon and Schuster, 1967), p. 208.

15. Feldman, "Notes for the Open Theatre Production," p. 204.

16. Richard Gilman, "Introduction," to Sam Shepard, *Seven Plays* (New York: Bantam Books, 1981), pp. xv–xvi.

17. Helene Keyssar, *Feminist Theatre: An Introduction to Plays of Contemporary British and American Women* (London: Macmillan, 1984), p. 53.

18. Dinah L. Leavitt, "Megan Terry" [Interview], in *Women in American Theatre: Careers, Images, Movements: An Illustrated Anthology and Sourcebook*, ed. Helen Krich Chinoy and Linda Walsh Jenkins (New York: Crown Publishers, 1981), p. 286.

19. Leavitt, "Megan Terry," p. 288.

20. Chaikin, *The Presence of the Actor*, p. 1.

13
No Place But the Funnyhouse: The Struggle for Identity in Three Adrienne Kennedy Plays

Susan E. Meigs

> I know no places. That is I cannot believe in places. To believe in places is to know hope and to know the emotion of hope is to know beauty. It links us across a horizon and connects us to the world. I find there are no places only my *funnyhouse*.
>
> —Adrienne Kennedy, *Funnyhouse of a Negro*

In 1960, while dramatists were forging a rhetoric of black theater from the emerging black power movement, twenty-nine-year-old Adrienne Kennedy travelled to Africa with her husband and son. The trip would prove to be the catalyst for her career as one of America's most complex contemporary playwrights. At the time of her trip, Kennedy had been writing stories and plays for nearly ten years and had received virtually no public attention. Her failure to establish herself as a writer was made more discouraging by the recognition her husband Joseph Kennedy received for his work in social psychology at Columbia. She felt increasingly that she "was just accompanying another person as he lived out his dreams" and that she had acquiesced "to another person's desires, dreams and hopes."[1] As she struggled to maintain her identity as a black woman author and attempted to invest herself in the Western literary tradition she embraced, Kennedy grew conscious of a buried African heritage. Africa opened to her a world of black artists and leaders, like Congo Prime Minister Patrice Lumumba, to match and challenge the Western literary figures and rulers she admired. The conflict between these two ancestral traditions would become one of the primary themes in Kennedy's complex, surrealistic psychodramas.

Although her rhetoric maintains a political agenda, albeit one aimed more at expressing black women's struggles, Kennedy's method draws from the mythic elements of traditional African ritual drama, particularly the Kuntu form described by Paul Carter Harrison. Ritual drama empowers its participants as they negotiate their roles within its theatrical community. Kennedy discovered, however, that these roles, designated like those in many black protest groups by men, fail to allow female participants self-determination. This dissonance in the fragmented black family/community impedes the collective expression of harmony required of ritual theater. "Having been fractionalized, [the black American's] rituals are often played out in a spiritual vacuum, [her] energies dissipated without the generative feedback of a stable society."[2] Kennedy's plays address the cultural and political fragmentation of black Americans that occurs when a dominant (white) social structure interrupts efforts to construct a black community.

Kennedy uses this damaged social identity in her plays as a symptom of the deeper psychological fragmentation black women suffer. Kennedy particularly uses the mask, a traditional symbol of power and mystery, as a device to develop what Michael Goldman calls "the double movement of dramatic elation—both escape from self and self-discovery."[3] Kennedy undermines this empowerment and elation, however, and transforms the mask into an image of imprisonment and terror. Many of her characters become trapped in the mask's freakish impersonality and are unable either to discover themselves fully or to escape from the horrifying selves they do discover.

In three of Kennedy's plays, *Funnyhouse of a Negro* (1964), *The Owl Answers* (1965), and *A Movie Star Has to Star in Black and White* (1976), the protagonists are black women who fail to unite the fragmented elements of their identities into harmonic, dynamic wholes. Their equally fragmented communities have failed to provide them with the ritual means for locating themselves and have made them feel guilty for recognizing the extra measure of alienation assigned to black women. These characters represent the community of women, largely excluded from the political mechanisms of black protest, who are nonetheless expected to sacrifice gender issues for racial concerns. In these three one-act plays, Kennedy exposes how black Americans, especially women, having been denied a social context and history, are therefore powerless to resolve the chaotic elements of their black female identities.

In *Funnyhouse of a Negro*, Sarah seeks to find herself among four historical figures who share her voice: Queen Victoria, the Duchess of Hapsburg, Jesus, and Patrice Lumumba. Although she lives in a brownstone with her Jewish boyfriend, she mentally inhabits the expressionistic settings suggested by these figures. After her mad mother introduces the play's action, Sarah and her selves confront her fear that her father will find and rape her as he did her mulatto mother. She imagines his various fates, including one in which she bludgeons him with an ebony mask. Herself a mulatto, Sarah's conflicting racial histories are illustrated but never resolved by the figures that serve as her masks. Far from empowering her, these character masks trap Sarah in a role of self-hatred, fear, and the inability to integrate her personality that leads to her suicide.

Kennedy introduces the mask motif in the play's first sequence. Sarah's mad mother passes before the closed curtain wearing an eyeless yellow mask that renders her not only blind but faceless. She gropes across the stage in a dreamlike state we later learn is death, separated from the "life" of the play only by the rat-eaten shroud of a white stage curtain. She carries before her a bald head, an image of weakness that recurs as Sarah's selves lose their wild, kinky hair throughout the play. Although Kennedy later introduces a bald head that drops and hangs from the ceiling to indicate the martyrdom of Christ and Lumumba, the baldness of Victoria and the Duchess is more "hideous" and frightening because it links them to Sarah's dead mother. For Sarah, baldness indicates not only death but also a life of repulsion, vulnerability, and madness. As her female selves lose their hair, the threat of her father's return, of a confrontation with her irreconcilable blackness, grows imminent. Unable to cope with the jungle's darkness, Sarah attempts to hide herself in a white city.

During the course of the play, two historical characters who represent her white heritage assume Sarah's psychological narrative. These alter-egos, Queen Victoria and the Duchess of Hapsburg, also wear white, expressionless death masks and are cast in a strong white light that contrasts with the stage's unnatural darkness. These other selves express Sarah's thoughts while the connotations of their historical identities comment on them. The sense of power and authority evoked by the two European rulers cannot be appropriated properly by Sarah, who is neither white nor black. Their imperialistic implications comment on the extent of Sarah's psychological oppression, one history a victim of the other. Nonetheless, she spends her days writing poetry that imitates Edith Sitwell's and dreaming of living in a white, European culture. She attempts to efface her black heritage not only by "killing" her father but by injecting herself into white society. She claims to need these white figures "as an embankment to keep me from reflecting too much upon the fact that I am a Negro. For, like all educated Negroes . . . I find it necessary to maintain a stark fortress against recognition of myself" (133).[4] The expressionless masks of the two rulers serve both to identify an aspect of Sarah's historical identity and to alienate her from it. In the play's final scene, Sarah is discovered hanging from the ceiling of her "funnyhouse" as the lights come up on the white plaster statue of Queen Victoria. Enshrined in Sarah's room, she is finally reduced to a voiceless, immobile image of "astonishing repulsive whiteness" (147). When Sarah dies, the masked figures that have given body to her voice are stripped of their narrative power. They become hollowed references to a history that is finally unavailable to Sarah.

The persona of Patrice Lumumba, whom Sarah both adopts and associates with her father, differs from the first two in that he is black and carries rather than wears his ebony mask. Because Lumumba acts as a bridge between Sarah and her father, he represents both the black man's noble efforts to save his race and her inescapable and damning blackness. Lumumba, murdered by African radicals who smashed his skull, appears in the play with a split and bleeding head. At one point, as Sarah explains how she killed her father, she confuses him with Lumumba: "No, Mrs. Conrad, he did not hang himself, that is only the way they understood it, they do, but the truth is that I bludgeoned his head with an ebony skull that he carries about with him. Wherever he goes, he carries out black masks and heads" (134–35). Sarah's previous statements about her desires to integrate into white society are repudiated by an unidentified black man who recalls Lumumba because he too carries his mask: "I am a nigger of two generations. I am Patrice Lumumba. . . . I am the black shadow that haunted my mother's conception. . . . It is my vile dream to live in rooms with European antiques and my statue of Queen Victoria" (139).

Because Sarah is a mulatto, she cannot wear the masks of both the Negro and the white woman simultaneously. As the mask signifies the character's fragmented identity, the mulatto bastard becomes a metaphor for the black woman's alienation from her gender and her race. Sarah attempts to reconcile her identity as a mulatto by claiming to have murdered her black father. She is unable to conceal her hatred of him for literally blackening her family. Sarah conflates her story with his story as she recalls how her grandmother encouraged her father to become a black Messiah. Sarah believes he betrayed her wish and his future family by marrying a light-toned woman with "hair as straight as any white woman's" (130). His mother "hoped he would be Christ but he failed. He had married [Sarah's] mother because he could not resist the light. Yet, his mother from the beginning in the kerosene lamp of their dark rooms in Georgia said, 'I want you to be Jesus, to walk in Genesis and save the race, return to Africa, find revelation in the black'" (144). To fulfill his mother's vision, he takes his white wife to Africa to pursue mission work. There she "falls out of live" with him and slowly goes mad, symbolized by her gradual hair loss. He rapes her when she denies him access to the marriage bed because he is black and creates a legacy of violence, madness, and failure for their daughter Sarah. " 'Forgiveness for my being black, Sarah. I *know* you are a child of torment. . . . *Forgive my blackness!*' " her father pleads (144). But Sarah can neither accept nor escape her own blackness: "before I was born," she laments, "he haunted my conception, diseased my birth" (131).

Sarah seeks to neutralize her blackness by living with her white boyfriend, Raymond Mann, whom she wishes she could love but doesn't, in an apartment run by a white landlady, Mrs. Conrad. These two white characters in Sarah's "funnyhouse" are modelled after the looming clownlike figures that guard an amusement park in Kennedy's hometown, Cleveland. The set for the scene in which Raymond and the Duchess of Hapsburg engage in a bizarre exchange includes a backdrop of mirrors, revealed only as Raymond alternately opens and closes the blinds that conceal them. The flashing mirrors recall the disorienting nightmare quality of what is ironically called a funnyhouse. Raymond and Mrs. Conrad laugh, in accordance with their roles as funnyhouse guards, at Sarah's bewilderment and failure to distinguish herself from her historical reflections. They mock her attempts to gain self-knowledge and control over the conflicting elements of her persona. When she is unable to do so, Sarah hangs herself. After discovering her body, Mrs. Conrad and Raymond suggest that Sarah's father is not dead but lives in a white suburb with a white prostitute. He and his "whore" join the other white characters in the funnyhouse who, in refusing to understand or sympathize with Sarah's internal struggle, derive ironic amusement from her desperate suicide. " 'She was a funny little liar,' " Raymond comments as he observes her hanging figure. Mrs. Conrad can only offer the unsympathetic remark, " 'The poor bitch has hung herself!' " (147). Sarah, ultimately powerless to reconcile and integrate her conflicting selves and incongruent historical narratives, chooses to abandon the white funnyhouse. That Sarah recognizes no escape other than suicide testifies to the insidiousness of her tragedy. Unable to move beyond feebly articulating her oppression, Sarah can neither appropriate the power of her masks, as Harrison might suggest, nor follow the mandate of Amiri Baraka's militant theater to create white-free spaces for blacks. To excise her whiteness would leave Sarah vulnerable to a terrifying blackness she cannot control.

Kennedy continues to explore the fragmented psyche of the female mulatto in *The Owl Answers*. Rather than function as mouthpieces for a single character's states of mind, however, the play's characters are each composed of multiple personae with a common voice. As the stage directions indicate, "The characters change slowly back and forth into and out of themselves, leaving some garment from their previous selves upon them always to remind us of the nature of SHE WHO IS CLARA PASSMORE WHO IS THE VIRGIN MARY WHO IS THE BASTARD WHO IS THE OWL'S world" (170).[5]

Like Sarah, Clara Passmore is the bastard product of an illicit relationship between "The Richest White Man in Town" and his black cook. After her mother dies, probably in childbirth, the cold Reverend and Mrs. Passmore adopt her. When her legitimate father dies and Clara is barred from the funeral, she travels instead to England to claim his British heritage. There she confronts three representatives of that heritage, Shakespeare, Chaucer, and William the Conqueror, who deny her access to it. Theirs is a white male tradition that finds little space for black women. Clara envisions her Negro heritage as a father, incarcerated and executed by the three masked figures, whose peeling white skin reveals a deeper, darker skin color. Clara's characterization of herself as "the ancestor of somebody that cooked for somebody and William the Conqueror" (179) further illustrates the conflict between her English heritage and the black ancestry it seeks to suppress. In the course of the play, her Dead Father, the white father who never acknowledged her as his child, encourages her to repudiate her "blackness": "He came to me in the outhouse . . . He told me you are an owl, ow, oww, I am your beginning, ow. You belong here with us owls in the fig tree, not to somebody that cooks for your Goddam Father" (178).

Goddam Father is concomitantly the Richest White Man in the Town, the Dead White Father, and the Reverend Passmore. Through her association with the Reverend Passmore and his "Holy Baptist church on the top of the hill" (179), She Who is Clara Passmore . . . becomes (the Virgin) Mary, to whom an altar is built in the course of the play. "The Reverend's Wife goes on building the High Altar with owl feathers, prays, builds, prays, stops, holds out her hand to She, puts up candles, puts up owl feathers, laughs, puts more candles on the High Altar" (183). The altar becomes a bed upon which a Negro Man attempts to seduce She. . . . In the final moments of the play, "They are upon the burning High Altar. He tried to force her down, yet at the same time he is frightened by her. The Dead Father who has been holding the candles, smiles" (186). Despite his attempts to "whiten" She . . ., he laughs in cruel recognition of her inability to be completely the mulatto bastard or Clara, the adopted daughter of the Reverend Passmore, the pure Virgin Mary, or the white "owl" of her (fore)fathers. She . . . is all and none of these. She . . . cannot conceal from the Negro Man who seduces her that underneath her clothing her body is black; yet one of the figures with which she is affiliated is Anne Boleyn, a white historical figure imprisoned and executed by a white patriarchy.

Representing that patriarchy, Chaucer, Shakespeare, and William the Conqueror wear masks that not only serve to identify them but allow them to oppress in anonymity. The mystery and power of the Kuntu mask is reserved for members of the white patriarchy and those complicit in it, who use its power to dominate and suppress the black and the woman. She . . .'s vision of a white history imprisoning and dismantling her black identity in the form of her Negro Father shatters her dreams of "love" and freedom from the internal conflict this domination creates.

> They took him away and would not let me see him. They who are my Black Mother and my Goddam Father locked me in the fig tree and took his body away and his white hair hung down.
>
> Now they, my Black Mother and my Goddam Father who pretend to be Chaucer, Shakespeare, and Eliot and all my beloved English, come to my cell and stare and I can see they despise me and I despise them . . .
>
> From my Tower I keep calling and the only answer is the Owl, God. I am only yearning for our kingdom, God. (185)

Kennedy's use of bird imagery is most poignant in her characterization of She . . . as the Owl. In contrast to the play's haunting raven and God's white dove, the owl can see through the darkness that empowers it. But for Clara, the silence of the darkness and of the owl's world undermines its power. Although She . . . struggles to define her own historical and psychological space, the play's surrealistic dreamscapes merge. Clara stands at the base of St. Paul's Chapel as she confronts a seducer on the subway platform, as she perches in the fig tree. She rebuffs the Negro Man on the burning high altar/bed with a knife covered in the owl's blood and feathers, which are her own. As she burns on Mary's altar, her feathers fly like the pages of her journal, and her silence is broken only by the echoes of the owl's unanswerable question "Ow . . . oww" whooo? (187).

In *A Movie Star Has to Star in Black and White*, Kennedy complicates the issue of masks and personae by incorporating movie stars who don the masks of film roles. This multiplicity of personae is emphasized and heightened as the film characters become mouthpieces for the protagonist, Clara, at the same time they constitute her personal history for the audience. Clara's characterization occurs through a complex and often ironic system of projections and transferences of voice and symbolic significations. Her internal monologues and dialogues are prompted by her brother Wally's near fatal accident that serves to reunite her with her divorced parents. Clara's own marital conflicts over her desire for a career as a writer and her husband Eddie's desire to pursue his academic career at Columbia while Clara raises their expanding family (she is carrying Eddie's child) are examined in light of her parents' failed marriage.

Clara's concerns are voiced by the movie stars Bette Davis, Jean Peters, and Shelley Winters, whose film characters and narratives in their respective films *Voyage Out*, *Viva Zapata*, and *A Place in the Sun* are superimposed on Clara's own narrative. The play takes on the dimensions and properties of the "well-made" Hollywood movie in the opening scene, in which the Columbia Pictures Lady appears in a brilliant light to introduce the "film's" stars and sets. The story is Clara's, but she plays only a bit part. Her perceptions and reflections make up the plot, yet the film characters who give them voice separate her from them.

As playwright or, rather, screenplay writer, Clara seeks to write/right the script of her life so that she may play a more active, starring role in it than mere spectator. She works to activate the desires she records in her diary and to construct a unifying narrative from the pieces of her voice that have been distributed among the female movie stars. Clara suppresses her desire to construct a coherent self that can "co-exist in a true union" with other selves, however, by casting herself as an "angel of mercy" in her parents' marriage (55–56).[6] Displaced from her own narrative and unable to dispel her fear that she will miscarry, as she did in her first pregnancy, Clara projects her despair onto her parents. Blaming herself for not being able to unify them, Clara laments her failure:

> When I came among them it seems to me I did not bring them peace . . . but made them more disconsolate. The crosses they bore always made me sad.
>
> The one reality I wanted never came true . . . to be their angel of mercy to unite them. (56)

Bette Davis voices these reflections on the ship set of *Voyage Out*. In the film, her character achieves a fulfilling transformation on her voyage, a bleak contrast to Clara's attempt to transform her (family's) life by journeying into her parents' past. As Bette Davis, Clara pores over her father's scrapbook and discovers her parents' journey of transformation. Their trip takes them from the rural, segregated South, where whites live on one side of the town and blacks on the other, to a more "progressive" Cincinnati. There, Clara's father becomes active in community work and receives a commendation from the city's mayor for his seven years of work on the New Settlement for the Negro community. His achievements in the North, like those of Bette Davis's character, however, are fleeting and ultimately unsatisfying. After an unsuccessful suicide attempt, he leaves Clara and her mother, returns to Georgia, and marries "a girl who talked to willow trees" (57). He tells Clara that he left her "yellow bastard" mother because she wouldn't accompany him back to Georgia and because she thought herself superior to him. "You know Mr. Harrison raised her like a white girl, and your mother, mark my word, thinks she's better than me" (67).

Her father's effort to escape the racial oppression of Georgia, like Clara's own attempt to reconstitute her family in her memories, like Bette Davis's character's attempt to maintain her transformed self in the face of her mother's neuroses, fails and leads to greater despair. Not only does Clara fail to unify her parents, she is unsuccessful in redeeming herself as harmonizer in her own marriage. The affirmation of the marriage union in the *Viva Zapata* wedding night scene, which is superimposed on the *Voyage Out* set, is ironically juxtaposed to the confrontations between Clara's parents and between her and Eddie. These marital conflicts are deviations from the Hollywood norm, epitomized in the union of Jean Peters's femininity and Marlon Brando's virility. Neither Clara's parents nor she and Eddie are able to live up to the social roles designated by the masks of Peters and Brando's characters.

While Clara suffers the weight of her own guilt, her mother believes that by failing to please her husband she contributed to the dissolution of her daughter's family. She urges Clara to return to Eddie because she is pregnant, despite Clara's insistence that Eddie does not understand her. Like Eddie, Clara's mother cannot understand how her desire to be a writer can supersede the desire to raise a family:

> *Mother.* Your family's not together and you don't seem happy. . . .
> *Clara.* I'm very happy mother. Very. I've just won an award and I'm going to have a play produced. I'm very happy. . . .
> *Mother.* When you grow up in boarding school like I did, the thing you dream of most is to see your children together with their families.
> *Clara.* Mother you mustn't think I'm unhappy because I am, I really am, very happy.
> *Mother.* I just pray you'll soon get yourself together and make some decisions about your life. I pray for you every night. Shouldn't you go back to Eddie especially since you're pregnant? (62)

Clara is trapped by social values that prove insufficient for expressing her identity as a black woman author. Because she and her mother cannot live up to white or black social expectations, they suffer for abdicating their designated roles as mother and wife.

Because the only roles that are available to Clara are those fashioned by a white patriarchy in Hollywood or a black patriarchy in New York, she initially accepts Jean Peters's role of self-sacrificing wife. She suppresses her awareness of its repressiveness and berates herself for not properly wearing its mask. Clara is finally unable to justify playing the role that provides her with so little satisfaction when she becomes increasingly aware of its "darkness" and her resulting "floating anxiety" (59). Because he relies on Clara to continue playing her proper role, however, Eddie is suspicious of her "obsession to be a writer" and dismisses it as unrealistic and unnecessary (66).

Nevertheless, despite her family's objection, Clara shifts the focus of her unifying efforts from her parents and her marriage to herself and works to unite her fractured and diffused self through her writings. Whereas Clara plays only a bit part in the play's narrative, she exerts some of the constructive power of the mask when she exchanges her wifely mask for that of the writer. Although her social environment forces her to choose between the two, she finally attempts to invest herself fully in the role that allows her the most power and fulfillment. Scattered throughout the play are excerpts from the play she is writing, which is Kennedy's play, *The Owl Answers*. As Jean Peters, Clara explains to her film husband Marlon Brando, "It's about a girl who turns into an Owl. Ow. (*Recites from her writings.*) He came to me in the outhouse, in the fig tree. He told me, 'You are an owl, I am your beginning.' I call God and the Owl answers. It haunts my tower, calling" (64). Following this description, Clara's slightly drunk father staggers toward her and her mother and rushes out of the hospital lobby where they have been waiting to see Wally. The image of the owl that represents the protagonist's white ancestry in Kennedy's earlier play is juxtaposed in *A Movie Star* to her black father, her "goddam father," who fails in the white northern city and retreats to the South. Although Clara's family and film stars silence and mask her, she hopes to voice publicly and thus resolve her despair by writing a play about it.

This desire to achieve self-actualization is represented by the character Shelley Winters portrays in *A Place in the Sun*. For Kennedy, Winters's role depicts the "essence of longing,"[7] a longing that persists throughout the last third of the play. Clara's desire for fulfillment is transposed onto Shelley Winters's character. None of the actresses takes on the role of Clara, although they voice her thoughts and feelings; the voice is Clara's. Nonetheless, the resonances of their characters and films are superimposed onto Clara's narrative in such a way that they simultaneously comment on it. The stage reflects the layering of characters and plots in that the "fantasy" sets and actors from the three films remain on stage alongside the corresponding "realistic" sets of the hospital lobby, Wally's hospital room, and Clara's old room from childhood. Clara's longing to act out her life in these secure movie sets is mirrored in Shelley Winters's obsessive desire for Montgomery Clift in *A Place in the Sun*. In the final moments of the play, a union of character and voice occurs when Clara and Winters speak in harmony about Wally's hopeless prognosis. Almost immediately following this union, however, Shelley Winters falls into the water on which her "dark" boat has been floating and drowns while Montgomery Clift looks helplessly on. That she can only call silently for help signifies the fleeting and precarious power of the theatrical/literary mask through which Clara tries to express her "floating anxiety."

The voicelessness of Montgomery Clift and the other male stars, Paul Henreid and Marlon Brando, indicates their inappropriateness as voices for Clara's identity. She cannot speak through them, and they cannot speak for or with her because she rejects them, finds them inaccessible. In her mental narrative, Clara does attempt to give voice to the play's most significant silent male, her brother Wally, around whom the play's surface action revolves. His silence not only is a result of his paralyzing accident but is noticeable particularly when he returns from duty on the German front in World War II. As Clara recalls,

> Once I asked you romantically when you came back to the United States on a short leave, how do you like Europe Wally? You were silent. Finally you said, I get into a lot of fights with the Germans. You stared at me. And got up and went into the dining room to the dark sideboard and got a drink. (pp. 60–61)

Later, in the persona of Jean Peters, Clara reveals that Wally was court-martialed for a crime he committed in the army in Germany. "He won't talk about it," she says. "I went to visit him in the stockade" (68). Her description of his shaven head and "vein that runs down his forehead" recalls his appearance in the hospital bed. She describes his successive failures to become an Olympic athlete: "I'm a failure he said. I can't make it in those schools. I'm tired. He suddenly joined the army" (68). Because of his lack of education, Wally cannot even appropriate the literary tools that represent his sister's hope for self-fulfillment. His wife graduates cum laude while he is a prisoner in the army stockade. Only by being silenced, or rather silencing himself, in an automobile accident, that renders him brain dead does Wally finally avoid the madness of coping not with a surplus of voices and roles but with a lack of viable identities.

In the postscript to her *People Who Led to My Plays*, Kennedy states that "my plays are meant to be states of mind." These states of mind not only are her own but belong to her entire race of "Negroes," whom she characterizes as "underdogs, and underdogs must fight in life."[8] In these plays, Kennedy exposes the barriers black women face in their struggle for power, voice, and unity. The double binds of race and gender produce the black anguish that afflicts the plays' protagonists. The roles that the white and black communities offer these women, like the masks they wear, threaten to silence them and efface their identities in a miasma of conflicting historical connotations.

Written during the black protest movements of the seventies, these plays evolved in the ideological space between the agitprop theater of Amiri Baraka and the ritual drama of Paul Carter Harrison. Although Kennedy recognized the political power of Harrison's theater to revitalize the black community spiritually and of Baraka's to incite it to militant protest, she cut to a deeper level of psychological oppression. Her plays reveal the disorientation and despair of black women who can find no other space for themselves but the funnyhouse.

Notes

1. Adrienne Kennedy, *People Who Led To My Plays* (New York: Alfred A Knopf, 1987), pp. 122–23.
2. Paul Carter Harrison, *The Drama of Nommo* (New York: Grove Press, 1972), p. xv.
3. Michael Goldman, *The Actor's Freedom: Toward a Theory of Drama* (New York: Viking Press, 1975), p. 47.
4. Adrienne Kennedy, *Funnyhouse of a Negro*, in *The Best Short Plays, 1970*, ed. Stanley Richards (Philadelphia: Chilton Book Company, 1970), pp. 125–47. Subsequent references are cited parenthetically by page number.
5. Adrienne Kennedy, *The Owl Answers*, in *Kuntu Drama: Plays of the African Continuum*, ed. Paul Carter Harrison (New York: Grove Press, 1974), pp. 170–87. Subsequent references are cited parenthetically by page number.
6. Adrienne Kennedy, *A Movie Star Has To Star in Black and White*, in *Wordplays 3: An Anthology of New American Drama* (New York: Performing Arts Journal Publications, 1984). Subsequent references are cited parenthetically by page number.
7. Kennedy, *People Who Led To My Plays*, p. 97.
8. Ibid., p. 11.

14
Whose Name, Whose Protection: Reading Alice Childress's *Wedding Band*

Catherine Wiley

In the first act of *Wedding Band*, a scene of reading and performance occurs that lies at the center of a feminist interpretation of the play. Mattie, a black woman who makes her living selling candy and caring for a little white girl, has received a letter from her husband in the Merchant Marine and needs a translator for it. Her new neighbor, Julia, the educated outsider trying to fit into working-class surroundings, reads the sentimental sailor's letter aloud. After her performance, in which the women listening have actively participated, Mattie tells Julia that, in addition to his love, her husband gives her what is more important, his *name and protection*. These two standards of conventional love are denied Julia because her lover of ten years is white; and even Mattie learns that because she never divorced her first husband, she is not now legally married and cannot receive marital war benefits. Neither woman enjoys a man's name or his protection, in part because the chivalry implied in such privilege was unattainable for blacks in the Jim Crow society of 1918 South Carolina. The women in *Wedding Band* learn to depend on themselves and each other rather than on absent men, a self-reliance born painfully through self-acceptance.

Wedding Band received mixed reviews when it opened off-Broadway in 1972. It was described both as "the play about black life in America that isn't a 'black' play"[1] and too much "like a story wrenched from the pages of what used to be known as a magazine for women."[2] Interesting for their racist and sexist connotations, these comments betray the reviewers' uncritical assumptions about who constitutes a theater audience. The play doesn't look "black" because its integrationist subtext surfaces only occasionally and its political urgency is dressed safely in realistic period costume. New York theater patrons of 1972 applauding the drama as entertainment alone could assure themselves that the play's World War I setting depicted a reality long past. The first reviewer assumes that a "black" play, one that speaks primarily to a black audience, is implicitly alien and uninteresting to a white audience. Representations of so-called minority lives told from a minority point of view cannot interest the rest of us, if we are white. Likewise, the pages of a women's magazine would bore us if we were men, because they focus on the small, private issues of home and heart. And although none of the liberal reviewers profess any shock over the play's important theme of miscegination, no New York producers would touch *Wedding Band* until 1972, six years after it was written and first performed, attesting to the subject's unpopularity.

My reading of the play argues that its subject is less interracial heterosexual relations than the relations between black women and between black women and white women in World War I–era South Carolina. That said, I must add that I perceive a certain danger in trying to read feminist rather than racial politics into Alice Childress's play. White feminists must take care not to offer our own invaluable "name and protection" to black women writers who do not need them. For a feminist criticism that is not limited to the privileged location of many of its practitioners, it is crucial that white feminists read the work of black women, especially those like Childress who have been all but ignored in academic theater. We might read in the same spirit of canon disruption inspiring the informal creation of a women's literary counter-canon, recognizing that in the same way white women writers were denied membership in the old canon on the basis of "greatness," we may be guilty of blocking black women writers for the same reason. The value of a literary text cannot be defined out of context. White readers should try to decentralize our historically majority context—to see ourselves, for once, in the margins with respect to the Afro-American women's literary tradition. I recognize with dismay the truth of Hortense J. Spillers's statement: "When we say 'feminist' with an adjective in front of it, we mean, of course, white women, who, as a category of social and cultural agents, fully occupy the territory of feminism."[3] But does including Afro-American women writers in the canon, which seems to be my project in writing for this book, imitate a colonizing gesture? Am I offering the protection of the canon to Alice Childress, protection on the canon's (and for now, white women's) terms? Instead of attempting to answer these questions now, I can only say that I am beginning to learn to read black women's plays in the same way many feminists ask men to read women's texts. Rather than seeing myself reflected in their work, I want to understand why my difference makes these plays a challenge to read.

Difference has become a feminist catch-word, complicated by its dual usage as what makes women different from men as well as what makes women different from each other. Teresa de Lauretis and Linda Gordon have argued recently that the first definition, which makes women's primary characteristic the fact that we are not men, risks becoming a substitute for women's opposition to men's discriminatory practice. This opposition, however, has always differed from one group of women to another, because our discrimination as women has always differed.[4] The various ways we have resisted male practice through history define women as much as what we have in common biologically. It is not enough for white feminists merely to tolerate women of color or invite them to join our canon, but to understand how we are different, to understand differences among women as differences within women. Because, in de Lauretis' words, "not only does feminism exist despite those differences, but . . . it cannot continue to exist without them."[5]

Many of these differences, especially between black women and white women in the United States, have been constituted historically. As Childress writes in the *Negro Digest* of April 1967, her newest play, *Wedding Band,* serves as a reminder of the many promises made in 1918 that are still unkept in 1967.[6] During the gap between the play's initial production in 1966 at the University of Michigan and today, most of the promises of integration have been fulfilled legally; however, we still have much to learn of the limits of the successes of the civil rights movement. Although the *Negro Digest* article refers specifically to the Jim Crow laws prohibiting intermarriage, Childress's play can be read today as a history lesson pointed at white women to remind them and us, in 1966 or now, that our vision of sisterly equality has always left some sisters out. Until the Civil War, the women's rights movement was essentially inseparable from the abolitionist movement. As Angelina Grimke, the southern white abolitionist, wrote in 1838:

> The discussion of the rights of the slave has opened the way for the discussion of other rights, and the ultimate result will most certainly be the breaking of *every* yoke, the letting the oppressed of every grade and description go free,—an emancipation far more glorious than any the world has ever yet seen.[7]

But the interests of women fighting for decades to assure themselves a voice in the political process could not be reconciled to those of white politicians eager to take advantage of black men's votes. Despite their political training as abolitionists, most of the white suffragists were quick to forgo interracial solidarity as their own movement foundered in the Reconstruction era.[8]

Black women's frustration heard an echo a century later as the civil rights movement shifted from its origins in the rural south to the industrialized north. Hundreds of black women in the south led the grassroots movement for desegregation and voter registration in the late 1950s, and in the early 1960s they trained younger white women who had come down from northern colleges to take part in the Freedom Rides. The early civil rights movement had been affected most dramatically by an army of nameless women: black women who honed their leadership skills in the only place available to them, their churches. But in 1964, an anonymous paper about women's position in the Student Nonviolent Coordinating Committee (SNCC) circulated at the Waveland Conference, although assumed to be written by a black woman, was written by two white women who were trying to inject the civil rights movement with theories of women's liberation. Although these white women had learned invaluable skills, including the courage to withstand jailings, beatings, and death threats, from the black women, their influence in the overall movement dwindled in the mid-60s, partly because of their sexual liaisons with black men.[8] The Waveland Conference position paper, which criticized the assumption of male superiority at work in SNCC by comparing it with white superiority, marked the move of white women out of the civil rights movement and into the women's movement. Sexual discrimination in the civil rights movement forced white activists to confront their differences from black women in a way they had not since the struggle over voting rights a century earlier. The result of this confrontation, according to many historians, was the same: white women abandoned Afro-American liberation to pursue a goal closer to home, that of a race- and class-specific women's liberation.[9]

Set chronologically midway between the poles of Reconstruction and civil rights, *Wedding Band* describes an era when lynching presented one answer to demands for equality in the south, while Harlem flowered as a mecca for black culture in the north. In the 1960s, white women and black men's sexual relations generated tension in the black community, but miscegenation as the white master's rape of his slave retains deeper historical ramifications for black women. Childress's drama, subtitled "a love/hate story in black and white," takes place on the tenth anniversary of Julia and her white lover in the small backyard tenement to which Julia has moved after being evicted from countless other houses. Determined to get along with her nosy but well-meaning neighbors, Julia seems to have won a guarded acceptance until her lover, Herman, visits her. He has brought her a gold wedding band on a chain, and they plan to buy tickets on the Clyde Line to New York, where Julia will proudly and legally bear Herman's name. But Herman succumbs to the influenza epidemic, and in the second act he lies in Julia's bed waiting for his mother and sister to take him to a white doctor. Julia's landlady has refused to help because it is illegal for Herman to be in Julia's house, and she cannot appear to sanction Julia's immoral behavior. Herman's mother sides with the landlady in preserving respectability even at the cost of her son's life, and she will not carry him to the doctor until it grows dark enough to hide him. In the last scene, Herman returns to Julia with the boat tickets, which she refuses to take because his mother has convinced her that blacks and whites can never live together. Finally she appears to relent so that Herman can die believing that Julia, even without him, will go north.

The secondary characters, however, more than the two lovers, underscore the drama's didactic politics. They are types, but not stereotypes, and their separate dilemmas and personalities describe the injustices blacks have endured in the south. The landlady, Fanny, the neighbors Mattie and Lula, Lula's adopted son, Nelson, and the abusive white traveling salesman give the stage community a historical idiosyncrasy missing from Julia and Herman's relationship. Fanny has proudly joined the middle-class by acquiring property and exploiting her tenants (in 1918 a relatively new possibility for black women) in the name of racial uplift. As homeworkers, Mattie and Lula exist bound to a variety of semi-skilled, low-paying jobs to feed their children. Nelson, as a soldier in the newly desegregated United States army, assumes that when the war is over he will be given the rights of a full citizen, even in South Carolina. He is a forerunner of the militant youth who would later provide the impatient voice to the nascent civil rights movement of the late 1940s, and whose dreams of integration would be realized only partially in the 1960s.

These characters who inhabit Miss Fanny's backyard tenement underscore the vexed issue of difference as explored by the feminist scholars cited above. Julia's problem throughout the play is less her white lover than her reluctance to see herself as a member of the black community. Although a mostly white theater audience would see her as a different sort of heroine because of race, her black neighbors perceive her as different from them for issues more complex than skin color. She assumes that her racial transgression with Herman will make her unwelcome among the women she wishes to confide in, but her aloofness from their day-to-day interests also serves as a protective shield. In this, Julia is similar to Lutie Johnson in Ann Petry's *The Street*, written in 1946.[10] Both characters are ostensibly defined by their unequal relations with men, but their potential for salvation lies in the larger community that depends on the stability of its women. Lutie Johnson is so determined to move off "the street" in Harlem she thinks is pulling her down that she refuses to join the community Harlem offers her, a community that in some ways defies the white society keeping it poor.

Neither poor nor uneducated, Julia finds herself defying the black community by asserting her right to love a white man, but this self-assertion is, in a larger sense, a more dangerous defiance of the white community. She wants her love story to be one of individual commitment and sacrifice, but it is that only in part. Julia's refinement in manners, education, and financial independence, which are middle-class, traditionally white attributes, make her and Herman available to each other. But theirs is, as the subtitle insists, a "love/hate" story, in which interracial love cannot be divorced from centuries of racial hate.

As *Wedding Band* opens, Julia sleeps on her bed in the new house while a little girl enters her yard weeping about a quarter she has lost. Her mother, Mattie, chases the girl, threatening to whip her unless she finds "the only quarter I got to my name," the quarter that was to buy the ingredients to make the candy she sells (78).[11] Julia tries to sleep through this scene, but she cannot hide from either the noise or the predicaments because the coin has rolled under her porch and Mattie is trying to knock it down to get at the money. When Julia tries to escape back into her private room after giving Mattie a quarter, Fanny follows her to discern whether or not the new tenant is "quality." In Fanny's eyes, Julia's ability to give quarters away without a second thought is an indication that her boarding-house business is improving. She gossips about the other women and says Mattie was low-class enough to have worked once washing "joy-towels" in a white whorehouse. Another neighbor, Lula, has her grown-up adopted son living with her, although the arrangement is in Fanny's eyes "'gainst nature" (80). Unmarried herself because she has to "bear the standard of the race" and "colored men don't know how to do nothin' right" (122), Fanny's notions of sexuality are as puritanical as they are ignorant. But according to the Bell Man who sold it to her, she is the first and only black woman in the country to own a silver-plated tea service, a symbol of her single-handed effort to improve the appearance of her race in the eyes of the white community.

The first white character to appear in the play is the Bell Man, a foil to Herman, who pedals dime-store merchandise in the poor neighborhood using the insidious installment system, "fifty cent a week and one long, sweet year to pay" (85). Recognizing Julia from another neighborhood, he comments sardonically that she moves a lot, invites himself into her bedroom, and bounces on the bed. "But seriously, what is race and color?" he asks. "Put a paper bag over your head and who'd know the difference" (86). When Julia chases him out with a wooden hanger, he calls her a "sick-minded bitch" because she refuses to play the historical role of the master's sexual toy, already bought and paid for on the slave market. Like the landlady, who also has pushed herself unwanted into Julia's rented room, the Bell Man objectifies Julia into a representative of her race. If for Fanny the proper black woman is to be asexual, for the salesman she is to be a body with a paper bag over her head, hiding not only her race but her existence as an individual with a face and a name. Fanny's attitude constitutes one legitimate response to centuries of white men's sexual abuse of black women. Julia's relationship with Herman should not leave her open to the insults of a traveling salesman, but in his eyes, and perhaps in Fanny's, that relationship makes her another black woman who "prefers" white men.

This scene points to the inseparability of racism and sexism, an issue that cannot be isolated from the historical relationship of the civil rights and women's movements. The fallacy of *sisterhood* as the word was used in the women's liberation movement of the 1960s lay in its assumption that oppression was universal. The signal white women's liberationists sent to black women echoed the one suffragists had sent to their abolitionist sisters a century earlier: your race matters less then your gender. As Bell Hooks puts it, "If we dared to criticize the movement or to assume responsibility for reshaping feminist ideas . . . our voices were tuned out, dismissed, silenced. We could be heard only if our statements echoed the sentiments of the dominant discourse."[12] If a black woman is to be a feminist, it appears she must cease to be black. Julia's treatment by Fanny and the salesman effects the opposite but equally insidious contradiction: she can be a member of the black race, but as such she cannot be an individual woman.

In stark contrast to the private and commodified vision of sexuality the salesman offers Julia, in which he fixes a price for his use of her body, Mattie's letter from her husband reminds Julia that human love also involves a community. Knowing that Mattie can't read the letter herself, Fanny snatches it from her and offers to read it aloud for a dime, but Mattie objects saying, "I don't like how you make words sound. You read too rough" (88). She would rather not hear the words at all than receive them through an unsympathetic voice, as the words themselves only partially represent the layers of meaning contained in the letter. Fanny would have excluded Mattie from her own letter by turning the reading of it into a business transaction. Julia's reading of it is inclusive, not exclusive, and brings out several dramatic levels in the text. One level is the author, October, writing a love letter from his ship in the middle of the ocean. He writes that he wishes he had a photograph of his wife and daughter to show the white men around him, to prove that although he looks different from them he's as good as they are and has a family to miss as much as they do. As Julia reads October's words about loving and missing his wife, Mattie responds in kind, as though he were beside her. Mattie embodies the spectator willing to suspend her disbelief; even third-hand, October's words are enough to bring him into her presence. When Julia reads, "Sometimes people say hurtful things 'bout what I am, like color and race," Mattie replied "Tell 'em you my brown-skin Carolina daddy, that's who the hell you are" (90).

The words Julia reads remind her of what she does not have with her lover: the social legitimation of the public bond racism denies them. Julia carries October's message to Mattie in her voice; her enactment of his text and Mattie's reactions to it reconfirm Julia's own insecurity. The irony of the women's voices turning a private, written text back into a communal text that is orally conveyed is completed later in the play when we learn that October's papers do not "match up" and Mattie cannot receive his benefits. The other significant missing papers are the divorce paper legally freeing Mattie from an abusive husband and the marriage paper realizing her bond with October. All of these legal documents are, of course, controlled by white institutions hostile not only to women's needs but to the Afro-American community historically barred from them. As Susan Willis argues, the southern rural tradition that most contemporary black women writers refer back to depends on oral communication and storytelling. Willis describes this as, unlike writing, a "noncommodified relationship to language, a time when the slippage between words and meaning would not have obtained or been tolerated."[13] Because the paper containing October's letter is marked with her name, Mattie owns it and the words inscribed in it, although she can't read it. Papers she has or does not have control her life, like the laws on "the books" of South Carolina keeping Julia and Herman from marrying.

At the close of his letter, October assures Mattie that he will be home as soon as he can: "Two things a man can give the women he loves . . . his name and his protection . . . The first you have, the last is yet to someday come" (90). For Mattie, "name and protection" ensure a man's responsibility toward his wife; otherwise she just lets him use her. In other words, a woman's options are limited to a heterosexual union sanctioned by a piece of paper enforcing not the man's responsibility but her connection to him. In Mattie and October's case, however, he cannot offer her the financial protection of his war benefits because he has never legally given her his name. The bonds of sisterhood, on the other hand, offer no name, but an unspoken, and, more importantly, unwritten protection.

In response to Mattie and Lula's warm reception of her letter-reading, Julia feels compelled to confess her sin of "keeping company" with a man for ten years without being married, and Mattie and Lula prescribe folk remedies to tie him down. Learning that Herman is white, the two women are initially shocked but cannot believe that Julia really loves him. As Mattie says about whites, "They're mean, honey. They can't help it: their nose is pinched together so close they can't get enough air" (92). But when Julia insists that she feels about Herman the way Mattie feels about October, she loses her sympathetic audience. Having entered their company by reading October's letter, Julia tries to forget the class difference she had earlier imagined separated her absolutely from Lula and Mattie, but the women will not allow her love for a white man to be the same as their love for their own men. Sisterhood is threatened by a traditional loyalty to men whether the men are present or not. One thing besides race that these women hold in common is their status as single women: whether by choice or circumstance they are independent, a situation shared by the two white women who appear in the second act, Herman's mother and sister. Although independence and the complications of sustaining legal heterosexual relationships carry different valences for black and white women, especially in the Jim Crow era, the failure of these relationships for all of Childress's characters can serve as a locus of understanding between them.

In act 2, Julia must face the consequences of Herman's illness and her estrangement from her neighbors. Fanny will not permit her to call a doctor for Herman because she knows the repercussion such publicity would have on everyone. She tells Julia sarcastically, "No, you call a doctor, Nelson won't march in the parade tomorrow to go back in the army, Mattie'll be outta work, Lula can't deliver flowers. . ." (105). Fanny's pragmatism comes through what initially sounds like selfishness, but when Herman wakes up and Fanny is described as "very genial" in the stage directions, addressing him as "Sir" and "Mr. Herman," her desire not to make waves changes its tone. She dons the mask of the happy slave here, a mask of subservient self-protection echoed by Lula in scene 2 as she tells Julia how she saved Nelson from the chain gang. On her hands and knees, she says she "crawled and cried, 'Please white folks, yall's everything. I'se nothin, yall's everything.' The court laughed—I meant for 'em to laugh. . ." (125).Julia responds with pity that a lady is not supposed to crawl, but Lula reminds her that she was saving her son's life. A black woman cannot afford the luxury of ladylike behavior when her son is treated like an animal, but no one should have to crawl. Fanny and Lula recognize, and Julia is learning to recognize, that dignity finds its limits in the respect accorded it by others. The doubleness of black women's existence that gets enacted through the play, the flexibility of demeanor needed to survive in a society in which an unguarded facial expression could kill you, is what Julia thinks she can escape in the north.

White women, however, need no acting ability to get by. Herman's sister, Annabelle, does not mask her discomfort entering the strange world of Fanny's backyard, wondering aloud if the little white girl in Mattie's charge and Mattie's daughter might be her brother's illegitimate children. Although she tells Julia "you look like one-a the nice coloreds" (109) and cannot call the other woman—her figurative sister-in-law—by her name, she admits to Herman her envy of his ten-year love affair. As dominated by their mother as her brother is, Annabelle blames Herman for not showing more solidarity with her on the one occasion she invited her sweetheart home. "You didn't even stay home that one Sunday like you promised. . . Mama made a jackass outta Walter. You know how she can do. He left lookin' like a whipped dog" (110). Like Julia, she only wants to escape the south and go to Brooklyn to marry the sailor she loves, but, like Herman, she cannot break her mother's apron strings.

The audience discovers the desire and disappointment Julia and Annabelle share as Annabelle confesses curiosity about the other woman to Herman, but Julia's real lack of difference from her black neighbors is articulated when Herman's mother faces her and insists that she can never escape the history she shares with all black women. Julia's neighbors may perceive her difference in terms of class, but to Herman's mother, and initially to Annabelle as well, black women are indistinguishable from each other. After throwing Julia out of her own house, the mother addresses her son privately:

> There's something wrong 'bout mismatched things, be they shoes, socks, or people.
> *Herman*. Go away, don't look at us.
> *Herman's Mother*. People don't like it. They're not gonna letcha do it in peace.
> *Herman*. We'll go North.
> *Herman's Mother*. Not a thing will change except her last name.
> *Herman*. She's not like others . . . (117)

The mother is perhaps typecast as an ignorant, dangerous "cracker," but she is right that integration did not abolish racism in the north. When Herman insists that Julia is not like the others, he belies his feeling that other black women are as bad as his mother describes them. Herman's response to his mother, telling her not to look, is as naive as Julia's desire to escape her problems in New York. He cannot make her hatred disappear, and it finally reminds him of his own. As he leaves, supported by his mother and sister, Julia shouts that she will scrub her home with hot water and lye, to "clean the whiteness outta my house," that they should leave her "to [her] own black self!" (120).

Julia's crisis is precipitated by her belated understanding that love does not allow Herman to transcend his racism. Made delirious by the pain medicine the women have been pouring down his throat, he spouts a speech he had recited at a Klan picnic as a little boy, a moment of which his mother has always been proud, although she whipped him into memorizing it: "It is a great and dangerous error to suppose that all people are equally entitled to liberty . . . It is a reward to be earned, a reward reserved for the intelligent, the patriotic, the virtuous and deserving; and not a boon to be bestowed on a people too ignorant, degraded and vicious . . ." (118). Far from enacting the language of inclusion, as Julia's reading of October's letter does, this spectacle reinforces centuries of exclusion based on bigotry. The speech works two ways given the anti-German sentiment of the World War I period. First, it reveals to Julia and the audience the depth of Herman's ambivalence over his love for a black woman, and, secondly, it points to the historical specificity of prejudice. Herman's mother's embarrassment over her first name, Frieda, prompts her to introduce herself to Fanny as "Miss Thelma." She has also planted a red, white, and blue flower garden and has posted a sign in her window announcing: "We are American Citizens." Although the effects of racism cannot be compared to a few decades of anti-German feeling, Herman's mother's ethnic vulnerability exacerbates her own racial hatred. Julia counters the white woman's accusations of "Black, sassy nigger" with "Kraut, knuckle-eater, and red-neck," but the name-calling effectively ends with Frieda's pronouncement that "White reigns supreme . . . I'm white, you can't change that" (120).

The urgency of integration as a method of combatting such engrained hatred marks Julia's turning point in the play. After Herman and his family are gone, she must face her own difficult reintegration into the community of Fanny's backyard. As the women prepare to escort Nelson to his proud participation in the soldiers' parade, the air of festivity inspires Lula and Julia to perform an impromptu strut dance to the music of Jenkin's Colored Orphan Band. They discover a small common space in the mutual performance of a "*Carolina folk dance passed on from some dimly-remembered African beginning*" (124). Later, to send Nelson on his way, Lula begs Julia to give him a farewell speech telling him "how life's gon' be better when he gets back . . . Make up what *should* be true" (125), whether Julia believes in her performance or not. Julia makes a speech proclaiming the abolition of the "no-colored" signs after the war and the new lives of respect awaiting Nelson and October after their return home. Although the stage directions do not specify this, according to reviews of the play, she addresses these words directly to the audience. Edith Oliver, writing for the *New Yorker*, called the speech "dreadful . . . like something out of a bad Russian movie,"[14] in part because by addressing the audience Julia moves the issue of racism north of the Mason-Dixon line. Breaking the fourth wall of realism brings the drama out of its historical context of 1918 into the present and makes Julia's words about integration harder for a northern audience to ignore.

At the end of the play, Julia gives her wedding band and boat tickets to Mattie and her daughter, finally admitting that "You and Teeta are my people . . . my family" (132). But the gesture is compromised by its implication that the only choice for Afro-Americans is to leave their homes in the South. It was still illegal for blacks and whites to marry in South Carolina in 1966, but, despite the laws, by that time blacks had already begun to reclaim their homes. As Alice Walker argues in her essay "Choosing to Stay at Home," one thing Martin Luther King gave his people was the possibility of returning to the South they or their parents or grandparents had left.[15] The civil rights movement recreated the South as a site of militant resistance, resistance enacted equally by black women and men. Set in South Carolina and staged in Michigan and New York, *Wedding Band* provides a site of resistance like the political movement from which it grew. Julia's decision to stay at home, to keep her own name, makes the spectator witness to her new-found ability to celebrate, as she says, her "own black self."

Despite her helplessness regarding her mother, Annabelle, the literal "white sister" in the play, is a character who, like Julia and Nelson, embodies hope for the future in the South. Like the audience, she witnesses Julia's articulation of her newly-won independence. Julia's curtain speech with Herman dying in her arms escapes sentimentality only through the staging of Annabelle's mute participation in it. Julia and Herman remain inside Julia's house, after she simply but irrevocably bars Annabelle, Herman's mother, and Fanny from entering. Everyone leaves the stage except for Annabelle, who moves toward the house, listening to Julia's words to her brother. Without entering the house, to which the black woman has denied her access, she hears the other woman's words and so manages to share silently the loss of Herman without translating it into white terms. As Julia comforts Herman by describing their pretend journey north on the Clyde Line Boat together, she says, "We're takin' off, ridin' the waves so smooth and easy . . . There now . . . on our way . . ." (133). Julia and Herman are not on their way, but perhaps Julia and Annabelle will someday be on *their* way to mutual respect. I can only read these words as a directive to the audience of college students at the University of Michigan in 1966, empassioned with the growing fervor of the anti-war and women's liberation movements and prepared in their innocence to change the world. They cannot do it, *Wedding Band* gently but firmly insists, as gently and firmly as Julia closes her door on the other women, without a renewed commitment to civil rights for all people in the United States, in the South as well as in the North. Sisterhood, especially from the point of view of white women learning to understand black women, begins with listening, not to what one wants to hear but to what is being said.

Notes

I would like to thank Jill Dolan, Trudy Palmer, and Fiona Barnes for their thoughtful and constructive criticism of earlier drafts of this article.

1. Martin Gottfried, "*Wedding Band*," *Women's Wear Daily*, 10 October 1972, reprinted in *New York Theatre Critics' Reviews* 1972, p. 164.

2. Douglas Watt, "*Wedding Band* a Pat Period Play," *New York Daily News*, 27 November 1972, reprinted in *New York Theatre Critics' Reviews* 1972, p. 163.

3. Hortense J. Spillers, "Interstices: A Small Drama of Words," in *Pleasure and Danger: Exploring Female Sexuality*, ed. Carole Vance (Boston and London: Routledge and Kegan Paul, 1984), p. 79.

4. Teresa de Lauretis, "Feminist Studies/Critical Studies: Issues, Terms, and Contexts," in *Feminist Studies/Critical Studies*, ed. Teresa de Lauretis (Bloomington: Indiana University Press, 1986), pp. 1–19, and Linda Gordon, "What's New in Women's History," in ibid. pp. 20–23.

5. de Lauretis, "Feminist Studies/Critical Studies," p. 14.

6. Alice Childress, "Why Talk About That?" *Negro Digest* 16 (1967): 17.

7. Angelina E. Grimke, *Letters to Catherine E. Beecher, in Reply to an Essay on Slavery and Abolitionism, Addressed to A. E. Grimke, Revised by the Author* (Boston: Isaac Knapp, 1838), p. 126, cited in Gerda Lerner, *The Grimke Sisters from South Carolina: Rebels Against Slavery* (Boston: Houghton Mifflin, 1967), p. 187. I am indebted to Linda Gordon for drawing my attention to the Grimke sisters' careers in anti-slavery and feminism.

8. Angela Y. Davis, "Racism in the Woman Suffrage Movement," in *Women, Race and Class* (New York: Random House, 1981), pp. 70–86. Votes for black women, interestingly enough, were not an issue for the suffragists.

9. Paula Giddings, *When and Where I Enter: The Impact of Black Women on Race and Sex in America* (New York: William Morrow, 1984), pp. 296–302. See also Sara Evans, *Personal Politics: The Roots of Women's Liberation in the Civil Rights Movement and the New Left* (New York: Alfred A. Knopf, 1979).

10. See Linda J. M. LaRue, "Black Liberation and Women's Lib," *Trans-Action* 8 (November-December 1970): 59–64, and Toni Morrison, "What the Black Woman Thinks About Women's Lib," *New York Times Magazine*, 22 August 1971, pp. 14–15, 63–64, 66.

11. Ann Petry, *The Street* (Boston: Houghton Mifflin, 1946).

12. Alice Childress, *Wedding Band*, in *9 Plays by Black Women*, ed. Margaret B. Wilkerson (New York: New American Library, 1986), pp. 69–134. Subsequent references are cited parenthetically by page number.

13. Bell Hooks, *Feminist Theory: From Margin to Center* (Boston: South End Press, 1984), pp. 11–12.

14. Susan Willis, *Specifying: Black Women Writing the American Experience* (Madison: University of Wisconsin Press, 1987), p. 16. Putting words on paper maintains the power of those who control the paper. For October, the fact that he has to write a letter to communicate to Mattie, even knowing that she cannot read it, complicates his access to her. Not only does the colonist, or the white politician in this case, in this way enforce the use of his own language, but he also makes real life issues such as marriage conform to those words on paper, available for interpretation only to the literate. For the reading of paper as a carrier of colonial power, see Hugo Blanco's work on the Quechua people of

Peru, cited in Barbara Harlow, *Resistance Literature* (New York and London: Methuen, 1987), pp. 12–13.

15. Edith Oliver, "The Seamstress and the Baker," *The New Yorker*, 4 November 1972, p. 105.

16. Alice Walker, "Choosing to Stay at Home: Ten Years After the March on Washington," in *In Search of Our Mothers' Gardens* (New York: Harcourt Brace Jovanovich, 1983), pp. 158–70.

15

"The Poetry of a Moment": Politics and the Open Form in the Drama of Ntozake Shange

John Timpane

Ntozake Shange's four best-known dramatic works appeared in the late 1970s. Her most popular work, *for colored girls who have considered suicide/when the rainbow is enuf*, began as a cycle of seven poems in 1974, and by 1976 it had reached Broadway. *a photograph* appeared in different versions in 1977 and 1979. *boogie woogie landscapes* appeared as a one-woman show in 1978 and in play form in 1979. *spell #7: geechee jibara quik magic trance manual for technologically stressed third world people* first appeared in 1979. This impressive burst of productivity took place largely during the Carter years; ten years later, these pieces, although not exactly dated, bear the stamp of a period of social transition, of frustrations and possibilities, of a sense of imminent change and the necessity for improvisation.

That decade's remove makes it clear that Shange's dramatic work, especially *colored girls*, represents a moment of crucial importance in black and American history. (An unrepeatable moment, I might add. One could no more write a *colored girls* now than one could write another *Brave New World*. In her own words, these are works "dealing with a period of time that hasn't existed . . . for very long"[1] and that underwent almost immediate change.) Writers with whom she is often compared, such as Imamu Amiri Baraka and Nikki Giovanni, seem to speak of a different, earlier moment. Where these and other writers attacked the obstacles to black self-realization, Shange's dramas represent the tortured moment of becoming itself, *the* moment of emergence and discovery. Ambivalence and paradox mark this moment; a dynamic world full of potential inhabits the same sphere as an old dead world in which nothing can change. The future for Shange's characters fluctuates

Reprinted by permission from *Studies in American Drama, 1945–Present* 4 (1989): 91–101.

between a positive, realizable potential, such as Marx envisioned, and a negative emptiness, such as Benjamin envisioned, which must be filled by individual effort and suffering. The process of becoming is Shange's subject, "our struggle to become all that is forbidden by our environment, all that is forfeited by our gender, all that we have forgotten."[2]

In *spell #7, boogie woogie landscapes,* and *colored girls,* there is no one outcome to the process of becoming, no one unifying end—but there is the process itself, in which all are engaged. What is more, communal expression may well be the only outlet for a certain range of feelings, according to Shange: "in addition to the obvious stress of racism in poverty/afro-american culture . . . has minimized its 'emotional' vocabulary to the extent that admitting feelings of rage, defeat, frustration is virtually impossible outside a collective voice."[3] Again and again, Shange's dramas wander through a maze of personal and collective experience, only to coalesce in a chant that unites the subjective and the intersubjective. The women of *colored girls* chant

> i found god in myself
> & i loved her / i loved her fiercely (63)[4]

and the actresses, singers, magicians, and gypsies of *spell #7* end with the chant "colored & love it / love it/ bein colored" (52),[5] which incorporates extremes of joy and pain. Even *boogie woogie landscapes,* which focuses exclusively on a single woman, ends with a chant:

> dontcha wanna be music / & ease into the fog
> dontcha wanna be like rain / a cosmic event / like sound . . . (142).[6]

None of these epiphanies—the discovery of "god" within one's self, the acceptance and love of being black, or the urge to be like music—"solve" the future, but they are communal starting points for a large number of possible futures.

There is, however, a paradox about Shange's work. As mentioned, her works are inscribed with the tensions of a very specific time and place. Further, these pieces announce themselves as being "for" a particular audience, such as colored girls or technologically stressed third world people. Those pieces contain a great deal of aggression toward an oppressive white culture, an aggression that begins with an attack on white English: "i cant count the number of time i have viscerally wanted to attack deform n maim the language that i waz taught to hate myself in."[7] "The mess of my fortune to be born black & English-speaking"[8] has motivated her to cultivate nonwhite orthography, syntax, and what she has called verbal "distortions."[9] Yet despite all this effort at exclusion, her works remain remarkably "open" texts—that is, they anticipate and welcome the indeterminacy of any dramatic text and the unavoidable variation of performance. As a result, a series of texts that are addressed to, dedicated to, and written for a particular audience nevertheless throw themselves open to a multiplicity of audiences and performances. In this essay, I examine this openness and its consequences for such a politically committed drama.

Texts are defenseless, most of all the text for a drama. No text can defend itself against being misread or misunderstood; the meaning of the text may change or be forgotten or be butchered over time, and no one can do anything about it. This is doubly true for a dramatic text, which at best is a trace of a suggestion about the way a group of people might choose to act out that text. Directors and troupes fling texts down and dance upon them. But *colored girls* seems to me to be the kind of "open text" that people have been writing about for the past critical generation. Its undeniable power as a piece of performance art derives from that openness, which is, ironically, its best defense against being "mis-cast," "mis-directed," or "misunderstood." Not that *colored girls* has no subject—on the contrary, it has a very self-conscious program—but that it anticipates the inevitability of variation and welcomes it, not, I think, as a means of defense against variation, but as a willing gesture toward it. The text of *colored girls* sets down a rhythm but only as an invitation to improvisation:

> dark phrases of womanhood
> of never havin been a girl
> half-notes scattered
> without rhythm / no tune
> distraught laughter fallin
> over a black girl's shoulder
> it's funny / it's hysterical
> the melody-less-ness of her dance
> don't tell nobody don't tell a soul
> she's dancin on beer cans & shingles (3)

These are the first ten spoken lines in the piece. There are no sentences until the sixth line, and the connections between the fragments are completely open to interpretation. Add to this that *colored girls* is a "choreopoem," meaning that the speaker will be dancing or moving in some fashion, also undetermined, while delivering the lines; the flexibility of dance is likely to open the possibilities of interpretation even further. The speakers/dancers—one cannot call them characters—are identified not by name but by color ("lady in purple," and so forth). At times they speak for themselves as centered personas, and at other times they narrate or act out the lives of others. In this second function, it is always clear that they are bearers of someone else's tale; there is always an alienation, for example, between the lady in purple, who declares she is "outside houston," and Sechita, whose story she tells later. As the play ends, the question of who these particular colored women really are has faded before their communal becoming.

Much in the history of *colored girls* contributed to Shange's discovery of the open form. For example, she evidently originally conceived of the women as anonymous entities: "the women were to be nameless & assume hegemony as dictated by the fullness of their lives."[10] From the beginning, the composition of *colored girls* was predicated on the unpredictability of performance—in a sense, the text apologizes for having to be written to give all the speaking and doing an origin. Such an origin is, after all, only a convention. Plenty of acting groups climb the stage nightly without a script. *colored girls,* despite its heavy program, gestures toward improvisational theater. It was born in bars and jazz dives, and Shange has written of the early performances: "the selection of poems chang[ed], dependent upon our audience & our mood, & the dance [grew] to take space of its own."[11] Jazz, dance, women's cooperatives, the Women's Studies Program at Sonoma State College, "The Raggae Blues Band giving Caribbean renditions of Jimi Hendrix & Redding"[12]—certainly these are conditions of possibility under which performance was thrown open to all arts and audiences. Even the word "choreopoem," meaning a piece that is part dance and part language, was coined to describe a kind of writing that "fits in between all" genres and does justice to "human beings' first impulses," which "are to move and to speak."[13]

Clearly, Shange and her associates were trying to give a great deal of autonomy to the work itself. She has written that "the most prescient change in the concept of the work" occurred when she gave up her role as director to Oz Scott. This, for Shange, was a way of subduing herself to the autonomy of the piece: "By doing this, I acknowledged that the poems & the dance worked on their own to do & be what they were."[14] Just as the piece seems to have anticipated the multeity of variations, so Shange, by resigning her directorship, anticipated the death of the author.

So far I have contrasted the political program in Shange's dramatic works with those works' openness. A closer examination of Shange's technique will reveal the paradox at closer range. Shange's most characteristic literary effects are those of collage. In the opening lines of *colored girls* and throughout her works, the fragment vies with the sentence, the image with the complete thought, as though the struggle between two grammars, one unofficial and one official, mirrored the struggle between two cultures. A passage from *boogie woogie landscapes* will serve as an example:

> yr hair is acorns / you rest on glass/ quick
> as a sailboat heeling / yr wine glass barely braizes yr lips /
> vermelho tambem / yr nails unpainted / ridiculously inviting
> you sit here in carved glass / in mirrors / on light /
> in sepia caves
>
> (121)

The aesthetic values of the fragment—that of disjunction, disruption, juxtaposition, sudden illumination or recontextualization—are also political values. That is because the complete sentence, complete plot, and complete character—all the hallmarks of the rage for closure—are associated with a white European theatrical tradition. To choose the disruption and fragmentation of collage is a strike at those values:

> as a poet in the american theater / i find most activity that takes place on our stages overwhelmingly shallow / stilted & imitative. that is probably one of the reasons i insist on calling myself a poet or writer / rather than a playwright / i am interested solely in the poetry of a moment / the emotional & aesthetic impact of a character or a line.[15]

Shange sees her choice of the "poetry of the moment" as a choice against the European bias of white American culture:

> for too long now afro-americans in theater have been duped by the same artificial aesthetics that plague our white counterparts / "the perfect play," as we know it to be / a truly european framework for european psychology / cannot function efficiently for those of us in this hemisphere[16]

If the European insistence on closure is not appropriate for white American playwrights, it is still less so for the poet in an Afro-American theater.

Collage is inherently subversive in that the artist who employs collage hopes to make meanings by disruption and juxtaposition rather than by the ordered sequence of signs prescribed by the rules of grammar—which is as much as to say that collage proposes a syntax to replace the standard syntax. Because of its subversive character, collage is a way of opening up the canon. It is used to challenge preconceived notions, show unexpected connections, and call forth the richness and dynamism of existence, as in *boogie woogie landscapes:*

> at the disco we shout the praises of the almighty
> i wrap my arms around you til the end (139)

At its least successful, collage can become merely associational, merely automatic: Castro / Santa Claus / Santa Cruz / the True Cross. Its very danger is that the number of possible connections is so very large, virtually infinite, while the number of meaningful connections is much smaller. Despite much critical support during the last twenty years, synchronic techniques such as collage have severe drawbacks as artistic tools. Synchrony can furnish flashes of light but is less effective as a means of developing or sustaining a continuous fire. For Shange, as for any literary bricoleur, the challenge is to fashion and sustain a drama that is not a single narration but a series of conflicts and collisions. Shange's solution has been to balance the potential anarchy of collage with a consistent political purpose.

An element of collage exists even in Shange's main dramatic technique, that of call and response, the monologue delivered against a chorus of voices. The magician lou begins *spell #7* with a bitter pastiche of a minstrel show, posing as Mr. Interlocutor while the rest of the cast is frozen kneeling. The piece is built on a series of monologues interspersed with various forms of group expression. *boogie woogie landscapes* is essentially a series of dialogues between layla and six "night-life companions," six aspects of her dreams and memories. As voices collide, so do images from personal history, world history, fashion, and literary and pop culture. In its juxtapositions and emphasis on improvisation, call and response is a dialogistic form of collage.

A crucial distinction must be made here. Shange's collage is not the undirected and autonomous collage of surrealism but a consciously motivated syncretism with a political agenda. After all, black history, be it African, Caribbean, or American, is characterized by collage and syncretism—just as white history is characterized by the myths of completion, racial unity, and progress. European theater thus insists on closure, while Afro-American theater, as Shange projects it, insists on the rough edge, the open, the fragment. The actor alec in *spell #7* recalls the tensions between past and present in his childhood. His family had become "paler" as it moved toward St. Louis, in "linear movement from sous' carolina to missouri / freedmen / landin in jackie wilson's yelp / daughters of the manumitted swimmin in tina turner's grinds" (10). Here, images of slavery collide with those of pop music. Sechita in *colored girls* combines the black connection with Egypt and her present as a dancer in a Creole carnival in Natchez: "sechita / goddess / of love / egypt / 2nd millenium / performin the rites / the conjurin of men / conjurin the spirit / in natchez / the mississippi spewed a heavy fume of barely movin waters" (25). The juxtapositions here are deliberate, the better to emphasize the richness and paradoxes of black history—even as they narrate the bitter experience of black individuals. There are moments in Shange that verge on surrealism, such as when in *boogie woogie landscapes* Fidel Castro is envisioned doing a "revolutionary rhumba" and Jimmy Carter, the Secret Service,

Leonid Brezhnev, and the Ayatollah Khomeini are seen dancing on the moon (125), but even here, the thrust of intention is too strong to overlook. These dignitaries dance on the moon, "all white n barren n free of anybody who looks like me" (125), because they have shown themselves incapable of such spontaneity or rhythm on earth. Carter and Khomeini and Brezhnev are made ridiculous to elevate layla, who lacks these men's power but surpasses them in spirit and spontaneity. Conversely, in *colored girls,* ancient Egypt, mystery religions, and the Mississippi are invoked to ennoble Sechita, who, while glamorous, is really just a carny dancer avoiding the coins flung between her knees.

Further, Shange's counterorthography—specifically, her rejection of periods and capital letters and her idiosyncratic use of the virgule—allows her collages to be even more abrupt, even more violent, than they would be had they been expressed in standard English orthography. The virgule, after all, is used to show, as in *spell #7,* that several alternatives may be appropriate simultaneously: "i waz a peculiar sorta woman / wantin no kisses / no caresses / just power / heat & no eaziness of thrust" (28). The proliferation of virgules in Shange shows that alternatives are always present, always in conflict or tension.

Thus, although collage is an "opening" technique, it is tamed, as it were, by a strong political program. The tendency toward closure (Shange's politics) somehow coexists with the tendency away from it (Shange's technique). In light of that tension, what happens to what many viewers value most in her drama—its content? These are, we must remember, dramatic events that thousands of spectators have *used.* These people attended these pieces because they had heard, expected, or been told that they would variously identify, vindicate, and validate them. These works served and are serving a purpose. Accordingly, the intended audience for *colored girls,* for example, considers it a holy thing, an object of reverence. What happens to that if we consider *colored girls* an open drama? Do we not deny that audience their special access, their special meaning?

As mentioned at the beginning of this essay, Shange's text shows the effort of exclusion. But I have never seen a performance of *colored girls* that singled out any kind of audience. In this way *colored girls* is distinctly democratic. There is plenty of *Publikumsbeschimpfung,* plenty of flaying of the male cock of the walk, plenty of moralism. But in these aspects, *colored girls* is firmly in the tradition of world drama, especially the tradition of the democracy of abuse as described by Bakhtin. Thus, the attacks against unfeeling males, stuck-up white women, the empowered classes, all these attacks that at times seem jejune or schoolgirlish in the text, work splendidly in performance because they establish that democracy of abuse. The persons in

Shange's dramas abuse one another as a means of establishing the dignity of each player. One is not allowed dignity until one is dressed down in public—and I cannot think of a more ancient ritual. No one audience is singled out. The women of *colored girls* will speak to anyone who will listen; the singers and dancers of *spell #7* will perform for anyone—"we're doin this for you" (19).

Is the chosen audience then deprived of their chosenness? Have we taken *colored girls* or *spell* or *boogie woogie landscapes* away from a particular group of people—women or blacks or black women or whoever—in giving it to whoever has ears and eyes? I don't see how. For one thing, an Afro-American woman wrote these pieces about and for colored girls and third-world people, her chosen audience, and any rights appertaining thereto are, of course, unimpeachable. The arrival of her work at a particular place and time was felicitous and crucial; it is rightfully valued by those it has helped. But that audience must, I think, take its place among all possible audiences, and its manifold interpretations of the manifold performances of *colored girls* or *spell #7* must take their places among all the other possible interpretations. Shange's most characteristic gesture is, as I have discussed, toward possibility rather than closure; her works evoke the complexity of human relations rather than the completion of given actions or characters. Her women, like her men, are unfinished and fallible and, therefore, worthy.

Shange's work suggests the kind of "canon" one might design for dramatic works. Let us not build a reading zoo and assign each work its cage. Instead, let us have a canon not of texts but of potential performance events. Perhaps we can say that a text of *colored girls* or *spell #7* or *boogie woogie landscapes*, like any script for any play, is just a template from which may be spun off a continuing series of performances. Let us identify the pieces whose texts suggest the greatest possibility of variation while retaining an integral character; let us say that such texts make up a group that we cherish. I nominate, not the text, but the unended group of performances indicated by the text of *colored girls* for inclusion into this nonexistent canon.

Notes

1. "Postscript with Ntozake Shange." Television interview with Charlene Hunter Gault following *for colored girls*, directed by Oz Scott, a co-production of WNET and WPBT, 1982.
2. Ntozake Shange, "A History: *for colored girls who have considered suicide / when the rainbow is enuf*," in *SeeNoEvil: Prefaces, Essays & Accounts 1976–1983* (San Francisco: Momo's Press, 1984), p. 17.
3. Ntozake Shange, "A Foreword to Three Pieces: (*Spell #7, A Photograph: Lovers in*

Motion, Boogie Woogie Landscapes) Unrecovered Losses/Black Theater Traditions," in *SeeNoEvil: Prefaces, Essays & Accounts 1976–1983* (San Francisco: Momo's Press, 1984), pp. 21–22.

4. Ntozake Shange, *for colored girls who have considered suicide / when the rainbow is enuf: a choreopoem* (New York: Macmillan, 1977). Subsequent references are cited parenthetically by page number.

5. Ntozake Shange, *spell #7: geechee jibara quik magic trance manual for technologically stressed third world people: a theater piece*, in *three pieces* (New York: St. Martin's Press, 1981), pp. 1–52. Subsequent references are cited parenthetically by page number.

6. Ntozake Shange, *boogie woogie landscapes*, in *three pieces* (New York: St. Martin's Press, 1981), pp. 109–42. Subsequent references are cited parenthetically by page number.

7. Ntozake Shange, "A Foreword," in *three pieces* (New York: St. Martin's Press, 1981), p. xii.

8. Ntozake Shange, "How I Moved Anna Fierling to the Southwest Territories, or my personal victory over the armies of western civilization," in *SeeNoEvil: Prefaces, Essays & Accounts 1976–1983* (San Francisco: Momo's Press, 1984), p. 35.

9. Shange, "A Foreword," p. xii.

10. Shange, "A History," p. 15.

11. Ibid.

12. Ibid.

13. "Postscript with Ntozake Shange."

14. Shange, "A History," p. 16.

15. Shange, "A Foreword," p. ix.

16. Ibid.

16
Comic Textures and Female Communities 1937 and 1977: Clare Boothe and Wendy Wasserstein

Susan L. Carlson

Although comedy's Lysistratas and Rosalinds have prompted general critical agreement that comedy promotes sexual equality, the women in two twentieth-century comedies by women suggest how easily such conclusions may be called into question. As they create all-female comic worlds, both Clare Boothe in *The Women* and Wendy Wasserstein in *Uncommon Women and Others* magnify some of the special dissonances which accompany the appearance of any woman in comedy. Neither Boothe's nor Wasserstein's is a major achievement, but as solid, successful plays, both tell us a great deal about the conventions and assumptions we depend on and respond to in all comedies. Specifically, the two plays disclose the kinds of female characters and communities comedy encourages or discourages.[1]

While Boothe's 1937 comedy *The Women* is a play full of women, it is not a woman's play. As a comedy it is troubled and troubling. Like a comedy, it is propelled by the humorous unmasking of human frailties and double standards. Like a comedy, it is neatly knotted at the end by marriage and an attitude of compromise that bravely point both characters and audience toward the future. Like many comedies, it is also laced with satire and irony that transmit double messages: its scintillating wit is both freedom and escape, its stage full of women at once a potential women's community and a backhanded endorsement of a male world. But the results of the satire and irony in Boothe's comedy are unusually disruptive.[2] While many have held Boothe accountable for the disconcerting effect of her female enclave, comedy itself is the cause of the disturbance in her play.

Reprinted by permission from *Modern Drama* 27 (December 1984): 564–73.

Displayed in a succession of exclusively female domains—a powder room, an exercise salon, a beauty shop, a kitchen, and others—the five central women in Boothe's play victimize themselves and one another in winner-take-all games of marriage, adultery, and divorce. Boothe maintains that she wrote the play to satirize only a "small group of ladies native to the Park Avenues of America,"[3] but nevertheless she fills her world with characters and encounters which make this play a much broader study of women's roles. The cast list alone underlines her concentration on women *in* roles and *as* roles. While Boothe's main characters have names (although even they dwindle into the roles "single" or "married" when Nancy is subtitled "Miss Blake," Sylvia "Mrs. Howard Fowler," etc.), a majority of the forty-four cast members are listed *only* as types or roles. There are hairdressers, pedicurists, salesgirls, models, a nurse, a cook, an instructress, a cutie, a society woman, a dowager, a debutante, and a girl in distress. These social, professional, and personal roles supply a busy backdrop for the playwright's central study of the roles most vital for her women: roles as wives, mothers, daughters, and friends. Comedy has always been fertile ground for the study of social roles, masks, and the often indistinguishable line between the two. Boothe adopts this comic concern with a vengeance.

First and foremost "the women" are wives. But as wives, the central character Mary and her four closest friends Sylvia, Nancy, Edith, and Peggy do not enact for us their half of a simple battle between the sexes. That basic comic battle has been superseded by a vicious battle *within* one sex *over* the other. Dubbed "odious harpies," "werewolves," "sluts," "barbaric savages," and "brazen hussies" by 1937 reviewers,[4] Boothe's women engage themselves in an endless and incestuous series of bruising encounters: for example, Mary loses Stephen to Crystal, who deserts him for Buck, who abandons the Countess, who has been married four previous times. Every time a community of women forms, it is splintered by the women's battles over their men, their battles to be wives.

The bold but unbecoming behavior of "the women" as wives works as flashy camouflage to cover the much more destructive self-hatred which grows out of the women's roles as mothers, daughters, and friends. The play's harsh attitude toward mothering is defined most specifically in Mary's role as mother to Little Mary. On her mother's arrival home from the beauty shop, Little Mary announces that she does not "want to be a dear little girl" anymore,[5] not only because girls are "silly," but because they never stop being so (121). Little Mary "hates" little girls, in part because she refuses to accept the yoke of a double standard that means "Daddy has more *fun* than you" (122). Mary, just returning home from the discovery of her husband Stephen's philandering, is perhaps uncharacteristically unprepared for this metaphysical crisis with which Little Mary greets her. But that circumstance alone cannot account for the mechanical emptiness of this mother's responses. In short, Mary has no soothing answer to Little Mary's questions because she lacks the self-consciousness such answers would demand. Throughout the play, the rebellion and self-hatred that Little Mary voices so unambiguously show themselves again and again in the twisted and perverted shapes they must take on in the mothers who have buried such emotions. Sylvia's explosive but fragile ego and Mary's battered one are but two results of such interment. Blindly accepting what they are told is their inferiority, the women fail as mothers.

As a daughter herself, Mary is but a passive receptor of the self-hatred her mother passes on. Mrs. Morehead instructs her daughter Mary to lie in order to win back her husband, and to divorce herself from other women—"Don't confide in your girl friends!" (125). Mary follows her advice. The battling that "the women" engage in as wives seems to have mined any possible strength or contentment in their roles as mothers and daughters who nurture and teach one another. What remains of these potentially powerful roles is only a residue of slushy sentiment.

These women's fierceness as wives and their failures as mothers and daughters contribute, finally, to their inability to be friends. Although the play's successive episodes study the permutations in one community of women, in every case the community is one in which sharing and concern give way to battles and rifts. The chatty bridge luncheon of the opening scene is subverted by Sylvia's vigilance for any new gossip, and succeeding exchanges follow suit. Even the camaraderie we glimpse at times in the service communities—the hairdressers, the models, the ladies'-room attendants—is undermined by infighting and backbiting. The sturdy, inward female communities Nina Auerbach tells us are common in all-female environs are completely absent.[6]

Like Mrs. Morehead, these women believe that women are the last to be trusted—with anything. Mary, Nancy, Peggy, and even Edith (it would be stretching matters to include Sylvia) do make sincere overtures of friendship. Their tunes fall on deaf ears, however, since "the women," to survive, have also had to assume that female friendships are foolish luxuries. Of course, they all fail to see the schizophrenia of both soliciting and rejecting friendship. When Mary defends her "friend" Sylvia to Nancy, protesting "she's a good friend underneath" (114), she exposes the clandestine form caring must take for these women. Nancy's latest novel about "Women I dislike" (115) more brazenly displays the embattled nature of female friendships. Mary's main lesson in the play is that Mrs. Morehead is correct in her assessment of friendship: Mary learns that the only clear road back to her marriage with Stephen is a lonely one on which she will shed not only her pride and graciousness, but also her friends. In her extremely cynical portrait of a female community, Boothe forges what seems to be an unnatural connection between comedy and a friendless female world.

But if we reconsider our most treasured, liberated comic heroines, we realize how the witty, conniving, sly, underhanded, two-faced women who appear so vile in the isolation of *The Women* are only slight exaggerations of the comic rule rather than exceptions to it. If we imagine Shakespeare's Rosalind and Beatrice, Shaw's Candida, and Aristophanes' Lysistrata collected around Mary's bridge table, we recognize how these women too—though much more vibrant than Boothe's—gain their power only *in reaction to* what the governess Miss Fordyce has surmised is a "man's world" (119). When such women are left alone together—as they are in *Lysistrata,* or as Helena and Hermia are in *A Midsummer Night's Dream*—they are likely to engage in vicious battles, almost always, as in *The Women,* battles over men.

Whereas Boothe seems only vaguely aware of a connection between her ugly portraits of women and the double standards of the "man's world" in which they must maneuver, Desmond MacCarthy sees Boothe's vile women as products of an unfair world: ". . . they [the women] are in a highly precarious position because they have to be carried by men *to whom they are not necessary. . . .*"[7] Most comedy exposes, with varying degrees of boldness, sexual double standards. Comedy's central role reversals are, in fact, based on the stereotypes that result from double standards: i.e., women gain control and men lose it because these are laughable inversions of normal roles. Such inversion endows most comic heroines with their memorable, freewheeling power to criticize and belittle an unfair world. This liberating criticism does not evolve in Boothe's play, however, even though *The Women* is full of women ruling in their worlds. Moreover, the liberating criticism does not evolve *because The Women* is full of women ruling in their worlds. For the women's sovereignty extends only over their own turfs—the beauty salons, the kitchens, the powder rooms. Instead of gaining freedom and power in comedy, Boothe's women are more than ever victims in their proscribed world. Trapped in a women's world which exists only because it is necessary to the men's, the women cannot choose to be other than they are. Boothe's play shows that the refreshing freedom of the sole comic heroine is not necessarily multiplied by the presence of multiple heroines, and that, actually, just the opposite may be true. The comic ending, supposedly comedy's final gesture in the conferral of social joy, becomes only the final severing of women's bonds to one another to ensure a happy, fully heterosexual ending.

As is typical in comedy, the "happy ending" is marriage, more precisely the remarriage of Mary and Stephen. As she claws her way to this personal happiness through the nasty social jungle in which "the women" must operate, Mary clearly demonstrates that success in Boothe's world is measured by one's ability to keep a man by fighting off other women. The irony is heavy, but as in most comedies, the heroine, Mary, ends by accepting the social games she had earlier scorned; her acknowledgment reinforces the social rules of this world and counsels acceptance of them for others. Yet the sinking feeling one has at the end of the play is a reaction Boothe has programmed the play to command. Boothe wants to expose these women who are "vulgar and dirty-minded, and alien to grace,"[8] and her ending is a conscious emphasizing of their hopelessness as redeemable human beings. The best Boothe can offer is Mary's unsatisfying final compromise because it is the best she *wants* to offer.

There is a second cause for the dissonance of this ending; Boothe was probably far less conscious of it, but it doubles the effect of what she *does* consciously provide in Mary's sad compromise. In exposing the double standards under which her women function (as she could not avoid doing in comedy), Boothe allows us to witness their vulnerability. Yet Boothe, whose life patterned for others one way out of such a confining miasma of stereotyped roles, persists in denying a connection between a double standard and her empty women. Because of this blind spot, she also persists in misreading the effects of "comedy" in her play. Boothe's text is full of the social criticism comedy encourages, but its object—"the women" themselves—confuses that criticism. Boothe forgets that she is criticizing the double standard that has made these women mean-spirited *as well as* criticizing the women. The effect is that her lampooning of the women seems cruel because it is practiced upon characters who are already the victims of comic and social convention. Thus, when the play ends with Mary's ambiguous triumph, and Sylvia and Crystal's hand-to-hair combat, we respond with as much pity as scorn.

Boothe's foreword to *The Women* is final evidence of the perplexing collision between dramatic form and authorial intent in this play. Although Boothe at times echoes the self-effacement of her women in this foreword by apologizing for certain aspects of the play, the fierce spirit of her defense shows that she senses, rightly, her innovation in the play. So the loose plot for which she takes "blame" is one of the play's greatest strengths, allowing for the development of the contexts and textures Boothe needs to develop her characters. The creation of such textures is a futile exercise in Boothe's "man's world," yet the persistence of the characters in building them—in spite of certain collapse—is the source of the small hope Boothe's play inspires. The heavily ironic ending is another attempt by Boothe to alter comic boundaries; and its failure is but another sign of her inability to free her comedy from the dramatic forms whose effect she never fully perceived. While Boothe labors in her foreword to allay charges that *The Women* is misogynous,[9] the misogyny she did not intend persists, embedded in her adoption of traditional comic attitudes to sexual double standards and social roles.

Wendy Wasserstein's 1977 comedy *Uncommon Women and Others* mirrors Boothe's in its all-female world and picaresque plot; and it borrows the earlier play's superstructure of five main characters playing out social roles against a backdrop of clearly typed characters. But the crucial difference is that Wasserstein shows how a comedy full of women no longer needs to be a bitter dead end.

As her subtitle documents, Wasserstein's text is "A Play About Five Women Graduates of a Seven Sisters College Six Years Later." While it begins and ends "Six Years Later" with the five women gathered at a restaurant for lunch, most of the action is a replay of scenes during the characters' senior year at Mount Holyoke. There is no plot. Instead of events and suspense, Wasserstein gives her characters time and peer audiences. As they drift in and out of the play's seventeen episodes, the five main characters set their own paces and create a dramatic forum in which they can leisurely, continually mold, test, and retest their lives and those of their friends. Wasserstein may have discarded the comic plotting that confined Boothe, even in her loosely plotted play, but the later dramatist has not discarded comedy. In a new mode, she presents the same comic search for a resolution, for the comfort of a happy ending.

Sometimes boldly, sometimes fearfully, the five Mount Holyoke seniors relentlessly confront their futures. Kate, a Phi Beta Kappa who loves trashy novels, collects men, and is headed for law school, is the other women's image of success, their Katharine Hepburn.[10] Although she is well on her way to becoming the successful career woman already typed by her friends, Kate has doubts about the "role" she has chosen for herself. She fears becoming "a cold efficient lady in a grey business suit" (62) and laments, "I don't want my life to simply fall into place" (63). "Six Years Later," Kate is still fighting against the constraints of her role as the career woman; she realizes that she has sacrificed as much as she has gained, but she remains admirable in her constant, honest battle within and against a role that isolates her.

Kate's bold insecurity is matched by Rita's willful perverseness. A mouthy, playfully radical feminist preoccupied with tasting her menstrual blood and lecturing her friends on the dangers of a society "based on cocks" (38), Rita refreshes the spirits of the others while restlessly searching for the experiences and feelings that will make her feel whole. Her constant, soon haunting refrain is to proclaim how amazing this group of women will be at ages twenty-five or thirty or forty-five—or somewhere down the road. Pressing achievement conveniently always just out of reach in the future, Rita squares her hope with her disappointments. With her unabating hatred of roles, Rita has not let society pigeonhole her, but she has not yet found a way to fashion a world without the old pigeonholes.

Muffet and Holly's searches for their futures are less frenetic than either Kate or Rita's. They wander in and out of Wasserstein's scenes, trying—in their more subdued ways—to fashion their lives somehow out of the old roles that remain the only ones they know and the undefined new ones no one else can describe for them. Wishing for the direction of a Kate or a Rita, Holly slips and slides between the despair and elation of growing up. Her long-distance telephone conversation "to" a man she has only casually met in a museum is touching evidence of her need for a man and her confusion over the preference for the comforting presence of Rita or Kate (68–70). Muffet confesses a similar need for men, and like Holly fears planning for the future as much as meeting it.

Holly and Muffet are openly insecure about a future they cannot seem to pattern for themselves; Kate and Rita are much less secure than they know they seem. Yet all four consciously confront a world in which women's role have become ambiguous and confusing. Unlike theirs, Samantha's position recalls Boothe's simpler, albeit harsher female world. Like Boothe's women, Sam opts for a very traditional marriage, one in which she can dedicate herself to her husband, Robert. She feels no shame about giving herself to her husband and, in fact, radiates self-confidence and contentment that the others all envy. Sam chooses life akin to the values and conditions Boothe traced in *The Women*, but hers promises happiness that life in *The Women* could not. Because she consciously chooses a traditional marriage as one of many options open to her, Sam has the potential of being happy as a satellite in Robert's world. The others envy her not because she can so easily choose an established role, but because she can fit into it: they could not. Wasserstein does not make the mistake of preaching that "new" types like Rita and Kate are any more acceptable than "old" types like Sam; she simply provides a context where all such roles coexist and can be studied, challenged, accepted, altered, or dropped.

Wasserstein's expansive plot, her concentration on characters and roles, and her weaving of texture are not unique. Any number of comic playwrights (and many great ones) have preceded her with such mixtures, yet usually without her success in transforming comedy's women. Although in time Wasserstein's transformations will come to seem a matter of degree and not radical alterations, the still significant difference between Wasserstein and predecessors like Boothe is consciousness. Wasserstein *is aware* that comedy's built-in easy answers to women's problems are deceptive and dangerous; she *is aware* that comic conventions in and of themselves pressure characters into a limited number of roles. And for now, her ability to translate this awareness to a comic practice that focuses on characters (not roles) and allows these characters to create unified female communities must be viewed as significant. For in creating her community, Wasserstein diffuses comic prejudice against female friendship. Sifting through her treasure chest of Mount Holyoke scenes and characters, Wasserstein allows real female friendships to develop, friendships that have been rare in comedy. Freed from the requirement that they bond only with men (and produce the traditional happy ending), Wasserstein's women can choose to bond with each other.

In the final scene of act 1, Rita—coordinating the others as usual—asks them which one woman they would marry if they could, if women married women. A joyous communal dance grows out of the touching, honest exchange that follows and is our cue that act 1 is over. While there are many other direct comments on female friendships in this play, none surpasses this marriage scene in its creation of believable, lasting relationships. Its direct substitution of female-female marriage for the traditional male-female kind must be read as a challenge to a world and comedy that expect otherwise. It is almost as if Wasserstein knew her play could not end this way, so she indulged her dreams and her characters' dreams of togetherness in this wish-fulfilling pseudo-ending. She provides enough evidence elsewhere that her female community is no utopia, for this group of women has its tensions and defections along with its Bacchic idylls.

Wasserstein deals directly with the fragility of such happy communes by creating two very distinct communities in the play. We focus on the five women who will meet again six years later in the restaurant frame of the play—Kate, Rita, Holly, Muffet, and Sam. Yet in our peripheral vision other students remain—Susie Friend, Carter, and Leilah—who are set off not only by their absence from the reunion, but also by the one-dimensional nature of their roles in the Mount Holyoke community. These misshapen shadows of outsiders and failed friendships keep Wasserstein's play from deteriorating into a facile celebration of sorority. Like the hairdressers, the cooks, and the attendants in *The Women*, who offered a background chorus of roles, these three outsiders put a damper on the soaring aspirations of the "uncommon women" by stubbornly reminding them of a world that is still not all that different from Boothe's.

The closing of *Uncommon Women and Others* is Wasserstein's final statement about these women's roles, as well as her final transformation of comedy. Because the playwright wants it this way, there is no end, only a stopping point. The indeterminateness of her ending is indicated both by the age of Wasserstein's matured women—still only twenty-seven—and by the constant transition they have learned, for better or worse, to accept in their lives. The stopping point of the end is marked as a pause also by Sam's announcement that "Robert and I are having a baby" (76). Sam's announcement is not intended as a parody of the traditional ending of comedy with marriage and the implicit future promise of babies; her solid, lovable character ensures that we respond to her news as warmly as the other women do. Moreover, in Sam's announcement, Wasserstein does not simply embrace the comfortable comic ending which returns the world to an established social order. By making Sam's future as a mother only one part of an otherwise diffuse ending, Wasserstein extracts the joy and assurance of the traditional comic ending without the encumbrance of comedy's predictable return to the status quo. In other words, Wasserstein protects the reactionary power of the traditional comic ending by setting Sam's future in the context of four other, much less defined futures. All five women, like Wasserstein, know that the happy endings promised in comedy are illusive, but that comedy's joy is not. In this they are uncommon.

Forming her characters as a social unit in a comedy of textures, Wasserstein demonstrates how the delicate relations of women to social roles may be best studied, may be *only* studied, in an altered comic form. Boothe's comedy about women generated bitterness, complaints, and brittle laughter; Wasserstein's comedy about women nurtures faith, concern, and warm, easy laughter. Community.

Two plays by women, about women, full of women. They are not unique, of course: Boothe had her companions in creating female worlds in the 1930s, just as Wasserstein has her companions now. Yet the two plays represent not only their ages, but a shift in our attitudes and consequently our comedy. I have been trying to show how Boothe's play exposes some of the limitations comedy imposes on its female characters; how comic conventions in themselves account for the types of women Boothe creates in her play; how Boothe would have found it difficult to model a female world much different from the one she produced. I have also attempted to demonstrate how Wasserstein, with her play's openness of form and retaliation against some of comedy's sexist assumptions, has avoided some of the limitations that cornered Boothe. With her dramatic textures, Wasserstein creates a comic world where women can work within a female community to challenge social roles. I would like to conclude, but cannot, that Wasserstein may have found a way to translate comedy from its inherent social conservatism without destroying comedy itself. Like Caryl Churchill, Pam Gems, Beth Henley, and other women now writing comedy, Wasserstein will have to keep experimenting before any such change becomes reality. Yet in this community of writers we may place our hope for comedy free of sexism. Boothe's play suggests why feminist comedies have been all too rare; Wasserstein's suggests that they no longer have to be.

Notes

1. I have purposefully avoided an elaborate discussion of comic theory anywhere in my essay because, for the purposes of my study of female comic communities, such a survey would only be a rehearsal of the failure of comic theorists to ponder the special problem of women in comedy. Although George Meredith's essay on comedy seems to accord to women in comedy a haven of equality, Meredith overlooks the conscription of a comic heroine's freedom by comedy's end. Most comic theorists since Meredith pay lip service to his comic equality as a way of avoiding any real talk about women in comedy. I would like to offer the following as a working list of studies in which the role of women in comedy is finally being re-viewed: Linda Bamber, *Comic Women, Tragic Men: A Study of Gender and Genre in Shakespeare* (Stanford, Calif.: Stanford University Press, 1982); Marilyn French, *Shakespeare's Division of Experience* (New York: Summit Books, 1981); Shirley Nelson Garner, "*A Midsummer Night's Dream*: 'Jack Shall have Jill; / Nought shall go ill,'" *Women's Studies* 9 (1981): 47–63; Marianne Novy, "Demythologizing Shakespeare," *Women's Studies* 9 (1981), 17–27; Nancy Walker, "Do Feminists Ever Laugh? Women's Humor and Women's Rights," *International Journal of Women's Studies*, 4 (January/February 1981): 1–9; Michelene Wandor, *Understudies: Theatre and Sexual Politics* (London: Methuen, 1981); Naomi Weisstein, "Why We Aren't Laughing . . . Any More," *Ms.*, November 1973, pp. 49–51, 88–90; Judith Wilt, "The Laughter of Maidens, the Cackle of Matriarchs: Notes on the Collision between Comedy and Feminism," *Women and Literature* 1 (1980): 173–96; several essays in *The Woman's Part: Feminist Criticism of Shakespeare*, ed. Carolyn Ruth Swift Lenz, Gayle Greene, and Carol Thomas Neeley (Urbana: University of Illinois Press, 1980).

2. Boothe's play is often categorized as satire and not comedy. Although the play's satiric bite is obvious, it is only part of a broader comedy that shows in Boothe's language, plot, character interaction, and attitude. The critical equation of the text with satire is just more evidence of the confused messages the play transmits. For a sampling of critical response to the play, see "The Women," *Time*, 4 January 1937, pp. 30–31; Stark Young, "Not a Review," *New Republic*, 7 April 1937, p. 263; Brooks Atkinson, review of *The Women*, *New York Times*, 28 December 1936, reprinted in *The New York Times Theatre Reviews 1920–1970*, vol. 4: 1935–1941; "Theatre," *Playboy*, August 1973, p. 39; Martin Gottfried, "The Women," *Women's Wear Daily*, 27 April 1973, reprinted in *New York Theatre Critics' Reviews* 1973, p. 287; Ellenore Lester, "'The Women': Older but not Wiser," *Ms.*, August 1973, pp. 42–45; and Jack Kroll, "The Girls in the Bank," *Newsweek*, 7 May 1973, p. 109.

3. Clare Boothe, Foreword to *The Women* (New York: Random House, 1937), p. vii.

4. See the list of such nouns Boothe compiles in Foreword to *The Women*, pp. ix–x.

5. Clare Boothe, *The Woman*, in *Plays by and about Women: An Anthology*, ed. Victoria Sullivan and James Hatch (New York: Random House, 1973), p. 120. Subsequent references are cited parenthetically by page number.

6. See Nina Auerbach, *Communities of Women: An Idea in Fiction* (Cambridge: Harvard University Press, 1978), especially "Introduction: The Communal Eye." Auerbach mentions *The Women* as an example of a persistent stereotype of the self-rejecting female group, a type she believes experience does not validate. It is a type that comedy does validate, however (pp. 12–13). Along the same lines, although Ellenore Lester attempts to defend *The Women* because of its all-female communities, the feminist hope she wistfully injects into the play is hers, not Boothe's (44).

7. Desmond MacCarthy, "Jungle-Red Nails," *New Statesman and Nation*, 19 April 1939, p. 646.

8. Boothe, Foreword to *The Women*, p. xii.

9. Ibid., pp. ix–xii.

10. Wendy Wasserstein, *Uncommon Women and Others* (New York: Avon, 1978), p. 68. Subsequent references are cited parenthetically by page number. For a sampling of the very positive response this play engendered, see Harold Clurman, review of *Uncommon Women and Others*, *Nation*, 10 December 1977, pp. 667–68; Douglas Watt, "Holyoke Hen Sessions," *New York Daily News*, 22 November 1977, reprinted in *New York Theatre Critics' Reviews* 1977, p. 139; Richard Eder, "Dramatic Wit and Wisdom Unite in *Uncommon Women and Others*," *New York Times*, 22 November 1977, reprinted in *New York Theatre Critics' Reviews* 1977, pp. 138–39; and Edith Oliver, review of *Uncommon Women and Others*, *New Yorker*, 5 December 1977, p. 115.

17
Gender Perspective and Violence in the Plays of Maria Irene Fornes and Sam Shepard

Catherine A. Schuler

In light of recent studies on the relationship between audience reception and gender, the plays of Maria Irene Fornes and Sam Shepard offer interesting opportunities for comparison. In the last several years, Shepard has found an increasingly wide audience for his work, but Fornes's name remains generally unfamiliar outside of elite feminist and/or avant-garde circles. Shepard has become a mass media icon and may have wider name recognition than any American playwright but Neil Simon. In marked contrast to Shepard, and regardless of the number of Obie awards she collects, Fornes remains on the fringe, known primarily to feminist scholars and to those dwindling audiences who will still pay the price of a ticket to be offended, bemused, and befuddled by the experimental theater experience.

This discrepancy is puzzling for several reasons. First, Shepard and Fornes are part of a handful of survivors of the alternative, experimental theater of the 1960s and 70s and thus share a history in the American avant-garde. Second, both have developed into skilled craftspersons whose plays reflect at least some similar social, political, and formal concerns. Fornes apparently believes that confused, hostile responses to her work are the inevitable result of her continuing desire to engage in radical experiments with form. In a recent interview, she stated: "I realized that what makes my plays unacceptable to people is the form more than the content. My content is usually not outrageous. I think it's mild!"[1] Although her argument may be a bit disingenuous, it contains at least a grain of truth. In 1924, in "The Dehumanization of Art," José Ortega y Gasset used a similar argument in his discussion of popular responses to modernism. He observed that large, popular audiences are generally hostile to radical experiments with form because they demand art that reflects their own lives in a recognizably realistic manner.

Ortega went on to say that any art form that is incomprehensible will be perceived as threatening, and the average spectator who feels threatened will respond with hostility.[2] In light of Ortega's observation, it is ironic that Sam Shepard's mass appeal has increased in direct proportion to his mastery of the well-made, linear plot.

Ultimately, however, Fornes's argument about form is not entirely convincing. With the possible exception of *The Danube*, her most recent plays, including *Fefu and Her Friends*, *Mud*, *The Conduct of Life*, and *Sarita*, are quite straightforward. Yes, *Fefu* requires a peripatetic audience, and photographic freezes punctuate the action of *Mud*, but, in general, these plays conform to relatively linear patterns of development that should be easily understood even by unsophisticated spectators. Perhaps the thematic content of her most recent work is *too* clear; because she is regarded in many circles as a feminist playwright, perhaps Fornes is being deliberately disingenuous when she insists that the mass audiences that currently flock to Shepard's latest plays and films reject her work on the basis of form rather than content.

Audience reception is problematic for many female authors, and a significant issue in spectator resistance to Fornes is the complex relationship between gender and response. Indeed, two of the most striking differences between Fornes and Shepard reveal themselves in choice of gender for the foregrounded characters and in the ways in which male characters are represented. In "Writing the Male Character," Margaret Atwood offers several relevant insights into the special problems of female authors who attempt to create male characters from authentic experience rather than from the ways men imagine themselves and wish to be seen. Indeed, one of the greatest challenges for women is to create "acceptable" male characters. Atwood sagely observes:

> For the female novelist, it means that certain men will find it objectionable if she depicts men behaving the way they do behave a lot of the time. Not enough that she may avoid making them rapists and murderers, child molesters, warmongers, sadists, power-hungry, callous, domineering, pompous, foolish or immoral, though I'm sure we will all agree that such men do exist. Even if she makes them sensitive and kind she's open to the charge of having depicted them as "weak". What this kind of critic wants is Captain Marvel, without the Billy Batson *alter ego;* nothing less will do.[3]

Bearing Atwood's observations in mind, I next examine three prominent factors that distinguish audience response to Fornes and Shepard: the gender of the central characters, the general depiction of male characters, and the depiction of male violence against women.

The gender of the principal characters is central to audience response, and popular taste demands maintenance of particular heroic male traditions and types. Looking at the broader social picture, it is painfully clear that, despite the proliferation of feminist analyses of the dynamics of patriarchal culture, we continue to be extraordinarily male focused. Even in the supposedly progressive latter half of the twentieth century, statistics still indicate that significantly larger percentages of couples, given the choice, prefer to have male children. A continuous stream of novels, films, and plays examines the moral, social, and sexual development of the male from birth through adolescence, young adulthood, middle-age, old-age, and death. Audiences flock to ogle the newest Rambo and Rocky films, and adolescent females swoon over tough but sensitive male heroes who reflect some ideal melding of Burt Reynolds and Robert Redford. Shepard's plays speak directly to this obsession. As Bonnie Marranca and other feminist critics have pointed out, Shepard's preoccupation with the psychic conflicts and emotional development (or lack thereof) of male characters renders him virtually incapable of imagining or depicting interesting, believable women; even *Fool for Love* and *A Lie of the Mind*, which include more fully developed female characters, still focus primarily on the moral and psychological development of the male. In *Fool for Love*, for example, May is a central figure, but the amount of time she spends offstage in the bathroom so that the action between Eddie and Martin can be developed indicates that Shepard's preoccupation continues despite his apparent desire to achieve a more heterogeneous world view.

In contrast, Fornes tends to foreground women and female experience. Because male characters are entirely absent from *Fefu and Her Friends*, it is unusual even in Fornes's oeuvre, but an anecdote about *Fefu*, related by the playwright, reveals one of the principal problems faced by female authors writing about women's experience: audience identification with the characters. Fornes explained that many male spectators who attended the New York production could not accept the absence of a male protagonist; thus they identified Phillip, Fefu's offstage husband, as the protagonist: they simply could find no interest in a production that featured women.[4] (Even more problematic is the possibility that female as well as male spectators view Fornes's work through the patriarchal imperative. There is convincing evidence that women have learned to "read" a performance from the dominant male perspective.) In a recent production of *Mud*, a male spectator insisted that Lloyd was the protagonist in contradiction to everything Fornes says about the play:

> I feel that what is important about this play is that Mae is the central character. It says something about women's place in the world, not because she is good or a heroine, not because she is oppressed by men . . . but simply

> because she is the *center* of that play. . . . It is because of that mind, Mae's mind, *a woman's mind*, that that play exists."

What is important, according to Fornes, is that a woman is "at the center of the universe."[5] Women are at the center of *Fefu, Mud, The Conduct of Life,* and *Sarita.* Because Fornes maintains a genuine commitment to placing women in the subject position, she does not compromise her point of view to please popular audiences who are unaccustomed to seeing women at the center of a dramatic situation and who resist receiving an image of the world and men through a woman's eyes.

In her most recent plays, Fornes replaces the male quest for self-actualization with the moral, social, and sexual conflicts typical of female experience. Because women have been peripheral to most male-authored sociocultural documents, both historical and theoretical, interest in their development as autonomous individuals has been minimal. Women who entertained ambitions beyond marriage and motherhood were, and perhaps are, beyond the male imagination. Given this historical and cross-cultural indifference to female development, Fornes's tendency to concentrate on female rather than male psychology may be responsible for the hostility engendered by her work. This, however, is only a partial explanation, and the issue of audience reception and gender transcends the mere centrality of female characters.

Similarly, Shepard's preoccupation with male characters provides a plausible but partial explanation for his current popularity. If simply foregrounding a particular gender constituted an instant formula for success, many obscure playwrights would be in strong competition with Shepard. The key to Shepard's popularity is that he created and exploited a particularly appealing male character type, marketing it with great success to the traditionally conservative, sentimental American public. Although this observation is not unique, it is apparently true that with characters like Lee in *True West,* Vince in *Buried Child,* Eddie in *Fool for Love,* Wes in *Curse of the Starving Class,* and Jake in *A Lie of the Mind,* Shepard has created a new American antihero: the disenfranchised cowboy who searches in vain for a range that has long since vanished; the round peg who refuses the square hole of middle-class, corporate America; the last true iconoclast who rejects bourgeois values of home, family, and stable career to wander the West, alone but self-sufficient; the sensitive male whose erratic and often violent behavior can best be understood as a futile gesture of revolt against an increasingly complex, incomprehensible universe. This image has a quality of nineteenth-century romanticism clinging to it. Indeed, I would like to propose that Shepard's antihero is really just a familiar

American icon dressed up in a new costume. This character type has a cyclical existence and reappears periodically in popular art and literature. As Barbara Ehrenreich noted in *The Hearts of Men,* the most recent wave of machismo rebellion occurred in the 1950s. In that era, the paradigm of conformity was the "grey flannel man," and that image drove "real men" to create counter images that reeked of ruggedly rebellious machismo individualism.[6]

Although they are grubby and frayed along the edges, rugged individualists are Shepard's specialty. Vince and Eddie, and to a lesser degree Wesley, Lee, and Jake, fit quite comfortably into that type. It might be argued that Shepard's perspective is satirical, but evidence from the plays provides tenuous support for that position. The contrasts he draws between Lee and Austin in *True West* and Eddie and Martin in *Fool for Love* clearly establish his point of view on desirable male lifestyle. Austin is a particularly instructive case. He is the spaniel, the domestic dog, the "good boy" who waters Mom's plants, supports a family, and runs the bourgeois rat race. Lee is the coyote, the quintessential "bad boy" who balances precariously, with one foot poised before the prison gates, on the fringes of civilized society. But although he is tempted by Austin's financial security, Lee does not dream of living Austin's life—it is Austin who hungers for an opportunity to escape the drudgery of middle-class respectability by joining his brother in the desert. The play's action and the character of Lee have immense appeal to audiences because together they embody a traditional male escape fantasy. Spectators may identify with Austin's desire, but the object of that desire is Lee's freedom. For all of Lee's disreputable degeneracy, he fulfills a role model function in *True West* just as Eddie does in *Fool for Love*. Eddie conforms to the best romantic traditions, and his attractions become even more obvious when Shepard deliberately contrasts him with the dreadfully dull, monochromatic Martin who, God forbid, actually allows the woman to choose the movie. Which character is the average spectator more likely to identify with—violent, crazy, irresponsible Eddie or wimpish Martin? The question is almost rhetorical.

Shepard plays to our cultural "Walter Mittyishness." We dream of escape into freedom and fantasize obsessively about the Vinces, Eddies, Wesleys, and Lees of the world. Women find their rough-hewn vulnerability attractive, and men imagine themselves into this image of the self-sufficient loner who bursts the chains of bourgeois conformity (chains which were forged primarily by women). Vince, the questing male hero of *Buried Child*, is the paradigm for this type; he is the most conspicuous example of the man outside who returns like a conquering savior to tear the rot out of what is left of his family. Consider the significance of the following action. Bemoaning the fate that has left her with a group of impotent, ineffectual, mentally disturbed males, Halie, Vince's grandmother, cries out for her lost child, Ansel: "He was a hero! A man! A whole man! What's happened to the men in this family! Where are the men!"[7] The words are hardly out of her mouth when the answer comes crashing through the ancient screen door—her grandson, Vince. He is drunk and disheveled, but there is no question that he is the "New Man" who will whip this dissipated, degenerate excuse for a family into shape. In a gesture reeking of patriarchal symbolism, Dodge wills the house to Vince and then conveniently dies, leaving the newly crowned superhero to ascend the patriarchal throne and create life in his own image. (Vince's girlfriend, Shelly, is conspicuously absent from this picture. Vince discards her as offhandedly as used tissue. This approach to women is typical of Shepard's antiheroes.)

Shepard's treatment of female characters raises the issue of violence. There is significant violence in most of the plays, but it is a pretend, boyish violence without real consequences. *Curse of the Starving Class* exemplifies Shepard's casual treatment of male violence against women. The play begins with a conversation between Wesley and his mother, Emma. Emma insists that on the previous night, Wes, her deadbeat husband, had threatened her physically—perhaps to the point of a brutal beating or even death—and that she was fully justified in locking him out of the house. Wesley denies this: "He wasn't threatening you. . . . He was just trying to get in."[8] Shepard manipulates the spectator into seeing the situation through the boy's eyes and accepting his point of view. Wesley's father is not a brutal wife beater, just a well-meaning disillusioned bumbler who is not dangerous. This pretend violence is evident in most of the "family" plays. In *Fool for Love,* Eddie stalks but never strikes, and although the suicide of May's mother is the result of the Old Man's unexplained absences and infidelity, his role in her madness and subsequent death is depicted as indirect and peripheral to the central interest of the play. Shepard apparently would have the audience believe that Eddie's final disappearing act is one of selfless renunciation and atonement for past wrongs after he acknowledges the validity of May's version of the family's history. Jake, the "hero" of *A Lie of the Mind,* brutally beats his wife, Beth, to the point of brain damage (out of love, he reminds us), but despite being virtually lobotomized, Beth finds truth, love, and happiness with Jake's gentle brother, Frankie. In a gesture reminiscent of Eddie's final act, Jake renounces his claim to Beth and disappears, perhaps to contemplate his newly found wisdom.

Whose reality is this? Is there any relationship between these situations and the reality of male violence against women? With the possible exception of *Curse of the Starving Class,* Shepard reveals himself as an essentially romantic playwright who rationalizes male violence and softens its consequences to appeal to the sentimentality of American audiences. He reinforces popular media images in the best Sylvester Stallone tradition. In place of an authentic exploration of male violence in general and male violence against women in particular. Shepard's texts offer the tired but still popular diatribe against mothers. The image of the American mother popularized by Philip Wylie has new life in Shepard's family plays, and they must continually shoulder the blame for any mental or emotional disturbances experienced by the adult males who were once their helpless victims.

Fornes resists these insidious, but unfortunately popular, fantasies by focusing insistently on the ugly consequences of gratuitous violence. A passage from *Fefu and Her Friends* reveals the general purpose of her work. Fefu, in discussing what she believes to be an almost involuntary but nonetheless universal attraction to revolting objects, illustrates her point by asking the other women if, after turning over a lovely rock that is resting in damp soil, they are not both fascinated and revolted by what is underneath: "You see, that which is exposed to the exterior . . . is smooth and dry and clean. That which is . . . underneath, is slimy and filled with fungus and crawling with worms. It is another life that is parallel to the one we manifest. It's there. The way worms are underneath the stone. If you don't recognize it . . . it eats you."[9]

Although audience resistance to Fornes's work may be explained partially by the centrality of female characters, more problematic is her invitation to the audience to view the underside of patriarchal culture through women's eyes (and, author's disclaimers aside, they are angry eyes). Fornes's mirror reflects disturbing images of patriarchy in general and of male behavior in particular, images that will be offensive to audiences who are hungry for traditional male heroism and who demand evidence that patriarchy is still a viable cultural system. Positive male characters do appear in Fornes's plays: Mark, in *Sarita,* is an obvious example, but he is also exceptional. More typical are Orlando in *The Conduct of Life,* Julio in *Sarita,* Lloyd and Henry in *Mud,* and even Philip, the offstage husband in *Fefu and Her Friends.*

There are several interesting parallels between *The Conduct of Life* and *A Lie of the Mind,* and they provide an opportunity to compare textual strategies for depicting male violence. The situations are similar: Orlando and Jake are men who physically abuse women, and both are married to women who love them regardless of their brutality. In *A Lie of the Mind,* the first character introduced is Jake, and the audience is invited to sympathize and identify with him: Jake, who believes he has just killed his wife; Jake, who has beaten her frequently in the past;

Jake, who is now a trembling little boy and who cannot live without the woman he nearly murdered. Frankie reminds him that, as a boy, he abused his pet goat, and Jake's response is revealing: "I loved that goat."[10] The message is clear: brutality, love, and need are intimately linked. Jake loved his goat, but he kicked her; Jake loved Beth, but he nearly beat her to death. She and the goat share a common history. Perhaps the goat motif was an unfortunate choice on Shepard's part if he wished to show Jake's vulnerability and sensitivity: equating the goat with Beth suggests that Beth is dehumanized to the level of a goat. Indeed, it seems that Jake cannot distinguish between goats and women. Even more frustrating is that Shepard manipulates the already credulous audience into identifying with Jake. The first action, a telephone conversation between Jake and Frankie, reveals Jake's suffering and emotional state. Thus the audience is asked to (please) understand this poor unfortunate soul who beats his wife because he just cannot help himself—and after seeing his mother, one understands why he turned out so badly.

Fornes deals quite differently with Orlando. Like Jake, he is the first character introduced, but Orlando does not win any sympathy with his opening monologue:

> Thirty three and I'm still a lieutenant. In two years I'll receive a promotion or I'll leave the military. I promise I will not spend time feeling sorry for myself.—Instead I will study the situation and draw an effective plan of action. I must eliminate all obstacles.—I will make the acquaintance of people in high power. If I cannot achieve this on my own merit, I will marry a woman in high circles. Leticia must not be an obstacle.—Man must have an ideal, mine is to achieve maximum power. That is my destiny.—No other interest will deter me from this.—My sexual drive is detrimental to my ideals. I must no longer be overwhelmed by sexual passion or I will be degraded beyond hope of recovery.[11]

Orlando is driven by his overwhelming ambition and hunger for power to join an "information gathering" arm of the government, and having learned the fine art of torture, he rises quickly to a position of authority. But his unfortunate inability to suppress his sexual drive leads him to kidnap a child, hold her in bondage, and subject her to repeated rape. His justification is astonishingly similar to Jake's:

> What I do to you is out of love. Out of want. It's not what you think. I wish you didn't have to be hurt. I don't do it out of hatred. It is not out of rage. It is love. It is a quiet feeling. It's a pleasure. . . . It is my most private self. And this I give to you.—Don't be afraid.—It is a desire to destroy and to see things destroyed and to see the inside of them.—It's my nature. I must hide this from others. But I don't feel remorse. I was born this way and I must have this.—I need love. I wish you did not feel hurt and recoil from me.[12]

Orlando's action are not entirely unmotivated: Fornes offers justification for his brutality, but, unlike Shepard's crafty presentation of Jake, it does not appeal to popular sentiment. It does not seek to excuse Orlando because he had a nasty childhood and his mother was guilty of poor parenting. Orlando's actions are based in a fundamental drive for power and an almost inhuman indifference to any needs but his own. Nena, the young girl kidnapped by Orlando, resembles Beth in that both women are dehumanized and reduced to the level of the goat. Orlando's needs are paramount, and his women are subject to his godlike will. They are his property, and he is fully convinced of his right to dispose of them as he pleases. In *The Conduct of Life*, Fornes exposes a dynamic of patriarchal culture that eludes Shepard: our society condones, encourages, and even venerates male brutality, and violence against women has for centuries been a strategic device that preserves traditional gender hierarchies.

Gender hierarchy and the operations of patriarchy are treated more directly in *Fefu and Her Friends*. Although Fornes prefers to leave the identity of "They" to the imagination of the spectator, "They" clearly will not tolerate women who challenge their authority and privilege. Fefu's friend, Julia, was the first victim. Suffering from physical paralysis and paranoia and tormented by violent fantasies, she finds relief only by reciting the following prayer:

> The human being is of the masculine gender. The human being is a boy as a child and grown up he is a man. Everything on earth is for the human being, which is man. To nourish him.—There are evil things on earth for man also. For him to fight with, and conquer and turn its evil into good. So that it too can nourish him.—There are Evil Plants, Evil Animals, Evil Minerals, and Women are Evil.—Woman is not a human being. She is: 1—A mystery. 2—Another species. 3—As yet undefined. 4—Unpredictable; therefore wicked and gentle and evil and good which is evil.—If a man commits an evil act, he must be pitied. The evil comes from outside him, through him and into the act. Woman generates the evil herself.[13]

Although Fornes resists ideological labels and refuses to align herself with any particular feminist position, it is impossible to ignore the explicit critique of patriarchy in *Fefu and Her Friends*. This critique is general, symbolic, and tends more toward radical feminism than do her most recent plays, but it is eminently clear that Julia's madness and genuine physical and mental anguish are the consequences of psychic violence perpetrated on all women who resist the unwritten rules of patriarchy. Mae, in *Mud*, and Sarita, in *Sarita*, suffer similar fates. Mae is destroyed by the insatiable demands of Lloyd and Henry, and Sarita, perhaps a victim of internalized oppression, destroys herself by maintaining a destructive relationship with the physically and emotionally abusive Julio. Violence against women remains the dominant issue, but in both of these plays, the radical feminist critique is considerably modified by the influence of class and ethnicity.

Regardless of specific ideological intent, Fornes's plays deconstruct the dynamics of gender hierarchy with profoundly disturbing results. Her images—violent, unsentimental, and unremittingly pessimistic—recall a statement by Marguerite Duras, who wrote: "I think 'feminine literature' is an organic, translated writing . . . translated from blackness, from darkness. Women have been in darkness for centuries . . . and when they write, they translate this darkness. . . ." Duras goes on to say that genuine women's writing is a new way of communicating; it uses a new language. There are, she admits, many female plagiarists—women who write to please men or in imitation of men, but this is not authentic feminine literature. True feminine literature "is a violent, direct literature."[14]

Fornes translates from this blackness. She turns the stone over and reveals aspects of male psychology and heterosexual intimacy that are profoundly disturbing. If Fornes remains on the periphery of the mainstream, it is because large, popular audiences come to the theater to have their most cherished beliefs reinforced, not challenged. They do not want to examine the implications of gender hierarchy or the dynamics of patriarchy too closely. Fornes's refusal to compromise, her refusal to write to please men, her rejection of romantic sentimentality ensures that she will remain on the fringe. Male heroics are absent from her plays, and she explores the consequences of physical, emotional, and mental abuse through the eyes of the victims. Fornes's plays reflect an essentialist world view, and average spectators will reject the proposition that males derive some mysterious pleasure from violence or that violence satisfies some innate desire for power; but a cursory glance through the first thirty pages of any given *Newsweek* reveals an unending parade of photographs of young men ecstatically waving their weapons and testifies to the validity of Fornes's perspective. Desperate to justify the morality of patriarchy, we prefer Shepard's romanticism. We demand assurances that Beth and May will live happily ever after, and that Eddie and Jake have gone to the mountain top. Is it any wonder that Fornes's work remains obscure? From the darkness of her vision, Mae and Julia die, Sarita is institutionalized, and Leticia wishes for death after she kills Orlando. There is no pretend violence in Fornes's plays. Big boys play dangerous games. Ted Bundy really exists and his childhood traumas and unsatisfactory relationship with his mother are irrelevant to the women he murdered. For Shepard, male violence is only a game; for Fornes, it is reality. I suspect that our reluctance to acknowledge this reality is at the root of spectator hostility to Fornes's work. After a recent production of *Mud*, an angry male spectator walked out muttering: "This play must have been written by a woman." Sugar-coating is not part of Fornes's recipe.

Notes

1. Kathleen Betsko and Rachel Koenig, *Interviews with Contemporary Women Playwrights* (New York: Beech Tree Books, 1987), p. 164.
2. José Ortega y Gasset, "The Dehumanization of Art," in *Dramatic Theory and Criticism: Greeks to Grotowski*, ed. Bernard Dukore (New York: Holt, Rinehart and Winston, 1974), pp. 756–60.
3. Margaret Atwood, *Second Words* (Boston: Beacon Press, 1982), pp. 419–20.
4. Conversation with Maria Irene Fornes, Tallahassee, Fla., 1986.
5. Betsko and Koenig, *Interviews with Contemporary Women Playwrights*, p. 166.
6. Barbara Ehrenreich, *The Hearts of Men: American Dreams and the Flight from Commitment* (Garden City, N.Y.: Anchor Books, 1984).
7. Sam Shepard, *Buried Child*, in *Sam Shepard: Seven Plays* (New York: Bantam Books, 1984), p. 124.
8. Sam Shepard, *Curse of the Starving Class*, in *Sam Shepard: Seven Plays* (New York: Bantam Books, 1984), p. 136.
9. Maria Irene Fornes, *Fefu and Her Friends*, in *Wordplays: An Anthology of New American Drama* (New York: Performing Arts Journal Publications, 1980), p. 9.
10. Sam Shepard, *A Lie of the Mind: A Play in Three Acts* (New York: New American Library, 1986), p. 13.
11. Maria Irene Fornes, *The Conduct of Life*, in *Maria Irene Fornes: Plays* (New York: Performing Arts Journal Publications, 1986), p. 68.
12. Fornes, *The Conduct of Life*, p. 82.
13. Fornes, *Fefu and Her Friends*, p. 25.
14. From an interview with Marguerite Duras, in *New French Feminisms: An Anthology*, ed. Elaine Marks and Isabelle de Courtivron (Amherst: The University of Massachusetts Press, 1980), p. 174.

18
The Ghosts of Chekhov's *Three Sisters* Haunt Beth Henley's *Crimes of the Heart*

Joanne B. Karpinski

In *Mississippi Writers Talking,* Beth Henley identifies herself more with an older tradition of playwrights than with her contemporaries (in a prose style that may cause the gentle reader to doubt the assertion):

> I mainly read old things. I missed a lot of reading when I was young, so I like to read more classical stuff . . . They told me, "They're not doing three-act plays anymore," and I went "They're not? Wow! Back when I was reading plays they were doing them."[1]

The name of Anton Chekhov is prominent in her discussion:

> I had read Tennessee Williams and Chekhov, and I think they're great . . . Chekhov and Shakespeare, of course, are my favorite playwrights. Chekhov, I feel he influenced me more than anyone else . . .[2]

Henley doesn't mention *Three Sisters* specifically, although in a telephone conversation with the author she did say she had *Three Sisters* in mind when writing *Crimes of the Heart.* It may seem premature to compare a playwright's first work (albeit a Pulitzer Prize winner) to the epitome of Chekhov's dramatic oeuvre, but similarities of plot, setting, theme, characterization, and comic technique invite such a comparison, and the results help to clarify the successes and shortcomings in Henley's art at this early stage of its development.

Perhaps the most obvious parallel between the two works is the presence in both of three sisters. The impetus for Henley's choice is biographical, although "my mother isn't dead with suicide, my sister hasn't shot her husband, you know, my sister doesn't have a missing ovary."[3] What Henley's dramatized siblings chiefly have in common with Chekhov's is a sense of blighted expectations about work and love. Lenny, like Olga, has aged prematurely in a self-defeating effort to carry out a nurturing role and never expects to have a man of her own; Babe, like Masha, feels stuck in an inappropriate marriage and finds a more sympathetic partner outside this bond; Meg, like Irina, gets sidetracked into a meaningless job despite lofty career aspirations and has doubts about making a commitment to a man who truly loves her.

The MaGraths and the Prozorovs both endure the "soul-killing ennui of a provincial town," but their efforts "to deal with the commonplace reality of life are ineffectual and unrealistic."[4] Despite the surface gaiety of their interactions,[5] the sisters reveal themselves as isolated to the point of desperation. Their isolation manifests itself in petty unkindnesses such as Meg's taking one bite out of each of Lenny's birthday chocolates or Olga's refusal to listen to Masha's confidence about falling in love with a married man.[6] All the sisters suffer the vexations of a more energetic, vulgar female antagonist, although Chick in *Crimes* functions more as an externalization of the MaGraths' self-doubts than as a genuine force of dramatic opposition. These female antagonists represent "lesser potentials, unworthy of realization according to Chekhov's [and Henley's] values":

> . . . their actual presence makes even more poignant the sense of deprivation resulting from the non-fulfillment of the greater potential. Thus, for instance, in *Three Sisters* Natasha and Kulygin fully realize their meagre, narrow potentials and feel themselves fulfilled, satisfied people. . . .[7]

Most important, both sets of sisters have inherited a suffocating value system, reenforced by their emotional ties to a dominating male figure not present on the stage. The MaGraths' nascent triumphs over their dreary heritage contrast with the Prozorovs' dispersal and defeat in the service of their glorious but paralyzing tradition. This difference in outcome results from the antithetical attitudes the two families hold about the past, and from what René Girard would characterize as the relative force that "mediated desire" exerts in the lives of Henley's and Chekhov's protagonists.

When Henley remarked, "Both are about overcoming ghosts of the past and letting go of what other people have said you are,"[8] she was characterizing the similiarity of theme in *Crimes* and her later work *The Miss Firecracker Contest*, but the description pertains to *The Three Sisters* as well. The Prozorov and the MaGrath sisters both begin the dramatic action under the sway of life expectations established by a patriarchal figure who never appears on stage. The Prozorovs' father has been dead for a year, and Old Granddaddy MaGrath lies comatose in the hospital, but the expectations engendered by these men continue to oppress the young women.

Olga, Masha, and Irina yearn to go to Moscow to take up the life of aristocratic culture for which their father trained them; this illusory prospect deters them from taking decisive action to improve their present circumstances. Lenny, Meg, and Babe suffer as they struggle to fulfill the roles assigned to them by Old Granddaddy's self-serving ambitions for them. Like Don Quixote in Girard's analysis, both sets of sisters desire *"according to Another"*[9] rather than choosing for themselves; like the Don, they look painfully foolish in this predicament. Ultimately, sisterly solidarity forms the basis for the MaGraths to break out of "mediated desire" into a more self-directed mode, but the Prozorovs remain imprisoned by their admittedly more seductive legacy of values.

Henley's play makes the mediated nature of the sisters' desire more apparent and more imposed than Chekhov does. Lenny remembers that Old Grandaddy said Zachery "was just the right man for [Babe] whether she knew it now or not" (22).[10] Meg overtly expresses resentment of Old Granddaddy's efforts to direct her life, but Lenny experiences his interference as well-meant:

> *Meg.* . . . I hate myself when I lie for that old man. I do. I feel so weak. And then I have to go and do at least three or four things that I know he'd despise just to get even with that miserable, old, bossy man!
>
> *Lenny.* Oh, Meg, please don't talk so about Old Granddaddy! It sounds so ungrateful. Why, he went out of his way to make a home for us, to treat us like we were his very own children. All he ever wanted was the best for us. That's all he ever wanted.
>
> *Meg.* Well, I guess it was; but sometimes I wonder what we wanted. (69–70)

Chekhov's three sisters are aware of their father's role in creating their values and aspirations, but they do not experience any dissonance about this. Only their brother Andrei has found parental expectation burdensome:

> Father—God rest his soul—oppressed us with education. It's ridiculous and stupid, but all the same I must confess that after his death I began to fill out, and now, in one year, I've grown fat, as if a weight had been lifted from my body. Thanks to Father, my sisters and I know French, German, and English, and Irina knows Italian besides. But at what a cost! (248)[11]

Masha responds that in their provincial setting the knowledge of three languages is "not even a luxury, but a superfluous appendage, like a sixth finger" (249), but she does not reject the appendage. Vershinin, the visiting colonel who had known their father and who will soon become Masha's lover, stipulates that "there is not and cannot be a town so dull and depressing that a clever, educated person would be useless" (249). Hearing this self-validation, Masha reverses her earlier decision to leave Irina's name-day party.

It is essential to the dramatic structure of *The Three Sisters* that the sisters more consistently experience their patrimony of education and culture as uplifting rather than deforming. The wave of the future, embodied in Natasha Ivanovna, is represented as vulgar, mean-spirited, and even immoral (it is strongly hinted that her second child is her lover's rather than her husband's). As a result, the audience sympathizes with the Prozorovs although it acknowledges that their passive clinging to the past is forlorn and foolish. In contrast, Old Granddaddy's desires *have* deformed the MaGraths: Lenny believes herself to be sterile and undesirable, Meg has had a brush with insanity, and Babe has been battered by "Mr. Right."

Unlike the Prozorovs, for whom the beautiful past forms a consolation for the banal present, all the MaGrath sisters' connections to the past are negative or truncated. Meg remembers their father, who walked out on them, as a bastard—"Really, with his white teeth. Daddy was such a bastard" (31).[12] Their mother sank into a depressed silence before she hanged herself and took the pet cat with her. Meg's singing talent has deserted her as she has abandoned her lover, Babe has shot her husband, and Lenny's horse has been struck by lightning. Consequently, the MaGraths have an incentive to look for new directions.

Furthermore, the MaGraths' chief antagonists in the present action embody the ghastly results of enacting Old Granddaddy's value system. On the one hand is Zackery Botrell, the pinnacle of Hazelhurst society, willing to beat, incarcerate, or institutionalize his wife to keep his dominant position. On the other is Cousin Chick, proud possessor of a husband, two children, and a modern home, who sees the sisters' actions not as consequences of a desperate emotional plight but as "trashy ways" that impede her social striving.

Finally, the MaGraths find (as the Prozorovs do not) an ally in their efforts to disrupt the cycle of mediated desire. With a baby face and awkward speech, Barnette Lloyd initially seems like no match for Zackery Botrell, acknowledged as the best lawyer around but not in a position to defend Babe against the charge of attempting to murder him. Although Barnette has just graduated from law school, and Lenny has hired him as a favor to a family friend, he has the shrewdness and drive that the sisters lack. By turning Botrell's effort at blackmail back on him (would Zackery like the citizens of Hazelhurst to see pictures proving his wife found him so inadequate that she had turned to the carnal consolations of a black teenager?), Barnette makes Babe's act of rebellion efficacious. This coup paves the way for Meg and Lenny to assert themselves.

Feminists may, with some justification, object to Henley's introduction of a male savior, particularly one who seems motivated by mediated desire (his "personal vendetta" against Babe's husband concerns some injustice inflicted on Barnette's father). Barnette's intervention only changes the tide of the external action, however; his maneuver sets the stage for Babe's triumph over her most severe internal crisis.

When she shot Zackery, Babe first had intended to kill herself, but then found the courage to redirect her despair toward its proper source, realizing "I wanted to kill him. . . . 'Cause I—I wanted to live!" (49–50). Botrell's threat to commit her to an insane asylum speaks to her deepest fear—that she really is crazy, like her suicidal mother. She is rescued from acting out this fear not by Barnette but by Meg, who convinces her that she is not alone, that she really wants to live and help celebrate Lenny's birthday. Barnette's actions only catalyze a *peripeteia* that the sisters accomplish for themselves.

This reversal of the MaGrath sisters' fortunes has a preliminary, conditional feeling. Lenny's candlelit vision of the three sisters laughing together "wasn't forever; it wasn't for every minute" (124), and Babe's legal problems are far from over when the curtain falls. Moreover, the more authentic desires toward which the sisters begin to strive remain fairly conventional: Lenny seeks marriage with Charley Hill, and Babe seems on the verge of establishing a relationship with a more suitable lawyer. Meg seems poised for a fresh start, but the play does not resolve the traditional split between a woman's achievement of a successful career and an emotional commitment; she regains her singing voice when she gives up the prospect of stealing Doc away from his wife and children.

Despite remaining bound up in traditional female expectations, the MaGraths' future prospects are considerably more optimistic than the Prozorovs'. In contrast to the vague but promising vision of the future that ends Henley's play, Chekhov's denouement confronts with brutal honesty the gender-related socioeconomic constraints that limit the sisters' claims on the future. The sisters' dream of going to Moscow is compromised not only by their own refined inertia but by their lack of financial control over their destiny.

By mortgaging the family home without his sisters' permission, Andrei traps Olga and Irina in the backwater mode to which he has already committed himself by marrying Natasha and going to work for the contemptible provincial council. Masha, too, has married a small town hack, to whom her loyalty seems as compelled as that of her lover to his suicidal wife. Irina's reluctant acceptance of Tuzenbach's proposal leads her even deeper into the provinces, to a prosaic job in a brickyard that she fatalistically plans to honor even after Tuzenbach's death theoretically sets her free. In default of the husband with whom she would willingly have spent her days at home, Olga achieves the pinnacle of her professional possibilities when she is made directress of the district girls' school, but her earnings only make it possible for her to liberate the family nurse from ending her life in the poorhouse rather than enabling them to begin a new life in Moscow.

In the fiscal powerlessness imposed on them by the gender-biased property laws of their time, Chekhov's three sisters *need* a male savior but don't get one. Nor does their love for each other form a sufficient basis of support and warmth to overcome the pain and anguish caused by their failure to achieve relationships based on romantic love.[13] In contrast to the MaGraths, the Prozorovs have neither the incentive nor the means to escape the beautiful prison-house built by their father's values. Ironically, they are evicted by the vulgar and materialistic Natasha, the antithesis to their mediated desires.

Here Chekhov achieves a level of dramatic tension beyond Henley's scope. In *Crimes of the Heart*, Chick's ambitions are comically belittled, and Old Granddaddy's are shown to be oppressive, but the MaGrath sisters' own values are poorly defined in contrast. Their freedom to choose seems taken as sufficient value in itself. Moreover, these choices are subjected to some of the same comic belittling as Chick's. Babe takes up the saxophone, not a classical instrument; Lenny meets Charley Hill through a lonely hearts club rather than by some more dignified means. Although these outcomes are consistent with the social fabric of the MaGraths' lives, they also create comic distancing between the audience and the presumed protagonists. This strategy makes it difficult to "enter the . . . female culture of [Henley's] characters and judge their actions *from within that world*."[14]

Another striking connection between *Crimes of the Heart* and *The Three Sisters* is their shared commitment to tragicomic tone. Chekhov firmly believed that "In life, there are no clear-cut consequences or reasons; in it, everything is mixed up together; the important and the paltry, the great and the base, the tragic and the ridiculous."[15] Henley points out (with the intense personalism that consistently distinguishes her viewpoint from Chekhov's more universalized perspective, exemplified in the reference to *all* "life," above) that she doesn't set out to write comedy:

> All these things that I feel inside are desperate and dark and unhappy. Or not *unhappy*, but searching. Then they come out funny. The way my family dealt with hardships was to see the humor or the ironic point of view in the midst of tragedy. And that's just how *my* mind works.[16]

Henley's and Chekhov's tragicomic mixtures have antecedents in the *comédie larmoyante*, but they differ from the French archetype in refusing both sentimental and moralistic closure.[17] No theatrical precedent existed for Irina's reaction to the threats of fire, foreclosure, eviction, and unattainable love by sobbing "I can't remember how to say window or floor in Italian" except in Chekhov's own earlier plays (289). This sublime non sequitur has few dramatic equals until the outburst of hysterical laughter that greets Meg's promise to tell the truth to Old Granddaddy even if it sends him into a coma (99).

Both plays contain examples of a beau geste that turns grotesque: Babe aims for Zackery's heart but instead shoots him in the stomach because her hands are shaking; Tuzenbach dies in a duel with a rival whose claims are rhetorical, not real. Henley, however, uses this device to emphasize comically the difference between the audience's expectations and her characters' actions (as when Babe mixes herself a pitcher of lemonade after she shoots Zackery and even asks him if he wants some), while Chekhov uses it to stress the ironic distance between what his characters hope for and what they achieve (as when Chebutykin, a doctor, copies a cure for hair loss out of a local newspaper).

Henley's deployment of the grotesque initially "allows the spectators to distance themselves from these characters and perhaps even to dismiss [their] challenge to male-defined reality as merely 'crazy,' "[18] whereas Chekhov's strategy connects audience to character in a moment of rueful recognition. Laughlin, however, sees a polemic method to Henley's flirtation with the madwoman stereotype:

> For example, the play clearly connects Babe's "madness" with her rejection of sex role stereotypes and especially the sexual assertiveness demonstrated in her affair with Willie Jay. . . . While Henley's script leaves itself open to a production which plays up the insanity and presumed irrationality of her central characters, the notion of madness . . . links *Crimes of the Heart* with similar devices in an entire tradition of women's writing.[19]

A side effect of the tragicomic tone in Henley's and Chekhov's plays is that both require a particular kind of acting ensemble for successful performance. Chekhov's *Seagull* expired uneventfully in the star-oriented, highly commercial Imperial theater, in reaction to which he became active in developing the Moscow Art Theater as an alternative. The development of regional and off-Broadway venues for plays by women made possible productions of *Crimes* that did not cater to female stereotypes. It is significant that *Crimes* won its Pulitzer Prize before its Broadway review, under a policy (first adopted in the year the play appeared) that allowed works from regional as well as New York theaters to be considered for the award. Several critics of the Broadway staging of *Crimes* felt that the actresses' exaggerated Southernness verged on parody, in contrast to the restraint exercised in the prize-winning Louisville production. As Helene Keyssar observed:

> Because the play's texture relies on the characterizations of the three sisters and the dialogue among them, it can only move the audience if the ordinariness of the women is made specific and honest in performance. In the Broadway production, however, each of the actresses parodied her role, exaggerating the "Southernness" of the women, the *naïveté* of Lenny, the brashness of Babe and the pseudo-urban sophistication of Meg. Laughing at these women is boring and allows a particularly dangerous condescension when the audience's frame is a play by and about women.[20]

For Henley, as for Chekhov, the tragicomic tone functions as a diagnostic and a healing device. Again, Henley approaches these functions from a personal perspective, while Chekhov's view is other-directed. Chekhov operates with the objectivity of a clinician ("My familiarity with the natural sciences and the scientific method has always kept me on my guard"[21]), tempered by the compassion of a general practitioner ("First of all, I'd get my patients into a laughing mood, and only then would I begin to treat them"[22]). Henley thinks like an (im)patient:

> Writing always helps me not to feel so angry. I've written about ghastly, black feelings and thoughts that I've had. The hope is that if you can pin down these emotions and express them accurately, you will be somehow absolved. I like to write characters who do horrible things, but whom you can still like . . . because of their human needs and struggles.[23]

The pursuit of objectivity may explain the Darwinian underpinning of the character struggles in *Crimes of the Heart* and *Three Sisters*. The passive, exhausted Prozorov sisters identify with the migratory birds that can fly away to more propitious climates although they themselves cannot set forth for Moscow. Their brother Andrei describes the family nemesis, his wife Natasha, as "a small, blind, sort of thick skinned animal" (301); that is, as a mole that has undermined the structure of their household. Which species seems better equipped to survive in the changing social environment depicted by the play?

Early in *Crimes of the Heart*, the MaGrath sisters are associated with images of extinction and decay (Lenny's horse struck by lightning, the family cat hanged by their suicidal mother, Meg's fascination with the illustrations of skin diseases in Old Granddaddy's medical books), but the balance of power shifts when Lenny sweeps the appropriately named Cousin Chick out of the family kitchen with a broom. Both plays also raise the Lamarckian question of whether acquired characteristics (a culture, a psychosis) determine the behavior of the next generation.

The struggle for survival depicted by Henley and Chekhov takes place on determinedly commonplace grounds. Chekhov described the rationale for the texture of his dramatic realism in this way:

> Let the things that happen onstage be just as complex and yet just as simple as they are in life. For instance, people are having a meal at table, just having a meal, but at the same time their happiness is being created, or their lives are being smashed up.[24]

Nancy Hargrove points out that Henley's realistic details "reinforce the idea that ordinary life is like this":

> Her characters unobtrusively but constantly are doing the mundane things that go on in daily life. . . . In fact, eating and drinking run all through the plays, not only because they are such ordinary and necessary parts of living but also because, in Henley's universe, they are among the few pleasures of life or, in certain cases, among the few consolations *for* life.[25]

Everyday activities serve the cause of characterization, too. The simple act of carrying a candle across the stage identifies Natasha as Lucifer or Lady Macbeth. A game of hearts emblemizes the MaGraths' troubled efforts to achieve sisterly bonding; they can scarcely remember the rules, except that "the Black Sister is the worst," and the game abruptly breaks up when Meg accepts Doc Porter's invitation. Both playwrights use gift-giving to establish relationships among characters. Chick's present of leftover Christmas chocolates shows how little she really thinks of Lenny, and at the other extreme the silver samovar presented to Irina by Chebutykin indicates that he sees her as an avatar of her dead mother.

Gift-giving participates in a larger context of ritual occasions serving as an ironic counterpoint to the developing dramatic situation. Lenny's thirtieth birthday should be celebrated as a lifegiving event, but even such comically offhand remembrances as the leftover chocolates and Lenny's candlelit birthday cookie get swept aside in the aftermath of Babe's attempt to kill her abusive husband. Irina's nameday party, which unpropitiously occurs on the anniversary of her father's death, unwittingly begins her downfall and her sisters', because it provides Andrei the opportunity to propose to the adorably flustered Natasha.

Chekhov gives much fuller scope to this idea than Henley, as successive acts show Natasha's increasingly malevolent ability to kill the Prozorovs' celebratory impulse. In act 2, she preempts the Mardi Gras celebration but goes off herself "for a drive" with her lover Protopopov. The fire in act 3 may be beyond her control, but she so joylessly opposes the domestic hubbub brought about by the sisters' relief efforts that Masha observes, "She goes about looking as if it were she who had started the fire" (290). By the end of the play, she has successfully evicted the sisters from their own home, and she even casts gloom over the farewell party by voicing her plans to cut down the trees in their garden. In this respect, *The Three Sisters* marks an advance even within Chekhov's *oeuvre* in the "technique of wringing symbol from apparent naturalism."[26]

Keeping a single set for her drama, Henley follows Chekhov in using setting to reveal character and situation in a more limited way. The MaGrath kitchen, the sentimentalized "heart" of a family's home, becomes the site of betrayed confidences that reveal the sisters' mutual isolation; in act 3, however, the sisters' growing solidarity is revealed by their ability to chase the intrusive Chick out of the house. The closing tableau of *Crimes*, with the sisters laughing and hugging in the glow of birthday candles, echoes in a brighter key the curtain tableau of *The Three Sisters'* farewell embrace.

Henley also provides a natural catastrophe as a metaphor for emotional crisis. She uses the device in less developed form than appears in *Three Sisters*, in which the fire gives physical immediacy to the tensions and longings that have suffused the emotional atmosphere of the play. She set the time of *Crimes of the Heart* as "five years after Hurricane Camille," making both the past event and the elapsed interval significant to the course of present action.

The tropical storm with a woman's name crippled Meg's lover when, with ironic literalness, it made the roof fall in on them. Meg subsequently abandoned Doc, re-enacting her own abandonment by her father in the same spirit of painful self-preservation that in childhood led her to consume double-dip ice cream sundaes while staring at the March of Dimes poster in the drugstore. Half a decade later, Meg has lost her ability to sing and has been driven to the brink of madness by her bad-faith effort to live out Old Granddaddy's vision of her as a Hollywood sensation. In this same time period, Babe has endured the abusive marriage arranged by Old Grandaddy to "skyrocket her to the heights of Hazlehurst society" (22), and Lenny, goaded to despair about her own desirability by Old Granddaddy's constant references to her shrunken ovary, has donned "the lime-green gardening gloves of a dead woman" (34) to assume Old Grandmama's role of self-effacing caregiver. This five-year interval can be seen as the eye of the storm, with Babe's murder attempt ushering in a new phase of turbulence that ultimately clears the air, but Henley does not ground the metaphor this specifically in her writing.

In *The Three Sisters*, the texture of everyday life acts as a ground for displaying and reversing theatrical conventions. A similar effect appears in *Crimes of the Heart*, although Henley disclaims this as a conscious intent, and her knowledge of the devices seems to have been absorbed from popular culture rather than theatrical experience.

As early as 1880, Chekhov demonstrated his command of the stock materials of popular theater in a list called "Things Most Frequently Encountered in Novels, Stories and Other Such Things." Of the twenty-six categories listed, at least ten appear in *Three Sisters*, including the "baron-neighbour" and the "foreign musician" (Tuzenbach), the "littérateur-liberal" (Solyony), the "doctor with a worried face . . . And where there is a doctor, there is . . . care of the wounded in a duel" (Chebutykin), the "servant who has been in service with the old masters, who is prepared to go through thick and thin for the master's family, even go through fire" (Anfisa), "a mortaged estate in the South," the "height of the skies, the impenetrable, boundless . . . distance . . . incomprehensible, in a word: nature!" and such standard props as "Chinese porcelain" (Irina's heirloom clock, shattered by Chebutykin) and "the gun that does not fire."[27]

Many of these features appear only to reverse the audience's expectations about them. The Baron does not marry the ingenue and thus rescue the mortgaged estate, the literary type turns out to be a villain, the doctor does not save the duellist when the prop gun is actually fired. Furthermore, the melodramatic crises of the play occur offstage, and the characters seem barely able to grasp them in their aftermath. When Andrei announces that he has mortgaged the girls' patrimony to pay his gambling debts, when Masha confesses that she loves the visiting colonel more than her boring husband, when Chebutykin reveals that Andrei's wife is having an affair with his boss and chief creditor (all these disclosures occurring while the town is burning down around them), the sisters don't even want to hear about it. Irina's fiancé is killed, Masha's lover departs with his regiment, the sisters are turned out of their own home, but the only resolution offered to these disasters is Olga's curtain line, "If we only knew, if we only knew!" (312).

To a certain extent, the characters in *Crimes of the Heart* present themselves as Southern Gothic stereotypes: Lenny the neurasthenic old maid, Meg the sultry temptress, Babe the slow-witted child-wife, Zackery the slick and Barnette the hayseed version of the rural lawyer, Old Grandaddy the fierce patriarch. The thread of grotesquerie epitomized by the mother hanging her cat along with herself is also a southern Gothic staple.

The play's resolution refutes these stereotypes, however, as Lenny makes a date with her mailorder beau, Meg learns that she can love Doc without possessing him, Babe escapes Zackery's malign influence and commences a healthier relationship with Barnette, who shrewdly uses Zackery's macho to neutralize his efforts to imprison or institutionalize his wife. Even the hanging of the cat is transformed from eccentricity to poignantly motivated action.

Henley incorporated southern Gothic motifs into *Crimes* intuitively rather than in polemic with a system of conventions:

> Well, I didn't, consciously like say that I was going to be like Southern Gothic or grotesque. I just write things that are interesting to me. I guess maybe that's just inbred in the South. You hear people tell stories, and somehow they are always more vivid and violent than the stories people tell out in Los Angeles.[28]

She had not even read Flannery O'Connor until one of her early reviews pointed out a similarity in the two writers' styles. Perhaps this is why she is less adept at exposing and dramatically manipulating stock expectations than Chekhov. Consequently, some critics experienced the texture of *Crimes* as unrealistic and clichéd:

> Henley's play . . . is like a tall tale. You don't believe a minute of it but you do want to know what happens next. . . . her characters never rise above cliché and the story, though funny, never seems true.[29]

Others, meanwhile, treated Henley's "pure vein of Southern Gothic humor" as a specialized form of realism rather than as a system of conventions:

> The playwright gets her laughs not because she tells sick jokes, but because she refuses to tell jokes at all. Her characters always stick to the unvarnished truth, at any price . . . the heightening is not achieved at the price of credibility.[30]

This unstable mixture of elements has proved a difficult challenge for directors. Henley notes that despite *Crimes*'s victory in The Actors Theater of Louisville's Festival of New American Plays, it was then "turned down all over town. I guess it's not an easy play for people to pick up the tone of—to know whether it's funny or sad."[31] Reviewers of the Broadway production were divided in their opinions (in the same week that *The Christian Science Monitor* called it "a perversely antic stage piece" that demonstrates "there is sometimes no accounting for awards," the *New York Post* hailed *Crimes* as "A prize hit that's all heart")[32] and could have refereed their differences by reference to the Chekhovian precedent. Chekhov's leading actress (later his wife) Olga Knipper and his leading director Konstantin Stanislavsky recalled that at the Moscow Art Theater's first formal reading of *Three Sisters* not only did nobody laugh, but several listeners shed tears. In the face of this reaction, Chekhov repeatedly muttered, "But what I wrote was a vaudeville!"[33] Clive Barnes may have captured best the volatile spirit of Henley's and Chekhov's tragicomedy when he noted that:

> Those Greeks had it absolutely right when they made their theatrical symbolic masks of tragedy and comedy identical except for the mouth. For so often, comedy is merely a tragedy that is happening to someone else.[34]

Some feminist critics object to the comic emphasis of *Crimes of the Heart* because it undermines the possibility of constructively changing the social relations it satirizes. As Helene Keyssar puts it:

> A common and not trivial attribute of these plays is their ability to make audiences laugh; each of these playwrights has a skill with dialogue and an eye for the absurd in ordinary life that make somber topics palatable and engaging. The weakness common to these plays is inherent in their particular strengths: no matter how serious the topic, they are all comedies of manners, revelations of the surfaces of sexual identity and sexism; they are not challenges to the deeper social structures that allow those manners to endure.[35]

Susan L. Carlson traces this difficulty not to particular dramatists but to comedy as a genre:

> In the upheaval of comedy's role reversals, women acquire a dominance they normally do not possess. We can laugh at that novel power as we laugh at the other role reversals and inversions of comedy because we are also assured by comedy that this world out of order will be—by the end of the play—comfortably set back in order. . . .
>
> For no matter how revolutionary a comedy may be, no matter how strong its women, no matter how battered its sexist double standard, no matter how ironic the happy ending, comedy as we know it can in the end only reflect the society it portrays. Its structure grows out of an old society, never the new one it may propose.[36]

Some of the aspects of comedy that trouble feminist critics may concern the economic constraints of commercial theater production. Asked if she felt that there is still discrimination against women playwrights in the American theater, Henley replied:

> Yes, I think there is. Simply because there are still a lot more men than women in charge of our theaters: producing, directing, managing, fund raising. That's where the power and the money are in this country. Men generally can't help but be more moved by a man's play because they relate to it in a personal way. Women are more used to identifying with men, because they're raised on it, they've got to be . . . In terms of the people who make decisions about play production, the closer these dreams are to their version of them-

> selves, the more chance they'll want to sit through a play or to find money to produce it.[37]

An additional problem arises from the necessity for plays to compete with other commercial media. Pam Gems, a British dramatist whose works are often contrasted to those of American mainstream women playwrights for their ability to bring feminist issues more assertively to the stage, presents the issue this way:

> Seriously, we do have a problem, not only because other people can stay at home . . . switch channels . . . but because whole generations are growing up accustomed to the quick elision of the visual mode . . . the quick transitions of movies and television. We have to elide. But a serious play is working at depth. So it ain't easy.[38]

Whatever causes might account for the emphasis on comedy in Henley's tragicomic mixture, comparison with Chekhov on this point suggests that depth need not be sacrificed to laughter in the work of a mature playwright. Chekhov's one-act comedies and even an early full-length play, *Ivanov,* shared some of the limitations of Henley's writing. They emphasized plot over character development and lacked the lyricism that in Chekhov's later dramas provides a poignant counterpoint to the banal lives depicted on the stage. His three sisters, on the other hand, "create images to embody their sense of an ideal life,"[39] and in general his later plays juxtapose poverty of circumstances with richness of metaphor. Moreover, Chekhov (with the essential cooperation of the Moscow Art Theater) was able to find a paying audience for his lyrical comedies at a time when Stanislavsky characterized the commercial theater as "controlled by restaurateurs on the one hand, and by bureaucrats on the others."[40]

At this point in her development as a playwright, Henley yearns for lyricism but does not feel confident of her ability to produce it. She worries about "what the world is going to be like when people won't talk anymore . . . because their minds are absorbed with electronic images" and contrasts that future with a turn-of-the-century past when even small town newspapers "use big words and twists of phrases that are poetic and much more literate than newspapers today," concluding, "I'm astounded when I think of what a dive we've taken in such a short time."[41] On the other hand, she hasn't tried prose or poetry because "I don't know if I could do them . . . I still don't have good grammar for putting like a whole novel or whole story together. I can just write dialogue."[42]

Although she's naive in reducing the problem to lacking good grammar, Henley puts her finger on the central weakness of her dramatic style when she says she just writes dialogue. Chekhov's dramaturgy may err on the side of prosiness—how is it possible to stage Chekhov's direction in *Uncle Vanya* that the map of Africa is "of no use to anyone here"? But at its best, Chekhov's dramatic writing combines the implicative power of narrative with the spontaneity of the spoken word in a way that Henley might learn to emulate.

When May Sarton went to see the film version of *Crimes of the Heart*, she recorded in her journal:

> I was a little disappointed in the text, written by the author of the play which was on Broadway last year . . . The clamor of voices for one thing, like sharp bird voices, put me on edge. It made me long for Chekhov, for something subtler, less obviously dramatic—but in these days no doubt there would be no audience if it were Chekhov.[43]

Sarton here implies that Henley is the Chekhov the present generation deserves. This judgment seems unduly stringent toward both the playwright and her public.

Henley's "clamor of voices" builds toward "a vision of feminine assertiveness and female bonding as an alternative to self-destruction,"[44] which Chekhov's soft-spoken protagonists cannot begin to imagine. Less subtle but more dynamic than Chekhov's infinitely nuanced social milieu, the one depicted by Henley seems more susceptible to beneficial change. This prospect of transformation makes *Crimes of the Heart* more accessible to contemporary audiences for whom the dramatic representation of life's unresolved texture produces the ache of familiarity rather than the sting of novelty. Sarton's bird metaphor, critical in its context, has a more positive aspect; while Chekhov's three sisters elegiacally celebrate the freedom of the migratory birds, Henley's help each other escape from the cage.

Notes

1. John Griffin Jones, "Beth Henley," in *Mississippi Writers Talking: Interviews with Eudora Welty, Shelby Foote, Elizabeth Spencer, Barry Hannah, Beth Henley*, ed. John Griffin Jones (Jackson: University Press of Mississippi, 1982), p. 180.
2. Ibid., pp. 181–82.
3. Ibid., p 184.
4. Nicholas Moravčevich, "Women in Chekhov's Plays," in *Chekhov's Great Plays: A Critical Anthology*, ed. Jean-Pierre Barricelli (New York: New York University Press, 1981), p. 206. Moravčevich here speaks specifically of Irina, but the criticism seems fairly applied to all the sisters.
5. Don Nelson, "*Crimes* is Heartwarming," *New York Daily News*, 5 November 1981, points out that:

> Even the frivolity makes a point. There is enough hugging and squealing and jumping about among the MaGraths to recall with dismay a host of sorority films; but these frolics do reveal an immaturity which is almost crippling.

6. Nancy D. Hargrove, "The Tragicomic Vision of Beth Henley's Drama," *Southern Quarterly* 2, no. 4 (Summer 1984): 54–70. Hargrove notes this pattern in *Crimes of the Heart*, but it occurs frequently in *Three Sisters* as well. Chekhov even has a scene in which one character eats up all of somebody else's chocolates!

7. Harai Golomb, "Music as Theme and as Structural Model in Chekhov's *Three Sisters*," in *Semiotics of Drama and Theater: New Perspectives in the Theory of Drama and Theatre*, ed. Herta Schmid and Aloysius Van Kesteren (Amsterdam/Philadelphia: John Benjamins Publishing Company, 1984), p. 175.

8. Kathleen Betsko and Rachel Koenig, *Interviews with Contemporary Women Playwrights* (New York: Beech Tree Books, 1987), p. 218.

9. René Girard, *Deceit, Desire, and the Novel: Self and Other in Literary Structure*, trans. Yvonne Freccero, quoted by Karen L. Laughlin, "Criminality, Desire and Community: A Feminist Approach to Beth Henley's *Crimes of the Heart*," *Women and Performance: A Journal of Feminist Theory*, no. 5 (1986), p. 38.

10. Beth Henley, *Crimes of the Heart* (New York: Viking Press, 1982). Subsequent references are cited parenthetically by page number.

11. Anton Chekhov, *The Three Sisters*, in *Chekhov: The Major Plays*, trans. Ann Dunnigan (New York: Signet, 1964). Subsequent references are cited parenthetically by page number.

12. Is the "big teeth" description a reference to the absent Daddy as a Big Bad Wolf?

13. Hargrove, "The Tragicomic Vision of Beth Henley's Drama," identifies this theme as "typical of Henley's realistic and uncompromising vision" (p. 61).

14. Helene Keyssar, *Feminist Theatre: An Introduction to Plays of Contemporary British and American Women* (London: Macmillan, 1984), p. 26.

15. Anton Chekhov, as reported by Alexander Kuprin, quoted in Vera Gottlieb, *Chekhov and the Vaudeville: A Study of Chekhov's One-Act Plays* (Cambridge: Cambridge University Press, 1982), p. 1.

16. Betsko and Koenig, *Interviews with Contemporary Women Playwrights*, p. 216.

17. Gottlieb, *Chekhov and the Vaudeville*, p. 39.

18. Laughlin, "Criminality, Desire, and Community," p. 46.

19. Ibid., p. 47.

20. Keyssar, *Feminist Theatre*, p. 158.

21. Chekhov, letter responding to request from Gregory Rossolimo (1899), quoted in Gottlieb, *Chekhov and the Vaudeville*, p. 10.

22. Chekhov, letter to Nikolai Leykin (1884), quoted in Gottlieb, *Chekhov and the Vaudeville*, p. 11.

23. Betsko and Koenig, *Interviews with Contemporary Women Playwrights*, p. 215.

24. Chekhov, quoted in Robert Brustein's foreword to *Chekhov: The Major Plays*, trans. Ann Dunnigan (New York: Signet, 1964), p. x.

25. Hargrove, "The Tragicomic Vision of Beth Henley's Drama," p. 64.

26. Richard Peace, *Chekhov: A Study of the Four Major Plays* (New Haven: Yale University Press, 1983), p. 75.

27. Anton Chekhov, "Things Most Frequently Encountered in Novels, Stories and Other Such Things" (1880), quoted in Gottlieb, *Chekhov and the Vaudeville*, p. 17.

28. Jones, "Beth Henley," p. 182.

29. Howard Kissel, *Women's Wear Daily*, 6 November 1981, in *New York Theatre Critics' Reviews* 1981, p. 140.

30. Frank Rich, "Beth Henley's *Crimes of the Heart*," *New York Times*, 5 November 1981, in *New York Theatre Critics' Reviews* 1981, p. 136.

31. Interview with Robert Berkvist, "Act I: the Pulitzer, Act II: Broadway," *New York Times*, 25 October 1981, pp. 4, 22.

32. John Beaufort, "A Play That Proves There's No Explaining Awards," *The Christian Science Monitor*, 9 November 1981, in *New York Theatre Critics' Reviews* 1981, p. 137.

33. Quoted in Maurice Valency, "Vershinin," in *Chekhov's Great Plays: A Critical Anthology*, ed. Jean-Pierre Barricelli (New York: New York University Press, 1981), p. 220.

34. Clive Barnes, "*Crime* is a Prize Hit That's All Heart," *New York Post*, 5 November 1981, in *New York Theatre Critics' Reviews* 1981, p. 138.

35. Keyssar, *Feminist Theatre*, p. 150. Other "hit shows" by and about women that Keyssar criticizes along with *Crimes* for staying on "relatively safe terrain" include Mary O'Malley's *Once a Catholic*, Wendy Wasserstein's *Uncommon Women and Others*, and Marsha Norman's *'night, Mother.*

36. Susan L. Carlson, "Women in Comedy: Problem, Promise, Paradox," in *Drama, Sex and Politics*, ed. James Redmond (Cambridge: Cambridge University Press, 1985), pp. 159–60.

37. Betsko and Koenig, *Interviews with Contemporary Women Playwrights*, p. 221.

38. Ibid., p. 206.

39. Beverly Hahn, "Three Sisters," in *Chekhov: New Perspectives*, ed. Rene and Nonna D. Wellek (Englewood Cliffs, N.J.: Prentice-Hall, 1984), p. 142.

40. L. Shestov, *Anton Tchekhov and Other Essays*, quoted in Gottlieb, *Chekhov and the Vaudeville*, p. 14.

41. Betsko and Koenig, *Interviews with Contemporary Women Playwrights*, pp. 219–20.

42. Jones, "Beth Henley," pp. 172–73.

43. May Sarton, *After the Stroke: A Journal* (New York: W. W. Norton, 1988), p. 252.

44. Laughlin, "Criminality, Desire, and Community," p. 35.

19
Disturbing Women: Wendy Kesselman's *My Sister in This House*

Bette Mandl

Christine and Lea, the maids of Wendy Kesselman's play *My Sister in This House*, first appear "side by side, as if framed in a photograph" (p. 7).[1] This image suggests both the intimacy of their shared world and the historical documents that would record their experience. Kesselman's drama had its genesis in the account of a murder by two servants of their mistress and her daughter in Le Mans, France in 1933. The playwright envisions the movement, gradual and then sudden, of these private lives into the realm of public attention.

In her autobiographical volume, *Prime of Life*, Simone de Beauvoir describes how compelling she and Jean-Paul Sartre found the newspaper reports of the crime and trial of Christine and Lea Papin. De Beauvoir explains that she and Sartre were fascinated by

> any upheaval which exposed the defects and hypocrisy of the bourgeoisie, knocking down the façade behind which their homes and hearts took shelter. Trials no less than crimes drew our attention: the grimmer sort raised the question of individual and collective responsibility. The bulk of the verdicts reached, too, fed our indignation, for in them society shamelessly declared its class-ridden, reactionary attitudes.[2]

The Papin sisters, in particular, seemed "both the instruments and the martyrs of justice in his grimmest guise."[3] Christine was sentenced to death, but then the decision was made to place her in an asylum for the rest of her life. Preferring to think of the violent acts of Lea and Christine Papin as heroic, de Beauvoir and Sartre were dismayed by the diagnosis of mental disorder in the sisters, but "obstinately persisted in our admiration for them."[4] They passed judgment on responses to the trial that they saw as manifestations of "the whole ghastly system that had made" the Papin sisters "what they were."[5]

The events that so stirred the public imagination and that lent themselves so readily to symbolic conceptualizations inspired Jean Genet's second play, *The Maids*, first performed in its original version in 1946.[6] Genet transformed the story into one that suited a treatment of compelling shifts between reality and illusion. The maids, here called Claire and Solange, sustain themselves through fantasy. Claire impersonates their stylish and benevolent mistress, and Solange plays Claire, in enactments of the dominations and submissions that are the substance of their lives. Omitting the daughter of the mistress from his cast of characters, Genet introduces a figure who is the mistress's lover and who influences the play's events although he remains offstage. Monsieur had been arrested. Madame, who doubts her lover's guilt, dreams of being his accomplice and accompanying him to Devil's Island or Siberia. For her as for the sisters, the criminal and the saint are the "eternal couple."[7] Because Claire anonymously sent the letter incriminating Monsieur, the sisters are at risk now that he is being released from jail. Although the sisters envision and attempt it, the murder of the mistress does not take place in *The Maids*. It is Claire, playing Madame, who ultimately chooses to take the poisoned tea they have prepared, providing Solange with the opportunity to take credit for the deed.

When Genet conceived the play, he hoped that the female roles would be played by men. Bettina Knapp links this intention, which he relinquished at the insistence of director Louis Jouvet, to Genet's preoccupation with truth and disguise:

> Genet is intrigued by the artifice and the sham of the theater as he had been by the betrayal and deceit of crime . . . Had the characters been played by men, the confusion between illusion and reality would have been that much greater. Men would have been playing at being women, who would in turn have been playing at being maids, who would themselves have been playing at being each other, who then would have been playing at being Madame, who would have been playing at being part of Madame's dream world.[8]

Sartre suggests that for Genet, "Appearance, which is constantly on the point of passing itself off as reality, must constantly reveal its profound unreality."[9]

Thus Genet's focus in *The Maids*, although its three principal characters are women, is not on the women themselves. As Sartre says, "Genet's poetic themes are, as we know, profoundly homosexual. We know that neither women nor the psychology of women interests him."[10] Although it may be more difficult than Sartre acknowledges here to disentangle Genet's several concerns in the play, the comment has validity.

Kesselman, on the other hand, found the same material that served Genet suggestive of possibilities for a drama that evokes the female world the four women inhabited. In *My Sister in This House*, which won the 1980 Susan Smith Blackburn Award, Kesselman focuses on the complex web of social and psychological elements that constitute the relationship of the maids and their mistresses.[11] She shapes the material to reveal its inherent power and heightens awareness that the fissures in this doomed house open between female servants and female "masters."

In the first scene, Christine sings a gentle lullaby of her own to her younger sister Lea. They have only recently come to work for the Danzards, and the arrangement is marked by mutual satisfaction. At the outset, all seems well in this hierarchical world, with no hint of either tyranny or rebellion. Christine is an excellent seamstress and a fine cook. Madame Danzard, although she has some reservations about Lea's youth and inexperience, appreciates Christine's skills. She tells her daughter Isabelle with enthusiasm: "Sisters! What could be better! And two almost for the price of one. We'll save on everything" (12). With such good servants, she expects to be the envy of her acquaintances. Christine is pleased as well, believing that she and Lea are lucky to have such a mistress: "Madame checks everything. I like that . . . It's better that way" (19).

The two sisters have a genuine affection for one another. They differ in this respect from the maids in Genet's play, in which Solange says to Claire:

> I want to help you. I want to comfort you, but I know I disgust you. I'm repulsive to you. And I know it because you disgust me. When slaves love one another, it's not love.[12]

Kate Millett describes Genet's characters as "outcasts in an emotional complicity with the ruling order," who "invent insults . . . exposing the poisonous effect their declared inferiority (agreed upon by others and agreed to by themselves) has had upon them."[13] Unlike Claire and Solange, who believe in "their superiors' edition of their lives,"[14] Christine and Lea are less persuaded by ideas of them that others hold. Nonetheless, the world they attempt to construct for themselves, contingent as it is on an increasing withdrawal from all around them, is inevitably fragile.

Resenting their mother, Christine encourages Lea's emotional separation from her. Christine recalls bitterly how their mother insisted on her return to the convent where they grew up when she used to escape from it:

> In the end all I wanted was to be a nun . . . But then of course she took me out. She hadn't expected that. That was against all her plans. I had to work. I had to make money. And she kept all of it. She placed me—and each time I

got used to it, she took me out again. Sometimes I'd run away. I ran back to the Sisters. They wanted to keep me. It was Maman, our beloved precious Maman, who would come and drag me out again. (25–26)

Rather than send their wages to their mother as they had, they decide to save toward a farm, a dream that occasionally punctuates their conversation. Although she was attached to the blanket crotcheted by their mother when she arrived at the Danzards, Lea later unravels it, playfully winding the yarn around Christine. The connection of the sisters comes to preclude all other attachments.

Christine devotes herself to Lea, indulging her with lingerie she sews for her: "undergarments trimmed with lace, nightgowns with fluttering ribbons, delicate ruffled chemises" (33). Their intimacy gradually slips into the erotic. Here, as elsewhere in the play, Kesselman draws on testimony from the trial. De Beauvoir says of the Papin sisters: "The papers told us that they were sexually involved with each other, and we mused on the caresses, and the hatred, that their lonely attic concealed."[15]

The servitude of Christine and Lea, rigidly defined, does not permit them to revise their assigned parts. Whenever they approach the limits imposed, they are reminded of the violation. At one point, Christine arranges for the two of them to have their photograph taken, urging this luxury, although the process makes them both uneasy. The photographer, whom we hear in a voiceover making unsuccessful efforts to engage Christine and Lea in conversation, says, "No one would ever know the two of you were servants" (38). His flattery has more than a kernel of truth in it and hints at the conflicts inherent in their situation.

By juxtaposing the experience of servants and mistresses, Kesselman manages to suggest, without didacticism, the arbitrary nature of the social arrangements that place Madame Danzard and Isabelle over Christine and Lea. The superficial exchanges between mistress and daughter, for example, during a game of cards when they bicker over whether Isabelle has cheated, indicate that their class privilege has not secured for them much more spacious lives than their servants have.

Because difference, particularly under such circumstances, is difficult to maintain, Madame Danzard is alert to the blurring of boundaries. When Lea wears a lovely sweater, Madame Danzard is outraged. Although Christine, who made the sweater for her sister to wear only within the confines of their attic room, realizes at once that Lea has made an error, the damage is done. Madame Danzard says to Isabelle: "What in heaven's name allows her to think she can wear a sweater like that in this house" (45). She is appalled by the extravagance of her servant: "Can you imagine if someone had seen. . . ." (47).

Tension mounts steadily. Madame Danzard, who has always been the kind of mistress who checks for dust with a white glove, becomes increasingly disdainful. A scene in which Isabelle is being fitted for a dress reveals the deterioration of the relations between the Danzards and the sisters. No longer appreciative of Christine's talents, Madame Danzard disparages her work and insists, "Next time we'll go to the dressmaker's" (54). In a Sunday morning conversation, the Danzards agree that the sisters' request for an extra blanket for their unheated attic room is "incredible" (57). Shortly afterward, when Christine and Lea return from church, Madame Danzard echoes the photographer, complaining to Isabelle: "They don't even look like maids anymore" (58).

There is an undercurrent of tension in the relationship of Christine and Lea as well. The increasing intensity of their attachment makes every threat to it loom large. Small gestures, such as Isabelle's offering a candy to Lea or asking Lea to brush her hair, upset Christine. She fears that Lea will follow Isabelle if the marriage that is rumored takes place. Christine pleads, "Promise me you won't go. When she goes." Lea, somewhat exasperated, says, "If she goes. She may never go. We've been over this a hundred times, Christine." But Christine persists: "You're all I have, little Lea. All I'll ever have" (55).

It becomes apparent that it would not take much to set off a conflagration here. An iron that blows a fuse and a blouse that is burned as a consequence suffice to set it off. Madame Danzard accuses Christine and Lea of deliberately causing the minor household accidents. When Christine tries to salvage her dignity and protect Lea by saying that they will leave the house, Madame Danzard says, "Not with the recommendation you get from me." She insinuates that she knows something of their intimate life: "Forgive me God for what I have harboured here" (64).

As the Danzards continue to insult them, Christine cries out repeatedly, "Not my sister, not my sister." Madame Danzard says, "You'll never work with your sister again" (65). The sisters respond swiftly and with stunning brutality to the threat of separation, which for them is a threat to their survival. Lea lifts a pewter pitcher above Isabelle's head, as Christine moves toward Madame Danzard with a violence accentuated, no doubt, by the anger against the mother that surfaced earlier in the play.

The murder of the Danzards takes place on the darkened stage. Kesselman is unflinching in her review of the details. The medical examiner, in a voiceover, reports in the final scene that "a single eye was found, intact, complete with the optic nerve. The eye had been torn out without the aid of an instrument" (65–66). Two other eyes had been torn out as well, and lay in a bloody wreckage of small possessions and fragments of bone and teeth. Isabelle's wounds suggest evidence of a sexual rage engendered, perhaps, by Christine's jealousy. In this circumscribed world, in which class has been the implicit issue, the sisters' futile impulses toward transcendence or revolution are all centered on the female body.

The judge, the third male whose voice is heard in a female domain that is nonetheless linked inextricably to the structures of the masculine public sphere, sentences Lea to ten years of hard labor and Christine to public execution. The sisters, now beyond violence and seemingly remorse, grieve for the loss of one another. Christine begs to be reunited with Lea, who sings for her sister the lullaby that Christine has at times sung to her. In the final moments of the play, the sisters appear once more as if in a photograph.

Between the familiar terrain where the sisters and their mistresses have co-existed and the anarchic wilderness that it briefly becomes is a wide gap, however successfully a production of the play leads the audience to sense the impending horror. Although the story of Christine and Lea as Kesselman recreates it is convincing, even haunting, it is nonetheless preserved as a conundrum to be pondered. The most disturbing element of the drama is its insistence that we link gender and violence in unfamiliar ways.

Throughout the scenes that precede the murders, the language and silence of the household reflect the private sphere of women's experience. Kesselman resists any impulse to present Christine or Lea as monsters or to suggest that Mme. Danzard and Isabelle have been much worse than conventionally domineering in their assertion of power. Because Kesselman is persuasive in presenting the servants and mistresses as women whose lives are recognizable to us, the conclusion of the play, although grounded in historical reality, seems unassimilable.

Kesselman's play has much in common with other works, such as Charlotte Perkins Gilman's story *The Yellow Wallpaper*, that are rich in insight into how subtle oppressions, related to gender, precipitate despair and breakdown. *My Sister in This House*, by confronting us directly with the furies that can be unleashed by banal torments—within a world of women—extends the tradition in which it can be located. In Gilman's piece, the main character, confined by her doctor-husband to a "rest-cure," zealously guards the wallpaper on which she projects her predicament: "no person touches this paper but me,—not *alive!*"[16] But her rage, unlike that of Christine and Lea, is turned inward. Rather than manifesting in violence, it develops into a version of the "female malady" that Elaine Showalter analyzes in her book of that title.[17]

There are significant resemblances between *My Sister in This House* and Susan Glaspell's *Trifles*.[18] Mrs. Wright, a farmwife, has murdered her husband by strangling him with a rope as he slept. Her neighbors, Mrs. Hale and Mrs. Peters, discern the motives for her seemingly unconscious act. A crooked seam on a quilt and an empty bird cage are among the domestic "trifles," unnoticed by the men investigating the crime, that provide these neighbors with clues to Mrs. Wright's frustration and isolation. The concerns of *Trifles*, however, distract us from the female violence that is inescapable in *My Sister in This House*. Glaspell's play focuses on the growing awareness of the neighbors of their own guilt in failing to be available to Mrs. Wright. Acknowledging their unwitting complicity in her crime, they shield her by concealing what they have learned.

Although *Trifles* sounds a promising note about the possibility of community among women, *My Sister in This House* offers a different challenge. The starkness of its conclusion demands a reassessment of an oversimplified conception of women as "an unalloyed force for good or as a unified sisterhood or nature."[19] As Helene Keyssar says of *My Sister in This House*, "The four women live together in a household that could breed affection and community, but class distinctions separate Madame and Mademoiselle Danzard from their 'maids.' "[20]

Kesselman's play acknowledges the impact of social realities as she develops characters of psychological complexity. As a result, she has created an effective work for the theater, which also contributes to a comprehensive vision of the diversity of women's experience. Theorists Judith Newton and Deborah Rosenfelt speak of the importance of a cultural analysis that

> encourages us to hold in our minds the both-ands of experience: that women at different moments in history have been both oppressed and oppressive, submissive and subversive, victim and agent, allies and enemies both of men and one another.[21]

The undeniable power of *My Sister in This House* is attributable, in large measure, to the playwright's willingness to embrace just such contradictions.

Notes

1. Wendy Kesselman, *My Sister in This House* (New York: Samuel French, 1982). Subsequent references are cited parenthetically by page number.

2. Simone de Beauvoir, *The Prime of Life*, trans. Peter Green (New York: Harper Colophon Books, 1976), pp. 107–8 (first published in Paris by Librairie Gallimard as *La Force de l'Age*, 1960).

3. Ibid., p. 108.
4. Ibid., p. 109.
5. Ibid., p. 108.
6. Jean Genet, *The Maids*, in *The Maids and Deathwatch: Two Plays by Jean Genet* (New York: Grove Press, 1954). For information on the early productions, see, for example, Richard N. Coe, *The Vision of Jean Genet* (New York: Grove Press, 1968). Coe also refers to the use of the story of the Papin sisters in the film *Les Abysses*, directed by Nico Paptakis (248).
7. Genet, *The Maids*, p. 63.
8. Bettina Knapp, *Jean Genet* (New York: Twayne, 1968), p. 110.
9. Jean-Paul Sartre, Introduction to *The Maids*, in *The Maids and Deathwatch: Two Plays by Jean Genet* (New York: Grove Press, 1954), p. 10.
10. Ibid., p. 13.
11. *My Sister in This House* was first produced by Actors Theatre of Louisville, 18 February–29 March 1981. In the same year, it was produced in New York by The Second Stage.
12. Genet, *The Maids*, p. 61.
13. Kate Millett, *Sexual Politics* (Garden City, N. Y.: Doubleday and Company, 1969), p. 351.
14. Ibid.
15. de Beauvoir, *The Prime of Life*, p. 109.
16. Charlotte Perkins Gilman, *The Yellow Wallpaper* (1899; reprint ed., Old Westbury, N.Y.: The Feminist Press, 1973), p. 33.
17. Elaine Showalter, *The Female Malady: Women, Madness, and English Culture: 1830–1980* (New York: Pantheon Books, 1985).
18. Susan Glaspell, *Trifles*, in *Plays by Susan Glaspell*, ed. C. W. E. Bigsby (Cambridge: Cambridge University Press, 1987), pp. 35–45.
19. Judith Newton and Deborah Rosenfelt, "Introduction: Toward a Materialist-Feminist Criticism," in *Feminist Criticism and Social Change: Sex, Class and Race in Literature and Culture*, ed. Judith Newton and Deborah Rosenfelt (New York: Methuen, 1985), p. xxvi.
20. Helene Keyssar, *Feminist Theatre: An Introduction to Plays of Contemporary British and American Women* (London: Macmillan, 1984), p. 181.
21. Newton and Rosenfelt, "Introduction: Toward a Materialist-Feminist Criticism," p. xxix. A "materialist feminist" theoretical approach, such as Newton and Rosenfelt develop, is considered in relation to feminist theater in Sue-Ellen Case's *Feminism and Theatre* (New York: Methuen, 1988).

20
The Demeter Myth and Doubling in Marsha Norman's *'night, Mother*

Katherine H. Burkman

Marsha Norman's Pulitzer Prize-winning play, *'night, Mother,* has been greeted by many critics as a major drama. Robert Brustein notes that the play is "chastely classical in its observance of the unities," and he welcomes Norman as one writing in "a great dramatic tradition" who, "young as she is, has the potential to preserve and revitalize it."[1] Another critic appreciates Norman's dissection of the "mythic relationship between mother and daughter"[2] in the play. Escaping the weaknesses of melodrama, Norman offers a drama that not only leads up to the carefully planned suicide of Jessie Cates, for which Jessie prepares her mother, Thelma, during the play, but one that also leads to a quickened sense of life. Departing from an overt dramatization of a split self in an earlier drama, *Getting Out* (1977), in which the author explored the relationship between Arlene, newly released from prison, and her earlier, juvenile delinquent self, Arlie, Norman offers in *'night, Mother* a dramatization of doubling between mother and daughter that leads to a character integration her earlier heroine sought in vain.

One way of approaching this drama is by looking at its banal surface in the context of the underlying mythic relationships of Demeter and Kore (Persephone), a relationship that offers clues to the mother-daughter relationship in the play. C. G. Jung and C. Kerényi, in their exploration of the Mysteries of Eleusis in *Essays On a Science of Mythology,* suggest an essential oneness of the Demeter and Kore figures in mythology, a oneness that is actually threefold, also embracing the third mythological figure, Hecate. Commenting on the identification of mother and daughter, Jung writes, "Demeter and Kore, mother and daughter, extend the feminine consciousness both upwards and downwards. They add an 'older and younger,' 'stronger and weaker' dimension to it and widen out the narrowly limited conscious mind bound in space and time, giving it intimations of a greater and more comprehensive personality which has a share in the eternal course of things."[3] Much of the power of Norman's play emerges from a mythical identification of mother and daughter that leaves Thelma bereft of the daughter she thought she had possessed but ironically at one with that daughter from whom she has derived new strength and life. More cathartic than depressing, the play reveals a bond between mother and daughter and a mythical sense of their oneness that allows for what Kerényi, commenting on Jung's ideas, calls *"being in death."*[4]

Although Jessie seems like a very different protagonist in her quiet determination and lack of pretension, she is, in some ways, descended from such self-destructive and flamboyant heroines as Ibsen's Hedda Gabler and Strindberg's Miss Julie. Like Hedda and Miss Julie, Jessie is her father's daughter (like Hedda, Jessie kills herself with her father's pistol), and she has identified with his kind of withdrawal: "I want to hang a big sign around my neck, like Daddy's on the barn. GONE FISHING" (27),[5] she explains to her mother. Like Hedda and Miss Julie, Jessie finds some measure of redemption in a suicide that is partly an escape from a world in which she lacks the strength to act with freedom or control; but her suicide also is a way of taking control by embracing a death that affords that freedom and fulfillment denied her in life.

What distinguishes Jessie from these former heroines is her reaching out to her mother in her last hours of life, recognizing her mother's greater appetite for life, arranging for the continued availability of the sweets her mother craves as a consolation for her empty existence but also offering her the more nourishing truths that may sustain her after her daughter's death. As she plays the role of mother to her mother, a role she has assumed after her husband has deserted her and she has moved into her mother's house, Jessie may be understood as both the Kore figure who feels used or raped and the Demeter figure who shares in that sense of loss and has lost the zest for life. As the drama progresses, however, we see not only the reversal of the Demeter-Kore role as daughter plays mother but also the common ground that binds the two, both in their shared sense of being used and in their deep feeling for each other. This kind of mutual participation in an archetype is that Jung suggests rescues the individual from isolation and restores her to wholeness.[6] Only a sense of incipient wholeness allows Jessie's mother to accept her daughter's death, to allow her that freedom, and to understand her choice.

The major difference between Jessie Cates and her mother seems to be a question of appetite. As Jessie readies herself for suicide and attempts to prepare her mother for her life without her, the focus is on food. Mama opens the play with her assertion of appetite.

> *Mama. (Unwrapping the cupcake.)* Jessie, it's the last snowball, sugar. Put it on the list, O.K.? And we're out of Hershey bars, and where's that peanut brittle? I think maybe Dawson's been in it again. I ought to put a big mirror on the refrigerator door. That'll keep him out of my treats, won't it? You hear me, honey? *(Then more to herself)* I hate it when the coconut falls off. Why does the coconut fall off? (5)

Mama is concerned with not running out of the sweets that sustain and console her in what we soon learn is an arid existence. Significantly, she addresses her daughter as sugar and honey here as well as in subsequent exchanges.

Although Jessie assures her mother that she has ordered a "whole case" of snowballs, she is intent in the opening moments of the drama on preparing for her death by locating her father's gun and collecting enough old towels for the mess her death will make. There is nothing sweet about Jessie as she determines that "garbage bags would do if there's enough" (6). Later, when she tries to explain her failed marriage to her mother and why her husband has chosen to leave her behind, Jessie notes: "You don't pack your garbage when you move" (61). What Jessie has bought in a "feed store" her brother Dawson told her about is bullets, not food.

The question of appetite is at the heart of Mama's choice for life and Jessie's choice for death. When they discuss Jessie's son Ricky, who has become a thief, Mama looks on the bright side and sees Ricky's redemption in terms of food. Ricky, she suggests, may simply be going through a bad period, mixing with the wrong people. "He just needs some time, sugar. He'll get back in shoool or get a job or one day you'll get a call and he'll say he's sorry for all the trouble he's caused and invite you out for supper someplace dress-up" (11). Such a proposition has no value for Jessie, however, who says, "Those two rings he took were the last valuable things *I* had" (11), and she insists she would turn him in if she knew where he was. Jessie knows she could choose to live rather than to die, but she lacks the appetite for the choice. She tells her mother that she wondered after her decision at Christmas time to kill herself what might make it worth while staying alive and says, "It was maybe if there was something I really liked, like maybe if I really liked rice pudding or cornflakes for breakfast or something, that might be enough" (77).

Appetite is also a major concern in the Demeter myth for both mother and daughter. When she learns of her daughter's rape by Hades, who has taken her to be queen of the Underworld, Demeter will neither eat nor drink. In the myth, however, the implications of this loss of appetite involve the fertility of the earth itself and the revolution of the seasons. As goddess of the corn, not only does Demeter refrain from eating; she also will not permit the crops to grow, depriving mankind as well as herself of food and the gods of their sacrifices. Only the restoration of her daughter will bring the return of spring. Persephone as Kore, the maiden, also refuses food in the Underworld, but her eating of pomegranate seeds just before her return to her mother ensures her marriage to Hades and her return for three months of each year to his abode.

Here the paradox of the myth may offer a clue to the paradox of the play. The pomegranate, although it ties the Persephone-Kore figure to the Underworld and thus to death, is associated with fertility and sexuality. Geoffrey Grigson describes the fruit as "enclosed by the enlarged calyx—a womb with an opening, a womb packed with seeds of translucent pink . . . The pomegranate, then, is the physical secrecy and portal of the feminine, whether for Aphrodite, or any related goddess of fertility and the sexual."[7] Not just a fruit of the Underworld, the pomegranate is one of Demeter's "fruits of the earth" as well, symbolizing marriage, in this case the marriage of Persephone and Hades for the winter of each year. The fruit is paradoxical in that it ties the daughter figure simultaneously to life on earth and to death in the Underworld—in other words, to life's cycle with its death and rebirth.

Although on one level the play deals with Mama as a Demeter figure trying to rescue her child from death, to talk her out of it, one senses as the play unfolds that on a deeper level it is about the reclamation of the mother from death, that it is about Thelma's rebirth. However, because there is a doubling of mother and daughter in the drama that is similar to its doubling in the myth, one senses at the end of the play a rebirth that combines mother and daughter as aspects of one entity.

Despite differences in Mama and Jessie's appetite for food and life and their different attitudes toward death, Mama fearing that which her daughter seeks to embrace, Norman establishes the similarity between mother and daughter early in the play. When Mama thinks Jessie is looking for her father's gun to protect them from thieves, she says, "We don't have anything anybody'd want, Jessie. I mean, I don't even want what we got, Jessie" (10). Jessie's "Neither do I," of course, has a more ominous meaning because one senses that the "protection" she seeks with the gun is not from thieves but from life even before she announces her intention to commit suicide. Still, neither woman values what she has.

Mother and daughter also share the sense of violation that permeates the Demeter myth. Some versions of the myth depict Demeter as herself raped by Poseidon, lord of the sea, while searching for her violated and kidnapped daughter.[8] In the play, mother and daughter feel violated by their respective husbands. Mama admits to Jessie that she didn't love her husband, who "wanted a plain country woman and that's what he married, and then he held it against me the rest of my life like I was supposed to change and surprise him somehow" (46). Although Jessie did love her husband, she expresses a similar feeling about their relationship, explaining to her mother that it was a "relief" when Cecil left. "I never was what he wanted to see, so it was better when he wasn't looking at me all the time" (61). As Jenny S. Spencer has noted, "Despite differences in personality and coping patterns, the two characters share similar attitudes toward the meaninglessness of their lives, toward the demands of their husbands and children."[9]

Even concerning appetite, one comes to see that the differences between mother and daughter are less profound than they would appear. Rather than having a true appetite for life, Mama's appetite for sweets symbolizes her need for a slave for her death-in-life existence, a way of filling up an emptiness and of hiding from her fear of life and death. One begins to see that she, like Jessie, also is in death's grip.

Although Jessie has no particular fondness for any food, Mama has rejected almost all nourishing foods. In her state of agony over her daughter's announced suicide, she even rejects the proferred sweets that are her main source of consolation if not nourishment, and she insists that she will not cook if Jessie carries through with her plan. She wants her daughter to throw out all but one pan: "I'm not going to cook," she explains, and adds, significantly, "I never liked it, anyway. I like candy. Wrapped in plastic or coming in sacks. And tuna. I like tuna. I'll eat tuna, thank you" (51).

Mama also informs Jessie that she doesn't like carrots, and after making cocoa at her daughter's request, she finds it as undrinkable, because of the milk, as her daughter does. "God, this milk in here" (45), Mama complains, and Jessie agrees; "I thought it was my memory that was bad, but it's not. It's the milk, all right" (45). When Mama tells Jessie she doesn't need to finish it, she might be talking about Jessie's life, which Jessie has decided not to finish.[10] Perhaps it is this shared and symbolic distaste for milk that helps Mama finally to accept and understand Jessie's decision.

Jessie's preparations for her mother's welfare, however, involve milk. She has told the grocer to deliver "a quart a week no matter what you said" (54), she informs Mama, thus insisting on offering her mother the nourishment that she herself rejects, recognizing in her mother a life force that she lacks. Mama's old glasses, it also turns out, are "in an old Milk of Magnesia box" (56), further information she garners from her daughter that suggests Thelma's gaining insight during the play as well as the nourishment that such insight affords her.[11] When she grasps the hot chocolate pan at the end of the play, holding *"it tight like her life depended on it"* (89), something Jessie has advised her to clean after hearing the shot, calling her son, and waiting for him to arrive, Thelma is doing what she said she would not and could not. She is finding a way to go on, a way pointed out to her by her daughter, who, by taking control of her life by killing herself, has also offered her mother a new sense of life and strength to live it.[12] One shares Mama's feelings of devastation at the end of the play but also feels a sense of her impending renewal.

The seeds of that renewal, like the pomegranate seeds of the myth, involve a quickened sense of life through the gaining of a quickened sense of death; Mama must face that death which Jessie chooses; must, so to speak, taste it, if she is to achieve a reversal of her death-in-life existence and achieve that "*being in death*" that Kerényi suggests is at the center of the Demeter-Kore myth.[13] Explaining her fear of death to her daughter, Mama describes death as "some killler on the loose, hiding out in the back yard just waiting for me to have my hands full someday and how am I supposed to protect myself anyhow when I don't know what he looks like and I don't know how he sounds coming up behind me like that or if it will hurt or take very long or what I don't get done before it happens" (77–78). Mama might be describing some modern version of Hades, waiting to pounce, violate her, and carry her off to the Underworld.

After this outburst, however, Mama confronts death in her own daughter, whom she now sees is beyond persuasion, "Who am I talking to? You're gone already, aren't you? I'm looking right through you!" (78). Only by coming to see her daughter as gone, unreclaimable, married to Hades, and by experiencing her daughter's acceptance of her own lostness and death can Mama undergo an integration with her daughter that is the only possible source of renewal at hand.

As she battles with Jessie over the impending suicide, partly blaming herself for urging Jessie to move in with her after her divorce, Mama senses in some profound way the doubling of herself and her daughter.

> *Mama*. Everything you do has to do with me, Jessie. You can't do *anything*, wash your face or cut your finger, without doing it to me. That's right. You might as well kill me as you, Jessie, it's the same thing. This has to do with me, Jessie. (72)

Here Mama is partly expressing her identification with Jessie as a part of herself—but as that part Jessie is also the antagonist, the killer. Otto Rank has discussed this aspect of doubling in which the double symbolizes death so that encountering one's double is a kind of encounter with one's own mortality. Although doubling, Rank explains, grows out of a narcissistic inability to love others and a fear of death, resisting exclusive self-love leads to the doubling and a projection of hate or fear onto the other self.[14] Mama's slow acceptance of Jessie's decision to die is a movement toward acceptance of her own mortality. That this is a life-giving experience becomes clear as Thelma begins to accept the impending separation and hence the death of her dependency. Mama's expression of identification with Jessie—"This has to do with me Jessie" (72)—is partly an expression of dependency. Realizing Jessie's loneliness—"How could I know you were so alone?" (88), she begs, addressing the now locked door—her final words after she hears the shot display a moment of true recognition. "Jessie, Jessie, child . . . Forgive me. *(Pause)* I thought you were mine" (89).[15] Mother and daughter merge as they separate, the death of one giving life to the other.

Similarly, it is only through an anticipated encounter with death, one that Jessie associates as a merging with her withdrawn father, a gentle and quiet Hades, that Jessie has been able to achieve the independence that she manages at last to pass on to her mother. When Thelma claims possession—"You are my child!"—Jessie explains that she is "what became of your child" (76). She has decided not "to stay" because she feels she has never shown up as a person and that she never will. Again, there is a paradoxical sense of identity here as Jessie, taking control and guiding her mother to acceptance, finally does seem to arrive as a person.

If Jessie were entirely calm as she approached her death, the play might lose some of the tension that comes from her vulnerability that lasts, despite her overall control, until the end; thus both Jessie and Mama experience growth during the play. Learning from her distraught and angry mother that the epilepsy she thought derived from a fall from a horse as an adult had been with her since childhood and was probably inherited from her father, who had similar seizures, Jessie feels that this knowledge was her right, that it was hers to know (70). She is hurt further to learn from her mother that her husband Cecil had another woman, the daughter of her mother's friend Agnes. Jessie's ability to digest these new hurts without loss of control is a measure of the sense of self she has achieved now that she has decided to protect herself from further hurt through death. Significantly, her seizures, which are like minor descents into the Underworld and represent a loss of control and self, have been brought under control by medication, and it has been more than a year since her last one. No longer overtaken by Hades and violated by him, she is choosing to consummate her union with him.

More information Jessie gains during the drama involves the somewhat comic Hecate figure, Agnes. In the Homeric Hymn to Demeter, the oldest account of the rape of Persephone, there is, according to Kerényi, a doubling not only of Demeter with Persephone but also with the moon goddess Hecate.[16] Hearing the cries of the raped Persephone in her cave, Hecate meets Demeter and together, torches in hand, they seek knowledge of the lost child from the sun. Various versions of the myth, according to Kerényi, depict now Demeter, now Hecate seeking Persephone in the Underworld, these different versions suggesting an underlying unity between the goddesses.[17] Because Hecate also is sometimes portrayed as queen of the Underworld, she may also be identified with Persephone. Despite her slight role in the myth, Kerényi suggests that Hecate may even be its primary goddess on some level.[18] Whether one considers her in her depictions as three-headed like her dog Cerberus, or as having influence over either the three realms of heaven, earth, and sea, or heaven, earth, and the Underworld, she may be understood as one who encompasses the other two figures in the myth.

Agnes, who is only discussed by Jessie and Mama in the play, seems to have more of the crone and witchlike attributes that Hecate has developed over time. Surrounded by birds and living on okra, even in the winter, Agnes is described by Thelma as being "as crazy as they come . . . a lunatic" (42)—hence her lunar aspect or association with the moon. She does not help Thelma with Jessie, avoiding the house when Jessie is home because she associates Jessie with death and she fears that it is catching (43). But if her avoidance of Jessie seems to preclude her Hecate role on the mythic level of the play's action, her setting fire to her houses may be associated with Hecate as a torch bearer bringing light. Agnes's behavior is akin to Jessie's suicide and is applauded by mother and daughter, although they consider it "crazy." Apparently Agnes has set eight fires already, waking up people so they won't be hurt and serving lemonade. Seeking to rationalize this behavior, Mama explains, "The houses they lived in, you knew they were going to fall down anyway, so why wait for it, is all I could ever make out about it. Agnes likes a feeling of accomplishment" (39). Jessie's "Good for her" (39) indicates her appreciation of Agnes deciding to terminate before termination date, a similar choice to her own, and when she expresses doubt that Agnes would burn down a house now since her dead husband could not build a new one, Mama also appreciates the act: "Be exciting, though, if she did. You never know" (40), is Mama's response.

Although Mama's picture of Agnes surrounded by birds, living on okra, and burning down houses may be an exaggeration, it has some of the festive quality that is associated not only with the torch-bearing Hecate but with Demeter in her role as goddess of the grain. One may liken the burning and rebuilding of houses to the dying and returning moon (Hecate) or the dying and returning corn (Demeter or Persephone). Kerényi reminds us that "Whether it is parched or baked as bread, death by fire is the fate of the grain. Nevertheless, every sort of grain is eternal."[19] In the Demeter myth, Demeter treats the child Demophoön with fire in an attempt to make him immortal, as though he were the grain.[20] Jessie recognizes Agnes's value for her mother, and despite being hurt by what she learns of Agnes's fear of her, she suggests that her mother may like to live with Agnes after she is gone. Thelma, however, doubtless will be able to live alone. In the midst of telling Jessie about Agnes, Thelma insists that three marshmallows are the best way, the "old way" to have hot chocolate. She is imbibing not only Jessie's strength but Agnes's strength as well. She will be the primary goddess among the three in this drama.

Marsha Norman surely did not attempt to make *'night, Mother* a modern version of the Demeter myth. The rhythms and resonance of that myth, however, give the play, despite its great sadness and sense of loss, its quickened sense of life. "Hades," it has been noted, "is the god presiding over our descents, investing the darkness in our lives, our depressions, our anxieties, our emotional upheavals and our grief with the power to bring illumination and renewal."[21] Jessie embraces this god, and it is he that she introduces to her mother, who perhaps is able to see him more clearly through the image of Agnes's fires, a torch that burns to help one find what is lost. Mama learns from Jessie what it is that she used to whisper about after dinner with her withdrawn father—"His life, I guess," Jessie reveals. "His corn. His boots. Us. Things. You know" (47). And now Mama does.

Notes

1. Robert Brustein, "Don't Read This Review!," *New Republic*, 2 May 1983, p. 25.
2. Patricia Basworth, "Some Secret Worlds Revealed," *Working Woman* 8 (October 1983): 204.
3. C. G. Jung, "The Psychological Aspects of the Kore," in C. G. Jung and C. Kerényi, *Essays on a Science of Mythology: The Myth of the Divine Child and the Mysteries of Eleusis*, trans. R. F. C. Hull (Princeton: Princeton University Press, 1969), p. 162.
4. C. Kerényi, "Epilegomena: The Miracle of Eleusis," in C. G. Jung and C. Kerényi, *Essays on a Science of Mythology: The Myth of the Divine Child and the Mysteries of Eleusis*, trans. R. F. C. Hull (Princeton: Princeton University Press, 1969), p. 182.
5. Marsha Norman, *'night, Mother* (New York: Hill and Wang, 1983). Subsequent references are cited parenthetically by page number.
6. Jung, "The Psychological Aspects of the Kore," p. 162.
7. Geoffrey Grigson, *The Goddess of Love: The Birth, Triumph, Death and Return of Aphrodite* (New York: Stein and Day, 1977), p. 202.
8. C. Kerényi, "Kore," in C. G. Jung and C. Kerényi, *Essays on a Science of Mythology: The Myth of the Divine Child and the Mysteries of Eleusis*, trans. R. F. C. Hull (Princeton: Princeton University Press, 1969), p. 123.

9. Jenny S. Spencer, "Norman's *'night, Mother*: Psycho-drama of Female Identity," *Modern Drama* 30, no. 3 (September 1987): 371–72.
10. This idea was suggested in an unpublished paper on *'night, Mother* written by Linda Brown, 1986.
11. Debbie McCormick, "The Use of Food in *'night, Mother*," unpublished paper, 1986.
12. Ibid.
13. Kerényi, "Epilegomena: The Miracle of Eleusis," p. 182.
14. Otto Rank, *The Double: A Psychoanalytic Study*, ed. and trans. Harry Tucker, Jr. (Chapel Hill: The University of North Carolina Press, 1971), pp. 71–73.
15. Inexplicably, the otherwise sensitive film version of *'night, Mother* leaves out this crucial line.
16. Kerényi, "Kore," pp. 110–11.
17. Ibid., p. 110.
18. Ibid., p. 113.
19. Ibid., p. 116.
20. Ibid.
21. Arianna Stassinopoulis and Roloff Beny, *The Gods of Greece* (New York: Harry N. Abrams, Inc., 1983), p. 187.

21
The Silver Lining in the Mushroom Cloud: Meredith Monk's Opera/Music Theater

Suzanne R. Westfall

> Let us begin . . .
> In the first generation
> It was decided that
> Form had to be maintained
> And we the people
> Began to investigate
> What this need meant
> —Meredith Monk and Ping Chong, prologue to *The Games*

Maintenance of form, particularly the forms canonized by western white patriarchy, Freudian psychology, and literary despotism, has provided more than one woman with her own "yellow wallpaper" in that attic room. In these days of post-structuralism and deconstruction, however, when marginalized texts and artists are beginning to be investigated, we notice enigmatic and omnipresent forms and begin to assess them. Since the sixties, feminist playwrights and performers have been stridently breaking the rules, producing in the process new methods of creation, new structures, new themes, and new production values—in short, the glimmerings of a new morphology.

Meredith Monk, in the forefront of the avant-garde theater/music/dance scene popularly known as "performance art," won the Obie Award for Sustained Achievement in 1985 for her years of testing the boundaries of traditional artistic structures. Unlike mainstream playwrights such as Marsha Norman, Wendy Wasserstein, and Beth Henley, Monk's methods resemble those of Megan Terry and Caryl Churchill, who focus on collaboration and nonlinear development; her production values seem in harmony with the prophetic and surreal style of Pina Bausch or Martha Clark, her sensibilities are as witty and keen as those of Laurie Anderson or Linda Montano, and her aesthetics are as daring as Judy Chicago's.

With these contexts in mind, I examine Monk's twentieth-anniversary work *The Games*, created with her long-time corraborator Ping Chong in November 1983 for the Schaubühne Theater in Berlin and restaged in October 1984 for the Brooklyn Academy of Music's Next Wave season. Although most of Monk's creations have been centered firmly on women's lives, in *The Games* Monk and Chong apply perspectives and techniques that spring from a feminist consciousness to consider the postapocalyptic world of all human beings.

It is no accident that Monk, like many women, has found acceptance and admiration in the avant-garde world of performance art. Many of us would like to ascribe the number and popularity of women performance artists to women being naturally more creative and courageous than their male counterparts, but the truth is probably a bit more pedestrian. Several reasons seem plausible for the fact that many women, from stand-up comics to female rock stars, are choosing to display their own works in their own ways with their own bodies.

First, a pragmatic explanation. Avant-garde theater is marginalized, not-for-profit theater, territory long familiar to women playwrights. Performance art is not threatening to mainstream Broadway and off-Broadway, because performances take place at smaller theaters and clubs, on limited budgets, with fewer risks. Consequently, women may find more spaces and funding, particularly when foundations for the arts are finally offering financial support for groups that have been disenfranchised for years.

Second, the avant-garde audience, which has been evolving gradually from the Dadaist movement of the early twentieth century,[1] is naturally willing and able to reach beyond traditional horizons of expectation and is eager to enter into complicity with revolutionary forms, concepts, and ideas. Women's morphologies, therefore, find more patient and accepting receivers here. New audiences, female audiences, also have been created as a result of the women's movement, increased financial and social freedoms for women, and increased credibility for feminist perspectives, forged through the diligent efforts of hard-thinking scholars and critics, assisted by a healthy bit of male Marxist guilt.

A third, and perhaps the most persuasive, reason for the success of female performance artists is historical. This form has been a woman's form for years, persisting even without public acclaim. I refer here to the tradition of the women's salon, which flourished in the eighteenth and nineteenth centuries, as a place where women were free to experiment with their own aesthetics in the supportive environment of friends within the safety of their own spaces, their own households.[2] These forms of what Sue-Ellen Case calls "personal theatre" evolve naturally into performance art, which is similarly based on first-person and first-hand accounts created and performed by the same body. Women's long-standing participation in community ceremonies and pageants, from Sunday school to the League of Women Voters, has provided similar impetus for the developing performance artist.[3]

Monk has always created portraits of the artist as a young woman, but she refuses to be identified by traditional forms or labels. Between the happenings she created in the sixties for such spaces as New York's Guggenheim Museum and what she now calls her "opera/music-theatre" performance art of the eighties, Monk created theater cantatas, movies, opera epics, and operas in an attempt to fracture audience expectations and thereby free interpretations.[4] In *Education of a Girlchild,* an elderly woman follows a moonlight path back to her own birth, "demonstrating the process of gender conditioning in reverse"[5]; in *Quarry,* restaged in 1985 at LaMama in New York, the terrified girlchild wakes screaming to a nightmare vision of the holocaust, which we see through her eyes with her mother as focus. *Acts from Under and Above,* a 1986 LaMama production, uses huge film closeups of the two indomitable protagonists, like "goddesses regarding the earth below, sometimes crying at what they see."[6] In *The Games,* Monk and Chong turn to science fiction, long a rich geography for the feminist imagination, creating a futuristic utopia that excavates its past (our present) for clues to its present (our future).

The audience is treated to a complex metatextual experience as our historical and sociological facts become the mythic ritual of our distant descendants, the survivors of a nuclear holocaust. These people play games to provide contiguity with their past and structure for their present. Monk's choice of game as the paradigm for ideological reconstruction is significant, because it suggests the recreation of children (with its attendant pedagogical effects), the re-creation of the theater, the fierce competition of organized sport, and, ironically, our game of survival. It is a curious paradox that folklorists, anthropologists, and theater theorists for years have viewed games as vital analogues of creation and paradigms for preserving culture, although paternalistic hierarchies relegate such pastimes to the implicitly inferior and powerless contexts of childhood and leisure, contexts traditionally associated with women's experience. Thus, in choosing a seemingly trivial yet psychologically loaded focus for her work, Monk begins to exploit her experience as a woman to construct her artwork.

The play begins with a series of children's games, such as red-light-green-light and musical chairs, played by natural deconstructionists, people who do not define the word *game* as we do, who do not understand the purpose of the action, who parrot words without understanding what they symbolize (the gamesmaster intones "swing ya padnah, doe see doe" as a foreigner mimics the sound but not the sense of English). With adult intensity and chillingly false postures of joy, the people play desperately but noncompetitively, an equivocal and ambiguous image of a society trying new ways to solve its problems without the saccharine promise of successes.

The second game, "Migration," reenacts the survivors' travails after the destruction, with the gamesmaster, played in her typical deglamorized style by Monk herself (a wonderful metaphor for the artist), alternately coaxing and bullying her charges through their sufferings. The third, "Memory," deconstructs the detritus of our culture; while a mislabeled clothespin flashes on the screen, trivial pursuit questions are asked: "what was lunch? who invented the question mark, and why?" Afterward, one woman chants, "I remember . . . ," while another intones, "I have forgotten. . . ." Things as trivial to us as morning coffee and as momentous as Shakespeare blend equally in the list, dramatically demonstrating the validity of reception theory, that meaning is created as the receiver interprets signs according to idiolectic criteria. Thus Monk achieves *Verfremdungseffekt*, "making the mundane look exotic" by wrenching it from context.[7]

The fourth game, "Fear" (an interlinguistic pun on *vier*), portrays the moment of nuclear destruction. All the games are enacted multimedially and simultaneously using music, song, dance, projections, and lights, accompanied by a smattering of text in several languages and non-languages.

The piece highlights feminist concerns from beginning to end, from its conception to its inception, design, and performance techniques. First, Monk had to go to Germany, where, to the shame of the Reagan administration, so many visionary artists, like Robert Wilson, are getting the financial and emotional support they require. Monk went to Berlin with the intention of creating a work about Roanoke, the lost colony of Virginia (which, incidentally, gave us our first American-born victim/heroine, little Virginia Dare) but ended up collaborating with the Schaubühne to create something different, in the process devoting three weeks of her long ten-week rehearsal period to acclimating herself to the actors and the actors to her style. She considered it vital that the actors not be subjected to übermarionette treatment. Although she stresses rigor and discipline, she wants the work to emerge organically and comfortably from and for her performers. Both the time commitment and the stress on process distinguish Monk's method (gestation) from the modus operandi of most male theater directors (programmed rehearsal).

In addition, this creative process represents what Marxist-feminist critics have noted about female methods of production in general: that women tend to create "material that is valued for itself, for its immediate physical and qualitative worth, and not for its abstract quantitative monetary or exchange value."[8] Monk's production methods certainly are not cost efficient and are far too concerned with integrating rather than alienating her labor force to be considered good business by patriarchal society. Furthermore, her reliance on collaboration, another particularly feminist method of creating, further distinguishes her work from the traditional theater, which since Meyerhold has been developing the notion of the author/director as dictator. Through their philosophy of collaboration, Monk and Chong ally themselves with playwrights such as Terry and Churchill and with countless feminist and lesbian theater collectives.

Even more feminist is the structure of *The Games*. One of the most pervasive and disturbing errors that women artists commit is to take a female hero and force her through the basic psychological/mythic quest pattern: separation from family, trial of physical/psychological strength, return to society reborn.[9] The problem is that this is a male pattern of individuation that has been so "canonized" (and I mean that word in both senses) as to be almost de rigueur in literary patterning. Using the same male pattern and merely changing the gender of the protagonist creates what I call the "hero in drag," not a woman hero but a woman who has learned to play by the boys' rules, who has assumed male problems and adopted male methods of dealing with them.[10] *The Games* is not structured linearly, nor is it concerned with quests. As Claudine Herrmann has argued, women perceive time differently than Western thought dictates: passage of time is not necessarily progressive, nor does it increase the levels of truth or complexity.[11] In true deconstructionist fashion, Monk chooses fragments in time and space, uniting them in the familiar feminine web or network[12] as variant views of experience rather than linking them in a plot that marches toward an inevitable ending. Consequently, *The Games* is nonlinear, its epilogue bringing it full circle, its sequence formed synchronically rather than diachronically, its unity provided by emotion and mood, not by plot or action. The characters act and react to situations that confront them rather than journeying out to slay monsters, claim treasures, and rescue helpless princesses, all methods of providing closure, a function many feminist structures avoid.[13] This intrinsically feminist structure stems from Monk's philosophy of theater, which reaches beyond the Western androcentric traditions:

> For me, theatre, in the broadest sense of the word, is really a place where you can take storytelling, acting, visual images, movement, and music, and put them into a form where these elements are not separated. And I think the only place where those things are separated is in Western culture. . . . All the elements in my work—the lighting, the text, the movement, the music, the visual images—are part of one mosaic which will hopefully form as full a perceptual, emotional, spiritual, kinetic entity as possible.[14]

Monk further resists the impulse to follow the typical patterns in her language. Obviously, sexist diction is conspicuously absent; the protagonist is the collective "we the people," the human race, enacted by gamesplayers who are pan-cultural and not sexually stereotyped in any way. Some feminists may find Monk's avoidance of woman as subject, as "I" with specific point of view, a bit recidivist or at least somewhat disappointing, but group identity and focus have long been women's concerns, and in *The Games* Monk and Chong are more concerned with exploring human processes through feminist means than in focusing on specifically gynocentric issues.

What text there is affirms Christiane Makward's observation that women's language is "open, nonlinear, unfinished, fluid, exploded, fragmented, polysemic . . . as opposed to . . . pre-conceived, oriented, masterly or 'didactic' languages."[15] Frequent and abrupt changes of topic, ellipses, disjointed conversations, litotes, various languages, nonverbal languages, and ultimately nonlanguages continually undermine audience expectation of traditional syntactics and semantics, yet the layering of images and the cyclic and repetitive pattern, intrinsic to female experience, effectively provide guides to the creation of new meaning. This morphology is invaluable to feminist theater, because it forcefully and directly prevents automatic cultural decoding, thereby sabotaging the traditional sign systems and their implicit meanings.

This new meaning, which serves the place of plot, embraces feminist politics. When the political games are played with the boys' rules, the results are inevitable—apocalypse. Without assigning blame or demanding vengeance, Monk and Chong poignantly stress the survival of our race and the reconstruction of civilization. With deliberate irony, they reflect how obsession with *logos* destroys human freedom through its insistence on the straitjacket arms of rules and order. At the same time, however, they pay tribute to human strength and sensitivity as they explore the relationships between and among survivors: people abandon each other, support each other, torture each other, comfort each other; the refreshing difference here is that it is not always the women who nurture and the men who oppress.

Despite the truth of these observations, Monk cannot and would not be called a realist. Many critics have pointed out that realism, with its valorization of linear overviews, family structures, and traditional cultural coding, is intrinsically a patriarchal form. The production values common to realism, furthermore, tend toward the traditional, concentrating on a few modes of expression, chiefly linguistic and proxemic. In marked contrast with the realists, many feminist artists, Monk among them, are inordinately aware of the multimediality of the theater, perhaps as a concretized reflection of their alinear or contiguous forms and free-flowing temporal and spatial constructs.[16] Monk is keenly aware that audiences can and do absorb many different codes and images simultaneously, and she exploits each level of communication at her disposal. Consequently, she is not content to express what passes for plot merely using dramatic text; the performance text reveals that visual, aural, and proxemic signs reenforce the poignancy of the futuristic culture she creates. This makes the creation of audience complicity both more complex and simpler, for although information flows out on a variety of levels, the overcoding should disarm audience fears of chaos and confusion.

To begin programming spectator response, Monk presents her actor/dancers in costumes that are uniform and sexually nonstereotypical, thereby avoiding traditional theater's tendency to focus on what E. Ann Kaplan calls "the male gaze."[17] The men and women in the chorus are all dressed in antiseptic white jumpsuits, bearing headgear that resembles EEG machines. The gamesplayers, three women and two men, are similarly dressed in blue jumpsuits more loosely fitted than the chorus costume. The gamesmaster, wearing green and sporting a backwards baseball cap, may be played by either a woman or a man with no change in character, movement, or musical score, a further tribute to the work's gender equality.

Gender differences, however, are not obliterated entirely; the cast is equal, not androgynous. Androgyny and transexualism have been popular ideas with many feminist science fiction writers such as Ursula LeGuin, Marge Piercy, and Joanna Russ[18]; the diegetic form of narrative prose allows a suspension of information that makes it possible to confuse the reader's concept of gender. But this confusion is not so easily produced through mimesis on stage, where the visual and aural perceptions of the audience are frequently (but not always) too sharp to be deceived. Rather than attempting such deception, Monk expects the audience to identify the genders of her players and to observe their interactions, thus treating spectators to another metatextual experience as they apply their own sociological and cultural gender-role expectations to characters who clearly have other concepts of sex roles and behaviors. Iconically, the characters are clearly male and female, but indexually and symbolically they are not, a seeming paradox that leads us to reexamine our own peculiar preconceptions and misconceptions.

For example, Monk's vocal score, which critic David Sterritt describes as having "evocative effects ranging from folksong to birdsong,"[19] is musical abstract expressionism, sung in German, French, Russian, Japanese, English, and gibberish. Because performers generally scat-sing rather than text-sing, content is obviously gender neutral. In addition, Monk's singers are so well trained that vocal range is not entirely dependent on gender; Monk herself sings from baritone to soprano, and her men are able to range from bass and baritone to mezzo to falsetto.

The gender neutrality that is established in design and score is reemphasized in proxemics and dance. Men partner men as frequently as they do women. None of the dance follows the patterns of classical or even modern ballet, in which men lift, throw, and take dominant physical roles while women flutter, float, roll on floors, and pirouette on point. In one episode, a man embraces and comforts his dying friend (brother? lover?); in another, a woman coldly shakes off the clinging duo (children? friends? parents?) who threaten her survival, leaving them to die. One of the most moving images occurs when a woman attempts vainly to convince an exhausted man to get up and move: she first harangues, then encourages, then beats, then begs. Finally, she squirms underneath him, using her body as a lever to force him to rise; then, in an astounding vision of strength, she bears him to safety on her back.

This forceful image demonstrates that Monk chooses not to ally herself with what Showalter has called "gynocriticism" and others have called "essentialism" or ghettoization, all of which maintain exclusivity: men cannot surrender their "paternal privileges" to read and experience as women do.[20] Refusing to assert separateness and difference and uninterested in the mission to establish a women's canon and to defend women's ways of thinking and knowing, Monk is nonetheless stridently feminist. She constructs a vision of feminism that has entered Betty Friedan's much maligned but appropriately named "second stage," when

> . . . we transcend the polarization between women and women and between women and men, to achieve the new human wholeness that is the promise of feminism, and get on with solving the concrete, practical, everyday problems of living, working and loving as equal persons. . . .[21]

Like Friedan, Monk's art in the sixties sounded dire warnings, but she now prefers "to offer an alternative—not in the sense of '60's alternative lifestyles, but in terms of ways of seeing things."[22]

These "ways of seeing things" may not, in a representative feminist structure, include answers or closure. Although the choreography of *The Games* is echoed in a technological code by markers on a projected grid upstage center, Monk's dancers move constantly across the stage but never really get anywhere, reenforcing the motif of the first game in which the adult children energetically play without producing winners. This endless cycle of movement is mirrored in the networked structure of the entire piece, for the epilogue enacts the arrival of the first generation of survivors, unrecognizable in space suits; the audience is thrown further back in time and space when this image is replaced by a medieval bagpiper. His mournful solo reminds us that apocalypses of different sorts have always hovered around us, but his presence onstage with figures representing the immediate and far future remind us that humans and humanity survive. *The Games*, with its revision of ideology and society, holds out the hope that this recurring pattern is, if not preventable, at least survivable: a slight, but not very comforting, silver lining.

In her artistic vision and methodology, Monk offers not only new ways for spectators to think about our society but new ways for women to construct and present art and new ways for audiences to interpret art, perhaps the traces of the feminist morphology that many critics seek to discover, uncover, and recover. Following the rich historical tradition of the salon performers, Monk takes a primary role as creator, producer, leading performer, director, choreographer, and composer. She is completely at ease with the technology of the traditional and nontraditional theater and secure enough to foreground technology itself as an art and artifact.

Most significantly, Monk's structures, her style, and her methodology reflect centuries-old traditions of women's aesthetics: collaboration and gestation; attention to gender issues; multimediality; and nonlinear, atemporal, disjointed vectors of experience without closure. By exploring these oxymoronic new/old paradigms for creative women, Monk reveals that we need not and should not rely on traditional ways and means if we wish to produce revolutionary art. Rather, we must recognize the subtle presence of androcentric influences, find mythic and psychological patterns that present human experience undistorted by the mirror of male perceptions, and we learn to convert these aesthetics into images. As Monk and Chong write:

> Let us reach completion . . .
>
> In The Games
> We remember the past
> And in this way
> Prevent the darkness and chaos that
> Plagued our ancestors
> Before the first generation

. . . Let us now honor
The courage and wisdom
Of our first generation
Who survived calamity
To bring us a new life thru the legacy
Of The Games

Let us reach completion by remembering this. . . .[23]

Notes

1. The term *performance art* is inordinately difficult to define. The 1989 *Readers Guide* or *Humanities Index* lists articles about Robert Wilson and Laurie Anderson. Go back two years, and you are directed to "see Theatre, experimental." In the 1980 listings, you are sent to "happenings"; before that, you are advised to consult "Art, modern." The most thorough historical survey and investigation of the form is RoseLee Goldberg, *Performance Art: From Futurism to the Present* (New York: Harry N. Abrams, 1988). For history and criticism of performance art by women, see Moira Roth, ed., *The Amazing Decade: Women and Performance Art in America 1970–1980* (Los Angeles: Astro Artz, 1983) and *Women and Performance: A Journal of Feminist Theory.*

2. Sue-Ellen Case surveys the history and influence of the salon in chapter 3, "Personal Theatre," of *Feminism and Theatre* (New York: Methuen, 1988).

3. Helen Krich Chinoy and Linda Walsh Jenkins, eds., *Women in American Theatre*, revised and expanded edition (New York: Theatre Communications Group, 1987). This ambitious work is a treasure trove of information about women as creators, directors, consumers, technicians, and critics. In addition, the volume provides thorough catalogues of practical information on women's collectives, production histories, awards, and countless other resources.

4. Alisa Solomon, "Doubly Marginalized: Women in the Avant-Garde," in *Women in American Theatre*, revised and expanded edition, ed. Helen Krich Chinoy and Linda Walsh Jenkins (New York: Theatre Communications Group, 1987), p. 366.

5. Jeanie Forte, "Female Body as Text in Women's Performance Art," in *Women in American Theatre*, revised and expanded edition, ed. Helen Krich Chinoy and Linda Walsh Jenkins (New York: Theatre Communications Group, 1987), p. 378.

6. Elizabeth Zimmer, "New York Reviews," *Dance Magazine* 60 (October 1986): 22.

7. Sally Banes, "Reviews," *Dance Magazine* 59 (January 1985): 39.

8. Josephine Donovan, "Toward a Women's Poetics," in *Feminist Issues in Literary Scholarship*, ed. Shari Benstock (Bloomington: Indiana University Press, 1987), p. 102.

9. The supposedly "universal" mythic pattern has been delineated by Lord Raglan in "Myth and Ritual" and by Claude Levi-Strauss in "The Structural Study of Myth," in *Myth: A Symposium*, ed. Thomas A. Sebeok (Bloomington: Indiana University Press, 1958), pp. 122–35, 81–106. Vladimir Propp, *Morphology of the Folktale*, trans. Lawrence Scott (Austin: University of Texas Press, 1968), assumes the same patterns in chapter 3, his discussion of the functions of the "dramatis personae" in folk and fairy tales. For the same pattern in its psychoanalytical incarnation, see Carl G. Jung's comments on the process of individuation in *The Archetypes and the Collective Unconscious*, vol. 9 of *The Collected Works*, trans. R. F. C. Hull (New York: Pantheon Books, 1959); C. G. Jung and C. Kerényi, *Introduction to a Science of Mythology: The Myth of the Divine Child and The Mysteries of Eleusis*, trans. R. F. C. Hull (London: Routledge & Kegan Paul, 1951), and C. G. Jung, *Man and His Symbols* (Garden City, N. Y.: Doubleday, 1964). Freud and Jung also assume that masculine patterns are applicable to women.

10. For an interesting and entertaining discussion of the problem, see Joanna Russ, "What Can a Heroine Do? Or Why Women Can't Write," in *Images of Women in Fiction:*

Feminist Perspectives, ed. Susan Koppelman Cornillon (Bowling Green, Ohio: Bowling Green University Popular Press, 1972), pp. 3–20.

11. Claudine Herrmann, "Women in Space and Time," in *New French Feminisms: An Anthology*, ed. Elaine Marks and Isabelle de Courtivron (Amherst: The University of Massachusetts Press, 1980), pp. 168–73.

12. In their attempts to discover a female morphology, many critics have noted the female pattern of weaving and networking from Penelope through *Quilters*. Case briefly discusses the phenomenon in *Feminism and Theatre;* for a more thorough overview, see Donovan, "Toward a Woman's Poetics," pp. 98–109.

13. Like weaving, lack or postponement of closure has been delineated as a specifically female technique, because women's lives are cyclical rather than linear, their activities "interruptable" rather than sacrosanct. See Case, *Feminist Theatre*, p. 116, and Donovan, "Toward a Women's Poetics," pp. 101–2.

14. Rob Baker, "New Worlds for Old: The Visionary Art of Meredith Monk," *American Drama* 1, no. 6 (October 1984): 4–9, 34. For reviews of *The Games*, see Mel Gussow, "Theatre: Next Wave Festival Opens," *New York Times*, 11 October 1984, sec. C, p. 16; Jack Anderson, "*The Games*—Serious Science Fiction on Stage," *New York Times*, 21 October 1984, sec. 2, p. 6. For Jon Pareles's interview with Monk, see "Meredith Monk, Two Decades Later" *New York Times*, 17 May 1985, sec. C, pp. 3–4.

15. Christiane Makward, "To Be or Not to Be . . . a Feminist Speaker," in *The Future of Difference*, ed. Alice Jardine and Hester Eisenstein (Boston: G. K. Hall, 1980), p. 96.

16. Case, *Feminist Theatre*, p. 126; Herrmann, "Women in Space and Time," p. 172.

17. E. Ann Kaplan, *Women and Film* (New York: Methuen, 1981), p. 23.

18. See such novels as Ursula K. LeGuin, *The Left Hand of Darkness* (New York: Chelsea House, 1987) and Marge Piercy, *Woman on the Edge of Time* (New York: Fawcett, 1986). Joanna Russ's short stories frequently concern gender identification; she writes forcefully about the issues in *How to Suppress Women's Writing* (Austin: University of Texas Press, 1983) and in *The Female Man* (Boston: Beacon Press, 1986).

19. Baker, "New Worlds for Old," p. 8.

20. Attitudes toward the practice of "reading as a woman" seem divided between radical feminists and materialist feminists. Sandra M. Gilbert, Susan Gubar, and Elaine Showalter are the leading, or perhaps the most vociferous, proponents of gynocriticism. See Showalter, "Toward a Feminist Poetics," in *The New Feminist Criticism: Essays on Women, Literature and Theory*, ed. Elaine Showalter (New York: Pantheon Books, 1985), pp. 125–43. Jane Marcus surveys the battlefront in "Still Practice, A/Wrested Alphabet: Toward a Feminist Aesthetic," in *Feminist Issues in Literary Scholarship*, ed. Shari Benstock, pp. 79–97. See also Donovan, "Toward a Women's Poetics." In her discussion of radical feminism and theater, Case explains the attitude of gynocritical opponents by examining the notions of cultural feminism, essentialism, biologism (63, 130).

21. Betty Friedan, *The Second Stage* (New York: Summit Books, 1981), p. 41.

22. Solomon, "Doubly Marginalized," p. 366.

23. Meredith Monk and Ping Chong, Prologue to *The Games*, in program, Schaubühne am Lehniner Platz, Berlin.

22
Canonizing Lesbians?

Lynda Hart

"The Master's Tools Will Never Dismantle the Master's House"

—Audre Lorde, in *Sister Outsider*

Following the directive of this book's title, *Modern American Drama: The Female Canon*, and my own project within it to write about lesbian theater, I might simply search the modern American dramatic canon for plays about lesbians by female authors. That procedure will readily turn up Lillian Hellman's *The Children's Hour*, and not much else. Starting there, I would have to see if this play fits the book's intentions. Hellman was female, so that seems to present no definitional problems; and her play is the most frequently anthologized, if not the *only*, drama "about lesbians" in the canon. But is *The Children's Hour* a lesbian play, or even a play about lesbianism? Hellman did not think so.

Protesting a bit too much, she declared in an interview: "I picked on a story that I could treat with complete impersonality. I hadn't even been to boarding school—I went to school here in New York." If that is not enough to discourage anyone who might question her motives for writing a play that seems to investigate lesbian desire, Hellman insists that the play "is really not a play about lesbianism, but about a lie. The bigger the lie the better, as always."[1] Nevertheless, if a hypothetical teacher were in search of a lesbian play to teach, he or she would be pressed to think of another play that would fit that bill in the modern American canon. Hellman's disclaimer would probably not discourage him or her, because critics have rarely relied much on authors' testimonies, even when authors were presumed to be living.

Suppose, however, this teacher attempted a distinction between a play about lesbians written by a heterosexual woman, which Hellman presumably was, and a "lesbian play." The thorny question of when a text is a "lesbian text" or its writer a "lesbian writer" becomes increasingly complicated as feminist theory and identity politics collide with poststructuralist accounts of the absent author and the multiple, shifting subject.[2] The relationships between biological sex, gender, sexual orientation (or preference), and subjectivity are highly contested. This volume's title seems to avoid some of these difficult questions by referring specifically to biological sex—"female"—specifying that the writers under consideration will all be female, but not necessarily the essayists. That editorial choice appears to uncomplicate the practical decisions, but the book is clearly about gender, not biology, and a feminist contributor would not make the mistake of collapsing these terms after decades of efforts to disentangle them. Sex, gender, and sexuality are difficult terms to think separately, but that is a crucial project for feminists. As Gayle Rubin, among others, has argued, the tendency to collapse these terms is the problem constituting a major stumbling block for feminist critics.[3] Lesbian and gay critics have learned an important lesson from observing feminist analyses that untangle sex and gender. When we consider sexuality, as opposed to biological sex traits, it is clearer that gender and sexuality are not as discursively fused as gender and sex. Eve Kosofsky Sedgwick writes:

> The most dramatic difference between gender and sexual orientation—that virtually all people are publicly and unalterably assigned to one or the other gender, and from birth—seems if anything to mean that it is rather sexual orientation, with its far greater potential for rearrangement, ambiguity, and representational doubleness, that would offer the more apt deconstructive object. An essentialism of sexual object choice is far less easy to maintain, far more visibly incoherent, more visibly stressed and challenged at every point in the culture, than any essentialism of gender.[4]

Lesbian sexual choice as "an apt deconstructive object" may offer feminists a way of thinking about gender and sexuality that avoids essentializing by observing the relatively less stable binary homosexual/heterosexual. However, the greater part of lesbian-feminist theory has been an effort to locate the lesbian subject with some specificity. If it is generally agreed that lesbians are females, there is scarcely a consensus about which females are lesbians, but feminists have exerted tremendous effort in locating that difference. Locating the lesbian subject has been, in part, an endeavor to counter the logic of heterosexuality which strives to claim that lesbians do not exist; it certainly has been said that lesbians are not "real women," a gender category that I would think most heterosexual feminists would aspire to be eliminated from as well. Marilyn Frye's guided tour through the lexicon of heterosexism shows us that lesbians are a category of the unthinkable because heterosexuality defines Lesbians as women who have sex with other women and sex is defined as genital union (intercourse) with a member of the opposite sex, and presumably of the opposite gender.[5] Furthermore, genital contact theories diminish the value and validity of erotic bonding between women from the Renaissance through the nineteenth century. The "female world of love and ritual" that Carroll Smith-Rosenberg has documented in Victorian America and the "romantic friendships," "Boston marriages," and "sentimental friends" that Lillian Faderman describes in British and European history are not consonant with late twentieth-century conceptions of lesbianism. Smith-Rosenberg's and Faderman's ground-breaking work has taught us the necessity of historicizing lesbianism.[6] These relationships might be read as "lesbian" to a contemporary reader, but it is not at all clear that sexual activity, what these women did with their bodies in relation to one another, was or was not at all like contemporary sexual practices. In a discussion of love between women in the time of Queen Anne, Kendall says: "We need new language to talk about old sex."[7] Certainly, we need new language to talk about new sex as well.

Using the term *female* might have been useful for our editor's purposes, but it enormously complicates mine because lesbians are not reducible to females (which really means *women* because this collection is not about bodies) and are perhaps only marginally at best (or worst) located within the gender category of women as it has been constructed. Even if I ignore or disregard the postmodern shifting and multiple subject, *identity* is an already problematized concept for lesbians. Postmodern theorists who proclaim the death of the author as do Barthes and Foucault, among others, merely complicate further what was already a difficult social subject to locate. If we accept Foucault's "transcendental anonymity," or Barthes's description of writing as "that neutral, composite, oblique space where our subject slips away," then Hellman's heterosexuality certainly slips away and we are left only with her femaleness, a biological difference that tells us little or nothing about her sexuality or subjectivity.[8] It is even possible to argue that, given some feminist definitions of lesbian, Hellman *was* a lesbian. I will return to this later.

First, let me shift my approach and ask if there is a lesbian in Hellman's text. Martha is the only likely candidate, and she is not so sure herself. Because she commits suicide after the possibility occurs to her, Hellman prematurely forecloses the question. Hellman does permit Martha to announce: "*I have loved you the way they said*" (emphasis in original), which might sound like a declaration of lesbian identity to a modern spectator.[9] But in this play's context, loving Karen "*the way they said*" means that Martha has harbored an unnatural, criminal, possibly contagious, and certainly unspeakable desire for her friend. I might then agree with Hellman that her play is not about lesbianism at all but about a lie, the lie constructed by nineteenth-century sexologists who constructed lesbianism as a pathological "inverted" desire.

My response to the play, however, is informed by a 1980s lesbian-feminist perspective and politics. Historically, the play was based on the 1811 trial of two Scottish schoolmistresses who were acquitted of the "crime" because their culture's judge and jury could not imagine the enactment of sexual activity between women.[10] Although I can be happy for the two schoolmistresses who escaped imprisonment, I hardly can be pleased with a play that represents lesbian love as unspeakable, unseeable, and unthinkable holding a position for over fifty years as the *only* canonized work in the modern American theater "about lesbianism."

This brings me to the second term of the title that is troublesome—canon. The canonization of *The Children's Hour* reveals an unquestionable complicity between heterosexism and the concept of canonization. The play serves heterosexism by occupying a space when no other play "about" lesbianism and no plays at all by self-identified lesbians have that dubious privilege. This is where the simplicity of using the word *female* proves not so simple after all. Hellman was female; theoretically, I cannot exclude the play on the grounds of the author's "identity"; but to claim that it does not address lesbian concerns at all, I would have to dehistoricize it. Contemporary critical theory blocks my political impulse to throw *The Children's Hour* out of the canon. Therefore, I seem to be in a position of taking Hellman's play seriously as a "lesbian" play or objecting to the notion of a female canon altogether.

Having come to this impasse, I must address certain terms that signify the conceptual framework for this collection. The term *female* may be intended as no more than a practical strategy, but it can never be just that. Strictly speaking, *female* connotes only bodies that are prelinguistic. What meaning can this biological difference have outside of historically determined discourses? A female canon might simply reverse the terms that feminist critics have demystified whereby women have been excluded and men included in canons, not because of their biology only, but because of a massive inscription of characteristics imposed on those bodies that construct the binary oppositional category of gender. Thus, even as a provisional designation, framed by quotation marks, a female canon risks suggesting that gender and sex are one, a problem that our editor is well aware of but nonetheless adopts reluctantly to appropriate the term *canon* for its political power. Henry Louis Gates Jr. has recently argued that we (the "rainbow coalition of contemporary critical theory"—"that uneasy, shifting set of alliances formed by feminist critics, critics of so-called minority culture and Marxist and post-structuralist critics generally") must engage in this kind of canon formation, "borrow a leaf from the right."[11]

This is a powerful argument, but if this appropriation is to be successful, it must be on new terms. *Female*, I think, is not the term for feminist canons; biology is not the link that supports women's community. Few critics would dispute that women's plays have been neglected, lost, hidden, erased, from the history of western theater. Most feminists, I believe, agree that canonization is a concept that has effectively permitted that erasure. Universality is evoked to justify excluding divergent and diverse viewpoints, and most of us know that heterosexuality is one of the primary terms of universality. The canon has been a white, male, heterosexual (or passing heterosexual) club that has mystified its terms for inclusion by establishing aesthetic criteria that suppress the sociohistorical context from which these aesthetic criteria emerge. Gaining admittance for marginalized others into that canon is slow, painstaking, and often results in token admissions.

But the alternative, constructing opposing canons, also is problematic, especially for lesbians, because it is unclear whether they would meet the criteria for inclusion in a female, a woman's, or even a feminist canon. Canons, by definition, must set certain limits; they must be formulated as this, but not this. They are thus inherently exclusionary. Lillian Robinson has described the "agony" of feminist critics who are torn between championing the quality of women's writing within the canonical economy or "radically redefining literary quality itself."[12] The latter strategy, so brilliantly argued by critics like Barbara Herrnstein Smith, seems to be the most hopeful effort.[13] Although projects posing a noncanonical theory of literary evaluation are underway, we still are faced with making practical decisions about course syllabi, in-class methodological strategies, and anthology formations. Avoiding formulations based on biological determinants that link all women writers together and flatten their multiplicities into a homogeneous mass is absolutely necessary. At the same time, however, we are reluctant to give up the idea of women as a community; and we do so, I think, at our political peril. This problem can, and must, be successfully negotiated. Feminists are at risk when we reinstate a new either/or—the multiplicity of women's experience, differences between and among women, *or* women as a cultural community. We need both, but we must work together to challenge each other's tendencies to construct oppositional accounts of either. Although the essays in this volume might not follow through on the title and introductory remarks' inclination, I am concerned that a female canon might place an emphasis exclusively on gender at the cost of minimizing racial, ethnic, religious, experiential, class, and sexual differences between and among women.

Our editor states clearly that the emphasis in this book is on gender, which she regards as a "testament to the moment." But surely this qualification/justification overlooks the title's complicity in constructing that response from contributors. Whose moment and what moment is this? By staged intent, it seems to be a moment when sexual difference reifies itself. Feminists certainly will never see any of their objectives realized if we think of ourselves as the passive recorders of history. Schlueter concedes that if this book had been written at another point in history (presumably the future), gender may not have been the predominant concern. But producing a book that privileges gender does not merely reflect a static moment in history; on the contrary, it shapes, creates, and maintains that advantage. If that future moment when gender is no longer a privileged category is ever to succeed, feminist writers must not only stop assuming that gender is an inherent property of bodies (although that is a crucial first step), but they must also think of history as a process created and maintained by their own discourses. For some feminist critics, that succession has already occurred, which would render this informing principle to a past historic moment.

Assuming that sexual difference is a natural construct immutably wedded to gender difference lends stasis to the feminist project if it does not create a reactionary backsliding. Teresa de Lauretis shows that gender, like sexuality, is "not a property of bodies or something originally existent in human beings, but [borrowing from Foucault's description of sexuality] 'the set of effects produced in bodies, behaviors, and social relations . . .' by the deployment of 'a complex political technology.' "[14] A female canon might imply that gender is an inherent property of bodies. To represent it unproblematized is to construct it.

Moreover, the two terms of the title that I find troubling, "female" and "canon," are intimately bound up with each other in ways that subvert rather than support feminist projects. When our editor asks "the inevitable question of whether there should be any sacred texts at all, any institutionalized body of literature that is presumed to express values that speak to all cultures at all times," the feminist answer, it seems to me, would be no. I believe feminists have more than satisfactorily demonstrated that traditional humanists locate that center audience as a small, privileged body of white, elitist, heterosexual males. Therefore, I am puzzled by the anxiety implicit in the "risk involved in women reading female texts from a feminist perspective [which might lead to] this provocative and productive critical approach [becoming] the exclusive property of female writers." This anxiety sounds like the echoes of prefeminist women who exhorted us to avoid the "unwomanly" assertion of our power. Betsy Draine's politically important observation "that a feminist literary *establishment* is by definition not feminist at all—unless . . . it has to confront the otherness of those without power, and learns (again) to be subversive," is exactly right but strangely out of place in this context in which a female canon threatens a narrowing of the field of investigation.[15] If I read Draine correctly, she is warning feminists that their politics must not only avoid creating a new monolithic category of women (that is white, middle-class, and heterosexual), but it must also learn new strategies of resistance to patriarchal recuperation of feminist discourse. If at first it seems contradictory that male writers are included for discussion in this "female canon," that apparent contradiction is understandable when we see that foregrounding gender as an unproblematized term wed to biological difference maintains the tenacity of sexual difference, thus making it virtually impossible to think about women outside the company of men.

Locating a place for lesbian representation within these constructs might be offensive if not impossible. Lesbians are wary of being included as tokens in books about gender and sexuality. Try to locate lesbians to include in a female canon, and you will find that they are slippery; they elude such categorization. A brief look at the history of defining lesbianism uncovers a mass of conflicting claims. Mary Daly reserved the term *lesbian* "to describe women who are woman-identified, having rejected false loyalties to men on all levels."[16] She distinguishes between the "female homosexual" who relates genitally to women but places her allegiances with men in other areas, and the lesbian who eschews loyalties to men in all areas of social and sexual life. Daly's work importantly emphasizes the activist politics in the enactment of lesbian desire, but she still seeks to define a coherent identity for lesbians. Phyllis Lyon and Del Martin claim that a lesbian's *primary* erotic, psychological, emotional, and social interest is in members of her own sex, a somewhat more inclusive category than Daly's.[17] Adrienne Rich expanded the definition further by posing her notion of a lesbian continuum as "a range—through each woman's life and throughout history—of woman-identified experience," which raised a great deal of controversy for its universalizing tendency.[18] Daly, Lyon, and Martin might be criticized for reserving the power to exclude some women from lesbian identity; Rich was criticized heavily for constructing an idea that seemed to include all women. On Rich's continuum, might it not be possible to locate Lillian Hellman? Rich is acutely aware of the risk she takes in positing a lesbian continuum. "Everything we write / will be used against us / or against those we love," she writes.[19] Half a century after Hellman composed *The Children's Hour,* Carl Rollyson indulges himself in homophobic speculations: "Exactly what did Julia mean to Hellman? What kind of commitment was Hellman expecting from her friend? It is a question that also might be asked of Martha Dobie in *The Children's Hour.* What does she want from Karen? Martha's rebelliousness, outspokenness, and irritability all seem modeled on the playwright's own traits."[20] No wonder, then, that in her 1952 interview Hellman felt compelled to defend herself from autobiographical implications in her first play.

Attempts to define lesbianism as an identity that can be determined only if the correct prerequisites can be uncovered strive to stabilize the terms so that there are multiple ways of being lesbian but still some "essence" that is somehow ontological. Rich's continuum, on the other hand, seeks to locate the "lesbian within" all women. Ironically, when one reads these conflicting claims together, lesbianism becomes radically relativized so that it is possible to argue that all women are lesbians, or that no women are lesbians. Identity theories thus are bound to a liberal humanist ideology that personalizes lesbianism and, unwittingly perhaps, depoliticizes lesbian sexual preference as an active choice with potentially radical disruption of patriarchy's cornerstone—heterosexuality.

In 1981 Monique Wittig declared, "Lesbian is the only concept I know of which is beyond the categories of sex (man and woman) because the designated subject (lesbian) is *not* a woman either economically, or politically, or ideologically," thus shifting the grounds of the debates by problematizing the term *woman,* thus crucially separating gender from sexual orientation and reinstating the political power of lesbian difference.[21] Wittig recognized that lesbianism must be theorized outside of (not against) the category of gender. When she says that "what makes a woman is a specific social relation to a man, a relation that we have previously called servitude, a relation which implies personal and physical obligation . . . a relation that lesbians escape by refusing to become or stay heterosexual," Wittig activates lesbian power by displacing the heterosexual bond as the primary site of sexual difference.[22] Wittig's conceptual shift is crucial; women, she insists, are not bound to enter into a heterosexual contract unwillingly. They have the power to refuse to participate in this social unit.

Wittig has significantly modified the field of inquiry by posing the noncoincidence of lesbians and women. If lesbians refuse the gender category of women, then my hesitancy to include lesbian representations within the political framework of this book might be understood as more than resistance to voicing another minoritized position, but indeed a rejection of the book's definitional logic. At best I feel rather like I've been invited to a party and upon arriving have discovered that I am the entertainment. I am nonetheless striving here to articulate a lesbian position within the concept of a female canon, indicating my own bind as a writer who has accepted to speak as a feminist and as a lesbian. Politically, I want to include lesbians as social subjects in a context that intends to document women's history in the theater. But theoretically, I cannot find a place from which to speak that does not reinscribe lesbians in patriarchal ideologies. De Lauretis describes this contradiction within feminist thought and finds it specific to, "perhaps even constitutive of, the women's movement itself: a twofold pressure, a simultaneous pull in opposite directions, a tension toward the positivity of politics, or affirmative action in behalf of women as social subjects, on one front, and the negativity inherent in the radical critique of patriarchal, bourgeois culture, on the other."[23] This contradiction is likely to remain intact as long as we are working within constructs like gender and canonization as they have been formulated for us. Deconstructing their content alone will not suffice; what is needed is deconstruction of their epistemologically privileged status. While the contradiction stands, however, feminists might be able to use it to its limited advantages. Like Marilyn Frye's stagehands who can interrupt the seamless fabric of the play not in spite of but because of their contradictory positioning, this twofold pressure may offer the feminist critic a site from which she can best view the workings of patriarchal ideologies even as she deconstructs and reconstructs alternatives.[24]

Having laid out the theoretical terms that complicate my project, and having exhausted the possibility for locating lesbian plays within the canon, I could follow the liberal-assimilationist strategy and search for a candidate among lesbian plays that have not been canonized. Even this political retreat will not yield much. Kaier Curtin identifies Sholom Asch's *The God of Vengeance* (1922) as the first play on the American stage about lesbians. This first "frank and sensual scene of lesbian lovemaking" on the American stage caused the entire cast to be arrested.[25] Rivkele, the chaste daughter of a jealous father, is seduced by Manke, a prostitute in the brothel managed by her parents. Rivkele and Manke play "husband and wife" as they make love, certainly not what a modern spectator would consider lesbian lovemaking but perfectly consonant with the sexologists' description of "inverts."

In an out-of-print anthology of plays by American women, a female canon of sorts, I find two plays that might be considered lesbian: *The Mothers* (1915) by Edith Ellis (Havelock Ellis's wife) permits a passionate kiss between two women and the husband of one's veiled accusation of lesbianism. The women conclude that they can only love men as mothers love their sons.[26] Rachel Crothers's *Criss Cross*, written in the

1930s, represents the agony of Ann, who loves her cousin Cecil but can't bring herself to name that love. The play ends as Ann sits miserably alone while the heterosexual couple go merrily off on their date.[27] These plays permit exceptional moments in which the merest hint of lesbian desire is momentarily released then quickly suppressed. Feminists might find in them some acknowledgement of the existence of lesbian desire even in the most inhospitable circumstances, but basically these are prurient stage images that accept the terms of a heterosexual contract.

It was not until 1985 that the American publishing industry produced a collection of plays that named themselves lesbian—Kate McDermott's *Places Please!* Published by a small feminist press, Aunt Lute, these plays have not received much institutional recognition, nor have they drawn much response from alternative presses. McDermott adamantly intended these plays to be not just woman-centered, not just feminist, but unquestionably lesbian, as her introduction explicitly announces:

> "Lesbian" meant a viable, workable piece of theater written by a Lesbian; a script which consciously, and explicitly, claims through a Lesbian character a Lesbian perspective of the play's events. A Lesbian perspective, in this matter, meant: a life-stance marked by a strong, assured awareness of the suitability of the Lesbian connection between women, and an awareness of the societal tools used to oppose these connections.[28]

McDermott was obviously trying to squeeze out any ambiguity—the plays would be by, for, and about lesbians—and furthermore they would combine the personal with the political, be conscious of the operations of oppression and the strategies for combatting it, and present affirmative images of lesbian experience. Certainly the political imperatives that motivate this project are commendable. But at once we run up against theoretical problems. First, McDermott's persistent capitalization of "Lesbian" might simply be a way of affirming the term; however, it could also indicate that lesbianism is a monolithic, ahistorical, and universally recognized concept. Second, McDermott reveals an underlying faith in an ontology of lesbianism in her tautological definitional prescriptions for the book: a lesbian, she seems to be saying, is a lesbian, is a lesbian.

Furthermore, McDermott resorts to naive aesthetic criteria when she explains why she chose certain plays and rejected others. As a director, she claims intimate, experiential knowledge of what constitutes good, workable theater as opposed to literature. She sought plays that would make a "visceral impact," entertain and challenge an audience. Thus even in this potentially politically radical project, the editor is holding out for a set of aesthetic universals. However, McDermott is aware of the politics of putting such a book together. She includes two interesting caveats: that she regrets the unavailability of lesbian plays by women of color, and that she does not intend the anthology to be representative of lesbian theater forms. Consequently, the first American Anthology of lesbian plays is primarily white, middle-class, and realistic. Lesbian plays in this context are likely to emerge as yet another canon that mystifies the processes of its own construction and represents a new monolithic Other.

The plays in the anthology unfailingly address social issues of concern for lesbians: homophobia in the workplace, coming out to parents and friends, coping with the loss of a partner, living with the constant presumption of heterosexuality. All of the plays could be classified as either "coming out" plays (to oneself or to others) or coping with homophobia plays. These are, of course, primary concerns for lesbians, and the success of these plays in production indicates that audiences desire "realistic" representations of these problems. Although none of the characters think of themselves as "abnormal," many of them have some difficulty accepting their "lesbian selves." Unquestionably, this anthology offers a great improvement over dramatic representations of "pathological" lesbianism in the past. Nevertheless, I have some problems with these plays, a few of which I will try to discuss here.

My primary concern is that these plays are "about" lesbianism, by which I mean that they are representations that present lesbian characters operating in a heterosexual framework that is interior as well as exterior. Too often the characters' questions concern how to adjust and integrate in a heterosexual world that appears nearly monolithic—except for themselves of course. The heterosexual world is critiqued in these plays; it is shown to be narrow, confining, oppressive, and in need of transformation through understanding. Yet often the plays suggest that this understanding can be achieved through recognition of the similarities between homosexuals and heterosexuals, at the expense of reducing the differences between and among lesbians to a minimum. My concern is that these characters are not shown as active, perceiving, creative subjects but rather as images of the way that the heterosexual world perceives them. If so, they unwittingly reify the structures that they ostensibly challenge.

The first play in the anthology, *Dos Lesbos,* by Carolyn Meyers and Terry Baum, enjoyed considerable success in the San Francisco Bay area when it was first performed in 1981. McDermott characterizes it as a sort of revue/play that incorporates a variety of performance styles. In seven short scenes, the characters, Peg and Gracie, act out responses to homophobia by performing different characters drawn from various historical periods and genres—for example, coming out to one's mother as a Restoration dramatic heroine only to discover that her mother is a lesbian too. In many ways, *Dos Lesbos* is the most satisfying play in the collection because it seems to have the potential for disrupting stable identities and problematizing the homosexual/heterosexual binary. By subtitling it a "Play By, For and About Perverts," Baum and Meyers intend to mock the pathological view of lesbianism while they reclaim celebratory status for the words "lesbian" and "dyke" by having their characters frequently and enthusiastically name themselves so; and this naming, as Cheryl Clarke has argued convincingly, is an act of passionate resistance.[29] Nevertheless, in my reading, this play does not succeed in its disruptive potentials. The role playing that Peg and Gracie enact is always carried out within the confines of heterosexism, which is ridiculed, but at the same time represented as monolithic and ahistorical. Whatever genre or historical period in which Peg and Gracie select to perform their oppression as lesbians, the responses are similar enough to suggest that lesbianism, as well as particular forms of oppression, transcend culture and history. Despite the use of some potential distancing devices, such as songs and role playing, these performances are captured in the conventions of realism—no real breaks with that form occur because the performances are always surrounded by the overarching frame of two women realistically role playing in the privacy of their home. Thus an audience's ability to associate freely with the performance is repressed.

Peg and Gracie begin and end the play by singing the song "I Don't Care," which is undercut by their dialogue and which reveals repeatedly that they do care and are deeply hurt that they cannot simply be accepted as "one of the gang." The totalizing strategy of liberal feminism informs this play—equal rights for lesbians on heterosexual terms. Locked into the familiar binaries that constitute the humanist subject—male/female, masculine/feminine, homosexual/heterosexual, biology, gender, and sexual preference—are conceptually deadlocked in this play's representations. The characters seem to desire a future in which everyone will be regarded as the same, rather than a future of differences. *Places Please!* marks an important departure from the pathological model of lesbianism, but the plays are unwittingly caught in a "gay affirmative" model that, as Celia Kitzinger argues, is founded on a liberal humanist ideology that "merely substitute[s] one depoliticized image of the lesbian with another."[30] The desire to formulate images of lesbians as "normal" concedes to locating lesbianism within a privatized sphere in which politics are diffused and the radical threat of lesbianism to patriarchy is diluted.

Perhaps we should not be surprised that printed plays, with lesbian subjects who are not imprisoned within a heterosexual economy, available for consumption, canonization, and production, are virtually non-existent. Few places within the American publishing industry are likely to permit inscription of the lesbian-feminist subject as Elaine Marks sees her:

> There is no one person in or out of fiction who represents a stronger challenge to the Judeo-Christian tradition, to patriarchy and phallocentrism than the lesbian-feminist. After the end-of-the-century wailings over the death of the ideal God, after the aesthetic retreats and constructions of the dandys in life and art, after the liberation of the male imagination through surrealist techniques, after the existentialist images of male fraternity . . . the women began, ever so slowly, to see connections between production and reproduction, to masturbate consciously, to explore the "dark continent," and to write. The most subversive voices of the century are, and will be, in their texts.[31]

Where might we find this subversive lesbian-feminist in the conservative arena of American theater? And if we find her, will she really be elsewhere, or will she be recuperated in the dominant discourse once she becomes visible?

Derrida has said that "even in aggressions or transgressions, we are consorting with a code to which metaphysics is tied irreducibly, such that every transgressive gesture reencloses us—precisely by giving us a hold on the closure of metaphysics. . . . One is never installed within transgression, one never lives elsewhere." He does, however, acknowledge that "by means of the work done on one side and the other of the limit the field inside is modified," and transgression can occur if not "as a *fait accompli*."[32] Feminist theorists continue to construct strategies for modifying the field and, Derrida notwithstanding, locating an "elsewhere." Elaine Marks has argued, for example, that performing the body and language in excess may sometimes resist recuperation and reabsorption into male literary culture.[33] Teresa de Lauretis's feminist critiques of gender as "ideologicotechnological production" also propose a "view from elsewhere."[34] Luce Irigaray proposes "disruptive excess" and "mimicry" to locate the elsewhere of female pleasure.[35] The overwhelming ambiguity of lesbian sexuality, its resistance to coherent identification, its radical contingencies, propose a site from which this elsewhere might be constructed most productively.

It is not in theory alone that these constructions can be located. Jill Dolan has opened up that view from elsewhere in the work of WOW café performers. In this lesbian performance context, "playing with fantasies of sexual and gender roles offers the potential for changing gender-coded structures of power."[36] WOW performers do not subject lesbian sexuality to the dominant discourses; rather, it is the latter's construction of gender that is demystified. Sue-Ellen Case locates a promising space outside of heterosexual ideology in high camp representations of the butch-femme "dynamic duo. . . . These are not split subjects, suffering from the torments of dominant ideology. They are coupled ones that do not impale themselves on the poles of sexual difference or metaphysical values, but constantly seduce the sign system, through flirtation and inconstancy into the light fondle of artifice, replacing the Lacanian slash with a lesbian bar."[37] Dolan writes that "the choice of lesbian sexuality is in some ways *a rejection of the female*, as that gender class has been culturally constructed."[38] Can we go so far as to say that lesbians are not female? Certainly we might agree with Judith Butler that "there is . . . nothing about femaleness that is waiting to be expressed."[39] The official discourse on sexuality, psychoanalysis, certainly constructs the lesbian subject as not female. As Irigaray points out, within the discourse of psychoanalysis, which builds on the a priori and idealist concept of sexual difference, *"it is only as a man that the female homosexual can desire a woman who reminds her of a man"* (author's emphasis).[40] But the lesbian subject will not be located within the discourse of psychoanalysis. On the contrary, psychoanalysis permits critics like Hélène Cixous to define the lesbian as "the latent 'man-within,' a man who is reproduced, who reappears in a power situation."[41] Such formulations collude completely with heterosexist misconceptions of lesbians as "male-identified," i.e., not "real women." In contrast, Monique Wittig's lesbian peoples, as Diane Griffin Crowder has argued, abolish the family, eschew the machinations of the Freudian/Lacanian unconscious (where Cixous's "man-within" is presumably located), and "liberate[s] female desire from its possessive, privatized forms."[42]

Femaleness, strictly speaking, connotes only bodies, which are prelinguistic. When the female enters into language and culture, she is already marked as "Woman." Because lesbians are not "women," they might certainly find themselves out of place in a female canon. Their elusiveness is their strength, indicating that they are somewhere else, where the dominant culture does not represent and reproduce itself. Perhaps that is why the lesbian detective has become a popular character in lesbian performances and fictions.

Holly Hughes is becoming one of the better known lesbian playwrights. Her play, *The Well of Horniness*, has appeared recently in a high-gloss anthology.[43] Hughes's play uses many of the disruptive strategies theorized by the critics mentioned above: mimicry, hyperbole, excessive inscription, to perform gender and sexuality. When Hughes's lesbian character, Georgette, lasciviously goes on the prowl for the newest girl in town and seduces her under a restaurant table where she is having dinner with her fiancé, heterosexist misperceptions of lesbians as male-identified sex maniacs suffer a parodic disruption. The narrator of *The Well of Horniness* keeps spectators informed in a mimicry of the "voice over" that is contradicted by her physical presence:

"Georgette cuts through the dining room as surely as a honey bee picks out the last wildflower in a field of crab grass."[44] The dissenting quality of this gross stereotype would be difficult for even a conservative heterosexual viewer to miss, but its full effect has been reserved for self-identified lesbian spectators who share not a biology or a gender, and certainly not a repression, but a community of self-constructed signs and experience that mutate as the dominant culture attempts to enclose them. *The Well of Horniness* relies in part on the "time-honored tactic among oppressed groups" that Tania Modleski describes: [the oppressed groups] "often appear to acquiesce in the oppressor's idea about it, thus producing a double meaning: the same language or act simultaneously confirms the oppressor's stereotypes of the oppressed, and offers a dissenting and empowering view for those in the know."[45] This tactic, however, remains enclosed too firmly in a structure that it seeks to elude. Hughes's play, I think, is coded not only to empower lesbian spectators but also to resist the ability of heterosexuals to view it as acquiescent. *The Well of Horniness* is both transgressive and *aggressive*—it assaults the audience with barrages of signs that insist on disrupting heterosexist conceptions of lesbian desire. Part of that strength derives from its obvious play on *The Well of Loneliness*, which has achieved a status in heterosexual culture as *the* book on lesbianism. To appreciate its codes fully, however, one must have some knowledge of lesbian histories, both literary and social, and I think one must finally have experienced lesbian sexuality.

The Well of Horniness does not fully escape de Lauretis's argument that "the discourses, demands, and counter-demands that inform lesbian representation are still unwittingly caught in the paradox of sociosexual (in)difference, often unable to think homosexuality and hommosexuality at once separately *and* together,"[46] but I believe it does make a significant gesture in that direction. Still caught in that paradox, it is not caught there "unwittingly." Any play that effectively challenges the hegemony of heterosexuality and the tenacity of sexual difference offers a hopeful new space of visibility for feminists. *The Well of Horniness* presents such possibilities. At this historical moment, it is located on the borderline, a place both there and not there. It is a delicate balance to maintain, but as long as it holds itself tautly in that tension, deferring totalization, elusively in motion, poised in a position of aggressive resistance, I would name that play lesbian.

Notes

I would like to thank Sallie Bingham and The Kentucky Foundation for Women for grant support while I was writing this article. I also wish to thank the following individuals for their helpful advice and criticism: Sara Beasley, Mary DeShazer, Jill Dolan, Betsy

Erkkila, Raima Evan, Phyllis Rackin, and Amy Robinson. I am, of course, solely responsible for the ideas contained in the essay.

1. Harry Gilroy, "The Bigger the Lie" [1952], in *Conversations with Lillian Hellman*, ed. Jackson R. Bryer (Jackson: University Press of Mississippi, 1986), p. 25.

2. Susan Sniader Lanser, "Speaking in Tongues: *Ladies Almanack* and the Language of Celebration," *Frontiers* 4 (Fall 1979): 39. For an overview of the complexities of this question, see Bonnie Zimmerman, "What Has Never Been: An Overview of Lesbian Feminist Criticism," in *The New Feminist Criticism: Essays on Women, Literature and Theory*, ed. Elaine Showalter (New York: Pantheon Books, 1985), pp. 200–24.

3. Gayle Rubin, "Thinking Sex: Notes for a Radical Theory of the Politics of Sexuality," in *Pleasure and Danger: Exploring Female Sexuality*, ed. Carole S. Vance (Boston: Routledge and Kegan Paul, 1984), pp. 267–319.

4. Eve Kosofsky Sedgwick, "Across Gender, Across Sexuality: Willa Cather and Others," *The South Atlantic Quarterly* 88, no. 1 (Winter 1989): p. 56.

5. Marilyn Frye, *The Politics of Reality: Essays in Feminist Theory* (New York: The Crossing Press, 1983), pp. 156–57.

6. Carroll Smith-Rosenberg, "The Female World of Love and Ritual: Relations Between Women in Nineteenth-Century America," in *Disorderly Conduct: Visions of Gender in Victorian America* (New York: Alfred A. Knopf, 1985), pp. 53–76. Smith-Rosenberg's ground-breaking article first appeared in *Signs* 1, no. 1 (1975). Lillian Faderman, "Love Between Women in 1928: Why Progressivism Is Not Always Progress," in *Historical, Literary, and Erotic Aspects of Lesbianism*, ed. Monika Kehoe (New York: Harrington Park Press, 1986), pp. 23–42. See also Faderman's fuller treatment of the subject in *Surpassing the Love of Men: Romantic Friendship and Love Between Women from the Renaissance to the Present* (New York: William Morrow, 1981).

7. Kendall, "Finding the Good Parts: Sexuality in Women's Tragedies in the Time of Queen Anne," unpublished paper presented at the "New Languages for the Stage" conference, The University of Kansas, Lawrence, Kansas, October 1988. See also Kendall's article "From Lesbian Heroine to Devoted Wife: Or, What the Stage Would Allow," in *Historical, Literary, and Erotic Aspects of Lesbianism*, ed. Monika Kehoe (New York: Harrington Park Press, 1986), pp. 9–22.

8. Michel Foucault, "What is An Author?", in *Language, Counter-Memory, Practice: Selected Essays and Interviews*, ed. Donald F. Bouchard, trans. Donald F. Bouchard and Sherry Simon (Ithaca: Cornell University Press, 1977), p. 120. Roland Barthes, "The Death of the Author," in *Image-Music-Text*, trans. Stephen Heath (New York: Hill and Wang, 1977), p. 142. For an excellent argument that the author's death is premature for women writers, see Nancy K. Miller, "Changing the Subject: Authorship, Writing, and the Reader," in *Feminist Studies/Critical Studies*, ed. Teresa de Lauretis (Bloomington: Indiana University Press, 1986), pp. 102–20.

9. Lillian Hellman, *The Children's Hour*, in *Plays By and About Women: An Anthology*, eds. Victoria Sullivan and James Hatch (New York: Random House, 1973), p. 89.

10. *The Children's Hour* must be considered in its historical moment. Because it was written in 1934, it is improbable that Hellman would have written a play about a lesbian relationship that was fully accepted as healthy and normal. Her play is based roughly on the 1811 trial of Miss Marianne Woods and Miss Jane Pirie, Scottish mistresses of a girls' boarding school who were accused and tried for "improper and criminal conduct." Hellman's source was William Roughead's book, *Bad Companions*, published in Scotland in 1930. Roughead's title alone indicates the sensationalized and negative approach to his subject matter. From a contemporary feminist reader's perspective, the historical record strongly indicates that Pirie and Woods were involved in a consciously active sexual relationship. However, the women's defense attorneys were able to prove them "innocent" due to the judge and jury's incapacity to believe that lesbian lovemaking could occur between two respectable, middle-class schoolteachers. Ironically, the defense insisted on the women's great love for each other to prove that there could not have been an erotic dimension to the relationship. The case finally rested on the conviction that a woman who slept with and embraced another inferred nothing because sexual desire between women was not just improbable but impossible. For a fuller treatment of this case see

Faderman, *Surpassing the Love of Men*, pp. 147–56. Hellman's revision of this material points to the historical shift that occurred after the late nineteenth- and early twentieth-century sexologists acknowledged the existence of lesbian desire and defined it as a category of abnormality, in response, as Faderman argues, to a growing fear of women's autonomy. In Hellman's play, the community's reaction to Martha and Karen reflects the acceptance of this nineteenth-century psychological fabrication; and in this historical moment, Hellman realistically depicts the women's ruin as a result of this charge. Although I am fully aware that Hellman's play cannot be called upon to account for its representation outside of its historical specificity, I want to point out that Hellman chose to show the play's events from the perspective of the homophobic community. A lesbian writer might have found subversive ways to affirm the relationship, whereas Hellman simply kills Martha off. But more importantly, fifty years after its initial inscription, this play remains canonized as the only play about lesbianism in American drama. Obviously, the conservative values of canonization are grounded in a heterosexism that perpetuates the notion of lesbianism erected by the sexologists a century ago.

11. Henry Louis Gates Jr., "Whose Canon Is It, Anyway?" *The New York Times Book Review*, 26 February 1989, pp. 1, 45.

12. Lillian S. Robinson, "Treason Our Text: Feminist Challenges to the Literary Canon," in *The New Feminist Criticism: Essays on Women, Literature and Theory*, ed. Elaine Showalter (New York: Pantheon Books, 1985), p. 111.

13. Barbara Herrnstein Smith, "Contingencies of Value," in *Canons*, ed. Robert von Hallberg (Chicago: University of Chicago Press, 1984), pp. 5–39.

14. Teresa de Lauretis, "The Technology of Gender," in *Technologies of Gender: Essays on Theory, Film, and Fiction* (Bloomington: Indiana University Press, 1987), p. 3. De Lauretis borrows Foucault's language but goes beyond him by using his words in this context: Foucault's "critical understanding of the technology of sex did not take into account its differential solicitation of male and female subjects, and by ignoring the conflicting investments of men and women in the discourses and practices of sexuality, Foucault's theory, in fact, excludes, though it does not preclude, the consideration of gender" (3).

15. Betsy Draine, "Academic Feminists Must Make Sure Their Commitments Are Not Self-Serving," *The Chronicle of Higher Education*, 10 August 1988, p. A40.

16. Mary Daly, *Gyn/Ecology: The Metaethics of Radical Feminism* (Boston: Beacon Press, 1978), p. 26n.

17. Del Martin and Phyllis Lyon, *Lesbian/Woman* (New York: Bantam Books, 1972), p. 1.

18. Adrienne Rich, "Compulsory Heterosexuality and Lesbian Existence," *Signs* 5, no. 4 (Summer 1980): 648–49. Rich's article is reprinted in *Blood, Bread, and Poetry: Selected Essays 1979–1985* (New York: W. W. Norton, 1986), pp. 23–75. For criticism of Rich's position see *Signs* 7, no. 1 (Autumn 1981): 158–99.

19. Adrienne Rich, "North American Time," in *The Fact of a Doorframe: Poems Selected and New: 1950–1984* (New York: W. W. Norton, 1984), p. 324.

20. Carl Rollyson, *Lillian Hellman: Her Legend and Her Legacy* (New York: St. Martin's Press, 1988), p. 61.

21. Monique Wittig, "One is Not Born a Woman," *Feminist Issues* 1, no. 2 (Winter 1981): 53.

22. Ibid.

23. Teresa de Lauretis, "Rethinking Women's Cinema: Aesthetics and Feminist Theory," in *Technologies of Gender: Essays on Theory, Film and Fiction* (Bloomington: Indiana University Press, 1987), p. 127.

24. Frye, *The Politics of Reality*, p. 172. Frye's stagehands are the women in an extended metaphor where phallocratic reality operates like the *mise en scène* of a realistic play. Just as the stage pictures of realism are constructed to keep the spectators fixed on the action within the proscenium frame, so patriarchy depends on the mystification of its ideology. The "stagehands" can interrupt the seamless fabric of the play not in spite of, but because of, their contradictory positioning, which is both inside and outside the representational apparatus. In Frye's metaphor, it is the woman who loves women, the lesbian, who holds the most power for this disruption.

25. Kaier Curtin, *"We Can Always Call Them Bulgarians": The Emergence of Lesbians and Gay Men on the American Stage* (Boston: Alyson Publications, 1987), p. 26.
26. Edith Ellis, *The Mothers*, in *A Century of Plays by American Women*, ed. Rachel France (New York: Richards Rosen Press, 1979), pp. 46–47.
27. Rachel Crothers, *Criss Cross*, in *A Century of Plays by American Women*, pp. 25–29.
28. Kate McDermott, ed., *Places, Please! The First Anthology of Lesbian Plays* (San Francisco: Spinsters/Aunt Lute, 1985), p. xvi.
29. Cheryl Clarke, "Lesbianism: An Act of Resistance," in *This Bridge Called My Back: Writings by Radical Women of Color*, 2d ed., ed. Cherríe Moraga and Gloria Anzaldúa (New York: Kitchen Table, Women of Color Press, 1983), pp. 128–37.
30. Celia Kitzinger, *The Social Construction of Lesbianism* (London: Sage Publications, 1987), p. 178, passim.
31. Elaine Marks, "Lesbian Intertextuality," in *Homosexualities and French Literature: Cultural Contexts/Critical Texts*, ed. George Stambolian and Elaine Marks (Ithaca: Cornell University Press, 1979), pp. 369–70.
32. Jacques Derrida, *Positions*, trans. Alan Bass (Chicago: University of Chicago Press, 1972), p. 12.
33. Marks, "Lesbian Intertextuality," p. 375. Marks argues that Monique Wittig's *The Lesbian Body* creates "through the incessant use of hyperbole and a refusal to employ traditional body codes, images sufficiently blatant to withstand reabsorption into male literary culture."
34. De Lauretis, *The Technology of Gender*, pp. 21, 25. " . . . that 'elsewhere' is not some mythic distant past or some utopian future history: it is the elsewhere of discourse here and now, the blind spots, or the space-off, of its representations. I think of it as spaces in the margins of hegemonic discourses, social spaces carved in the interstices of institutions and in the chinks and cracks of the power-knowledge apparati" (25).
35. Luce Irigaray, *This Sex Which Is Not One*, trans. Catherine Porter (Ithaca: Cornell University Press, 1985), pp. 78, 76.
36. Jill Dolan, *The Feminist Spectator as Critic* (Ann Arbor: UMI Research Press, 1988), p. 68.
37. Sue-Ellen Case, "Toward a Butch-Femme Aesthetic," in *Making a Spectacle: Feminist Essays on Contemporary Women's Theatre*, ed. Lynda Hart (Ann Arbor: The University of Michigan Press, 1989), p. 283.
38. Dolan, *The Feminist Spectator as Critic*, p. 63.
39. Judith Butler, "Performative Acts and Gender Constitution: An Essay in Phenomenology and Feminist Theory, *Theatre Journal* 40, no. 4 (December 1988): 530. "There is," Butler continues, " . . . a good deal about the diverse experiences of women that is being expressed and still needs to be expressed, but caution is needed with respect to that theoretical language, for it does not simply report a pre-linguistic experience, but constructs that experience as well as the limits of its analysis" (530-31).
40. Irigaray, *This Sex Which Is Not One*, p. 194.
41. Hélène Cixous, "Rethinking Differences, An Interview," in *Homosexualities and French Literature: Cultural Contexts/Critical Texts*, ed. George Stambolian and Elaine Marks (Ithaca: Cornell University Press, 1979), p. 74.
42. Diane Griffin Crowder, "Amazons and Mothers? Monique Wittig, Hélène Cixous and Theories of Women's Writing," *Contemporary Literature* 24, no. 2 (Summer 1983): 124–25.
43. Holly Hughes, *The Well of Horniness*, in *Out Front: Contemporary Gay and Lesbian Plays*, ed. Don Shewey (New York: Grove Press, 1988), pp. 221–51.
44. Hughes, *The Well of Horniness*, p. 227.
45. Tania Modleski, "Feminism and the Power of Interpretation: Some Critical Readings," in *Feminist Studies/Critical Studies*, ed. Teresa de Lauretis (Bloomington: Indiana University Press, 1986), p. 129.
46. Teresa de Lauretis, "Sexual Indifference and Lesbian Representation," *Theatre Journal* 40 (May 1988): 177.

Contributors

JUNE SCHLUETER, associate professor of English at Lafayette College, is author of *Metafictional Characters in Modern Drama* (1979); *The Plays and Novels of Peter Handke* (1981); with James K. Flanagan, *Arthur Miller* (1987); and, with James P. Lusardi, *Reading Shakespeare in Performance: King Lear* (1990). With Paul Schlueter, she has edited *The English Novel: Twentieth Century Criticism*, Vol. 2, *Twentieth Century Novelists* (1982), *Modern American Literature, Supplement II* (1984), and *An Encyclopedia of British Women Writers* (1988). She has also edited *Feminist Rereadings of Modern American Drama* (1989) and, with Enoch Brater, *Approaches to Teaching Beckett's "Waiting for Godot"* (1990). She has published numerous essays and reviews on modern drama and Shakespeare and is coeditor of *Shakespeare Bulletin*. In 1978–79, she held a Fulbright lectureship in West Germany.

DORIS ABRAMSON is professor emeritus at the University of Massachusetts at Amherst, where she taught in the performance and dramaturgy areas of the Department of Theater. She is perhaps best known for her pioneering study *Negro Playwrights in the American Theatre, 1925–1959*, published in 1969. Professor Abramson has been theater editor of the *Massachusetts Review* since 1959. She is currently co-owner of the Common Reader Bookshop in New Salem, Massachusetts.

LEONARD R. N. ASHLEY is professor of English at Brooklyn College of The City University of New York. His latest books are *Elizabethan Popular Culture* (1988) and *What's in a Name?* (1989). In 1988, he published revised editions of the critical biography *Colley Cibber* and the anthology *Nineteenth-Century British Drama;* and his *The Wonderful World of Superstition, Prophecy, and Luck* (1984) and *The Wonderful World of Magic and Witchcraft* (1986) appeared in a combined volume, *The Amazing World . . .* (1988). He is the author of more than one hundred scholarly articles and has contributed to many reference books including Freedley and Reeves' *History of the Theatre*, Gassner and Quinn's *Reader's Encyclopedia of World Drama*, the Salem encyclopedia of short fiction, *Reference Guide to American Literature*, *Great Writers of the English Language*, and *An Encyclopedia of British*

Women Writers. He has twice been president of the American Name Society and once of the American Society of Geolinguistics and serves on the editorial board of several scholarly journals.

JENNIFER BRADLEY teaches academic and journalistic writing at UCLA Writing Programs, where she has also been supervisor of graduate teaching assistants for the Department of English. Associate editor of two anthologies, *Writing at Century's End* (1987) and *Making Connections Across the Curriculum* (1986), Bradley is also on the editorial board of *Writing on the Edge.* She is working on a biography of Zoë Akins.

KATHERINE H. BURKMAN is professor of English at Ohio State University. She has published extensively on modern drama and has dealt with ritual approaches to drama in *The Dramatic World of Harold Pinter: Its Basis in Ritual* (1971), *The Arrival of Godot: Ritual Patterns in Modern Drama* (1986), and an edited collection, *Myth and Ritual in the Plays of Samuel Beckett* (1987). She is currently working on a book on doubling in dramatic literature.

BARBARA L. BYWATERS is nonfiction editor for the *Mid-American Review* and has been a bibliographer for the *MLA International Bibliography* since 1986. Her current work examines the relationship between Jane Austen and modern women writers.

SUSAN L. CARLSON is associate professor of English at Iowa State University. She has published a book on Henry James's plays and is completing a book on women and British comedy. She has also published on contemporary women playwrights, women's theater groups, contemporary comedy, Shakespeare, D. H. Lawrence, and Henry Green.

CHARLOTTE GOODMAN is professor of English at Skidmore College, where she teaches courses on American literature, drama, and women writers. She has written about many twentieth-century women authors, including Harriette Arnow, Willa Cather, Edith Summers Kelley, Joyce Carol Oates, Tillie Olsen, Katherine Anne Porter, and Anzia Yezierska. Her critical biography of Jean Stafford is to be published in 1990.

LYNDA HART is assistant professor of English at the University of Pennsylvania. She is the author of *Sam Shepard's Metaphorical Stages* (1987) and editor of *Making a Spectacle: Feminist Essays on Contemporary Women's Theatre* (1989). Her articles and reviews have appeared in

The Southern Quarterly, Studies in the Literary Imagination, Contemporary Dramatists, Modern Drama, and *Theatre Journal.*

JOANNE B. KARPINSKI is assistant professor of English at Regis College, where she chairs the English department. She has delivered conference papers and published on contemporary women's theater and nineteenth-century women's fiction, concentrating especially on Mary Shelley and Charlotte Perkins Gilman. Her article on *Quilters* appeared in *Women in Performance.*

ANN E. LARABEE is assistant professor of American Thought and Language at Michigan State University. She has published articles on Djuna Barnes and Susan Glaspell and is currently at work on a study of women's theater in the early part of this century.

BETTE MANDL is associate professor of English at Suffolk University in Boston, where she also teaches Women's Studies. Her publications include articles on Doris Lessing, James Joyce, and Eugene O'Neill. Her current project is a book-length study of O'Neill from a feminist perspective.

MARY MCBRIDE has taught language and literature for more than forty years. She is currently on the faculty at Texas Tech University. Her published research includes two books and numerous articles, among which are studies of the works of dramatists Thomas Shadwell, Thomas Godfrey, Thornton Wilder, and Tennessee Williams.

SUSAN E. MEIGS, who received an M.A. from Texas in 1988 and a B.A. from Florida State University in 1985, is currently a doctoral student in English at the University of Texas working in modern drama. She is serving as editorial assistant for *Theatre Journal.*

BARBARA OZIEBLO teaches American Literature at the University of Malaga, where she is head of the English department. She attended the 1985 session of the School of Criticism and Theory, which kindled her interest in women's texts and led her to Susan Glaspell. She is presently writing a critical biography of Glaspell, authorized by the Glaspell Estate. She has written and given papers in Spain and in the U.S. on Salman Rushdie, Jerzy Kosinski, Glaspell, Edith Wharton, and feminist criticism and theory. In 1988, she was awarded a Visiting Fellowship by the Beinecke Rare Book and Manuscript Library, Yale University.

DINNAH PLADOTT is on leave from teaching at Tel Aviv University. She spent a sabbatical year at New York University working on a book on modern American drama, 1900–1930. She has published numerous articles on American literature and on the semiotics of theater.

MARY ANNE SCHOFIELD has published widely in eighteenth-century feminism. She has written *Eliza Haywood* and *Masking and Unmasking the Female Mind. Disguising Romances in Feminine Fiction, 1713–1799* and co-edited *Fetter'd or Free? Eighteenth-Century British Women Writers* and *Curtain Calls, Eighteenth-Century British and American Women Writers and their Relationship to the Theatre;* she has also edited numerous texts of eighteenth-century feminine novels and romances. Her breadth of interests is suggested by *The Barbara Pym Newsletter* (which she founded and coedits) as well as the new collection of essays, *Cooking by the Book: Food in Literature and Culture.* She has published articles in *Ariel, ELN, Tulsa Studies in Women's Literature, Studies in Eighteenth-Century Culture, The Windsor Review* and other journals.

CATHERINE A. SCHULER is assistant professor of theatre history and dramatic theory and criticism at The University of Maryland. She has written feminist analyses of the plays of George Bernard Shaw and Bertolt Brecht, and her article on spectator response to performance artist Karen Finley will appear in *The Drama Review.* Her principal current interest is in Russian and Soviet theater, and she is preparing a book on women directors, playwrights, producers, and designers of the Silver Age.

JOHN TIMPANE has taught at Rutgers University and the University of Southampton and is presently teaching at Lafayette College and Princeton University, focusing on composition, Renaissance drama, and the theory of comedy. His composition textbook, *Writing Worth Reading* (1986; 2nd ed. 1989), was coauthored with Nancy Packer. He also has written extensively for medical and scientific publications.

SUZANNE R. WESTFALL, assistant professor of English at Lafayette College, is the author of *Patrons and Performance: Early Tudor Household Revels* as well as articles and reviews on Renaissance and contemporary theater in such journals as *English Literary Renaissance, The Journal of Dramatic Theory and Criticism, Theatre Journal, Shakespeare Bulletin,* and *Theatre Survey.* Besides teaching Renaissance literature and interdisciplinary courses, she has directed and acted in plays from the medieval Mystery Cycles to contemporary performance art.

CATHERINE WILEY is a doctoral candidate in the English Department at the University of Wisconsin-Madison. Her dissertation, on the representation of women in late nineteenth-century British drama, is provisionally titled "Looking Elsewhere: Staging the New Woman as Feminine Subject." She has published articles on Brian Friel in the *Journal of Dramatic Theory and Criticism* and on the New Woman and drama in *Themes in Drama*, as well as reviews in *Literary Magazine Review* and *Theatre Insight*.

Index